Thomas Power O'Connor

The Parnell movement

with a sketch of Irish parties from 1843

Thomas Power O'Connor

The Parnell movement
with a sketch of Irish parties from 1843

ISBN/EAN: 9783744740777

Printed in Europe, USA, Canada, Australia, Japan

Cover: Foto ©ninafisch / pixelio.de

More available books at **www.hansebooks.com**

THE PARNELL MOVEMENT

By T. P. O'CONNOR, M.P.

POPULAR EDITION.

Ward & Downey, Publishers,

TEETH LIKE PEARLS,

white and sound teeth, perfect freedom from decay, a healthy action of the gums, and delightfully fragrant breath can best be obtained by discarding gritty tooth powders and acid washes and using daily

Rowlands'

or Pearl De   the Oriental
herbal, and   nd preserves
the teeth,   and gives a
pleasing fr   es exercise a
highly bene   er washes or
pastes can   a pure and
non-gritty   if. The box
has on it a   ree from any
injurious

ROW   a colour for
fair and go

ROW   ll cutaneous
defects, an   )WLANDS'
articles, of

AS   **EL**

In Ve   nary,
A   R,
For FUR   nd IRON

FOR THE   CHT, THE

IN TI   Free.
Also for   ATER,
In Snow   st Free.

ASPINALL'S ENAMEL WORKS,
Peckham, London.

SIX-SHILLING NOVELS.

A Terrible Legacy. By G. Webb Appleton.

In Jeopardy. By George Manville Fenn.

The Master of the Ceremonies. By G. Manville Fenn.

Double Cunning. By G. Manville Fenn.

The Lady Drusilla: A Psychological Romance. By Thomas Purnell.

Tempest Driven. By Richard Dowling.

The Chilcotes. By Leslie Keith.

A Mental Struggle. By the Author of "Phyllis."

Her Week's Amusement. By the Author of "Phyllis."

The Aliens. By Henry F. Keenan.

Lil Lorimer. By Theo. Gift.

Louisa. By Katharine S. Macquoid.

A Lucky Young Woman. By F. C. Philips.

As in a Looking Glass. By F. C. Philips.

That Villain, Romeo! By J. Fitzgerald Molloy.

The Sacred Nugget. By B. L. Farjeon.

Proper Pride. By B. M. Croker.

Pretty Miss Neville. By B. M. Croker.

The Prettiest Woman in Warsaw. By Mabel Collins.

Three-and-Sixpenny Novels.

Two Pinches of Snuff. By WILLIAM WESTALL.
The Confessions of a Coward and Coquette. By the Author of "The Parish of Hilby," &c.
A Life's Mistake. By Mrs. LOVETT CAMERON.
In One Town. By E. DOWNEY.
Anchor Watch Yarns. By E. DOWNEY.
Atla. By Mrs. J. GREGORY SMITH.
Less than Kin. By J. E. PANTON.
A Reigning Favourite. By ANNIE THOMAS.
The New River. By SOMERVILLE GIBNEY.
Under Two Fig Trees. By H. FRANCIS LESTER.
Comedies from a Country Side. By W. OUTRAM TRISTRAM.

Two-Shilling Novels.

In a Silver Sea. By B. L. FARJEON.
Great Porter Square. By B. L. FARJEON. 7th Edition.
The House of White Shadows. By B. L. FARJEON. 5th Edition.
Grif. By B. L. FARJEON. 10th Edition.
Social Vicissitudes. By F. C. PHILIPS.
The Last Stake. By MADAM FOLI.
Snowbound at Eagle's. By BRET HARTE. 4th Edition.
The Flower of Doom. By M. BETHAM-EDWARDS. 2nd Edition.
Viva. By Mrs. FORRESTER. 3rd Edition.
A Maiden all Forlorn. By the Author of "Molly Bawn." 4th Edition.
Folly Morrison. By FRANK BARRETT. 4th Edition.
Honest Davie. By FRANK BARRETT. 3rd Edition.
Under tS. Paul's. By RICHARD DOWLING. 2nd Edition.
The Duke's Sweetheart. By RICHARD DOWLING. 2nd Edition.
The Outlaw of Iceland. By VICTOR HUGO.

THE PARNELL MOVEMENT.

ج

THE
PARNELL MOVEMENT.

BY

T. P. O'CONNOR, M.P.,

AUTHOR OF

'GLADSTONE'S HOUSE OF COMMONS,' 'THE LIFE OF LORD BEACONSFIELD,' ETC.

NEW AND REVISED EDITION.

LONDON:
WARD AND DOWNEY,
12, YORK STREET, COVENT GARDEN, W.C.

CONTENTS.

CHAPTER		PAGE
I.	THE FALL OF O'CONNELL	7
II.	THE COMING OF THE FAMINE	15
III.	THE FAMINE	30
IV.	THE GREAT CLEARANCES	45
V.	THE GREAT BETRAYAL	84
VI.	RUIN AND RABAGAS	111
VII.	REVOLUTION	134
VIII.	ISAAC BUTT	139
IX.	FAMINE AGAIN	164
X.	THE LAND LEAGUE	175
XI.	THE COERCION STRUGGLE	212
XII.	THE FRUITS OF COERCION	240
XIII.	THE TORY-PARNELL COMBINATION	264
XIV.	THE HOME RULE STRUGGLE	274

THE PARNELL MOVEMENT.

CHAPTER I.

THE FALL OF O'CONNELL.

THE main purpose of these pages is to describe the movement which is associated with the name of Mr. Parnell. That movement cannot, however, be understood without some acquaintance with other movements, of which it is the child and successor. To the history of events in our own day, I have thought it best, accordingly, to prefix a sketch of some of the events by which they were preceded and prepared. For various reasons I have deemed it sufficient to start at the year 1843.

The Irish people had good reason for the honour they paid to O'Connell after he had won for them Catholic Emancipation. When he arose, they were literally aliens in their own country.

The passionate prejudices of the greater and stronger nation were against the Catholics; the Protestant section of their own countrymen held all the land and all the positions of trust and power; the Catholics were unarmed, and opposed to them were all the resources by land and sea of one of the world's greatest empires: and against all this, O'Connell, by the sheer force of his intellect, and with no other weapon than his voice, had succeeded. He was proclaimed the Liberator of his country; all other forces in the nation and all other men were overshadowed by his single name; and he established, without the assistance of a bayonet or of a musket, an omnipotence over the democracy as unquestioned and unquestionable as that of a Czar with millions of soldiers behind him.

It was not long before O'Connell and the nation found that the glories of Catholic Emancipation were but a mockery and an illusion. He had calculated that with this lever he would have been able to wring with promptitude all the other reforms which he deemed necessary; and the evils for which he demanded redress were sufficiently pressing. The tithes still existed; and the clergymen of the opulent Protestant Establishment gathered their dues of wheat from a poverty-stricken Catholic peasantry, backed by soldiers and police and guns, and sometimes amid scenes of mad passion and much bloodshed. O'Connell, in order to gain Emancipation, had committed the terrible mistake of consenting to the abolition of the forty-shilling freeholder: this had taken away from the landlords one of the most effective reasons for sparing the tenant at will; and evictions were perpetrated on an unusually large scale. In short, the material condition of Ireland was worse in the years succeeding than it had been for several years before the Act of Emancipation.

O'Connell's attempts to change all this through the Imperial Parliament proved miserably abortive; he determined to enter on a new agitation—this time the object being the Repeal of the Act of Union: and this brought the second of his great disillusions. He had throughout his career been the staunchest of Liberals; to every measure of Liberal reform he had given his passionate adhesion; of the Reform Act of 1832 he was one of the most effective advocates: and now the Liberal Party failed him. He had no sooner entered upon the agitation for the Repeal of the Union than he came into collision with the representatives of English Liberalism in Ireland. The association which he founded was declared to be illegal; the Marquis of Anglesey, the Liberal Lord-Lieutenant, proclaimed his meetings; his letters were opened by the hands of Liberals in the Post Office;[1] and he was finally brought by Liberal law officers before an Orange judge and a packed Orange jury. Declining to plead, he was convicted, but was never called up for judgment. It was under the exasperation caused by these high-handed acts that he hurled at the then Liberal Administration the words which have often since been quoted with rare delight by Irish speakers. He spoke of the Ministry as the 'base, brutal, and bloody Whigs.'

But these experiences had their effect upon him; and still more the bitter experiences he had in Parliament. He brought forward his motion (April 23, 1834) in favour of Repeal of the Union; it was laughed at by both sides of the House; and when he went into the lobby, he was supported by but 40 votes.

Then he made, perhaps, one of the worst, though one of the most natural, mistakes of his life. Instead of keeping the attention of his countrymen and of the Legislature fixed upon Repeal—which, if granted, involved the redress of every other grievance—he determined to reverse the process. He tried to make the removal of other grievances the stepping-stone to gaining Repeal, instead of standing by Repeal as the be-all and end-all of national rights. He had an additional reason for hoping for the redress of grievances, in the promises of the Liberal statesmen of the period. They had declared over and over again their readiness to place Ireland on a perfect equality with England; and O'Connell, before long, got strong evidence of the reality of the promise. In spite of continued opposition by the Conservatives and of repeated rejections by the House of Lords, an Act was passed which threw open the municipal councils of Ireland to the Catho-

---

[1] During the fierce excitement caused in 1845 by the opening of the letters of the brothers Bandiera to Mazzini by Sir James Graham, a Parliamentary Return was ordered of the various Ministers who had exercised the power of opening the letters of private persons. According to this return, Mr. Secretary Littleton (afterwards Lord Hatherton) had done so in 1834, and Lord Mulgrave (afterwards Marquis of Normanby) in 1835. In 1836 the same noble Marquis inspected private Irish correspondence, with the assistance of Mr. Drummond, the Irish Secretary. In 1837 Mr. O'Connell's private letters to his friends were opened by order of Lord Chancellor Plunket and Dr. Whately, Archbishop of Dublin and a Member of the Privy Council, the seals or envelopes being softened by the application of steam, and skilfully resealed after the letters had been copied. In 1838 the same sort of espionage was carried on by Lord Morpeth (afterwards Lord Carlisle), in 1839 by Lords Normanby and Ebrington and General Sir T. Blakeney, and again by Lord Ebrington in 1840.—(Parliamentary Return, Session of 1845. Papers relating to Mazzini.)

lics; and which enabled O'Connell himself to be elected Lord Mayor of Dublin. The spectacle of their great leader clothed in the robes of the chief magistrate of the metropolis was a sight that proved delightful to the Catholics of Ireland at that period, in a way that few people can now understand. The Corporation of Dublin had been the great home of Orange Conservatism; and its aldermen were among the most prominent spokesmen of the insulting and maddening creed of Protestant ascendancy. To see O'Connell in the seat that up to this time had been uninterruptedly occupied by one of their bitterest enemies appeared to the people the visible sign of a momentous triumph. But here, again, a great concession was accompanied by a villainous proviso. Neither O'Connell nor the people, in their enthusiastic welcome of municipal reform, attached much importance to the condition that the appointment of the high sheriff should rest in the hands of the Crown. By-and-by the importance of the provision was brought home to O'Connell when he was placed on his trial; and the High Sheriff of Dublin, as the man charged with the impanelling of the jury, held O'Connell, and through O'Connell the fate of all Ireland, in his grip.

The grant of municipal reform by the Whigs once more threw O'Connell into their hands; and he trusted that other reforms would follow. He spoke warmly on behalf of the Ministry of Lord Melbourne; and called upon the Irish people to rally around it. But in 1841 the period of Liberal ascendancy came to an end; and Sir Robert Peel—the bitter and uncompromising enemy of all Irish Reform—came to the head of the Government with a huge majority behind him. O'Connell lost all hope of redress from the Imperial Parliament, and once more started the Repeal agitation.

O'Connell's first move was to raise a debate on Repeal in the Corporation of Dublin. His speech on the occasion is regarded by competent critics as perhaps one of the finest of his whole life. It may still be read with advantage as an epitome of the case against the Union, and as a syllabus of the hideous ruin which that ill-starred Act has inflicted upon the Irish people. A full and interesting description of it will be found in Sir Charles Gavan Duffy's 'Young Ireland' (pp. 191-207). The chief antagonist of O'Connell on this occasion was a man who afterwards played an important part in Irish history, and who will often appear in these pages. Isaac Butt, at this time a young man of thirty years of age, was the rising hope of the Irish Orange Party, and was thought of so highly as to be put forward as a worthy antagonist of the great agitator. O'Connell's motion was carried by 45 votes to 15. This debate gave the new agitation an extraordinary stimulus. The subscriptions rushed up from £239 in March, the week after the debate, to £683 in the beginning of May; many classes of the population which had held back flocked in; a number of the bishops gave their adhesion to the movement either openly or silently; and as time went on Repeal of the Union was the passionate cry of a unanimous nation.

Doubt is still felt in many minds whether when he first started on this new enterprise O'Connell really meant to persevere with it; or whether he intended to use the larger demand of Repeal as a lever for obtaining the smaller reforms of tenant right, the disestablishment of the Irish Church, and other reforms. Whatever his original motives, the story of the Repeal agitation, which he now started, was that it was strong almost from the very commencement; that its strength increased in geometrical progression; and that finally it reached proportions so gigantic that it controlled its leader instead of being controlled by him.

The most significant and imposing sign of the hold which the new agitation had taken upon the country were the popular gatherings. These, from the immense numbers that attended them, came to be known as the 'monster meetings,' and probably were the largest assemblages of human beings that a political cause ever drew together in the history of the world. These meetings were held in almost every part of Ireland, and gathered volume as they went along ; until at Tara, sacred with the most ancient and proud memories of the Irish nation, there was a demonstration which numbered half a million of human beings.

The assembling together of so many hundreds of thousands of people, all inspired by the same thought, excited something like a national frenzy. The country was quivering in every nerve, and there was a state of excitement that made everybody anticipate a morrow either of complete victory or of an outbreak of baffled hate. The condition of England was one of excitement almost as intense. The attention of Sir Robert Peel was called in Parliament by some of his Irish Orange followers to these meetings ; and, after a certain amount of shilly-shallying, he had distinctly pledged himself that these meetings were seditious, and that the agitation for the Repeal of the Union should, if necessary, be drowned in blood. 'I am prepared,' he said, 'to make the declaration which was made, and nobly made, by my predecessor, Lord Althorp, that, deprecating as I do all war, but above all civil war, yet there is no alternative which I do not think preferable to the dismemberment of this Empire.'

The effect of these words was to exasperate public opinion on both sides of the Channel. It roused by insult the anger of the Irish people, and by provocation the anger of the English. The two nations stood, in fact, opposed to each other, maddened by all the fierce national passions that immediately precede sanguinary warfare.

It is O'Connell's action at this hour that has given rise to the most frequent and bitter controversies over his career. His enemies and many of his warmest admirers have ever since declared that he proved unequal to the situation ; that he had victory in his own hand, and threw it away, from want of courage and want of insight.

He would be a very unsympathetic or a very unimaginative man who would not pity the great agitator at this supreme crisis of his career. Never, perhaps, had a political leader graver difficulties, more perplexing problems—a responsibility so vast, so overwhelming, so undivided. On the one side he saw the great resources of the Empire arrayed against him : and Peel and the Duke of Wellington had taken care that the reality of these resources should be brought home to the mind of O'Connell and the Irish nation in a manner the most galling and the most palpable. Troops were poured into the country until there were no less than 35,000 men in Ireland ; and there were ships of war around the whole coast. O'Connell knew that to all this force he had nothing to oppose but the bare breasts of a brave but also an unarmed and an undisciplined people. On the other hand, there was the whole nation, with strained eye and ear, wanting something, they knew not what—filled with wild hopes and passions, longings, and dreams. And high uplifted above all these surging and strained millions he stood : worshipped as an inspired and resistless prophet ; omnipotent over their destinies, their hearts, their lives ; gigantic, solitary, most miserable.

For it is now certain that at this period O'Connell knew moments of perhaps deeper anxiety than ever he had experienced during the many chequered years of his previous life. When the last shout had died away ; when he had been proclaimed, amid such tumults of cheers, the uncrowned King of Ireland, and he found himself once more with a single companion to whom he could show the nudity of his soul, he frequently uttered in a cry of anguish and despair, 'My God, my God! what am I to do with this people?'

His habits at this period throw a considerable light on his motives and on the history of his country. In spite of occasional laxity of moral conduct, he was all his life a devoted member of the Catholic Church; and towards the end of his days, his daily life was that rather of an anchorite in a state of ecstasy than of a fierce politician in the midst of a raging and relentless struggle. He used not only to attend mass, but also to receive Holy Communion every morning of his life; and it was marked as indicative of his whole theory of political duty that he always wore on these occasions a black glove on his right hand—the hand that, having shed the blood of D'Esterre in a duel, was unworthy to touch even the drapery associated with the mysteries of his religion.

On the other side, there was the fierce democracy demanding excitement, encouragement, inspiration; and O'Connell would have been more than human if the fumes of this incense from millions did not occasionally disturb his brain, and if he were not now and then carried away on the spring-tide of so vast and enthusiastic a movement. Finally, O'Connell's hot language was often the outcome of the cold calculation of a most astute, experienced, and successful politician. For Peel he had a feeling of both loathing and contempt. He thought him at once a hypocrite and a coward. His smile, he used to say, was like the silver plate on a coffin. With Peel and Wellington a bold game had been played before; and had forced Catholic Emancipation, with hundreds of broken promises and abandoned principles, down their throats. The tactics that had won Emancipation might win Repeal.

These are the various considerations that account for the strange inconsistency of O'Connell's language and acts during this momentous time. At one meeting he spoke in terms of enthusiastic loyalty—indeed, he never was anything but loyal in his language to the throne—and he preached the doctrine that he would not purchase the freedom of Ireland by shedding one drop of human blood. Soon after, stung by some insult from the authorities to the people, he burst forth in language of vehement defiance. There was one speech of the latter kind which especially attracted notice, and afterwards was used against him with much effect. Speaking at the banquet in the evening after a meeting in Mallow, he used these remarkable words: 'Do you know,' said O'Connell, 'I never felt such a loathing for speechifying as I do at present. The time is coming when we must be doing. Gentlemen, you may learn the alternative to live as slaves or die as freemen. No; you will not be freemen if you be not perfectly in the right and your enemies in the wrong. I think I see a fixed disposition on the part of our Saxon traducers to put us to the test. The efforts already made by them have been most abortive and ridiculous. In the midst of peace and tranquillity they are covering our land with troops. Yes, I speak with the awful determination with which I commenced my address, in consequence of news received this day. There was no House of Commons on Thursday, for the Cabinet were considering what they should do, not for Ireland, but against her. But, gentlemen, as long as they leave us a rag of the Constitution we will stand on it. We will violate no law, we will assail no enemy; but you are much mistaken if you think others will not assail you.' (A voice, 'We are ready to meet them.') 'To be sure you are. Do you think I suppose you to be cowards or fools?'

And a little later on in the speech he used almost the best-remembered words of his life: 'What are Irishmen,' he asked, 'that they should be denied an equal privilege? Have we the ordinary courage of Englishmen? Are we to be called slaves? Are we to be trampled under foot? Oh, they shall never trample me—at least, ('No, no!') I say they may trample me, but it will be my dead body they will trample on, not the living man!'

Whatever O'Connell may have meant by these words, the interpretation put upon them by at least all the young and enthusiastic and brave men of the country was, that they were meant to be a threat of violence in answer to Peel's threat of violence. The Repeal movement, O'Connell was understood to say, was a constitutional movement, conducted by legal and constitutional methods, and if an attempt were made to deprive the Irish citizens of their constitutional right of public meeting for advancing this movement, the attempt would be resisted by force.

Meantime O'Connell's words became bolder and more encouraging as he went along. He declared at the monster meeting in Roscommon that the close of the struggle had almost come. 'The hour,' he said, 'is approaching, the day is near, the period is fast coming, when—believe me who never deceived you—your country shall be a nation once more.'[1] 'And this poetry of the orator,' sardonically adds Sir Charles Gavan Duffy, 'was translated into unequivocal prose by Mr. John O'Connell at the next meeting of the association. "The Repeal of the Union," he declared, "could not be delayed longer than eight or ten months."'[2]

The moment at last came when O'Connell's power and determination were to be put to the test. A meeting was announced for Sunday, October 5, 1843, at Clontarf—a suburb of Dublin made glorious in Irish hearts by the decisive victory of Brian Boru over the Danish invaders. The Ministry made up their minds to strike the blow which they had been long preparing: they proclaimed the meeting; took every means to carry out their order by force—or, as some people even said, to provoke violence in order to make bloodshed inevitable. The meeting had been in preparation for weeks; but it was not until half-past three o'clock on the Saturday before the meeting that the proclamation was issued. It was only by the despatch of special mounted messengers that the people, who were swarming in from the surrounding country, were told of the action of the Government.

There had already grown within the ranks of O'Connell's own following a section which bitterly differed from his policy, and in time broke his power. The *Nation* newspaper had been founded in October, 1842, by Mr. (now Sir) Charles Gavan Duffy, and he had among his assistants Thomas Davis, John Dillon, and subsequently John Mitchel. The Young Irelanders, as they were called, represented an entirely new phase in Irish politics. The *Nation* for the first time presented the Irish people with a journal of real literary merit; and the writers acquired an influence over the popular mind hitherto unknown in Irish journalism. Even in those days of high-priced newspapers and ill-developed communication, it circulated largely in the remotest towns in Ireland. It was devoured, not read. It convinced; it inspired; it roused loftiest hopes and fiercest passions. The writers, joining the Repeal Association of O'Connell, soon brought a new force into its councils. In the first place, they were determined not to sub-

---

[1] Gavan Duffy, 'Young Ireland,' p. 349. [2] *Ib.*

mit with the same passiveness as was generally the custom to the dictatorship of O'Connell. This brought them into collision, not only with O'Connell himself, but with the formidable group of men he had gathered around him. Many of these intimates of the great agitator were broken in health and fortune and character; but O'Connell stood by them with the natural constancy of a man of keen affections to old retainers; and one of the bitterest quarrels between him and the Young Irelanders was over the continuance in salaried positions of these men. The Young Irelanders made demands for the publication of accounts, which, though accompanied by strong professions of loyalty to O'Connell himself, produced, not unnaturally, irritation in his mind. In short, for the first time in his life, the experienced veteran found himself face to face with young foes who had not the same regard as their elders for his past services, who depended not on his will, and who wielded an influence outside his control. There was in addition to these causes of personal difference a more important and fundamental difference of principle. The Young Irelanders maintained that they were pushed by other forces, and especially by O'Connell himself, into the doctrine of physical force: at this moment the struggle over that question had not arisen. There was, however, the difference in the preference of the younger section for resolute, and the older for moderate courses.

John Mitchel, one of the Young Irelanders, writing many years after O'Connell's death, and in another land, deliberately repeated the opinion he held at the time as to O'Connell's duty on the day of the Clontarf meeting. 'If I am asked,' he writes, 'what would have been the very best thing O'Connell could do on that day at Clontarf, I answer: To let the people of the country come to Clontarf—to meet them there himself, as he had invited them; but, the troops being almost all drawn out of the city, to keep the Dublin Repealers at home, to give them a commission to take the Castle and all the barracks, and to break down the canal bridge and barricade the streets leading to Clontarf. The whole garrison and police were 5,000. The city had a population of 250,000. The multitudes coming in from the country would, probably, have amounted to almost as many. . . . There would have been horrible slaughter of the unarmed people without, if the troops would fire on them—a very doubtful matter—and O'Connell himself might have fallen. . . . It were well for his fame if he had; and the deaths of five or ten thousand that day might have saved Ireland the slaughter by famine of a hundred times as many.'

These words represent the gospel of a large section of Irishmen for many a day afterwards; they led to the almost contemptuous tone in which O'Connell's memory was treated by a vast number of his countrymen during a considerable period after the first outburst of worship after his death; they formed the fundamental idea of the love of revolutionary methods and the hatred of Parliamentary leaders which is the undercurrent of much of the Irish history that followed; above all, they added to the hideous disaster of 1846 and 1847 another element of woe in the thought of what might have been.

The immediate consequence was the break-up of O'Connell's mighty movement. He himself and several of his colleagues were immediately afterwards prosecuted; and the most shameful methods were adopted for obtaining a conviction. Out of the entire panel one slip, containing mostly Catholic names, was lost; when finally there were left eleven Catholics out of a panel of twenty-four, the Crown used their full power of challenge;

every single one of the eleven was driven from the box, and the jury consisted exclusively of Orange Conservatives, who were as impartial in deciding the case of O'Connell in those days as would be a jury of Southern slave-holders in the case of an Abolitionist immediately before the Civil War in America. Then the judges were notoriously partisan. An accidental phrase is still remembered which brought this out in full relief. Chief Justice Pennefather, in alluding to the counsel for the defence, spoke of them as 'the other side.' Of course, before such a judge and such a jury, conviction was a foregone conclusion. Everybody cried out shame on the iniquitous proceedings; O'Connell walked into the House of Commons amid the debate upon the trial, which was at the moment being denounced by English Liberals as vehemently as it could have been by himself. It was generally expected that the verdict would be reversed on appeal—as it was; and an effort was made to have a Bill passed which would have allowed O'Connell to remain out on bail until the case was finally decided. But the Bill was rejected—principally through the efforts of Brougham, who had a violent hatred of O'Connell; and the end of it all was that O'Connell had to go to gaol. This was the beginning of the end.

But it did not look so at the time. In his prison O'Connell held levees more like those of a prince than the unofficial head of a democracy; bishops, priests, town councillors, rushed to see him from all parts of Ireland. 'Here,' writes Mitchel of the imprisonment of O'Connell and his companions in Richmond, 'they rusticated for three months, holding levees in an elegant marquee in the garden; addressed by bishops; complimented by Americans; bored by deputations; serenaded by bands; comforted by ladies; half smothered with roses; half drowned in champagne.'[1] And when the case was brought before the House of Lords the verdict was reversed; Chief Justice Denman denounced the proceedings of the law officers as reducing trial by jury to a 'mockery, a delusion, and a snare:' and O'Connell was released from prison amid circumstances of wild triumph.

But all the same, the fact remained that O'Connell's conviction broke up his movement. The mighty dictator—to whom millions of men looked up, for whom thousands would have willingly died—had been dragged at the tail of a policeman; and the hero of a thousand fights had been beaten for the first time in his life. The prestige of unbroken victory was gone.

'The Repeal year,' as Mitchel pointedly puts it, 'had conducted, not to a parliament in College Green, but to a penitentiary in Richmond.' O'Connell, too, left the prison physically and mentally a broken man. It was discovered after his death that he had been for years suffering from softening of the brain, and the date generally assigned for the first appearance of the disease was that of his imprisonment. He was besides, as we have since learned, involved in domestic trouble.[2]

But though the fearful excitement of the Repeal agitation had broken down his robust frame, he remained still the same to his people. Keen observers remarked the feebleness of his own defence at his trial; and when he began to address meetings again after his release, he was noted to carefully avoid all subjects upon which the people were most eagerly desirous of information and direction. Here, again, most of the critics of O'Connell declare that he lost a great opportunity. Mitchel, and many men still

[1] 'Last Conquest of Ireland.'
[2] Duffy, 'Young Ireland,' pp. 530-32.

living, and with the hot blood of youth cooled by mature years, declare that he ought to have called upon the people to make some stand, and that the people not only would have obeyed, but at the time panted for the word. The population of Ireland at this period was eight and a half millions; and though there was terrible poverty in the country, there had, as yet, not been anything like universal starvation. The masses of men who marched to the demonstrations are universally described as stalwart, bold, and well drilled; and it is argued that by mere force of overwhelming numbers, and a frenzy that was national, they would have borne down the defences of the Government. In support of this view, and against the damning testimony of subsequent abortive attempts at insurrection, the argument is used that the means and methods of warfare have been revolutionized since that period. Soldiers in those days were armed with no better weapon than the 'Brown-Bess;' and, as an ancient revolutionary may now in many a part of Ireland be heard to exclaim, with a sigh: 'In those days every man had his pike.' The first charge might have killed hundreds; but after the first charge, soldiers at that time would have been impotent against a resolute people a hundred-fold more numerous.

But, wisely or foolishly, O'Connell was determined not to permit any bloodshed. His courage was proved on too many a scene to be open to question; but it was not the desperate courage that stakes life, fortune, and a whole national issue upon a single cast of the die. Then his whole training had been that of a man who had found in words weapons more potent than armies and navies. The victories he had obtained were victories in law courts, and in deliberative assemblies; and possibly, and probably, he honestly thought he would still be able to utilize the enthusiasm of the people in wringing from Parliament, if not Repeal, a blessing so great and so needed as security to the tenant-at-will from starvation and eviction.

There was one fatal obstacle to his success in a Parliamentary movement; and this is a fact which should always form a central consideration with those who criticise adversely O'Connell's career. The half-million of people who gathered around him at Tara were not those to whom he had to appeal for the most potent weapon in the Parliamentary conflict. He had to pass away from them to the miserable handful of voters who, in all the smaller constituencies, had the fate of elections in their hands; and at that time, and for many a day afterwards, personal interests begot of abject poverty, a spirit of clique or other mean or subsidiary motives, exercised deeper influence than great national issues. In the year 1843, when he was still at the very height of his power, his supporters in the House of Commons did not reach beyond the miserable total of twenty-six members.

From this time forward the history of O'Connell is the history of Repeal decay. Arms Acts and Coercion Acts meantime took from the people what few weapons they had, and the Government filling gaols with prisoners, accelerated the break-up of that tide of passion, enthusiasm, and desperate courage, which, if taken at its flood, might then have led on to fortune.

With disaster comes inevitable disunion. Between him and the Young Irelanders the quarrel that had been long smouldering had at last broken into open flame. Sir Robert Peel, by the concession of a larger grant to Maynooth, still further disintegrated the forces of O'Connell by bringing pressure on the Vatican, and through the Vatican on some of the bishops; and so, O'Connell's power began gradually to melt away.

CHAPTER II.

THE COMING OF THE FAMINE.

WHILE thus all the national forces of Ireland were being reduced to impotence, there was coming over the country a calamity which was to complete the work of national destruction; to inflict on Ireland one of the most widespread and one of the most terrible disasters recorded in human history; and to prove the need of a native legislature by the tragic testimony of a starving nation.

There never was an event in human history which could have been more clearly foreseen, or that was more frequently foretold, than the Irish famine of 1846-47. The circumstances of which it was the final outcome had been in progress for centuries. The destruction of the Irish manufactures by the legislation of the British Parliament had thrown the entire population for support on the land; and the fierce competition thus induced had raised the rents to a point far beyond anything the tenant could ever hope to pay. On the other side, the landlords, brought up to no profession, spendthrift, separated from the tenant by creed, race, and caste, aggravated all the evils of the system. According to testimony as unanimous as that on any human affair, they left to the tenant the whole improvement of the farm : the fencing, the building of houses and offices—all the work that from time immemorial had been done in England by the landlord; and then, when the tenancy was determined either by the lease or by caprice, they rewarded the tenant by eviction, or a rise in the rent. The complaints of the neglect of their duties by the Irish landlords run with a monotonous iteration through the extensive literature of the Irish land question. Spenser railed against the Irish landlord in 1596 for his preference of tenancies at will to the grant of leases. The exactions of the landlords, and the terrible want thereby caused among the people, suggested to Swift his perhaps most terrible satire—'The Modest Proposal' —and his bitterest passages. In 1729 Mr. Prior wrote a pamphlet to expose the evils which absenteeism inflicted. In 1791, the Protestant Bishop, Dr. Woodward, denounced rack-renting and the 'duty-work' which the landlords exacted; and so on with scores of writers on the subject.

The land question had been the stock subject of politicians as of *littérateurs*; innumerable Parliamentary committees had sat and investigated and reported upon it. To begin with the period after the Union, a Parliamentary committee, appointed on the motion of Sir John Newport in 1819, reported that there was great want of employment; that the want of employment was due to the want of capital; and that the want of capital was caused on the one hand by the absenteeism of a number of the landlords, and on the other through the consumption of all their capital by the tenants on the improvement of their holdings. In 1823, another committee drew attention still more emphatically to the difference between the action of the English and the Irish landlords, and denounced strongly the prevalent rack-renting. In 1829 there was another committee which considered a Bill brought in by Mr. Brownlow in favour of the reclamation of waste lands and the drainage of bogs—a favourite remedy of those days. In 1830 a committee reported that 'no language could describe the poverty' in Ireland, and recommended the settlement of the relations of landlord and tenant on 'rational and useful principles.'

There is an equally embarrassing riches both of speeches and of Bills.

In November, 1830, Mr. Doherty, the then Solicitor-General for Ireland, described the houses of the tenantry as such as the lower animals in England would scarcely, and as a matter of fact did not, endure. The Duke of Wellington denounced the evils of absentee landlordism in the same year; and in the following year Lord Stanley—afterwards, as Lord Derby, the obstinate advocate of the landlord party—called scornful attention to the fact that during a crisis of awful distress in Mayo there had been but a subscription of £100 from two persons out of a rental of £10,400 a year, and described the rents at the same time as exorbitant. In the same year Lord Melbourne, who had been Chief Secretary for Ireland, maintained that all the witnesses examined before the different Select Committees on the subject had united in the statement that the disturbances in Ireland were due to the relations between the landlords and tenants.

In the same manner Bill after Bill had been proposed. Mr. Brownlow's Bill was brought in in 1829. It passed through the House of Commons; it passed the second reading in the House of Lords; it was referred to a Select Committee; but they, on July 1, reported that at such an advanced period of the session it was impossible to proceed any further.[1] In the following year Mr. Henry Grattan called upon the Government to bring in a Bill for the improvement of the waste lands. In the next year, 1831, Mr. Smith O'Brien introduced a Bill for the relief of the aged, hopeless, and infirm. In 1835 Mr. Poulett Scrope asked in vain for a Land Bill; in the same year Mr. Sharman Crawford brought in a Bill.[2] In the following year Mr. Crawford got leave to introduce his Bill again; but it never got further than that stage. In the following year a Mr. Lynch recurred to the old proposal of a Bill for the reclamation of waste lands; but he also failed. In 1842 a small attempt was made to deal with the question of the waste lands by the Irish Arterial Drainage Act. In 1843 came the Devon Commission; this caused a pause in the efforts to amend the law. The Devon Commission recommended, as is known, legislation in the most emphatic manner; but no legislation came. In 1845 Lord Stanley brought in a Bill. The Bill was read a second time, was referred to a Select Committee, and was then abandoned. In the same session Mr. Crawford reintroduced his Bill, but had to abandon it. The next session, after some severe pressure, the Earl of Lincoln introduced a Bill; this was destroyed by the resignation of the Ministry.

It will be seen from this rapid sketch that the conditions of the problem were intimately known; that all parties—except a few of the Irish landlords themselves—were in favour of a change in the law; that attempt after attempt had been made to create this change, and that attempt after attempt had failed. Meanwhile, landlords and tenants were carrying on their warfare after their own lawless fashion. Allusion has been already made to the great clearances which followed the abolition of the forty-shilling freeholder; eviction had also been made easy by legislation, of which more presently. In 1843 there were no less than 5,244 ejectments, with 14,816 defendants, from the Civil Bill Courts, and 1,784 ejectments from the Superior

---

[1] 'Parliamentary History of the Irish Land Question,' by R. Barry O'Brien, pp. 36-7.
[2] This Bill put no restriction whatever on the power of eviction; it simply asked that when a tenant was evicted he should receive compensation for those permanent improvements which he had made with the consent of his landlord. In the case of improvements made without the consent of the landlord, the chairman of Quarter Sessions was to decide whether they presented a case for compensation. This was the basis of all the Land Bills which followed; it was the high-water mark of Land Reform in those days. Mr. Sharman Crawford's Bill will often recur in these pages.

Courts, with 16,503 defendants—making a total of 7,028 ejectments and 31,319 defendants. And in the five years from 1839 to 1843, no less than 150,000 'tenants had been subjected to ejectment process.'[1] Unprotected by the law from robbery, and face to face with starvation, the tenants formed secret and murderous organizations, and assassination and eviction accompanied each other in almost arithmetical proportion. As poverty increased indebtedness, and indebtedness increased eviction, times of poverty and times of disturbance were synonymous terms. With disturbance the Legislature showed itself ready and eager to deal—when the remedy applied took the shape, not of remedial legislation, but of Coercion Acts. The year was the exception in which Ireland was living under the ordinary law. The Habeas Corpus Act was suspended in 1800, in 1801, in 1802, in 1803, in 1804, in 1805; it was suspended again from 1807 till 1810; from 1814 to 1817; from 1822 to 1828; from 1829 to 1831; again from 1833 to 1835. Side by side with the suspension of the Habeas Corpus Act there were other and special Coercion Acts; frequently there were two Coercion Acts in the same year, sometimes in the same session: in the very first year of the Union Parliament no less than five exceptional laws were passed. These Coercion Acts were of a ferocious character: many of them abolished trial by jury; some of them established martial law; transportation, flogging, death, were the ordinary sentences.

It is a singular and instructive commentary on the Act of Union, that the Union Parliament had not only passed five Coercion Acts in its first session, but that it had sat for but two months when it passed a Coercion Act severer than any passed even in the stress of the rebellion of 1798. This was one of the terrible code known as the Insurrection Acts. Under the Act of 1800, courts-martial had the right to try prisoners; two-thirds of the officers could pronounce sentence, and the sentence might be the sentence of death. To encourage these tribunals in doing their duty, the officers were instructed, in the words of the Act, 'to take the most vigorous and effective measures;' and they received still further encouragement by being made absolutely irresponsible; 'no act,' decreed the Legislature, 'done by these tribunals shall be questioned in a court of law.' In 1817 a modified Insurrection Act was passed, which in some respects was worse than the preceding Acts. A body of justices—that is, of landlords—were entitled to form a tribunal if they were presided over by a Serjeant-at-law or a Queen's Counsel, and this tribunal had the right to pass sentences varying from one year's imprisonment to seven years' transportation; they were, like the courts-martial, irresponsible, for there was no appeal and no *certiorari*. These courts were employed in the trial of persons described as 'idle and disorderly,' and the 'idle and disorderly' were included in the following extensive category:

(1) Anyone found out of his or her dwelling-house between two hours after sunset and sunrise, who could not prove to the satisfaction of the tribunal that he or she was upon his or her 'lawful occasions'—the mere fact of being out was sufficient authority to a policeman to arrest and detain till trial; (2) persons taking unlawful oaths, or

---

[1] This is how O'Connell puts it (Hansard, lxxxv., p. 520). By tenants, he probably means heads of families. Mr. Bernal Osborne, who spoke in the same debate subsequently to O'Connell, puts the figures in another way. 'There were,' he said, '70,982 civil bill ejectments between 1839 and 1843, exclusive of the number of individual occupiers served with process. Counting,' he added, 'five for a family, this would show a total of 354,910 persons evicted in this period' (*Ib.*, p. 534). It will be seen presently what became of the persons evicted, and how they helped to bring about the Famine.

(3) having arms, or (4) found between 9 p.m. and 6 a.m. in a public-house or unlicensed house in which spirituous liquors were sold and not being inmates or travellers ; (5) persons assembled 'unlawfully and tumultuously'; (6) persons hawking 'seditious papers,' unless they disclose the persons from whom they received them.

It would, of course, be assumed by many readers, especially English readers, that these statutes were severe only in wording or intention and not in practical operation. But there was not one of these Acts which was not carried not only to the full lengths authorized by the words and intentions of the Act, but to a large extent farther. In order to make the dread provisions of the Insurrection Act just described applicable to a locality, it had to be proclaimed; and this is an instance of how such a proclamation was brought about:

'I am perfectly acquainted with that part of Kilkenny now under proclamation adjoining the Queen's County,' said Mr. John Dunn, a witness examined before the Lords' Committee of 1824.

'Had there been any disturbance,' asked one of their lordships, 'at the time the Act was put into execution?' 'Not in the barony of Innisfadden adjoining the Queen's County; I am aware of none.'

'Can you state,' goes on the examination, 'on what ground it was the Insurrection Act was applied for, so far as respects that barony, and the circumstances attending it?' 'I understand that some few trees—some two or three—had been felled in the domain of Lady Ormonde, and I am not aware of any other transaction at all that would justify the application of such a measure.'[1]

Thus the felling of two or three trees was sufficient to expose everybody in this Kilkenny barony to the chance of being transported for seven years by a Queen's Counsel and a body of landlords to whom he was for any reason obnoxious, if he only happened to stay beyond nine o'clock in a public-house.

An Irish writer who has written an excellent article on the coercive legislation of Ireland in the *Pall Mall Gazette* of September 18, 1885, will doubtless appear far-fetched when he says of the Insurrection Act of 1822-25, that if 'it had been in force in England during the Anti-Corn Law agitation, Mr. Cobden and Mr. Bright might have been transported for seven years by justices or landlords interested in maintaining the tax on food.' But the illustration is literally and strongly justified, for in 1814 the Insurrection Act was used by Sir Robert Peel to put down the Catholic Board and to prevent popular demonstrations; that is to say, to suppress all agitation against the exclusion of the millions of Irish Catholics from any share in the government of their own country; and that was an agitation as legitimate, legal, and constitutional as that for the repeal of the Corn Laws.

There were several Acts for the purpose of putting down the disturbances which the terrible sufferings of the tenantry generated, and some of these Acts permitted the sentence of 'whipping.' Here, again, it will be thought that the words were formal and minatory; but, says O'Connell, who lived all through these coercion laws, 'I have known instances where men have been nearly flogged to death.'[2]

Besides the Insurrection Acts, supplemented by suspensions of the Habeas Corpus, there were special Coercion Acts for every form of defence that the tenantry could devise. It has become the fashion of modern English statesmen to eulogize O'Connell; when he was alive, English statesmen met him at every point in his career by every agency of coercion

[1] Report Lords' Committee, 1824, p. 432. Quoted by O'Connell (Hansard, lxxxv. p. 503).
[2] Hansard, lxxxv., p. 503.

that the Legislature could devise. It has been seen how the Insurrection Act was employed by Peel in 1814 to put down the Catholic Board in which O'Connell had a part. Between 1825 and 1836 no less than four Acts of Parliament were passed for the purpose of suppressing political organizations which he had founded, and as the organizations were under the control of O'Connell, it is needless to say that they were legal, constitutional and peaceful in their methods. The Irish people, driven from open agitation, were then met by a disarming code, lest they should seek their emancipation by force; and when, finally, they thought of secret organization, they were confronted by another code of laws with terrible penalties. Anybody who administered or aided in administering an oath for what were called 'seditious purposes' might be transported for life by one of the tribunals consisting of landlords and a Queen's Counsel, and anybody who took the oath might be transported for seven years.

Nor does this represent the complete case in the contrast between the action of the Legislature towards the landlord and the tenant. While every attempt had failed—no matter how moderate—to improve the condition of the tenant, the Legislature had passed law after law to increase the power of the landlord. Thus the 56 Geo. III., cap. 88, gave to the landlord a power of distraint which he never had enjoyed up to this period. Under this Act the landlord could distrain the growing crops of a tenant, could keep them till ripe, could save and sell them when ripe, and could charge the tenant with the accumulated expenses. This terrible Act was the starting-point of the great evictions which have been the chief causes of agrarian crime in Ireland. Two years afterwards came another Act to complete the evil work begun. The 58 Geo. III., cap. 39, established the power of civil bill ejectments. The previous Act had given the landlord the means of ruining the tenant by the seizure of his crops; this Act enabled the landlord to complete the ruin by turning the tenant off his holding. The 1 Geo. IV., cap. 41, extended still further the power of civil bill ejectment; the 1 Geo. IV., cap 87, enabled the landlord to get security for costs from defendants in ejectments—that is to say, took away in a large proportion of cases any chance from the tenant of resisting the demand for the verdict of eviction; the 1 and 2 Wm. IV., cap. 31, gave the landlord the right of immediate execution in ejectment cases; the 6 and 7 Wm. IV. gave still further facilities for civil bill ejectments; and thus the whole eviction code was made entirely complete, without chink, without flaw, without possibility of improvement.[1] These, then, were the legislative benefits by which the Irish people were taught the enormous gain of having their interests attended to by an Imperial and United Legislature. It should also be remarked that these Eviction Acts, and some of the worst of these Coercion Acts, were passed when the late Sir Robert Peel was Chief Secretary; for, as we are told in Cates's 'Dictionary of General Biography,' 'in 1812 Peel was made Chief Secretary for Ireland—an office which he held with much advantage to the country till 1818.'[2] The 'advantage' to the country was the preparation of the famine.

Let us now put the whole case in tabular form by way of making it more intelligible.

FOR THE LANDLORD.

1800. Habeas Corpus suspended; Coercion Act.
1801. Habeas Corpus suspended; two Coercion Acts.

---

[1] O'Connell, in Hansard, lxxxv., pp. 522, 523. [2] P. 857 (second edition).

1802. Habeas Corpus suspended; two Coercion Acts.
1803. Habeas Corpus suspended; two Acts
1804. Habeas Corpus suspended.
1805. Habeas Corpus suspended; one Coercion Act.
1807. February 1, Coercion Act.
   ,,   Habeas Corpus suspended; August 2, Coercion Act.
1808. Habeas Corpus suspended.
1809. Habeas Corpus suspended.
1814. Habeas Corpus suspended; one Coercion Act.
1815. Habeas Corpus suspended; Insurrection Act continued.
1816. Habeas Corpus suspended; first Eviction Act; Insurrection Act continued.
1817. Habeas Corpus suspended; one Coercion Act; second Eviction Act.
1818. Second Eviction Act.
1820. Third Eviction Act; same year, fourth Eviction Act.
1822. Habeas Corpus suspended; two Coercion Acts.
1823 to 1828. Habeas Corpus suspended, and one Coercion Act in 1823.
1829. Habeas Corpus suspended.
1830. Habeas Corpus suspended; Importation of Arms Act.
1831. Whiteboy Act; Stanley's Arms Act; fifth Eviction Act.
1832. Importation of Arms and Gunpowder Act.
1833. Habeas Corpus suspended; Suppression of Disturbance Act; Change of Venue Act.
1834. Habeas Corpus suspended; Suppression of Disturbance Amendment and Continuance Act; Importation of Arms and Gunpowder Act.
1835. Public Peace Act.
1836. Another Arms Act; sixth Eviction Act.
1838. Another Arms Act.
1839. Unlawful Oaths Act.
1840. Another Arms Act.
1841. Outrages Act; another Arms Act.
1843. Another Arms Act; Act consolidating all previous Coercion Acts.
1844. Unlawful Oaths Act.[1]

FOR THE TENANT.

1829. Mr. Brownlow's Bill dropped in House of Lords.
1830. Mr. Grattan's demand for an Improvement of Waste Lands Bill refused.
1831. Mr. Smith O'Brien's Bill for the Relief of the Aged dropped.
1835. Mr. Sharman Crawford's Bill dropped.
1836. Mr. Sharman Crawford's Bill dropped.
   ,,   Mr. Lynch's Reclamation Bill dropped.
1842. Irish Arterial Drainage Act passed.
1845. Lord Stanley's Bill dropped.
   ,,   Mr. Sharman Crawford's Bill dropped.

Nor had outraged Nature neglected to give abundant warning of the Nemesis she exacts. The famine of 1846-47 differs in degree only from the famines which had recurred at almost regular intervals in preceding periods of Irish history. Beginning with the last century, it was the chronic starvation among a considerable portion of the people that drew from Swift in 1729 the savage satire already alluded to; and in the year of the publication of 'The Modest Proposal' there had been three years of dearth, and the people were reduced to the last extremity. In 1725, 1726, 1727, and in 1728 the harvests were very bad; and in 1739 there was a prolonged frost that produced in the following years a famine which was

---

[1] This list I have compiled from O'Connell (Hansard, lxxxv., p. 505), and from a pamphlet by Mr. I. S. Leadam, quoted by Mr. Healy in his pamphlet, 'Why there is a Land Question and an Irish Land League,' pp. 68, 69, first edition. O'Connell's calculation is that there were seventeen Coercion Acts up to August, 1887. There were nearly double that number—if not of Acts generally called Coercion, at least of Acts of an exceptional and restrictive character. Thus O'Connell enumerates three Coercion Acts in the first year after the Union: there were five. Nor does he include Arms Acts in his list; though, of course, Arms Acts are Coercion Acts. Thus, in 1807, he mentions two Coercion Acts; there were, besides, two Arms Acts.

one of the worst on record. Of that famine—the famine of 1740-41—we have many contemporaneous descriptions. According to one writer, four hundred thousand persons died. Bishop Berkeley has left behind touching descriptions of the misery that came before his own eyes and smote his loving heart; and another writer gives a picture as terrible as any even in the history of famines. 'I have seen,' says this writer, 'the labourer endeavouring to work at his spade, but fainting for want of food, and forced to quit it. I have seen the aged father eating grass like a beast, and in the anguish of his soul wishing for his dissolution. I have seen the helpless orphan exposed on the dunghill, and none to take him in for fear of infection; and I have seen the hungry infant sucking at the breast of the already expired parent.'[1]

In 1822 there was again a serious famine of considerable dimensions. Colonel Patterson, stationed at the time in Galway, tells how hundreds of half-starved wretches arrived daily from a distance of fifty miles, many of them so exhausted by want of food that means taken to restore them failed, owing to the weakness of their digestive organs (quoted from John Mitchel's 'History of Ireland,' p. 15). And certain official returns of the time state that in the month of June, in Clare County alone, 99,630 persons subsisted on daily charity; and in Cork, 122,000 (Alison's 'History of Europe,' quoted in John Mitchel's 'History of Ireland,' p. 154). Yet there was in 1821 a good grain crop, amounting to 1,822,816 quarters, and in 1822 to more than 1,000,000 quarters (Thom's 'Directory,' quoted by John Mitchel, p. 123).[2]

It was the peculiarity of the Act of Union and of the land legislation that it was ultimately a curse as great to the landlord as to the tenant. In the pages which immediately follow there will be terrible stories of cruelty by the Irish landlords; and these stories will often tempt the reader to ask whether the men who perpetrated such crimes could have had the same flesh and blood as himself. The landlords of Ireland were no less human beings than the Southern planters who upheld the slavery of the negro, or than the *noblesse* whose tyranny produced the horrors of the French Revolution. Like their serfs, they were the victims to some extent of circumstances. Behind their action in the days of the famine, there stood at least a century of extravagance. In the last century the Irish squire never dreamt that the time would come when the native Parliament of Ireland would be destroyed, and acted as if Ireland were to be always his chief home, and Dublin always the capital to which the Parliament of his country would bring the fashion and the society of Ireland. The result was that he spent more in proportion to his means on the construction of his house than probably his English brother. The aristocratic mansions in Dublin—which, if they be fortunate, are now occupied as public offices, and if unfortunate, have sunk to the degradation of tenement houses—were finer in the days before the Union than most of the houses which were then occupied by the aristocracy that dwelt in London.

[1] Lecky, 'History of England,' ii. 218, 219.
[2] Cobbett, in his 'Register,' remarked upon this strange phenomenon of abundant food and widespread starvation. 'Money it seems,' he wrote, 'is wanted in Ireland. Now, people do not eat money. No, but the money will buy them something to eat. What? The food is *there*, then. Pray observe this, and let the parties get out of the concern if they can. *The food is there:* but those who have it in their possession will not give it without the money. And we know that the food is there: for since this famine has been declared in Parliament, thousands of quarters of corn have been exported every week from Ireland to England.'—Quoted in Mitchel's 'History of Ireland,' p. 153.

Then came the Union; the price for which a large number of the Irish nobility betrayed the liberties of their country was a step in the peerage. With the departure of the Irish Legislature Dublin ceased to be the seat of Irish fashion; the Irish peer suddenly found himself obliged to live in the richer and more expensive country, in the larger and more expensive metropolis; and then began the creation of debt, alleviated occasionally by the Irishman's proverbial luck in the capture of a rich *parti*. When the famine came, a vast number of the Irish landlords were inextricably in debt; the Encumbered Estates Act had not yet been passed; and accordingly there was no means whatever of rescue. It often happened, therefore, that the nominal and the real owner were two different persons. The nominal owner was an O'Flaherty or a Blake; the real owner was the Hebrew gentleman resident in London from whom the O'Flaherty or the Blake had borrowed as much, or more, than the estate could bear. The Irish landlord of the period—as to a very recent date—was insolent, tyrannical, ignorant; a spendthrift, a gambler, often a drunkard; but he often stood to be shot at for deeds which were the natural sequence, not of his own follies and vices, but of the follies and vices of those who had gone before him.

The future of Ireland which all these causes were preparing was forecast in several of the official reports already alluded to, and above all in the Report of the Devon Commission.

A few extracts from these reports will complete the picture of Ireland in the days before the famine. These extracts will be very few and very brief, but they are sufficient to justify the assertion already made, that the famine was inevitable without land reform; and that its advent could fail to be foreseen only by invincibly ignorant Ministers and Parliaments.

'I have seen a great deal of the peasantry,' said the well-known engineer Alexander Nimmo, whose name is perpetuated by a pier in the town of Galway, in his evidence before the committee of 1824. 'I have sometimes slept in their cabins, and had frequent intercourse with them, especially in the south and west of Ireland. I conceive the peasantry in Ireland to be in the lowest possible state of existence; their cabins are in the most miserable condition, and their food is potatoes, with water, very often without anything else, frequently without salt; and I have frequently had occasion to meet persons who begged of me on their knees, for the love of God, to give them some promise of employment, that, from the credit, they might get the means of supporting themselves for a few months until I could employ them.'

'Nothing can be worse than the condition of the lower classes of the labourers, and the farmers are not much better,' said Mr. J. Driscoll before the 1824 committee. 'They have nothing whatever, I think, but the potatoes and water; they seldom have salt.'

The committee before whom this and the like evidence was brought reported:

That a very considerable proportion of the population, variously estimated at a fourth or a fifth of the whole, is considered to be out of employment; that this, combined with the consequences of an altered system of managing land, is stated to produce misery and suffering which no language can possibly describe, and which it is necessary to witness in order fully to estimate.[2]

The situation of the ejected tenantry, or of those who are obliged to give up their small holdings in order to promote the consolidation of farms, is necessarily most deplorable. It would be impossible for language to convey an idea of the state of distress to which the ejected tenantry have been reduced, or of the disease, misery, or even vice which they have propagated where they have settled; so that not only they

---

[1] P. 226 of the Report. Quoted by O'Connell (Hansard, lxxxv., p. 507).
[2] Pp. 380, 381 of the Report of 1824. Quoted by O'Connell (Hansard, lxxxv., p. 508).

who have been ejected have been rendered miserable, but they have carried with them and propagated that misery. They have increased the stock of labour, they have rendered the habitations of those who have received them more crowded, they have given occasion to the dissemination of disease, they have been obliged to resort to theft and all manner of vice and iniquity to procure subsistence; but what is perhaps the most painful of all, a vast number of them have perished of want.[1]

The Poor Law Inquiry of 1835 reported that 2,235,000 persons were out of work and in distress for thirty weeks in the year.[2]

Finally, the Devon Commission reported that it 'would be impossible to describe adequately the sufferings and privations which the cottiers and labourers and their families in most parts of the country endure,' 'their cabins are seldom a protection against the weather,' 'a bed or a blanket is a rare luxury,' ' in many districts their only food is the potato, their only beverage water.'[3]

The evidence which I have now quoted as to the Land question may be best summed up in the words of Mr. Mill: 'Returning nothing,' he writes of the Irish landlords, ' to the soil, they consume its whole produce minus the potatoes strictly necessary to keep the inhabitants from dying of famine.'[4]

It was this state of relations between landlord and tenant that gave to the potato its fatal importance in the economy of Irish life. The compromise between the two sides was that all the wheat and oats which were grown on the land and all the stock should go to the payment of the rent; and also so much of the potato crop as was not required to keep the tenant and his family from absolute starvation. The potato was found to be particularly well suited for the position of the tenant. It produced a larger amount per acre than any other crop ; it suited the soil and the climate ; it supplied a vegetable which, alone among vegetables, supported life without anything else. The potato meant abundant food or starvation, life or wholesale death. It was the thin partition between famine and the millions of the Irish people.

The plant that had so dread a responsibility had its bad qualities as well as its good; it was fickle, perishable, liable to wholesale destruction, and more than once already had given proof of its terrible uncertainty. It will be seen by-and-by that the readiness of the potato to fail played a very important part, and, indeed, was the main factor in Irish life, not merely in the epoch with which we are now dealing, but in a period a great deal nearer to our own time.

There was, however, no anticipation of disaster in 1845. The fields everywhere waved green and flowery, and there was the promise of an abundant harvest. There had been whispers of the appearance of disease, but it was in countries that in those days appeared remote—in Belgium or Germany, in Canada or the Western States of America. It was not until the autumn of 1845 that it made its appearance for the first time in the United Kingdom. It was first detected in the Isle of Wight, and in the first week of September the greater number of the potatoes in the London market were found to be unfit for human food. In Ireland the autumnal weather was suggestive of some calamity. For weeks the air was electrical and disturbed : there was much lightning, unaccompanied

---

[1] Quoted by O'Connell, ib. Report of Select Committee of 1830, p. 8. Quoted by O'Connell, ib., pp. 508, 509.
[2] Quoted by Mr. Labouchere, ' Annual Register,' 1847, p. 9.
[3] Quoted by O'Connell (Hansard, lxxxv., p. 509).
[4] Quoted in Healy, ' Why there is a Land Question,' etc., p. 55.

by thunder. At last traces of the disease began to be discovered. A dark spot—such as would come from a drop of acid—was found in the green leaves; the disease then spread rapidly, and in time there was nothing in many of the potato-fields but bleached and withered leaves emitting a putrid stench.

The disease first appeared on the coast of Wexford, and soon reports of an alarming character began to come from the interior. It was still a hopeful sign that a field of potatoes remained sound long after all the surrounding fields had been touched by the blight. The plague, however, was stealthy and swift, and a crop that was sound one day, the next was rotten. As time passed on, the disaster spread; potatoes, healthy when they were dug and pitted, were found utterly decayed when the pit was opened. All kinds of remedies were proposed by scientific men—ventilation, new plans of pitting and of packing, the separation of the sound and unsound parts of the potato. All failed; the blight, like the locust, was victor over all obstacles, omnipotent over all opposing forces.

O'Connell and the public bodies of the country called the attention of the Government to the impending calamity. The Royal Agricultural Society—an association of landlords—declared that a great portion of the potato crop was seriously affected. The Dublin Corporation called a public meeting under the presidency of the Lord Mayor, which O'Connell attended. He there drew attention to one of the facts which excited the most attention, and, afterwards, the fiercest anger of the time. This was, that while wholesale starvation was impending over the nation, every port was carrying out its wheat and oats to other lands. Side by side with the fields of blighted potatoes in 1845, were fields of abundant oats. In one week—according to a quotation from the *Mark Lane Express* in O'Connell's speech—no less than 16,000 quarters of oats were exported from Ireland to London. O'Connell joined in the proposal that the export of provisions to foreign countries should be immediately prohibited, and that at the same time the Corn Laws should be suspended, and the Irish ports opened to receive provisions from all countries.

Here it is well to pause for a moment on this point. In favour of the proposal of closing the ports, O'Connell was able to adduce the example of Belgium, of Holland, of Russia, and of Turkey under analogous circumstances. Testimony is as unanimous and proof as clear as to the abundance of the grain crop as they are to the failure of the potato crop. 'Everyone,' said Lord John Russell, in a letter he wrote to the Duke of Leinster in 1847, 'who travels through Ireland observes the large stacks of corn which are the produce of the late harvest.'[1] This corn was scattered far and wide. John Mitchel quotes the case of the captain who saw a vessel laden with Irish corn at the port of Rio in South America. On this point, more will be said by-and-by.

The complaint of the Irish writers is that this wholesale exportation was not arrested, and on this they founded charges against the Ministers of the period, some grotesque, but some most true. It is grotesque to charge it as a crime against the English people that they ate the food which was supplied to them from Ireland: they obtained the right to eat the food by having paid for it. But the charge is just that it was the land legislation which the Imperial Parliament had passed and maintained that rendered necessary the export of these vast provisions amidst all the stress and

---

[1] Quoted in 'History of the Irish Famine,' by Rev. J. O'Rourke, p. 248.

horrors of famine. There was scarcely a single head of all these cattle, there was scarcely a sheaf of all this corn, the price of which did not go to pay the landlord over whose exorbitance and caprice the Legislature had again and again refused to place any legislative restraint. The Irish land system necessitated the export of food from a starving nation. The Imperial Parliament was the parent of this land system; the Imperial Parliament was then responsible for the starvation which this exportation involved.

The appeals which O'Connell, the Dublin Corporation, and other bodies in Ireland addressed to the Government, grew in intensity and urgency as the crisis advanced, and as the reports began to reach Dublin of numerous cases of starvation throughout the country. These appeals met with dilatory answers. The Government were noting all that took place; then they were inquiring; finally they had appointed a scientific commission to investigate the facts of the case; and so on. Meantime the destroying angel was advancing with a certain and swift wing over the doomed country.

It was one of the necessary consequences of the Legislative Union that Ireland was inextricably involved in the struggles of English parties. And at this moment England was in the very agony of one of her greatest party struggles. The advent of the Irish famine was the last event that broke down Peel's faith in protection. When these warnings of impending disaster and these urgent prayers for relief came from Ireland, Peel was in the unfortunate position of being convinced of the danger, and at the same time impotent as to the remedies. He was at that moment in the midst of his attempts to carry over his colleagues to free trade; and so his hands were tied. He did propose that the ports should be opened by Order in Council, but to this proposal he could not get some of his colleagues to agree. Then there came a Ministerial crisis: Peel resigned; Lord John Russell was unable to form an Administration; and Peel again resumed office. The result of these various occurrences was that the ports were not opened and that Parliament was not summoned; and thus three months — every single minute of which involved wholesale life or death — were allowed to pass without any effective remedy.

Assuredly under such circumstances, O'Connell and the other leaders of the National Party were justified in drawing a contrast between this deadly delay and the promptitude that a native Legislature would have shown. 'If,' he exclaimed at the Repeal Association, 'they ask me what are my propositions for relief of the distress, I answer, first, *Tenant-right*. I would propose a law giving to every man his own. I would give the landlord his land, and a fair rent for it; but I would give the tenant compensation for every shilling he might have laid out on the land in permanent improvements. And what next do I propose? Repeal of the Union.'[1]

And then he went on with still greater force: 'If we had a domestic Parliament, would not the ports be thrown open — would not the abundant crops with which Heaven has blessed her be kept for the people of Ireland — and would not the Irish Parliament be more active even than the Belgian Parliament to provide for the people food and employment?'[2]

But Ireland had not won her Legislature; and she had accordingly to wait patiently until January 22, when it suited the English Premier to call Parliament together. The mysterious replies of the Ministers — the perfect paralysis of independent effort which these suggestions had caused in

---

[1] 'History of Ireland,' by John Mitchel, ii. 205.   [2] *Ib.*

Ireland—all tended to turn the eyes of the Irish people with feverish longing and expectation to this event. The opening hours of the session were sufficient to damp all these hopes. On means of affording relief the Queen's Speech was vague; but on the question of coercion it spoke in terms of unmistakable plainness. 'I have observed,' said that document, 'with deep regret, the very frequent instances in which the crime of deliberate assassination has been of late committed in Ireland. It will be your duty to consider whether any measures can be devised calculated to give increased protection to life, and to bring to justice the perpetrators of so dreadful a crime.' I will deal with the justification for the new Coercion Bill when I come to describe the memorable struggle that took place on that measure. Meantime, let it suffice to say that the characteristic contrast between the tender solicitude of the Government for the landlords, and its half-hearted regard for the tenants—at the moment when of the tenants a thousand had died through eviction and hunger for every one of the landlords who had met death through assassination—roused the bitterest resentment in Ireland. 'The only notice,' exclaimed the *Nation*, 'vouchsafed to this country is a hint that more gaols, more transportations, and more gibbets might be useful to us. Or, possibly, we wrong the Minister; perhaps when her Majesty says that "protection must be afforded to life," she means that the people are not to be allowed to die of hunger during the ensuing summer—or that the lives of tenants are to be protected against the extermination of clearing landlords—and that so "deliberate assassinations" may become less frequent—God knows what she means—the use of Royal language is to *conceal* ideas.'

The measures proposed by the Government for dealing with the distress were, first the importation of corn on a lowered duty through the repeal of the Corn Laws; and, secondly, the advance of two sums of £50,000, one to the landlords for the drainage of their lands, and the other for public works. The ridiculous disproportion of these sums to the magnitude of the calamity was proved before very long; but to all representations the Government replied in the worst and haughtiest spirit of official optimism. 'Instructions have been given,' said Sir James Graham, 'on the responsibility of the Government to meet any emergency.'[1] Only one good measure was covered by the generous self-complacency of this round assertion. Under a Treasury minute of December 19, 1845, the Ministry had instructed Messrs. Baring and Co. to purchase £100,000 worth of Indian corn. This they introduced secretly into Ireland, and its distribution proved most timely.

Still the Irish members pressed for more definite assurances and larger proposals. But their suggestions and Peel's beneficent intentions were frustrated by the fatal entanglement of Irish sorrows in the personal ambitions and the partisan warfare of St. Stephen's. Peel had put forward the Irish famine as the main reason for his change of opinion on the Corn Laws; and the Irish famine became one of the great debatable topics between the adherents of free trade and of protection. All the Protectionist Party in Parliament, all the organs of the landlords in Ireland, united in the statement that the reports of distress were unreal and exaggerated. 'The potato crop of this year,' wrote the *Evening Mail* of November 3, 1845, 'far exceeded an average one;' 'the corn of all kinds is so far abundant'—which, indeed, was quite true—'the apprehensions of

---

[1] Mitchel, ii. 205.

a famine are unfounded, and are merely made the pretence for withholding the payment of rent.' Some days after it repeated, 'there was a sufficiency, an abundance of sound potatoes in the country for the wants of the people.' 'The potato famine in Ireland,' exclaimed Lord George Bentinck, 'was a gross delusion—a more gross delusion had never been practised upon any country by any Government.'[1] 'The cry of famine was a mere pretence for a party object.'[2] 'Famine in Ireland,' said Lord Stanley, was 'a vision— a baseless vision.'[3]

The second great obstacle to the proper consideration of measures to meet the distress was the Coercion Bill. It was quite true that there had been several atrocious murders in Ireland; but the provocation to outrage had been terrible. A passion—that looked something like an epidemic of homicidal mania—had seized many of the landlords for wholesale clearances at the very moment when the people were confronted with universal hunger. One of the very worst of these cases had taken place within a few days of the discussion on the Coercion Bill. A Mr. and Mrs. Gerard had turned out in one morning the entire population of the village of Ballinglass, in the county of Galway—270 persons in number. Neither the old, the young, nor the dying had been spared; and even after the eviction the tenants had been pursued with a frenzied hate. The roofs had been taken off their sixty houses; and when the villagers took refuge under the skeleton walls they were driven thence, and the walls were rooted from their foundations. Then they took shelter in the ditches, where they slept for two nights huddled together before fires—some of them old men eighty years of age, others women with children upon their breasts. They were forced from the ditches as from their hearths. The fires were quenched, and the outcasts were driven to wheresoever they might find a home or a grave.

The proposals of the Coercion Bill of the Government were certainly startling. Under the Bill the Lord-Lieutenant could proclaim any district, and could order every person within it 'to be and to remain' within his own house from one hour before sunset to one hour before sunrise. No person could with safety visit a public-house, or a tea or coffee-shop, or the house of a friend. A justice of the peace had the power to search for and drag out all such persons. The penalty was as terrible as the offence. Any person outside his own house, whether wandering on the highway or inside another house, was liable to be transported beyond the seas for seven years. 'From four or five o'clock,' said Earl Grey, criticising the Bill in the House of Lords,[4] 'in the afternoon, till past eight on the following morning, during the month of December, no inhabitant of a proclaimed district in Ireland was to be allowed to set his foot outside the door of his cabin without rendering himself liable to this severe punishment. He might not even venture from home during that time to visit a friend, or to enjoy at any place a few hours of harmless recreation. Nay, he dared not even go to his work in the morning, or return from his work in the evening, so as to gain the advantage of the hours of daylight, without rendering himself liable to arrest at the will of a police-constable, and to be kept in confinement, in default of proving what no man could prove—that he was out with innocent intentions.'

Such a Bill, ferocious at any time, was still more ferocious in the circumstances of Ireland at that moment. The man found outside a house between sunset and sunrise was liable to transportation for seven years; and in this

---

[1] Quoted by O'Rourke, p. 104. [2] 'Annual Register,' 1846, p. 68.
[3] Ib., p. 80. [4] Hansard, lxxxiv., p. 697.

year the roads of all Ireland were crowded with wanderers, houseless, homeless, starving, and dying. Then the Bill enabled the Lord-Lieutenant to inflict taxation on the proclaimed district for additional police, for additional magistrates, for compensation to the relations of murdered or injured persons; and it was especially enacted that the taxation could be levied by distress, and levied on the occupiers only. The landlords, who, through absenteeism, or rack-renting, or the clearances, were the direct authors and instigators of the despair that led to the crimes, were especially exempted from all taxation.[1] Every tenant was liable; and so resolute were the Government to inflict the tax, that the merciful exemptions by the Poor Law were abrogated. Under the Poor Law all persons in houses under £4 valuation were free from the rates; under the Coercion Bill the occupier of any house, whether above £4 or under £4, was liable to the tax. And this at the moment when the inhabitants of the greater number of the houses in Ireland had not one meal of potatoes a day!

But cruel as was such a Bill at such a time, it would have been passed with a light heart, and by huge majorities from all English parties, if the exigencies of English party warfare had not at this moment produced a curious and a not very moral alliance between the English Whigs, the English Protectionists, and the O'Connellites. The English Whigs were anxious to return to office; the Protectionists raged with the desire to be avenged on Peel for the abandonment of protection; and the two parties saw in a combination against this Bill an opportunity of attaining their different ends. There were some slight obstacles, it was true, in the way. Lord John Russell had voted for the first reading of the Bill, and Lord George Bentinck, in response to some overtures to use it against the Ministers, had responded with fierce indignation and a vehement defence of the measure. But Lord John Russell had a counsellor in his own ambition, and Lord George Bentinck as sinister an adviser in Mr. Disraeli: with the result that each performed a *volte-face* as prompt as it was shameless. They both condescended, of course, to supply most excellent and strictly decorous reasons for their change of attitude. Lord John Russell announced the discovery—made with the suddenness, and, as will be seen by-and-by, lost again with the suddenness of a modern miracle—that coercion aggravated instead of curing the evils of Ireland; and Lord George Bentinck, declaring that the Government had displayed insincerity in postponing the Bill so long, proceeded to prove his own sincerity by taking care that it should be postponed to the Greek Kalends. It was under conditions like this that an Irish Coercion Bill was defeated for the first, and up to the present, for the last, time in the whole history of the Imperial Parliament.

On June 26, 1846, the second reading of the Coercion Bill was rejected by 292 votes to 217. On June 29 Sir Robert Peel announced his resignation. In the opinion of the majority of the Irishmen who survive from

---

[1] Earl Grey: 'It was not just to exempt the landlords; though they were not the cause of these outrages and evils, Ireland never would have got into its present state, the existing state of society there would never have been such as it was, if the landlords, as a body, had done their duty to the population under them; . . . . . he believed that of late years an improvement had taken place in the conduct of the landlords of Ireland towards their tenantry; but if they looked to the past history of that land, the awful state of things now existing would be seen to be a direct consequence of the dereliction of their duty by the upper classes of that country, which was an historical fact known not only to England but to all Europe.'—Hansard, lxxxiv., pp. 694, 695.

that period, the change of Administration was dearly bought by Ireland, even by the defeat of a Coercion Bill. The steps that had been taken by Peel were certainly grossly insufficient; but the disaster with which he had to deal was small in comparison with that which confronted Lord John Russell; and the opinion of posterity—at least of Irish posterity—is that, as a Minister, Lord John Russell was vastly inferior to Peel, and, therefore, much less competent to deal with the terrible crisis which had now come upon Ireland.

Amidst the throes of these great struggles, Ireland was entering upon a new and a still more terrible chapter in her tragic annals. The Famine of 1846 was coming!

CHAPTER III

THE FAMINE.

NOTHING brings the desperate position of the Irish tenant home with more terrible clearness to the mind than the fact that the awful warning of 1845 was, and had to be, unheeded. The potato was still cherished as the only friend, the one refuge, the single resource of the peasant. He stuck, then, to the plant—not with the tenacity of despair; not with the obstinacy of incurable fatuity; but because, in his circumstances, the potato, and the potato alone, offered him hope.

Strangely enough, it was in no spirit of apprehension that the tenantry set to work in the preparation of the potato crop of 1846. Contemporary testimony is unanimous in describing them as working at that period with an energy that was frantic, with a hopefulness that was tragic—with a determination to risk all on the one cast that exhibited for once a nation carried in the maelstrom of the gambler's desperation. 'Although,' writes Mr. A. M. Sullivan,[1] 'already feeling the pinch of sore distress, if not actual famine, they worked as if for dear life; they begged and borrowed on any terms the means whereby to crop the land once more. The pawn-offices were choked with the humble finery that had shone at the village dance or christening feast; the banks and local money-lenders were besieged with appeals for credit. Meals were stinted; backs were bared.'

The signs of the seasons were watched throughout the year with fierce anxiety. The spring was unpromising enough. Snow, hail, and sleet fell in March; and in Belfast there was snow as late as the first week in April. But when the summer came, it made amends for all this. The weather in June was of tropical heat; vegetation sprang up with something of tropical rapidity; and everybody anticipated a splendid harvest. Towards the end of June there was again a change for the worse. The weather broke; in Limerick there was on the 19th a sudden downfall of copious rain; then came thunder and lightning, and after that intense cold. So also in July, there was the alternation of tropical heat and thunderstorm, of parching dryness and excessive rain. St. Swithin's Day was looked forward to with great eagerness. There was a continuous downpour of rain; and on the following day a fearful thunderstorm burst over Dublin. Still the crop went on splendidly; and all over the country once again wide fields of waving green and flowery stalks promised exuberant abundance of the staple product of Ireland.

[1] 'New Ireland,' p. 59 (eighth edition).

It was in the early days of August that the first symptoms of the coming disaster were seen. The calamity was heralded by a strange portent that was seen simultaneously in several parts of Ireland, and that at once suggested the ghastly truth to those who had carefully watched the signs of the previous year. A fog—which some describe as extremely white, and others as yellow—was seen to rise from the ground; the fog was dry, and emitted a disagreeable odour. A Mr. Cooper saw it on the Ox Mountains in Sligo; Justin McCarthy remembers to have seen it in Bantry Bay in county Cork. Mr. Cooper at once suspected the real truth, and caused inquiries to be made. The companion who was with Mr. McCarthy at the time at once exclaimed that the blight was coming. And they were right; the fog of that night bore the blight within its accursed bosom. The work of destruction was as swift as it was universal. In a single night and throughout the whole country the entire crop was destroyed, almost to the last potato. 'On the 27th of last month' (July), writes Father Mathew, 'I passed from Cork to Dublin, and this doomed plant bloomed in all the luxuriance of an abundant harvest. Returning on the 3rd instant (August), I beheld with sorrow one wide waste of putrefying vegetation.'[1]

The meaning of the dread calamity burst upon the people at once; but the suffering was yet to come. In the meantime, they gave way to the poignancy of their grief or to the apathy of their despair. 'In many places,' writes Father Mathew, 'the wretched people were seated on the fences of their decaying gardens, wringing their hands and wailing bitterly the destruction that had left them foodless.'[2] 'Blank stolid dismay, a sort of stupor, fell upon the people,' writes Mr. A. M. Sullivan, 'contrasting remarkably with the fierce energy put forth a year before. It was no uncommon sight to see the cottier and his little family seated on the garden fence, gazing all day long in moody silence at the blighted plot that had been their last hope. Nothing could arouse them. You spoke; they answered not. You tried to cheer them; they shook their heads. I never saw so sudden and so terrible a transformation.'[3]

'Famine advances on us with giant strides,'[4] wrote Captain Wynne, one of the officials of the time, from Ennis in the autumn of 1846; and his words were soon confirmed. Towards the end of August the calamity began to be universal, and its symptoms everywhere to be seen. Some of the people rushed into the towns; others wandered listlessly along the highroads, in the vague and vain hope that food would somehow or other come to their hands. They grasped at everything that promised sustenance; they plucked turnips from the fields; many were glad to live for weeks on a single meal of cabbage a day.[5] In some cases they feasted on the dead bodies of horses and asses[6] and dogs;[7] and there is at least one horrible story of a mother eating the limbs of her dead child.[8] In many places dead bodies were discovered with grass in their mouths and in their stomachs and bowels.[9] In Mayo, a man who had been observed searching for food on the seashore was found dead on the roadside, after vainly attempting to prolong his wretched life by means of the half-masticated turf and grass which remained unswallowed in his mouth. Nettle-tops,

---

[1] 'The Census for Ireland for the Year 1851.' Part V. 'Table of Deaths,' vol. i. p. 270.
[2] Ib.
[3] 'New Ireland,' p. 69.
[4] O'Rourke, p. 366.
[5] Census Commissioners, p. 273.
[6] O'Rourke, pp. 390, 391.
[7] Census Commissioners, p. 243.
[8] Ib., p. 310.
[9] Ib., pp. 243, 283.

wild mustard, and watercress were sought after with desperate eagerness. The assuaging of hunger with seaweed too often meant the acceleration of death, but seaweed was greedily devoured,[1] so also were diseased cattle,[2] and there were inquests in many places on people who had died from eating diseased potatoes.[3] Another general effect of the famine was that the characteristic merriment of the peasantry totally disappeared.[4] People went about, not speaking even to beg, with 'a stupid despairing look ;'[5] children looked 'like old men and women ;'[6] and even the lower animals seemed to feel the surrounding despair ; 'the few dogs,' says a visitor to Mayo, 'were poor and piteous, and had ceased to bark.'[7] Even the ties of kindred were rent asunder. Parents neglected their children, and in a few localities children turned out their aged parents.[8] But such cases were very rare, and in the most remote parts of the country. There are, on the other hand, numberless stories of parents willingly dying the slow death of starvation to save a small store of food for their children.[9]

The workhouse was then, as it is now, an object of dread and loathing. Within its walls were accustomed to take refuge the rustic victims of vice and the outcasts of the towns. Entrance into the workhouse then was regarded not merely as marking the advent of social ruin, but of moral degradation. Thus it came that fathers and mothers died, and allowed their children to die along with them within their own hovels, rather than seek a refuge within those hated walls.[10] But the time came when hunger and disease swept away these prejudices, and the people craved admission to the once-dreaded bastilles. Here again, however, hope was cheated ; the accommodation in the workhouses was far below the requirements of the people. At Westport 3,000 persons sought relief in a single day, when the workhouse, though built to accommodate 1,000 persons, was already 'crowded far beyond its capacity.'[11] It was this town that Mr. Forster described as showing 'a strange and fearful sight like what we read of in beleaguered cities : its streets crowded with gaunt wanderers sauntering to and fro with hopeless air and hunger-struck look.'[12] At Carrick-on-Shannon there were 110 applications in one day ; there were thirty vacancies.[13] Driven from the workhouses, the people began to die on the roadside, or, alone in their despair, within their own cabins. Corpses lay strewn by the side of once-frequented roads, and at doors in the most crowded streets of the towns. 'During that period,' writes Mr. Tuke, 'roads in many places became as charnel-houses, and several car and coach drivers have assured me that they rarely drove anywhere without seeing dead bodies strewn along the roadside, and that in the dark they had even gone over them. A gentleman told me that in the neighbourhood of Clifden one inspector of roads had caused no less than 140 bodies to be buried which he found along the highway.'[14] 'In our district,' writes Mr. A. M. Sullivan,[15] 'it was a common occurrence to find on opening the front door in early morning, leaning against it, the corpse of some victim who in the night-time had rested in its shelter. We raised a public subscription, and employed two men with horse and cart to go around each day and gather up the dead.'

---

[1] Census Commissioners, p. 272. [2] Ib., p. 243.
[3] Ib., pp. 271, 277. [4] Ib., p. 242. [5] Ib., p. 283.
[6] Ib., p. 273. [7] Ib., p. 284.
[8] Ib., p. 242. [9] Ib., p. 242 ; O'Rourke, pp. 401, 402.
[10] Census Commissioners, p. 92. [11] O'Rourke, p. 503.
[12] Census Commissioners, p. 283. [13] Ib., p. 273.
[14] O'Rourke, p. 384. [15] 'New Ireland,' p. 65.

The scenes that were revealed when some of the cabins were entered were even more horrible. When the inmates found that death was inevitable, they made no further struggle, sought the assistance neither of the Government nor of their neighbours; and occasionally, as Mr. Tuke tells us, the last survivor of a whole family 'earthed up the door of his miserable cabin to prevent the ingress of pigs and dogs, and then laid himself down to die in this fearful family vault.'[1] Men entering the cabins found the dead and the dying side by side—lying on the same pallet of rotting straw, covered with the same rags. 'The only article,' says an eye-witness of a scene in Windmill Lane, Skibbereen, 'that covered the nakedness of the family, that screened them from the cold, was a piece of coarse packing stuff which lay extended alike over the bodies of the living and the corpses of the dead; which served as the only defence of the dying and the winding-sheet of the dead.'[2]

'The first remarkable sign,' writes Mr. A. M. Sullivan, 'of the havoc which death was making was the decline and the disappearance of funerals.'[3] The annals of the time are full of the instances of this sinister change in the habits of Christian lands. The bodies of those who had fallen on the road lay for days unburied. Husbands lay for a week in the same hovels with the bodies of their unburied wives and children. Often when there was a funeral it bore even ghastlier testimony to the terror of the time. 'In this town,' writes a special correspondent of the *Cork Examiner* from Skibbereen, 'have I witnessed to-day men, fathers, carrying perhaps their only child to its last home, its remains enclosed in a few deal boards patched together; I have seen them, on this day, in three or four instances, carrying those coffins under their arms or upon their shoulders, without a single individual in attendance upon them; without mourner or ceremony—without wailing or lamentation. The people in the street, the labourers congregated in the town, regarded the spectacle without surprise; they looked on with indifference, because it was of hourly occurrence.'[4] A Catholic priest, who was a curate in county Galway during the famine, tells a story of meeting a man with a cart drawn by an ass, on which there were three coffins, containing the bodies of his wife and two children. When he reached the churchyard he was too weak to dig a grave, and was only able to put a little covering of clay on the coffins. The next day the priest found ravenous dogs making a horrid meal from the corpses.[5] In another part of the country a woman with her own hands dug the grave of her dead son.[6]

Meantime, what had the Government been doing? They had, to put it briefly, been aggravating nearly all the evils that were reaping so rich a harvest of suffering and death in Ireland. The measures which Sir Robert Peel had taken during the recess of 1845 and in the early portions of the session of 1846 have been already mentioned. As time went on he had taken other steps to meet the crisis. Donations to the amount of £100,000 had been given from the Treasury in aid of subscriptions raised by charitable organizations. A still more important step was the setting on foot of works for the employment of the destitute.

The initial blunder of Lord John Russell was suddenly to close the works which had been set on foot by Peel. At the time when this decree went forth there were no less than 97,900 persons employed on the relief

---

[1] O'Rourke, pp. 384, 385.   [2] *Ib.* p. 272.
[3] 'New Ireland,' p. 64.   [4] O'Rourke pp. 272, 273.
[5] *Ib.*, p. 379.   [6] *Ib.*, p. 405.

works; and the effect of adding this vast army of unemployed to the population whose condition has just been described, can easily be imagined.

The speech in which Lord John Russell announced his own policy followed on August 17, 1846; and, well-intentioned as it doubtless was, there was scarcely a sentence in it which did not do harm, not a proposal that did not work mischief. The first important statement was that the Government did not propose to interfere with the regular mode by which Indian corn and other kinds of grain might be brought into Ireland. The Government proposed 'to leave that trade as much at liberty as possible.' 'They would take care not to interfere with the regular operations of merchants for the supply to the country or with the retail trade.'[1] Then he described the new legislation which he proposed. Relief works were to be set on foot by the Board of Works when they had previously been presented at presentment sessions. For these works the Government were to advance money at the rate of 3½ per cent., repayable in ten years. In the poorer districts the Government were to make grants to the extent of £50,000. This Bill, when it became law, was known as the 'Labour Rate Act.'

The evil effects of this speech and this legislation were not long in showing themselves. The declarations with regard to non-intervention with trade were especially disastrous. The price of grain at once went up, and while the deficiency of food was thus enormously increased, speculators were driven to frenzy by the prospect of fabulous gains. Strange and almost incredible results followed. Wheat that had been exported by starving tenants was afterwards reimported from England to Ireland; sometimes before it was finally sold it had crossed the Irish Sea four times—delirious speculation offering new bids and rushing in insane eagerness from the Irish to the English and from the English to the Irish market in search of the daily increasing prices. Stories are still told in Ireland with grim satisfaction of the abject ruin that was the Nemesis to the greedy speculators in a nation's starvation. More than one Shylock kept his corn obstinately in store while the people around him were dying by the thousand, and when he at last opened the doors found, not his longed-for treasure-house, but an accumulation of rotten corn, which had to be emptied into the river. 'A client of mine,' writes the late Master Fitzgibbon,[2] 'in the winter of 1846-47, became the owner of corn cargoes of such number and magnitude that if he had accepted the prices pressed upon him in April and May, 1847, he would have realized a profit of £70,000. He held for still higher offers, until the market turned in June, fell in July, and rapidly tumbled, as an abundant harvest became manifest. He still held, hoping for a recovery, and in the end of October he became a bankrupt.'

'The Government,' said Lord John Russell, 'did not propose to interfere with the regular mode by which Indian corn might be brought into Ireland.' What was the result of this? According to a report from Commissary John Hewetson, dated December 30, 1846, Indian corn which had been bought for £9 or £10 a ton was selling for £17 5s. in Cork; was not to be had for any price in Limerick, but, in the shape of meal, was fetching from £18 10s. to £19 a ton. 'These,' said he, 'are really famine prices;'[3] and then he tells how in Cork alone one firm was reported to have cleared £40,000 and another £80,000, from corn speculations.

[1] Hansard, lxxxviii., p. 776.   [2] 'Ireland in 1868,' p. 205.   [3] O'Rourke, p. 171.

The reason for the non-intervention with the supply of Indian corn was that the retail trade might not be interfered with; and that at this period retail shops were so few and far between for the sale of corn that the labourer in the public works had sometimes to walk twenty or twenty-five miles in order to buy a single stone of meal.[1]

It will be seen, presently, how the inflated price of corn, and the difficulty of obtaining it at any price high or low, co-operated with some provisions of the Labour Rate Act to enormously increase the sum of suffering and the total of deaths.

These were the days when free trade was a doctrine professed with all the exaggeration and misconception of a new faith. The reader need not fear that I am about to inflict upon him any of the senseless and utterly unmeaning abuse of free trade and political economy with which ignorant or half-educated writers are in the habit of vexing intelligent men. The free trade under which Lord John Russell and his subordinates justified their fatal errors in 1846 and 1847 was not free trade, but a ghastly travesty of the doctrine, and a hideous misunderstanding of the teachings of sound political economy. It will be seen by-and-by that Lord John Russell and all his subordinates had themselves to make this acknowledgment, and to announce a palinode as shameful as any in Parliamentary history. But in the end of 1846 they were still unshaken in their crazy misunderstanding of the subject—and indeed lectured the starving Irish nation with the supremacy of superior beings and the remote calm of dwellers on Olympian heights. The offensiveness of the attitude and the absurdity of the doctrines were a good deal intensified by the fact that, with characteristic tenderness for Irish feeling, the preachers selected to announce those doctrines were self-sufficient English or Scotch civil servants, with more than the usual amount of the rancorous dogmatism characteristic of their race.[2]

There was to be no interference with the ordinary operations of trade. Thus, it was decreed that the food which was in the food depôts that had been established at various points in Ireland should not be sold at moderate prices—and, in fact, should not be sold at all until the autumn. The result was, that people died with money in their hands, knocking at the doors of the Government stores, and vainly begging for food.[3]

The Labour Rate Act was made even worse in operation by the rules of these same officials. First, the whole policy of the Act was to make the famine a Government business. It was Government that had the carrying out of all the works; the Government had to be consulted about everything, to give their approval to everything. The result was, that all independent initiative and effort were stifled; local bodies in their paralysis were sent from one department of the circumlocution office to another; then, in their despair and distraction, did nothing. The rule of Red Tape was established with plenary powers and disastrous results. In

---

[1] O'Rourke, p. 172.
[2] As an instance: a deputation waited on Sir R. Routh, head of the Commissary Department, from Achill, representing the total destruction of the potatoes there, the absence of green crops, and asking for a supply of food from the Government stores, for which the inhabitants were ready to pay. The reply of Sir R. Routh was a peremptory refusal, coupled with the statement that 'nothing was more essential to the welfare of a country than strict adherence to free trade.' Then he 'begged to assure the reverend gentleman'—meaning one of the deputation—'that if he had read carefully and studied Burke, his illustrious countryman, he would agree with him (Sir R. Routh).'—O'Rourke, pp. 222, 223
[3] O'Rourke, p. 226.

April, 1846, Messrs. Jones, Twistleton and Co. were able to report that they had sent to Ireland 'ten thousand books, besides fourteen tons of paper.' 'Over the whole island,' writes John Mitchel, 'for the next few months, was a scene of confused and wasteful attempts at relief—bewildered barony sessions striving to understand the voluminous directions, schedules, and specifications under which alone they could vote their own money to relieve the poor at their own doors : but generally making mistakes—for the unassisted human faculties never could comprehend these ten thousand books and fourteen tons of paper ; insolent commissioners and inspectors and clerks snubbing them at every turn and ordering them to study the documents ; efforts on the part of the proprietors to expend some of the rates at least on useful works—reclaiming land, and the like—which efforts were always met with flat refusal, and a lecture on political economy. . . . plenty of jobbing and peculation all this while.'[1]

With a view to prevent competition with private enterprise, the money was all to be devoted to exclusively 'unproductive works,' by which were excluded railways, reclamation, and the like. The positive and negative results of this restriction were equally prejudicial. There were railways demanding extension ; millions of acres of waste land demanding reclamation ; miles of marsh ready to be drained—all such work was forbidden. The look-out was then for unproductive work ; and unproductive work, in a sense a good deal more literal than the Government wanted, was discovered. The stories told of the kind of work done under these loans would be incredible if they were not so well attested—among other things, by solid monuments that exist to this day. Roads were made leading to nowhere ; hills were dug away and then were filled up again ; and so utterly useless was this kind of labour, that sometimes good roads were actually spoiled, and traffic was impeded for some time by these supposed improvements. Hardly any of the roads were ever finished. 'Miles of grass-grown earth works,' writes Mr. A. M. Sullivan,[2] 'throughout the country now mark their course and commemorate for posterity one of the gigantic blunders of the famine time.' 'While on the subject of mistakes,' said the Knight of Glin, a well-known landlord of the period, 'he might mention on the Glin Road some people are filling up the original cutting of a hill with the stuff they had taken out of it. That,' he added naïvely, 'is another slice of our £450 '—the sum lent to Shanagolden Union for relief works.

Even this useless work:—as has been seen—was not allowed to be done without the maddening preliminaries of vexatious and imbecile official delays. But this was not from the want of a sufficiently large staff. There were no less than 10,000 officials ; and these appointments were given from the most corrupt motives. This example of corruption at the top had a good deal to do with the disastrous and universal spirit of corruption below. And the most heart-rending feature of it all was that all this machinery, all this vast army of officials, all these vast sums of money, not only did no good, but were productive of an increase, instead of a diminution, of the miseries of the country. As to a large portion of the people, the relief—such as it was—came too late. 'The wretched people were by this time too wasted and emaciated to work. The endeavour to do so under an inclement winter sky only hastened death. They tottered at daybreak to the roll-call, vainly tried to wheel the barrow or ply the

[1] 'History of Ireland,' ii. 215. [2] 'New Ireland,' p. 64.
[3] Mitchel, ii. 216.

pick, but fainted away on the cutting, or lay down by the wayside to rise no more.'[1]

But officialism was not convinced, and insisted on making the Act still more cruel by the regulations under which it was to be worked. 'Those who choose to labour may earn good wages,' wrote Colonel Jones to Mr. Trevelyan [2]—the one head of the Board of Works, the other the representative of the Treasury; and in accordance with this superfine dictum of the official mind, it was decreed that the work done should be task-work. In other words, the feebler a man was, the less help he was entitled to receive; the nearer to starvation, the more quickly he should be pushed by labour into the grave. Hapless wretches, often with wives and several children dying of hunger at home—sometimes with the wife or one of the children already a putrid corpse—crawled to their work in the morning, there drudged as best they could, and at the end of the day often had as their wage the sum of fivepence—sometimes it went as low as threepence.[3] To earn this sum too, it often happened that the starving man had to walk three, four, five, eight Irish miles to, and the same distance from, his work. Finally, owing to blunders, he was frequently unable even to get this pittance at the end of the week or fortnight; and then he returned to his cabin to die—unless, as often happened, he died on the wayside.[4]

Even when he was paid, the meal-shop was miles away—for the retail trade, with which the Government would not interfere, existed only in Government imagination; and meal-shops were only to be found at long intervals. Or, if he reached the meal-shop, Government measures again had raised the price of meal beyond the reach of relief work wages; and if he knocked at the doors of the Government depôts, a harsh and alien voice replied that in the name of political economy he should die.[5]

Finally, the evil done by the Labour Rate Act was in attracting from the cultivation of their own fields nearly all the farmers of the country. The prospect of immediate wages proved more enticing than the uncertainty of a remote and fickle harvest; and the universal peculation, combined with the absolute uselessness of the works done, spread a spirit of hideous demoralisation. The farmers flocked to them 'solely,' as Mr. Fitzgibbon puts it, 'because the public work was in fact no work, but a farcical excuse for getting a day's wages.'[6] The labourers, having the example of a great public fraud before their eyes, are described by Mitchel as 'themselves defrauding their fraudulent employers—quitting agricultural pursuits and crowding the public works, where they pretended to be cutting down hills and filling up hollows, and with tongue in cheek received half wages for doing nothing.'[7]

The Conservative organs of the period, which were no friends of the national newspapers, joined them in the descriptions of the hideous demoralisation which these works were producing: and they foretold with a fatal accuracy the effects of it all on the following year. 'There is not a labourer employed in the county except on public works,' wrote the *Dublin Evening Mail*, 'and there is prospect of the lands remaining untilled and unsown for the next year.' 'The good intentions of the Government,' wrote the *Cork Constitution*, 'are frustrated by the worst regulations— regulations which, diverting labour from its legitimate channels, left the fields without hands to prepare them for the harvest.'[8] To sum up the

---

[1] 'New Ireland,' p. 64.
[2] O'Rourke, p. 209.
[3] Ib., p. 206.
[4] Ib., p. 258.
[5] Ib., p. 225.
[6] 'Ireland in 1868,' p. 206.
[7] 'History,' ii., p. 215.
[8] 'History,' ii., p. 216.

case in reference to this effect of the Labour Rate Act—the means that were taken to meet the famine of 1846 proved the precursors and the preparers of the famine of 1847.

The records of the sufferings from hunger in 1847 are almost more revolting and terrible than those of 1846.

Meantime, another and a bitter calamity was added to those from which the people were already suffering. Pestilence always hovers on the flank of famine, and combined with wholesale starvation, there were numerous other circumstances that rendered a plague inevitable—the assemblage of such immense numbers of people at the public works and in the workhouses, the vast number of corpses that lay unburied, and finally the consumption of unaccustomed food. The plague which fell upon Ireland in 1846-47 was of a peculiarly virulent kind. It produced at once extreme prostration, and everyone struck by it was subject to frequent relapses; in Kinsale Union, out of 250 persons attacked, 240 relapsed.[1]

The name applied to it at the time sufficiently signified its origin. It was known as the 'road fever.'[2] Attacking as it did people already weakened by hunger, it was a scourge of merciless severity. Unlike famine, too, it struck alike at the rich and poor—the well-fed and the hungered. Famine killed one or two of a family; the fever swept them all away. Food relieved hunger; the fever was past all such surgery.

Many of the people, worn out by famine, had not the physical or mental energy even to move from their cabins. The panic which the plague everywhere created, intensified the miseries of those whom it attacked. The annals of the time are full of the kindly but rude attempts of the poor to stand by each other. It was a common custom of the period to have food left at the doors or handed in on shovels or sticks to the people inside the cabins; but very often the wretched inmates were entirely deserted. Lying beside each other, some living and some dead, their passage to the grave was uncheered by one act of help, by one word of sympathy. Here is a brief but complete picture of this dread phase of the days of the plague: 'A terrible apathy hangs over the poor of Skibbereen; starvation has destroyed every generous sympathy; despair has made them hardened and insensible, and they sullenly await their doom with indifference and without fear. Death is in every hovel; disease and famine, its dread precursors, have fastened on the young and the old, the strong and the feeble, the mother and the infant; whole families lie together on the damp floor devoured by fever, without a human being to wet their burning lips or raise their languid heads; the husband dies by the side of the wife, and she knows not that he is beyond the reach of earthly suffering; the same rag covers the festering remains of mortality and the skeleton forms of the living, who are unconscious of the horrible contiguity; rats devour the corpse, and there is no energy among the living to scare them from their horrid banquet; fathers bury their children without a sigh, and cover them in shallow graves round which no weeping mother, no sympathising friends are grouped; one scanty funeral is followed by another and another. Without food or fuel, bed or bedding, whole families are shut up in naked hovels, dropping one by one into the arms of death.'[3]

The fever-stricken wretches who had energy enough to crawl from their own homes and seek a refuge, became the heralds of disease wherever they

---

[1] Census Commissioners, p. 304. [2] Ib., p. 278.
[3] *Cork Examiner.* Quoted by Census Commissioners' 'Tables of Death,' vol. i., p. 272.

went, and often suffered tortures more prolonged and darker than those who had lain down and died by their own hearthstones. Many of them directed their steps to the towns. 'From the commencement of 1847,' writes Dr. Callanan, 'Fate opened her book in good earnest here, and the full tide of death flowed everywhere around us. During the first six months of that dark period, *one-third* of the daily population of our streets consisted of shadows and spectres, the impersonations of disease and famine, crowding in from the rural districts and stalking along to the general doom —the grave—which appeared to await them but at the distance of a few steps or a few short hours.'[1]

'In cases succeeding exhaustion from famine,' says another writer, 'the appearances were very peculiar—the fever assuming a low gastric type, indicated by a dry tongue, shrunk to half its size, and brown in the centre; lips thin and bloodless, coated with sordes; skin discoloured and sodden; general appearance squalid in the extreme, and hunger-stricken. These symptoms, and a loathsome, putrid smell emanating from their persons, as if the decomposition of the vital organs had anticipated death, rendered these unhappy cases too often hopeless. They used to creep about the city while their strength allowed, and then would sink exhausted in some shed or doorway, and often be found dead.'[2]

The workhouses and the hospitals were besieged more than ever; and death now raged with a terrible promptness and universality. There was the same difficulty as when starving thousands clamoured for admission and help in buildings in which only hundreds could be attended to; and there are descriptions of scenes enacted outside the hospitals and workhouses so revolting as to be almost incredible. 'Before accommodation for patients,' writes the Census Commissioners, 'approached anything like the necessity of the time, most mournful and piteous scenes were presented in the vicinity of fever hospitals and workhouses in Dublin, Cork, Waterford, Galway, and other large towns. There, day after day, numbers of people, wasted by famine and consumed by fever, could be seen lying on the footpaths and roads waiting for the chance of admission; and when they were fortunate enough to be received, their places were soon filled by other victims of suffering and disease!'[3]

'At the gate leading to the temporary fever hospital, erected near Kilmainham, were men, women, and children, lying along the pathway and in the gutter, awaiting their turn to be admitted. Some were stretched at full length, with their faces exposed to the full glare of the sun, their mouths open, and their black and parched tongues and encrusted teeth visible even from a distance. Some women had children at the breast who lay beside them in silence and apparent exhaustion—the fountain of their life being dried up; whilst in the centre of the road stood a cart containing a whole family who had been smitten down together by the terrible typhus, and had been brought there by the charity of a neighbour.'[4]

'Fever,' writes the Freeman's Journal, 'has increased in Galway and Loughrea; numbers may be seen lying in rags or straw in the streets in the height of disease.' 'Alarming spread of fever in Dublin,' is the language of the same journal; 'crowds lying on the ground at Glasnevin and in Cork Street waiting for admission to the hospital.'[5]

Outside the workhouses similar scenes took place. The case of Westport workhouse has been mentioned already, where as many as three

---

[1] Census Commissioners, p. 301.   [2] *Ib.*, p. 302.
[3] *Ib.*, p. 248.   [4] *Ib.*, p. 297.   [5] *Ib.*

thousand, suffering from hunger and fever, sought admission on the same day. 'Those who were not admitted—and they were, of course, the great majority—having no homes to return to, lay down and died in Westport and its suburbs.'[1] Mr. Egan was clerk of the union at the period, and in a conversation with Father O'Rourke, pointing to the wall opposite the workhouse gate, said : 'There is where they sat down never to rise again. I have seen there of a morning as many as eight corpses of those miserable beings who had died during the night. Father G—— (then in Westport) used to be anointing them as they lay exhausted along the walls and streets, dying of hunger and fever.'[2]

Admission to the fever hospital, and, still more, to the workhouse, was but the postponement, and often the acceleration of death. Owing to the unexpected demands made upon their space, the officials of these institutions were unable to adopt the primary and fundamental measures for diminishing the epidemic. The crowding rendered it impossible to separate the sick and the healthy, sometimes to separate even the dead and the dying ; there were not beds for a tithe of the applicants : and thus the epidemic was spread and intensified, instead of being alleviated and diminished. 'Inside the hospital enclosure' (the fever hospital at Kilmainham), says a writer already quoted, ' was a small open shed, in which were thirty-five human beings heaped indiscriminately on a little straw thrown on the ground. Several had been thus for three days, drenched by rain, etc. Some were unconscious, others dying ; two died during the night.'[3] ' We visited the poorhouse at Glenties ' (county of Donegal), says Mr. Tuke in the 'Transactions of the Relief Committee of Friends,' ' which is in a dreadful state ; the people were, in fact, half starved, and only half clothed. They had not sufficient food in the house for the day's supply. Some were leaving the house, preferring to die in their own hovels rather than in the poorhouse. Their bedding consisted of dirty straw, in which they were laid in rows, or on the floor—even as many as six persons being crowded under one rug. The living and the dying were stretched side by side beneath the same miserable covering.' The general effect of all this is summed up thus pithily but completely in the report of the Poor Law Commissioners for 1846 : 'In the present state of things nearly every person admitted is a patient ; separation of the sick, by reason of their number, becomes impossible ; disease spreads, and by rapid transition the workhouse is changed into one large hospital.'[4]

The workhouses and the hospitals were not the only public institutions which were filled to overflowing. The same thing happened to the gaols. The prison came to be regarded as a refuge. Only smaller offences were at first committed ; and an epidemic of glass-breaking set in. But as times went on, and the pressure of distress became greater and the hope of ultimate salvation less, graver crimes became prevalent. Thus sheep-stealing grew to be quite a common offence ; and a prisoner's good fortune was supposed to be complete if he were sentenced to the once dreaded and loathed punishment of transportation beyond the seas. The Irishman was made happy by the fate which took him to any land—provided only it was not his own. And Botany Bay was transformed in peasant imagination from the Inferno of the hopeless to the Paradise of sufficient food and a great future.

But here again the refugees were confronted by the same horrors which

---

[1] O'Rourke, p. 393.   [2] Ib.
[3] Census Commissioners, p. 272.   [4] Ib.

awaited those who obtained admission to the workhouses and the fever hospitals. The prisons, without a tithe of the accommodation necessary for the inmates, became nests of disease; and often the offender who hoped for the luck of transportation beyond the seas, found that the sentence of even a week's imprisonment proved a sentence of death. In 1846, the Inspectors-General of Prisons reported that the increase of committals in that year over 1845 sometimes amounted to one hundred per cent., and then stated that 'in a very great number of instances small crimes have been committed for the purpose of obtaining that support in prison which could not be procured elsewhere.'[1] In 1847 they write: 'The terrible catastrophe which has disorganised the whole framework of society in Ireland fell with its full force on establishments under our charge. Disease and death increased to a degree that could never be contemplated by those acquainted with the usual orderly and healthy state of our gaols. The crowding together of 12,883 prisoners in gaols only calculated to contain 5,655, increased the deaths in the Irish prisons, in a single year, from 131 to 1,315.'[2] 'In March,' writes Dr. Browne of the Castlebar Gaol, 'our county gaol was crowded to more than double its capability, those committed being in a state of nudity, filth, and starvation.' Typhus broke out, and 'by the end of April we were in a state of actual pestilence. Every hospital servant was attacked, and from our wretched overcrowded state the mortality was fearful—fully forty per cent.; .... not a few of those committed were inmates of the fever wards a few hours after committal.'[3]

The years 1848 and 1849 present the same features. The increase of committals in 1848 over those of 1847 was no less than 34,105.[4]

In 1849 there was again an increase of committals, to the extent of 3,466 on the previous year, and the Inspectors-General comment on this significant phenomenon, 'The evil thus produced is so enormous as to threaten the total demoralisation of the lower orders, showing itself in the abolition of all distinction between right and wrong, and germinating a habit of committing crimes either for the sake of obtaining board and lodging in a gaol, or else for the remoter advantages of superior diet in the convict prisons, and the ultimate benefit of gratuitous emigration.'[5]

---

[1] Census Commissioners, p. 304.   [2] *Ib.*, pp. 304, 305.   [3] *Ib.*, pp. 300, 301.

[4] This is the comment of the Inspectors-General: 'The calamitous visitation of the last few years, operating with no exclusive pressure—affecting the most opulent and the humblest poor alike—suspending employment, and staying the hand of charity—has sorely tried the integrity of our people. *Larcenies have multiplied*, because, ordinarily, men will steal food rather than die; but to such as have made criminal compliance with necessity must be added vast numbers who, without means of earning subsistence, and unable to procure charitable aid, *notoriously appropriated articles of trifling value* that they might obtain the shelter of a prison under the guise of a commitment for a criminal offence.'—Report of Inspectors-General of Prisons: Census Commissioners' 'Tables of Deaths,' p. 311.

Here is a grim description of a prison of the period; it is written of Galway Gaol, under date February 8, 1848: 'It presented the appearance not only of a prison, but that of a poorhouse and infirmary. The prisoners were, in general, the most wretched class of human beings I ever beheld—badly clothed, and emaciated from the destitution to which they had been exposed, and from which many sought refuge in the gaol by asking alms and by the commission of petty crimes. Fever and dysentery are prevalent amongst the prisoners, and some die before they can be brought to the hospital, which is filled with the sick and the dying. Clad in miserable rags, crowded together during the day and heaped together during the night, contagious disease has taken root within the prison walls; and an extensive mortality was apprehended as the speedy and inevitable result.' It is added that, of the 888 inmates, more than 120 were suffering from fever and dysentery.—*Ib.*

[5] *Ib.*, p. 322.

Thus the plague worked—within the cabins, on the roads, in workhouses, in hospitals, in gaols. Of the numberless proofs of its dread activity let the following specimens suffice :—

Fever first demands attention. In one week 50 persons died in the workhouse at Castlerea.[1] In Carrick-on-Shannon there were, on April 16, 1847, 300 cases of fever. The weekly deaths were 50.[2] In one hospital in Dublin, Cork Street, 12,000 cases applied in ten months.[3] At Cork there were 174 deaths in seven days, or more than a death every hour.[4] In one day in the beginning of February, 1847, there were 44 corpses in the workhouse in the same city, and on the 10th of the same month in that year, 100 bodies were conveyed for interment to a single graveyard outside the town.[5] In the week ending April 3, 1847, of the entire number of inmates in the Irish workhouses—viz. 104,485—26,000 were sick, and of these 9,000 were fever patients.[6] During that week the number of deaths was 2,706, and the average of deaths in each week during the month was 25 per thousand of the entire inmates.[7]

Fifty-four, out of one hundred workhouse officials who were attacked with the fever, died between January 1 and April 2, 1847.[8] Of the entire medical staff employed in the different institutions of the country, one-fifteenth died in the same year.[9] 'Taking the recorded deaths from fever alone,' write the Census Commissioners,[10] 'between the beginning of 1846 and the end of 1849, and assuming the mortality at one in ten, which is the very lowest calculation, and far below what we believe to have occurred, above a million and a half, or 1,595,040 persons—being one in 4·11 of the population in 1851—must have suffered from fever during that period.' 'But,' continued the writers, 'no pen has recorded the numbers of the forlorn and starving who perished by the wayside or in the ditches, or of the mournful groups, sometimes of whole families, who lay down and died one after another upon the floor of their miserable cabin, and so remained uncoffined and unburied till chance unveiled the appalling scene.'[11]

The deaths from fever in 1845 were 7,249. From that figure they rose to 17,145 in 1846 ; to 57,095 in 1847. In 1848 they were 45,948 ; in 1849 they numbered 39,316 ; in 1850 they fell to 23,545. Finally, the total deaths between 1841 and 1851 from fever were 222,029. But, allowing for 'deficient returns, 250,000'—a quarter of a million of people—'perished from fever alone.'[12]

The famine and the fever were naturally accompanied and followed by all those other maladies which result from insufficiency and unsuitability of food. The potato blight continued with varying virulence until 1851, its existence being marked by the prevalence in more or less severe epidemics of dysentery, which carried off 5,492 persons in 1846, 25,757 in 1847, the annual totals swelling, until in 1849 the deaths from this disease alone amounted to 29,446 ;[13] of cholera, which destroyed 35,989 lives in 1848-49 ;[14] of small-pox, to which 38,275 persons fell victims in the decennial period between 1841 and 1851.[15] The deaths from small-pox, however, did not greatly swell the total of mortality between 1845 and 1851. It should be added that as a direct consequence of the famine many thousands suffered severely from

---

[1] Report of Inspectors-General of Prisons : Census Commissioners' 'Tables of Deaths,' p. 278.
[2] Ib., p. 296. [3] Ib., p. 298. [4] Ib., p. 284. [5] Ib., p. 282.
[6] Ib., p. 304. [7] Ib. [8] Ib., p. 293. [9] Ib., p. 30.
[10] Ib., p. 243. [11] Ib. [12] Ib. [13] Ib., p. 251.
[14] Ib., p. 252. [15] Ib.

scurvy, and that the recorded cases of ophthalmia swelled from 13,812 in 1849, to 45,947 in 1851.[1]

In addition to this appalling loss of life from actual disease, the number of deaths registered by the Census Commissioners under the heading of 'Starvation' were 6,058 in the year 1847, and 21,770 during the decennial period. Only 117 deaths from starvation were registered in the previous decennial period.[2] Under heading 'Infirmity, Debility, and Old Age,' the Commissioners record 10,609 deaths in 1845, 23,285 in 1847, and from 1841 to 1851 inclusive, a total of 133,923; but they acknowledge that many of these cases would be more appropriately ranked among the deaths from 'starvation.'[3]

It was the terrible mortality of these epidemics, and especially of the fever, that led to the most sinister invention of the time. This was the hinged coffin. The coffin was made with a movable bottom; the body was placed in it, the bottom unhinged, the body was thrown into the grave, and then the coffin was sent back to the workhouse to receive another body. Sometimes scores of corpses passed in this way through the same coffin. The hinged coffin was used extensively in Cork. Justin McCarthy, a youth of seventeen, just then started on his professional career as a reporter on the *Cork Examiner*, many times saw the hinged coffin in actual use. In Skibbereen, which was one of the worst scourged places or districts, the hinged coffin was perhaps more largely used than in any other district. The traveller is to-day pointed out, as historic spots of the town, two large pits, in which hundreds of bodies found a coffinless grave.

Appalled by the spread of death, the Ministry were compelled in 1847 to change their whole procedure. New legislation was introduced; all the ideas were abandoned to which the Government had adhered with an obstinacy that the deaths of tens of thousands of people could not for months change. The Irish Relief Act was the official title of the new enactment: it was familiarly known as the Soup Kitchen Act. Relief committees were to be formed throughout the different unions: they were to prepare lists of persons who were fit subjects for relief: food was to be given—at reasonable prices to some, gratuitously to the absolutely destitute. Here was a departure with a vengeance from the solid principles of political economy that had been preached with such unction to the benighted Irish, with references to Burke, by the official prigs who had undertaken to manage Irish affairs for the Irish people, and had managed them with such disastrous results.

But here again the good intentions of the Government and their legislation were defeated by characteristic blunders. One of the objects of the Government was to induce the people to till their own fields so as to avoid the repetition in 1848 of the loss of the harvest that had followed the blundering legislation of 1846; and, accordingly, it was ordered that the relief works should be gradually dropped, and that relief through the soup kitchens should take their place. At the end of March the number of persons employed was to be reduced by twenty per cent., and by May 1 the works were to be entirely discontinued. It was intended, too, that by the time the relief works came to an end the soup kitchens would be in existence; and thus the people would be supplied with a substitute.

The number of people employed on the relief works was gigantic. In the week ending October 3, 1846—the first week of the relief works—the

---

[1] Census Commissioners, p. 253. As a result, Ireland had the largest proportion of blind, compared with its population, except Norway.—*Ib.*
[2] *Ib.*, p. 253.
[3] *Ib.*, p. 246.

number of persons employed was but 20,000 ; but in March, 1847, when the number on the works began to be reduced, the total had reached the enormous number of 734,000. The disarrangement of a scheme on which so many people depended for food was a project of strange rashness, and, as usual, it was carried out by the officials of the Government in a manner to aggravate all the evil tendencies of the original plan. The intention of the Government was that the reduction of twenty per cent. was to take place in the aggregate, and not in each place—the object, of course, being that regard should be had to the different conditions of each locality : the officials lowered the number of persons employed in every district with perfect uniformity. Then the intention of the Government was that the Soup Kitchen Act should be in full working order when the relief works came to an end. By May 1, when the whole mighty army of three-quarters of a million of people were turned away from work, there was not a single relief committee in full working order, not a single can of soup had, in all probability, been manufactured. The result was that there was in 1847, as there had been in 1846, a hideous interregnum during which some of the worst sufferings of the famine days were repeated.

But when the scheme did get into working order, it proved on the whole effective and beneficial. Deaths from starvation came to an end ; fever grew less intense in the hospitals ; and the fields were fairly well tilled. Thus the severest verdict on the early incompetence of the Government was passed by the result of their own later legislation. And, indeed, with an appalling candour, the Ministers themselves confessed to their own tragic mistake. In the preamble to the Soup Kitchen Act the measure is justified : it has become necessary because, 'by reason of the great increase of destitution in Ireland, sufficient relief could not be given' under the Labour Rate Act.[1] M. Jules Sandeau tells in one of his stories how a royal prince gave the child of a faithful Breton family a smile ; the royal smile, he bitterly comments, had been purchased by three lives. The preamble to the Soup Kitchen Act had been purchased by many and many thousands of lives that might have been saved.

But all these things came too late, and especially too late to retain the population. Emigration received a terrible impetus, and the people fled in a frenzy of grief and despair from their doomed land. But even in their flight they were pursued by the demons they had endeavoured to leave behind. The brotherhood of humanity, powerless to frame just laws and to give national rights, asserted itself in disease and death. To England, as the nearest refuge, the Irish exiles first fled. No less than 180,000 are said to have landed in Liverpool between January 15 and May 4, 1847.[2] In Glasgow, between June 15 and August 17, 26,335 arrived from Ireland. Many were 'aged people unfit for labour ;' out of 1,150 patients in the Glasgow fever hospital at the period, 750 were Irish.[3] At last the Government had to interfere to protect the English people from the horrors which the errors and folly of British administration had created in Ireland.

---

[1] The testimony is overwhelming that if the policy of the Soup Kitchen Act had been originally adopted, a large amount of the horrors of the famine would have been prevented. 'The cost of the Kenmare soup-kitchen,' reports the Relief Committee, 'from April 25 to September 1, amounted to £2,205 13s. 4d.; the amount of money paid for public works in the same district from November 23, 1846, to May 1, was £5,583, during which time the people were dying on the roads and dropping in the streets. Since the soup-kitchens were set on foot, *we can safely affirm that not one human being died from starvation.*'—Census Commissioners, p. 290.

[2] *Ib.*, p. 305. [3] *Ib.*

An Order in Council was issued by which deck passengers were subjected to quarantine. Shortly afterwards, at the request of the Government, the fares for deck passengers were increased by the owners of four steamships plying between England and Ireland. These passengers were all Irish tenants, fleeing from their farms, voluntarily or by compulsion, through hunger or through eviction.

Vast masses tried to make their way to America. In the year 1845, 74,969 persons emigrated from Ireland; in 1846 the number had risen to 105,955; during 1847 it rose to 215,444. No means were taken to preserve these poor people from the rapacity of shipowners. The landlords, delighted at getting rid of them, made bargains for their conveyance wholesale, and at small prices; and in those days emigrant-ships were under no sanitary restrictions of any effectiveness. Thus the emigrants, already half-starved and fever-stricken, were pushed into berths that 'rivalled the cabins of Mayo, or the fever-sheds of Skibbereen.' 'Crowded and filthy, carrying double the legal number of passengers, who were ill-fed and imperfectly clothed, and having no doctor on board, the holds,' says an eye-witness, 'were like the Black Hole of Calcutta, and deaths in myriads.'[1]

The statistics of mortality bear out these words. Of 493 passengers during the year in the *Queen*, 136 died on the voyage; of 552 in the *Avon*, 236 died; of 476 in the *Virginius*, 267 died; of 440 on the *Larch*, 108 died and 150 were seriously diseased. 89,783 persons altogether embarked for Canada in 1847. The Chief Secretary for Ireland reported with regard to these that 6,100 perished on the voyage; 4,100 on their arrival; 5,200 in hospital; 1,900 in towns to which they repaired. 'From Grosse Island up to Port Sarnia, along the borders of our great river, on the shores of Lakes Ontario and Erie, wherever the tide of emigration has extended, are to be found one unbroken chain of graves, where repose fathers and mothers, sisters and brothers, in a commingled heap, no stone marking the spot. Twenty thousand and upwards have gone down to their graves.'[2]

CHAPTER IV.

THE GREAT CLEARANCES.

It was at the moment when Ireland was being scourged with all these plagues that her political leaders aggravated her sufferings by their dissensions.

It has already been told that the rise of the *Nation* newspaper introduced into the counsels of O'Connell a new element, which he found it impossible to control. As disaster came upon the country these differences were bound to increase; defeat outside being always the solvent of unity inside a political organization. The hideous magnitude of the sufferings of Ireland at this moment, too, was another element which was bound to increase the tendency to discord. The young and strong and brave can never reconcile themselves to the gospel that there is such a thing in this world as inevitable evil. The sight of so many thousands of people perishing miserably naturally suggested a frenzied temper, and the extreme course

---

[1] Sir Charles Gavan Duffy, 'Four Years of Irish History,' p. 531.
[2] *Ib.*, p. 532.

that such a temper begets. Among the young men, therefore, who gathered round the leaders of the *Nation* newspaper, there was a constant feeling that enough was not being done to save the people. O'Connell, on the other hand, was now approaching the close of a long and busy life. As has been already mentioned, he had been at the period when the famine broke out already suffering for some years from the depressing influence of brain disease. It would take me far beyond my purpose to go through the details of the many questions upon which the two sides came into collision. One of the great causes of the split between Young and Old Ireland was in reference to what are called the 'peace resolutions.' Some of the utterances of the Young Irelanders had suggested the employment of physical force under certain circumstances; and O'Connell, whose alarms were fed and increased by disreputable retainers, and by his son John—an intellectual pigmy of gigantic ambition—insisted upon the Repeal Association solemnly renewing its adhesion to the resolutions. These resolutions, passed at its formation, laid down the memorable doctrine that no political reform was worth purchasing by the shedding of even one drop of blood. It is hard to believe that O'Connell ever did accept in its entirety the doctrine that physical force was not a justifiable expedient under any imaginable circumstances. There is no record in his speeches—at least, none that I remember—of his reprobation of the American Colonies for having laid the foundation of their liberty and of their present greatness in armed insurrection. There is a famous speech, which formed part of the case of the Crown against him, in which he spoke of himself as the Bolivar of Ireland—and the triumphs of Bolivar were not gained without the shedding of blood. All O'Connell probably meant to say, in the moments when he was free from a certain kind of devotional ecstasy, was that Ireland was so weak at that time when compared to England, that a resort to physical force could have no possible chance of success, and that it was as well to reconcile the people to their impotence by raising it to the dignity of a great moral principle. The Young Irelanders left the Repeal Association; and from this time forward there were rival organizations, rival leaders, and rival policies in the National Party.

O'Connell did not survive to see the complete wreck of the vast organization which he had held together for so long a period. Rarely has a great, and on the whole successful, career ended in gloom so appalling and so unbroken. The imprisonment of 1843 was so ignoble an ending to the glorious promise and the wild and tempestuous triumph of that period, that it probably gave his spirit a shock from which it never recovered. He worked on as energetically as ever, for he was a man whose industry never paused. But both he and his policy had lost their prestige. The young and ardent began to question his power, and still more to doubt his policy. Then came 1846 and 1847, with the people whom he had pledged himself to bring into the promised land of self-government and prosperity dying of hunger and disease, fleeing as from an accursed spot, and bound to the fiery wheel of oppression more securely than ever. In breaking health and with broken spirits the old man fought doggedly on. On April 3, 1846, he delivered a lengthened speech to the House of Commons, of which an historic but an entirely inaccurate description is given in Lord Beaconsfield's 'Life of Lord George Bentinck.' The speech, whether supplied to the newspapers, as suggested by Lord Beaconsfield, or not, appears in 'Hansard,' and, however much the voice and other physical attributes of O'Connell may have appeared to have decayed, this speech, in its selection of evidence, and in its arrangement of facts and its presentation of the whole case against the land system of Ireland, may be read even to-day as the completest and most convincing speech of the times on the question. In Dublin, too, the old man attended the relief committees day after day. He spoke in the House of Commons for the last time in February, 1847, and then it was that he displayed that utter debility which is transposed in the 'Life of Bentinck' to the April of the previous year. He was next day seriously ill, and was ordered change of air. He went abroad, and was everywhere met by demonstrations of respect and affection. But his heart was broken. A gloom had settled over him which nothing could shake off. He did not even reach the goal of his journey. He died at Genoa on May 15, 1847. His last will was that his heart should be sent to Rome, and his body to Ireland. He lies in Glasnevin Cemetery.

Meantime, the removal of his imposing personality from Irish politics aggravated the dissensions between Old and Young Ireland. O'Connell was largely dominated in his later years by his son, John O'Connell; and the father bent much of his efforts towards handing on to his son the dignity of popular leader. But there is no divine right in popular command, except that which is given by supreme talents; and John O'Connell was utterly devoid of qualifications for the new position. He was weak, vain, and shallow, and the disproportion between his pretensions and his abilities did much to aggravate the bitterness and accelerate the rupture between the two schools of political thought.

The evils of the country grew daily worse; hope from Parliamentary agitation died in face of a failure so colossal as that of O'Connell; and some of the Young Irelanders, seized with a divine despair, resolved to try what physical force might bring.

The first important apostle of this new gospel was John Mitchel—one of the strangest, most picturesque, and strongest figures of Irish political struggles. He was the son of an Ulster Unitarian clergyman; and he was one of the early contributors to the *Nation*. He separated in time from Sir (Mr.) Charles Gavan Duffy, and started a paper on his own account. In this paper insurrection was openly preached; and especially insurrection against the land system. The people were asked not to die themselves, nor let their wives and children die, while their fields were covered with food which had been produced by the sweat of their brows and by their own hands. It was pointed out that the reason why all this food was sent from a starving to a prosperous nation was that the rent of the landlord might be paid, and that the rent should therefore be attacked; afterwards he advised an attack upon some of the taxes.

The Ministry, in order to cope with such writing and the other results of a period of universal hunger and disease, succeeded in having a whole code of coercion laws passed. The Cabinet had changed its political complexion. The fall of Peel had, as has been seen, been brought about by the defeat of his Coercion Bill through a combination of the Whigs, the Protectionists, and the O'Connellites. Lord John Russell had been the leader of the Whigs in the triumphant attack on coercion; and Lord John Russell, now transformed from the leader of Opposition to the head of the Government, brought in Coercion Bills himself.

Mitchel was the first of the Young Irelanders who was attacked. He was brought to trial; Lord John Russell, questioned in the House of Commons about the trial a few days before it took place, pledged himself that it should be a fair trial. He had written, he declared, to his noble friend (Lord Clarendon) that he trusted there would not arise any charge of any kind of unfairness as to the composition of the juries, as, for his own part, 'he would rather see those parties acquitted than that there should be any such unfairness.' Most Englishmen who read this statement came to the conclusion—the very natural conclusion—that the word of an English Prime Minister thus solemnly pledged was carried out ; and if there were any complaints by Irish members afterwards, they were dismissed as the emanations of the hopeless mendacity or the incurable folly of a race of persistent grumblers. Yet was the pledge most flagrantly broken; and the packing of the jury of John Mitchel under the premiership of Lord John Russell was as open, as relentless, as shameless, as the packing of the jury of O'Connell under the premiership of Sir Robert Peel. The Crown challenged thirty-nine of the jurors—of these thirty-nine, nineteen were Catholics, the rest were Protestants suspected of National leanings—with the final result that there was not a single Catholic on the jury, and that the Protestants were of the Orange class who would be quite willing to hang Mitchel, or any other man of his opinions, without the formality of trial, or without any evidence at all.

With such a jury Mitchel was, of course, convicted. He was sentenced to fourteen years' transportation ; in a few hours after the sentence he was in a Government boat, on the way already to the land to which he was now exiled. One of the questions debated at the time most seriously was whether Mitchel should be allowed to be taken out of the country without some attempt at rescue. His own expectation was that the Government would never be allowed to conquer him without a struggle, and that his sentence would be the longed-for and the necessary signal for the rising. But it was deemed wisest by the other leaders of the Young Ireland Party that the attempt at insurrection should be postponed until the people were organised and armed. By successive steps these men were in their turn driven to extremities, and to the conviction that an attempt at insurrection should be made.

The leader of this movement was Mr. Smith O'Brien. Mr. O'Brien was the member of an aristocratic family. His brother afterwards became Lord Inchiquin, and was the nearest male relative to the Marquis of Thomond. For years he had been a member of the English Liberal Party, honestly convinced that the Liberal Party would remedy all the wrongs of the Irish people. But as time went on, and all these evils seemed to become aggravated instead of relieved, he was driven slowly and unwillingly into the belief that the Legislative Union was the real source of all the evils of his country ; and he joined the Repeal Party under O'Connell. By successive steps he was driven into the ranks of Young Ireland, and by degrees into revolution. When he, Mr. John Blake Dillon (father of the John Dillon of our own day), Mr. D'Arcy M'Gee, and Mr. (now Sir) Charles Gavan Duffy were finally forced into the attempt to create an insurrection, they probably had a strong feeling that the attempt was hopeless, and that they were called upon to make it rather through the calls of honour than the chances of success. The attempt at all events proved a disastrous failure. After an attack on a police barrack at Ballingarry, the small force which O'Brien had been able to call and keep together was scattered. He and the greater number of the leaders were arrested after a few days, and were put on their trial. The juries were packed as before, the judges were partisans of the Orange school, and O'Brien and the rest were convicted, were sentenced to death, and, this sentence being commuted, were transported. Dillon and M'Gee succeeded in escaping to America.

This was the end of the Young Ireland Party. The party of O'Connell did not survive much longer. In 1847 there was a general election. The graphic account of that election in Sir Charles Gavan Duffy's book is one of the most depressing and most instructive chapters in Irish history, and makes several years of Irish history intelligible. The election was fought out between the Young Irelanders and Conciliation Hall—the place where O'Connell's Repeal Association used to meet—on the principle whether there should or should not be a pledge against taking office.

The idea of Gavan Duffy and the other Young Irelanders was an independent Irish Party—independent of Whig as of Tory Governments. But O'Connell's heirs, as he himself, taught a very different creed. It was O'Connell's persistent idea that his supporters were justified in taking offices under the Crown. It is easy to understand, though it may be hard to forgive, his reasons for adopting such a policy. When O'Connell started, as to a large extent when he ended, his political career, every post of power in Ireland was held by the enemies of the popular cause. The Lord-Lieutenant, the Chief Secretary, all the judges, all the county court barristers, all the sheriffs, all the men in any public position, great or small, were Protestants, and most of them Orange Conservatives. Irish history teaches this lesson, if no other, that apparently popular and even Liberal institutions may exist in name and be the mask for the worst vices of unchecked despotism. Ireland had all the forms which in England are the guarantees of freemen and freedom, but these forms became the bulwarks and instruments of tyranny. It was in vain that there were in Ireland judges who had the same independence of the Crown as their brethren in England, if, from violent political partisanship, they could be relied upon to do the behests of the Government as safely as if they were the creatures of the Crown. Trial by jury was a 'mockery, a delusion, and a snare,' if it meant trial, not by one's peers, but by a carefully selected number of one's bitterest political and religious opponents. And no laws could establish political or social or religious equality when their administration was left to the unchecked caprice of a hierarchy of unscrupulous political partisans.

O'Connell found how true this was in the days that succeeded Catholic Emancipation; and he thought, therefore, that one of the first necessities of Irish progress was that the judiciary and the other official bodies of the country should be manned by men belonging to the same faith and sympathizing with the political sentiments of the majority of their countrymen.

There were some other reasons, too, of a less creditable character. O'Connell was the leader of a democratic movement with no revenue save such as the voluntary subscriptions of his followers supplied. It was not an unwelcome relief to his cause if occasionally he was able to transform the pensioners on his funds into pensioners on the coffers of the State. It is to be remembered, too, that at this period the Irish leader had a much more circumscribed class from which to draw his Parliamentary supporters than at the present day. The property qualifications still existed; a member of Parliament was obliged to have £300 a year to be a borough, and £600 a year to be a county member. There are many amusing and many sad stories of the strange characters which this necessity compelled O'Connell to introduce as advocates of the sacred cause of Irish nationality. There were large classes of the population who, while they had the property qualification, were in other respects entirely unsuited for the position of members of a popular party. The landlords were almost to a man on the side of existing abuses, and the greater number of the members of this body whom O'Connell was able to recruit to his ranks were *déclassés*. They were usually men of extravagant habits and of vicious lives, and politics was the last desperate card with which their fortunes were to be marred or mended. Next, the constituencies of Ireland had at this moment a very narrow electorate. It was all very well for half a million of people to meet O'Connell at Tara, or at any other of the monster meetings, and to show that he commanded, as never did popular leader before, the affections, the opinions, and the right arms of a unanimous nation. But when it came to the time for obtaining a Parliamentary supporter—the only available weapon for his struggle with English Ministries—it was not upon the voice of the people that the decision rested. He could carry many of the counties, even though support of him meant sentences of eviction, and, through eviction, of death or of exile, to thousands of his adherents. In the boroughs it was half a dozen shopkeepers, face to face with the always impending bankruptcy of small towns in an impoverished country, who had the decision of an election in their hands. This is a central fact in the consideration of O'Connell's career, and must always be taken as supplying at least some explanation of his many mistakes, and his many disastrous failures.

The result of this theory of O'Connell's was the creation in Ireland of a school of politicians which has been at once her dishonour and her bane. This was the race of Catholic place-hunters. Throughout the following pages men of this type play a large part; it will be found that in exact proportion to their success and number were the degradation and the deepening misery of their country: that for years the struggle for Irish prosperity and self-government was impeded mainly through them; and that hope for the final overthrow of the whole vast structure of wrong in Ireland showed some chance of realization for the first time when they were expelled for ever from Irish political life.

The way in which the system worked was this. A profligate landlord, or an aspiring but briefless barrister, was elected for an Irish constituency as a follower of the popular leader of the day and as the mouthpiece of his principles. When he entered the House of Commons he soon gave it to be understood by the distributors of State patronage that he was open to a bargain. The time came when in the party divisions his vote was of consequence, and the bargain was then struck—the vote from him, and the office from them.

Under O'Connell this hideous system had not reached the proportions to which it afterwards attained; but it had gone so far as to create a vast scandal; and, along with the wretched tail which in the course of his long struggle O'Connell had gathered about him, gave that uncleanness to his proceedings which excited the just indignation of the young and ardent and high-minded men who formed the Young Ireland Party. The final event that made separation between O'Connell and the Young Irelanders inevitable was the struggle between the demand for an independent Irish Party, with no mercy to place-hunters, and the resolve of O'Connell to stand by the old and evil system of compromise. Richard Lalor Sheil, one of the most eloquent colleagues of O'Connell in the old struggle for Catholic Emancipation, had never joined in the agitation for Repeal, had kept out of all popular movements—some said because the despotic will of the great tribune made life intolerable to any but slaves—and had in time sunk to the level of a Whig office-holder. In 1846, having been appointed Master of the Mint in the Ministry of Lord John Russell, Sheil stood for Dungarvan, and the Young Irelanders demanded that he should be opposed by a man who was in favour not of the government of Ireland by English Ministers, whether Whig or Tory, but of the government of Ireland by the Irish people themselves. O'Connell stood by his old associate and his old creed, and Sheil was elected.

The struggle on this point, which had raged in the days of O'Connell, burst out with even greater fury when he was dead; and the Young Irelanders had to contend with his puny and contemptible successor. The Young Irelanders proposed that no man should be elected who did not pledge himself to take no office under the Crown. And assuredly if such a pledge were ever necessary or justifiable it was at that moment. Between Parliament and Ministers, between the land laws and the landlords, the Irish nation was being murdered; and the demand for relief should come, not from beggars seeking the pence of the Treasury, but from independent men caring only for the redress of the hideous wrong and the cure of the awful suffering of their country.

But Mr. John O'Connell and the Repeal Association refused to accede to any such pledge; and at this supreme crisis raised those false side-issues which are the favourite resort of unscrupulous traffickers in political struggles. A favourite expedient was to whisper doubts of the religious orthodoxy of the Young Irelanders; and their proposals being first described as revolutionary, dread warnings were by an easy transition drawn from the sanguinary teachings and acts of the revolutionaries of France. But the great side-issue was the attitude the Young Irelanders had adopted towards O'Connell. They were described as having 'murdered the Liberator.' The disappearance of O'Connell, especially in circumstances of such tragic and pitiful gloom, had produced on the whole Irish people the impression which Mrs. Carlyle so well describes as her feeling when the news came to England that Byron was dead. It seemed as if the sun or moon had suddenly dropped out of the heavens. In such a condition of the popular mind it was easy to raise a howl of execration against the men who had opposed his policy; the Young Irelanders were everywhere denounced; in many places they were set upon by mobs, and were in danger of their lives.

The revulsion of public feeling against them threw great difficulties in the way of the policy which they recommended; and that policy did not receive anything like a fair hearing. Their candidates were everywhere defeated, and in their stead were chosen men who were openly for sale. The one title for election in many cases was a hasty adhesion to the Repeal Association just before the general election. The subscription to this body was £5; hence these men came to be known as the 'Five Pound Repealers.' Thus, instead of seventy independent and honest Irish representatives, there was returned a motley gang of as disreputable and needy adventurers as ever trafficked in the blood and tears of a nation. The expected result soon followed. Of the entire number no less than twenty afterwards accepted places for themselves, and twenty more were continually pestering the Government Whips for places for their dependents. Mr. John O'Connell himself had refused to take the pledge against office-taking, on the ground that if the name he bore was not a sufficient guarantee, he would condescend to no more. The guarantee was scarcely trustworthy;

for he had at the time a brother and two brothers-in-law, and a train of cousins in office. He himself, within a short time afterwards, was being trained as a captain of militia to fight against the men whom the sight of their country's ruin was driving to the desperate resort of rebellion ; and, finally, ended as Clerk of the Hanaper.

Thus the Repeal Party broke up, and Ireland was left without an advocate in Parliament. The ruin and helplessness of the country were now complete. Insurrection had been tried and had failed ; constitutional agitation had produced a gang of scoundrels who were ready to sell themselves to the highest bidder. Ireland, starving, plague-stricken, disarmed, unrepresented, lay at the mercy of the British Government and of the Irish landlords. It will not be uninstructive to see what use the two classes made of their omnipotence over the country which death, hunger, and plague, abortive rebellion and political treachery, had given over to their hands.

First as to the landlords. The potato crop in 1848 and 1849 had again failed, and there were throughout the country the same scenes—especially in 1849—of starvation and plague as in 1846 and 1847. In 1848, 2,043,505 persons received poor-law relief—610,463 being in the workhouses, and 1,433,042 receiving outdoor relief.[1] Fever and dysentery raged in the workhouses,[2] the gaols,[3] the schools,[4] and in some places along the western coast with such destructiveness as to almost entirely depopulate them. 'Along the coast of Connemara,' says a medical writer, 'for near thirty miles, where the villages are very small and hundreds of cabins detached, sickness and death walked hand-in-hand until they nearly depopulated the whole coast.'[5] In Mayo hundreds of people died of starvation ;[6] in the townland of Moyard, County Galway, five persons—four sons and a daughter—died in one family ;[7] in Ballinahinch, in the same county, six persons in the same family died—the husband, two daughters, and three sons ;[8] in Ballinasloe, in the same county, eight persons died in the same family. 'The survivors have endeavoured to live on nettles and watercresses.'[9] Though there were 41,083 fewer deaths than in 1847, the total reached the enormous figure of 208,352, and of these 97,076 died of epidemic—that is, of famine-produced diseases.[10] And eventually, although there was a decrease of 37,285 on the emigration of 1847, no less than 178,159 persons left Ireland in 1848.

The failure was not so complete in 1848 as in 1847, but still it was very extensive, and there was terrible and widespread suffering. In 1849 the blight worked more disastrously. The potatoes were 'almost universally blighted.'[11] The year 1849 was thus a return to the greater ghastliness and more multitudinous horrors of 1847. As in previous years, the harvest began with promises of abundance. In May the crops looked 'luxuriant and flourishing' ;[12] but as early as June the blight appeared in County Cork and County Tipperary ; in July and August it appeared in several other counties. By the 18th of the latter month, in passing along the roads in the Mourne district of County Down, 'the peaty smell —a symptom of the fatal disaster—was perceived distinctly.' By September 14 the report was : 'The potato blight has now become unmistakable, changing in one night's time the green and healthy-looking appearances

---

[1] Census Commissioners, p. 310. [2] Ib., p. 310. [3] Ib., p. 311.
[4] Ib. [5] Ib., p. 312. [6] Ib.
[7] Ib., p. 311. [8] Ib. [9] Ib., p. 312.
[10] Ib., p. 31 [11] Ib., p. 319. [12] Ib., p. 315.

of the potato-stalk to blackness and decay.' October 1 : 'The potatoes are bad everywhere.'¹

As in the autumn of 1845, the people had staked their all on the success of the potato crop. 'Should the crop fail,' wrote the *Irish Farmers' Gazette*, 'the country will be in a wretched condition, for the poor people have risked their all in the planting of potatoes this year.'² One of the agricultural instructors sent out by the Lord-Lieutenant to lecture on improved methods of farming, reports from Roscommon instances of people having 'sold their only cow to procure seed potatoes, and of persons having sold their beds for the same purpose.'³ Another instructor makes a statement which it will be well to remember in reading an account of the working of landlordism some pages further on : 'They'—the tenants —'have nothing now left but the shelter of a miserable cabin, and themselves and the land in a corresponding state of misery ; though they are still clinging to their huts with the greatest tenacity, and seem better pleased to perish in the ruins than surrender what they call their last hope of existence.'⁴

The same suffering as in 1847 followed the failure of the staple crop. 'The earlier months of 1849,' report the Poor Law Commissioners, 'were marked by a greater degree of suffering in the western and south-western districts than any period since the fatal season of 1846-47. Exhaustion of resources by the long continuance of adverse circumstances caused a large accession to the ranks of the destitute. Clothing had been worn out and parted with to provide food or seed in seed-time.'⁵

Reports of all kinds present pictures as terrible as those of 1847, with deeper elements of tragedy in many cases, as the evils of 1849 came upon a people already exhausted by their dread experiences of the previous years. Then there had been added another burden to the famine-stricken people in the additional taxation imposed by the legislation of the Imperial Parliament, for the people had to pay for the legislation that had so terribly aggravated their sufferings, and that had murdered instead of saving hundreds of thousands of the nation.

'The people,' reports one of the agricultural instructors, 'complain bitterly [of the immense poor rate] ; they say it will be impossible for them to stand the payment of the taxes for another season. They likewise say,' adds this instructor, 'that if they improve their farms, they know in their hearts they are doing so for other persons.'⁶

And now for a few pictures of the state of things which existed among the people.

'The state of the country here,' writes one of the instructors from Clifden, Connemara, 'as in many other places, is utterly hopeless, and exhibits the most horrifying picture of poverty and destitution. The neglected state of the land—the death-like appearance of the people crawling from their roofless cabins . . . . the pitiful petitions of the desponding poor craving that charity which the "rate" of 23s. 1d. to the pound puts out of the power of humanity to bestow—some may conceive, but few can describe. It is not very likely, indeed, that any good can accrue to such people from my visits. "We will not sow, for we cannot work without food," is the general answer made to me by those patient sufferers.'⁷

'Anything,' writes another instructor from the Ballinrobe Union, County Mayo, 'to equal the misery and starved appearance of the people here I have not yet seen—no more sign of tillage, or any preparation for it, than on the top of a barren mountain, though very fine land . . . . I begged of them to prepare the land ; their reply was, " How can a hungry man work, sir ? we are all nearly starved ;" and really they had starvation in their worn faces . . . I met half-starved creatures in the fields everywhere, picking weeds and herbs to eat them. I have no hesitation in saying that five out of six of the really destitute will be dead on July 1.'⁸

---

¹ Census Commissioners, p. 315. ² *Ib.*, p. 319. ³ *Ib.*, p. 317.
⁴ *Ib.* ⁵ *Ib.*, p. 320. ⁶ *Ib.*, p. 317. ⁷ *Ib.*, p. 321. ⁸ *Ib.*

'Deaths from starvation occur almost daily,' writes another instructor from Ballinahinch Estate, Connemara, ' and the remains of hunger's victims are quietly laid in the ground unrecorded.'[1] In the neighbouring islands, 'which had quite run out of cultivation,' the inhabitants were 'either dead or supported by public relief and by that system of petty theft which unfortunately pervades the country, as the food supplied is barely sufficient to enable the living skeletons to go in search of a further supply.'

Finally, here are a few extracts from the newspapers of the time. 'The distress in the west of Ireland was very great; many died of want.' 'Great destitution at Athlone; never were the poor in so deplorable a condition.' 'A family of six lived for one week upon the carcase of an ass in the parish of Ballymackey, County Tipperary.' 'Great distress in Ulster—people eating ass-flesh.' Deaths from starvation were reported from Cong, County Mayo, from Lettermore, County Tipperary, and also from the County Clare. 'January 17: Twenty-two deaths from famine and destitution reported throughout the country.'[2]

As has already been stated, the epidemic of cholera was added to the other scourges which, in the latter part of 1848 and all through 1849, followed on the other epidemics. The total number of deaths in 1849 was 240,797, being the greatest number for any one year in the decennial period between 1841 and 1851 except 1847. The deaths from zymotic diseases were larger than in 1847, being 123,386, which is 7,021 more than in 1847.[3]

Such, then, was the state of Ireland in these two years. I now proceed to describe the conduct of the landlords. It would be easy to quote the general denunciations of their conduct all over the country, which appeared in the speeches and newspapers even of England, but I have thought it a better plan to take up one particular district and show the landlords at work there.

To anybody, then, who desires to obtain a detailed and realistic picture of what Irish landlordism in the days of the famine really meant, the perusal of the paper No. 1089, entitled 'Reports and Returns relating to Evictions in the Kilrush Union,' will be of absorbing interest. The Ministers, in order to give Parliament some idea as to the merits of the controversy between them and the landlords, presented in this volume a series of extracts from the Report of Captain Kennedy, who had been sent down to this union as representative of the Poor Law Commissioners. These extracts begin on November 25, 1847, and conclude on June 19, 1849. They tell over and over again the same tale, until the heart grows sick with the repetition of ghastly and almost incredible horrors. Kilrush was one of the unions in which neither famine nor fever worked with such deadly effect as in some other parts of the country.

The following extracts from Captain Kennedy's report are given without comment, and may be trusted to speak for themselves:

'*November* 25, 1847.—An immense number of small landholders are under ejectment, or notice to quit, even where the rents have been paid up.[4]

---

[1] Census Commissioners, p. 321.
[2] *Freeman's Journal* and *Saunders's Newsletter*, quoted by Census Commissioners, pp. 320, 321.
[3] Census Commissioners, pp. 323, 324.
[4] Blue-book No. 1089: Reports and Returns relating to Evictions in the Kilrush Union, 1849, p. 3.

'*February* 11, 1848.— ... Upwards of 120 *houses have been* "*tumbled*" *on one property* within a few weeks, containing families to a greater number, many of whom are burrowing behind the ditches, without the means of procuring shelter.[1]

'*March* 16, 1848.—We admitted a considerable number of paupers, among whom were some of the most appalling cases of destitution and suffering it has ever been my lot to witness. The state of most of these wretched creatures is traceable to the numerous evictions which have lately taken place in the union. *When driven from their cabins, they betake themselves to the ditches or the shelter of some bank, and there exist like animals, till starvation or the inclemency of the weather drives them to the workhouse. There were three cartloads of these creatures, who could not walk, brought for admission yesterday, some in fever, some suffering from dysentery, and all from want of food.*[2]

'*March* 23, 1848.—Whole districts are being cleared and re-let in larger holdings.[3]

'*March* 28, 1848.—*Cabins are being thrown down in all directions*, and it is really extraordinary and, to me, unaccountable where or *how the evicted find shelter.*[4]

'*March* 30, 1848.— . . . The pressure is coming, and will continue; and this will not surprise the Commissioners when I state my conviction *that* 1,000 *cabins have been levelled in this union within a very few months.* The occupants of many of these were induced to give them up on receipt of a small sum of money; and that once spent, they must seek the workhouse or starve.[5]

'*April* 6, 1848.—*The destitution in degree and character is, I trust, unknown elsewhere; improvident, ignorant, thriftless parents, scarcely human in habits and intelligence, only present themselves, with nine or ten skeleton children, when they themselves can no longer support the pangs of hunger and their wretched offspring are beyond recovery.* The state of this union must be seen to be believed or comprehended.[6]

'*April* 6, 1848.—While hundreds are being turned out houseless and helpless daily on one small property in Killard division, *no less than twenty-three houses, containing probably one hundred souls, were tumbled in one day,* March 27. I believe the extent of land occupied with these twenty-three houses did not exceed fifty acres. *The suffering and misery attendant upon these wholesale evictions is indescribable.*[7] *The number of houseless paupers in this union is beyond my calculation; those evicted crowd neighbouring cabins and villages, and disease is necessarily generated. On its first appearance, the wretched sufferer, and probably the whole family to which he or she belongs, is ruthlessly turned out by the roadside.* The popular dread of fever or dysentery seems to excuse any degree of inhumanity. The workhouse and temporary hospital are crowded to the utmost extent they can possibly contain; the crowding of the fever hospital causes me serious anxiety. The relieving officer has directions to send no more in: yet, notwithstanding this caution, *panic-stricken and unnatural parents frequently send in a donkey-load of children in fever a distance of fourteen or fifteen miles for admission.* How to dispose of them I know not.[8]

[1] Blue-book No. 1089: Reports and Returns relating to Evictions in the Kilrush Union, 1849, p. 3.
[2] Ib.   [3] Ib.   [4] Ib., p. 4.   [5] Ib.
[6] Ib., p. 4.   [7] Ib., p. 5.   [8] Ib.

'April 8, 1848.—*I calculate that 6,000 houses have been levelled since November, and expect 500 more before July.*[1]

'April 13, 1848.—These wholesale evictions are most embarrassing to the guardians. The wretched and half-witted occupiers are too often deluded by the specious promises of under-agents and bailiffs, and induced to throw down their own cabin for a paltry *consideration of a few shillings*, and an assurance of "outdoor relief."

'*June 27th, 1848.—Several of these wretched dens were without light or air, and I was obliged to light a piece of bog-fir to see where the sick lay, while many good and substantial houses lay in ruins about them. Whatever the necessity, or whatever future good these clearances may effect, they are productive of an amount of present suffering and mortality which would scare the proprietors were they to see it.* And the evil still goes on. During the last week about sixty more souls have been left houseless on one small property, to crowd into the already overcrowded cabins and create disease.[2]

'July 5, 1848.—Twenty thousand, or one-fourth of the population, are now in receipt of daily food, either in or out of the workhouse. Disease has unfortunately kept pace with destitution, and the high mortality at one period since last November, in and out of the workhouse, was most distressing. I have frequently been astonished by the sudden and unexpected pressure from certain localities; this naturally induced an inquiry into the causes, and eventually into a general review of the whole union. The result of this inquiry has convinced me *that destitution has been increased and its character fearfully aggravated by the system of wholesale evictions which has been adopted;* that a fearful amount of disease and mortality has also resulted from the same causes, I cannot doubt. I have painful experience of it daily. To make this understood, I may state, in general terms, that *about 900 houses, containing probably 4,000 occupants, have been levelled in this union since last November*. The wretchedness, ignorance, and helplessness of the poor on the western coast of this union prevent them seeking a shelter elsewhere; and, to use their own phrase, "they don't know where to face;" *they linger about the localities for weeks or months, burrowing behind the ditches, under a few broken rafters of their former dwelling, refusing to enter the workhouse till the parents are broken down and the children half starved, when they come into the workhouse to swell the mortality one by one.* Those who obtain a temporary shelter in adjoining cabins are not more fortunate. Fever and dysentery shortly make their appearance, when those affected are put out by the roadside as carelessly and ruthlessly as if they were animals; when frequently, after days and nights of exposure, they are sent in by the relieving officers when in a hopeless state. These inhuman acts are induced by the popular terror of fever. I have frequently reported cases of this sort. *The misery attendant upon these wholesale and simultaneous evictions is frequently aggravated by hunting these ignorant, helpless creatures off the property, from which they perhaps have never wandered five miles. It is not an unusual occurrence to see forty or fifty houses levelled in one day, and orders given that no remaining tenant or occupier should give them even a night's shelter.* I have known some ruthless acts committed by drivers and sub-agents, but no doubt according to law, however repulsive to humanity; *wretched hovels pulled down, where the inmates were in a helpless state of*

[1] Blue-book No. 1089: Reports and Returns relating to Evictions in the Kilrush Union, 1849, p. 5.   [2] *Ib.*, p. 7.

fever and nakedness, and left by the roadside for days. As many as 300 souls, creatures of the most helpless class, have been left houseless in one day, and the suffering and misery resulting therefrom attributed to insufficient relief or maladministration of the law: it would not be a matter of surprise that it failed altogether in such localities as those I allude to. When relieved, charges of profuse expenditure are readily preferred. The evicted crowd into the back lanes and wretched hovels of the towns and villages, scattering disease and dismay in all directions. The character of some of these hovels defies description. *I not long since found a widow, whose three children were in fever, occupying the piggery of their former cabin, which lay beside them in ruins; however incredible it may appear, this place, where they had lived for weeks, measured five feet by four feet, and of corresponding height.* I offered her a free conveyance to the workhouse, which she steadily refused; *her piggery was knocked down as soon as her children were able to crawl out on recovery, and she has now gone forth a wanderer.* I could not induce any neighbour to take her in, even for payment; she had medical aid, and all necessary relief from the union.[1]

'*August* 13, 1848.—*I regret to say that these monster evictions still continue.* During the last week forty-four families were evicted, and the houses levelled, on one property. . . . A band of paupers, taken from some distant stone-breaking depôts, and armed with spades, crowbars, and pickaxes, completed this work of destruction. . . . These helpless creatures, not only unhoused but *driven* off the *lands*, no one remaining on the lands being allowed to lodge or harbour them. . . . When winter sets in these evicted destitute will be in awful plight, as their temporary sheds, behind ditches or old fences, are quite unfit for human habitation, and *if they attempted to build anything permanent they would be immediately abolished.* If the records of the sheriff's office connected with the union for the last nine months were produced, they would account for much of the death and destitution of the union.[2]

'*August* 25, 1848.—In reply to your communication of the 24th instant, I have the honour to inform you that the band of paupers therein adverted to were hired by the sub-agent, and taken away from the stone-breaking depôt for the purposes I have stated. They, of course, received no relief for the day they were absent, nor for some days after, as the relieving officer ascertained that they received a high rate of wages for this service. I did not intend to convey that the implements used by these paupers were union or public property.[3]

'*August* 27, 1848.—Numerous evictions have taken place during the last week: the numbers and particulars will be forwarded on an early day. The ultimate fate of this class is a matter of curious speculation when their utter destitution and helplessness are fully understood.'[4]

Extract from the Vice-Guardians' Report.

'*October* 21, 1848.—*The number of houses now thrown down, and of families thereby rendered totally destitute, is daily increasing to a fearful extent.*'[5]

---

[1] Blue-book No. 1089: Reports and Returns relating to Evictions in the Kilrush Union, 1849, pp. 7, 8.
[2] *Ib.*, p. 19.   [3] *Ib.*, p. 20.   [4] *Ib.*, p. 23.   [5] *Ib.*, p. 30.

Extracts from Report of Captain Kennedy.

'*December* 4, 1848. — My acquaintance with the state of this union does not allow me to believe that the numbers becoming chargeable to the rates will stop short of 20,000. This can hardly be a matter of surprise when I state (what the Commissioners are in possession of) that I have forwarded *returns of the eviction of* 6,090 *souls since last July*.[1]

'*January* 22, 1849.—*I cannot estimate the evictions in the union much under* 150 *souls per week*.[2] . . . The destitution in this union is a mighty and fearful reality: it is in vain to strive to falsify or forget its existence; yet no combined effort, and hardly an individual one, is made to alleviate or arrest it. A few philanthropic individuals continue to afford their unit of relief and employment, but their example is not taking. There is a general lack of energy; the better part of the community seem, for the most part, as apathetic as if the country were comparatively prosperous; while demoralization, disease, and death are spreading like a cancer. *I see the masses of the people starving, and the land, which could be made to feed treble the number, lying all but waste.*'[3]

Extract of Report from the Vice-Guardians.

'*January* 22, 1849.—*Evictions and throwing down houses continue to be carried on to large extent, and the Quarter Sessions, now going on, shows that a large number of ejectments are in process; and we know that within a fortnight upwards of* 800 *beings have been evicted from their houses.* We cannot, therefore, make any calculation that may come near the amount, but are of opinion that at least 2,000 persons will be added in some parts of the intermediate season, and that about the same number will be off the list in the months of April to June; they increase from that to October.'[4]

Extract from Report of Captain Kennedy.

'*April* 3, 1849.—*On one farm alone, in Kilmurry (the most miserable district in the union), where there were seventy-three houses within the last ten months, there are now but thirteen.* I also enclose a petition marked "E," being one of hundreds which I have received to the same purport. This houseless class becomes more embarrassing daily, and I fear a money allowance for lodging, in addition to food, will ere long be forced upon the Vice-Guardians.'[5]

The following is the petition:

'*The humble petition of Patt Lumane*,

'Showeth,

'That he has neither house nor home, nor place to shelter him; no person would admit him, or give him a night's lodging. He has five in family, exposed to all sorts of persecutions; therefore he applies to the Board of Guardians to admit him and family into the workhouse to shelter them.

'He was upon outdoor relief, and had no asylum to eat it.'[6]

---

[1] Blue-book No. 1089: Reports and Returns relating to Evictions in the Kilrush Union, 1849, p. 36.
[2] *Ib*., p. 43.   [3] *Ib*., p. 45.   [4] *Ib*.   [5] *Ib*., p. 43.   [6] *Ib*., p. 46.

EXTRACT FROM REPORT OF CAPTAIN KENNEDY.

'*May* 7, 1849.—I find that my constant and untiring exertions make but little impression upon the mass of fearful suffering. *As soon as one horde of houseless and all but naked paupers are dead, or provided for in the workhouse, another wholesale eviction doubles the number, who, in their turn, pass through the same ordeal of wandering from house to house or burrowing in bogs or behind ditches, till, broken down by privation and exposure to the elements, they seek the workhouse, or die by the roadside.* The state of some districts of the union during the last fourteen days baffles description; *sixteen houses, containing twenty-one families, have been levelled in one small village in Killard division, and a vast number in the rural parts of it.* As cabins become fewer, lodgings, however miserable, become more difficult to obtain; *and the helpless and houseless creatures, thus turned out of the only home they ever knew, betake themselves to the nearest bog or ditch, with their little all, and, thus huddled together, disease soon decimates them.*

'Notwithstanding that fearful and, I believe, unparalleled numbers have been unhoused in this union within the year (probably 15,000), it seems hardly credible that 1,200 *more have had their dwellings levelled within a fortnight.*

'I have a list of 760 completed, and of above 400 in preparation. It appears to me almost impossible to successfully meet such a state of things; and the prevailing epidemic, or the dread of it, aggravates the evil. None of this houseless class can now find admittance, save into some overcrowded cabin, whose inmates seldom survive a month. I have shown Dr. Phelan some of these miserable nests of pestilence, which I am at a loss to describe.

'*Five families, numbering twenty souls, are not unfrequently found in a cabin consisting of one small apartment.* At Doonbeg, a few days since, I found three families, numbering sixteen persons, one of whom had cholera, and three in a hopeless stage of dysentery. The cabin they occupied consisted of one wretched apartment, about twelve feet square. It was one of the few refuges for the evicted, and they were unable to reckon how many had been carried out of it from time to time to the grave.'[1]

There are one or two further extracts which illustrate very forcibly the working of the land system. Thus, the following extracts from Captain Kennedy's report show the manner in which the excessive competition for land brought up prices far beyond their value and far beyond the capacity of the tenant to pay:

'Hundreds of instances occur where an acre of land worth 15s. is let for £3, and the occupier, in default of full payment, bound to give 140 days' labour to his lessor during spring and harvest, when the occupier himself requires them most; this would (valuing his labour at 8d. per day) amount to £4 13s.'[2]

The farmer, oppressed himself, naturally acted in like manner with regard to the labourer:

'The same system obtains as to the letting of cabins; 100 or 120 days' labour, during the only period the wretched labourer would earn, is exacted for a cabin worth perhaps 7s. 6d. a year.'[3]

---

[1] Blue-book No. 1089: Reports and Returns relating to Evictions in the Kilrush Union, 1849, p. 46.   [2] *Ib.*, p. 4.   [3] *Ib.*, p. 5.

And here is a definition of an able-bodied labourer that suggests curious reflections:

'.... There are but few who realize any idea of an able-bodied labourer; the great mass of them are called so, more in relation to their years than their physical power, or in contradistinction to those who are in the last stage of disease or existence. Men are called able-bodied here who would not be so designated elsewhere.'[1]

Then, as to the action of the landlord, here are two extracts which give a curious idea of his feelings and conduct:

'*The lands have been already literally swept for rent.* I frequently travel fifteen miles without seeing five stacks of grain of any kind; all threshed and sold. *Rent has seldom or ever been looked for more sharply, and levied more unsparingly, than this year.*'[2]

'Of the proprietors there are but few resident. I cannot speak of their means; I only know that there has not been any amount of poor-rate levied in this union seriously to injure them; no more than any man of common humanity ought voluntarily to bestow in disastrous times. That they are, generally speaking, embarrassed, I fear is a melancholy truth, and goes far to account for the existing want of employment and consequent destitution.'[3]

The result of these wholesale clearances was to extort from Parliament an Act which compelled the landlord to give forty-eight hours' notice to the Poor Law Guardians of his district, so that they might be able to make provision for giving food and shelter to those whom his eviction had left starving and homeless. The Act was called 'An Act for the Protection and Relief of the Destitute Poor evicted from their Dwellings in Ireland.' There is no Act of the Legislature which throws so ghastly a light on the social condition of Ireland. The first section enacts that notice of an eviction must be given forty-eight hours before to the relieving-officers, and prohibits evictions two hours before sunset or sunrise, and on Christmas Day and Good Friday! The seventh section makes the pulling down, demolition, or unroofing of the house of a tenant about to be evicted a misdemeanour. The fact that such an Act could be passed through two Houses of Parliament in either of which the landlord interest was predominant is the strongest evidence of the dread condition of things then existing in Ireland. But even the merciful provisions of this extraordinary Act, small as they were, the landlords and their agents managed to evade. The correspondence between Captain Kennedy and the Poor Law Commissioners abounds with instances of inquiries with regard to the violation of the law in this respect. But the landlords ultimately found out the way in which the Act might be evaded, as will be seen from the following extract from the Vice-Guardians' Report, dated October 21, 1848:

'In most instances the plan adopted by the landlords has been to proceed by civil bill against the person of the tenant, and, on his being arrested, to discharge him from gaol on his having the house thrown down, and possession given to landlord by the remainder of his family, or by his

---

[1] Blue-book No. 1089: Reports and Returns relating to Evictions in the Kilrush Union, 1849, p. 44.
[2] Ib.
[3] Ib. pp. 44, 45.

friends; in other cases, a small sum is given to the tenant, and discharge from all claim of rent, on the house being thrown down and possession given up. In both these cases the landlord is not obliged to give notice; nor does he incur any penalty, as no ejectment or legal process has been instituted for the recovery of the lands and premises, and the object intended by the Act, "to allow preparation to be made for the reception or subsistence of the families," is totally defeated.'[1]

As Captain Kennedy observed:[2]

'It may be asked why the occupier submits to what is illegal? The answer is simply that the great mass are tenants-at-will, and dare not resist; and on many properties notice to quit is served every six months, to enable the lessor to turn out the occupiers when he pleases. This is a ruinous system, and one much complained of.'

An extract from the report of Mr. Phelan, one of the Poor Law officials, dated May 16, 1849, shows even more plainly than do the many extracts from Captain Kennedy that it was eviction rather than famine and fever which was accountable for the horrible condition of the people. He says:

'I have, in many of the western and southern unions, seen sights of the most harrowing description, but I do not think that I have ever seen so much wretchedness arising from destitution as in these places in 1847-48. Epidemic fever and dysentery, produced, it is true, in considerable measure by want, caused great misery; but here, in the absence of fever and of dysentery, except that arising from want of food, destitution, although endeavoured to be met by indoor and outdoor relief, has assumed a shape which even in Clifden was not, I think, presented. Families are here literally naked, and at the same time progressing surely and quickly to the grave by diarrhœa and dropsy.'[3]

Extract from Report of Captain Kennedy.

'*May* 7, 1849.—In a cow-shed adjoining this wretched cabin, I found "Ellen Lynch" lying in an almost hopeless stage of dysentery. She had been carried thither by her son when "thrown out" of her miserable lodging, and was threatened with momentary expulsion from even this refuge by the philanthropic owner of it; her only safety rested in the fears of all but her son to approach her. I was ankle-deep in manure while standing beside her. This poor woman is nearly related to an elective member of the Ennis Board of Guardians, and also to one of the late Kilrush Board. Her husband had been lately evicted, and died. I had all conveyed to the workhouse. They were all in receipt of out-relief, and had even got medical assistance.

'While inspecting a stone-breaking depôt a few days since, I observed one of the men take off his remnant of a pair of shoes and started across the fields; I followed him with my eye, and at a distance saw the blaze of a fire in the bog. I sent a boy to inquire the cause of it, and the man running from his work, and was told that his house had been levelled the day before, that he had erected a temporary hut on the lands, and while his wife and children were gathering shell-fish on the strand, and he stone-breaking, the bailiff or "driver" fired it. These ruthless acts of barbarity are submitted to with an unresisting patience hardly credible.'[4]

[1] Blue-book No. 1089: Reports and Returns relating to Evictions in the Kilrush Union, 1849, p. 30.
[2] *Ib.*, p. 5.   [3] *Ib.*, p. 47.   [4] *Ib.*

Extract from Mr. Phelan's Report.

'*May* 16, 1849.— .... Many of these wretched creatures have not the benefit of a one-roomed house, nor even of a hut. I felt it my duty to go into several temporary shelters got up on the roadside, in fields and in bogs, which shelters were merely a few hurdles thrown across from the ground to the ditch or wall, with some loose straw or rushes or *scraws* laid on. These places can only be entered on hands and knees; the utmost height is not above three feet, even a boy or girl cannot stand up in them; yet I found a family of four or five in these places, usually all or most sick. But in some I have found the children naked in bed, the mother gone for the "relief," and the father "stone-breaking."[1]

In order to make the picture complete, I will give some few names from the nominal lists of the evicted which Captain Kennedy was in the habit of appending to his reports, with the observations made upon them.

[1] Blue-book No. 1089: Reports and Returns relating to Evictions in the Kilrush Union, 1849, **p.** 48.

EVICTIONS IN THE KILRUSH UNION.—PARISH OF KILLARD.—PROPERTY OF STACKPOOLES, MINORS;

ALL WITHIN THE LAST THREE MONTHS.

From List of Names and Number of Families evicted and driven from the Lands of Clohanes, Rhineagonnaut, and Doonbeg.[1]

No.	Heads of Families.	No. in Family.	Males.	Females.	How dispossessed.	Cause.	Title.	Quantity of Land.	Yearly Rent.	Arrears.	Observations.
43	Widow Gallagher	6	2	4	Evicted	—	Non-title	House	—	—	House thrown down, though built by her husband.
44	John Kelly	2	1	1	„	—	„	„	—	—	House thrown down, though built by himself.

From List of the Number of Families ejected and Houses thrown down on the Lands of Tullyroe and Shinaganah, Sub-divisions of Querin, by the Messrs. Burroughs.[2]

| 32 | Joanna Hoare (widow) | 2 | 1 | 1 | Evicted | — | — | — | — | — | Died in the workhouse while there the house was thrown down, though the rent was paid. |

From List of Families ejected and expelled from the Lands of Tullybrack, the estate of Mr. Westby.[3]

									£ s. d.		
1	Widow Flahert	6	5	1	Ejected	No title	At will	5 acres	1 18 0	—	These were ejected, having no title; no rent due; a gale's rent tendered to Mr. Marcus Keane, the agent, but refused.
2	Michael Nugen	10	4	6	„	„	„	13 „	2 15 0	—	
3	Widow McMah n	5	3	2	„	„	„	3 „	1 10 0	—	
4	Michael Mulquenny	5	3	2	„	„	„	4 „	2 0 0	—	
62	Connor Gaven	9	5	4	„	„	„	5½ „	4 0 0	—	House thrown down. This man paid £16 fine last year.

[1] Blue-book No. 1089: Reports and Returns relating to Evictions in the Kilrush Union, 1849, p. 9.   [2] *Ib.*, p. 10.   [3] *Ib.*, p. 15.

MOYARTA ELECTORAL DIVISION.

From List of Persons evicted and their Houses levelled on the Lands of Clolanmechy, in the Electoral Division of Kilmurry, the property of Sir John Reed. John Kelly immediate Lessor under the Court of Chancery.—August 14, 1849.[1]

No.	Heads of Families.	No. in Family.	Males.	Females.	How dispossessed.	Cause.	Title.	Quantity of Land.	Yearly Rent.	Arrears.	Observations.
9	Michael Consitin	2	1	1	—	Non-payment	At will	2 acres	£ s. d. 2 14 0	—	This man, in consequence of having land, could not be relieved. His wife and nine children died of actual want; some before and some since he was dispossessed or forced to give up his land.

From List of Evictions and Houses levelled on the Lands of Brisla, Kilmaeduane Electoral Division, Kilrush Poor Law Union, County of Clare, on August 10, 1848, the property of Mr. John McDonnell, New Hall.[2]

No.	Heads of Families.	No. in Family.	Males.	Females.	How dispossessed.	Cause.	Title.	Quantity of Land.	Yearly Rent.	Arrears.	Observations.
19	Widow McTurry	6	3	3	—	Non-payment	At will	6 acres	5 5 0	—	
20	Peter Kiniry	3	2	1	—	"	"	3 "	2 10 0	—	When in the poorhouse last March, where two of his children died, his house was levelled, and the land sold to another person.
21	Martin Kiniry, Pat	4	2	2	—	"	"	3 "	2 11 0	—	
22	John Keary	2	1	1	—	"	"	" "	" "	—	

From List of the Number of Families ejected and Houses thrown down on the Townsland of Coolmen, Steiendooly, Parish of Killofin, Barony of Clonderlaw.[3]

No.	Heads of Families.	No. in Family.	Males.	Females.	How dispossessed.	Cause.	Title.	Quantity of Land.	Yearly Rent.	Arrears.	Observations.
3	Edward Kelly, jun.	5	3	2	Ejected	Non-payment	At will	1 acre	3 0 0	—	Himself and three children died in the poorhouse.
12	Stephen Helfernan	4	2	2	"	"	"	¼ "	1 0 0	—	This man and his wife dead.

From List of the Names and Number of Families evicted and driven from the Lands of Gunnacatesky, since November 1 last, the property of Mr. Marcus Keane, Middleman to Miss Hickman, Parishes of Kilmaeduane and Kilrush.[4]

No.	Heads of Families.	No. in Family.	Males.	Females.	How dispossessed.	Cause.	Title.	Quantity of Land.	Yearly Rent.	Arrears.	Observations.
1	Simon O'Donnell	7	3	4	Ejected	Non-payment	At will	6 acres	7 4 0	—	Two dead; house levelled; his corn was sold for arrears before ejectment; now in poorhouse.

[1] Bluebook No. 1089 : Reports and Returns relating to Evictions in the Kilrush Union, 1849, p. 24. [2] Ib., p. 21. [3] Ib., p. 17. [4] Ib., p. 12.

KILLOFIN ELECTORAL DIVISION.

From List of Persons evicted, expelled their Houses, and Houses levelled, on the Lands of Lahill, Millpark, and Ballina, the property of John Westropp, Esq.—May 7, 1849.[1]

No.	Heads of Families.	No. in Family.	Males.	Females.	Quantity of Land.	Yearly Rent.	Cause of Eviction.	Title.	Observations.
14	Pierce McMahon	7	3	4	Cabin	—	—	At will	McMahon's wife and child died from exposure to cold since put out.
15	James Cox	6	3	3	,,	—	—	,,	Cox lodged with above. Cox and one child died from same cause.

KILMICHAEL ELECTORAL DIVISION.

From List of Persons evicted, and Houses levelled, on the Lands of Boulanamocle, the property of John Westropp, Esq., Attyflyune.—May 9, 1849.

No.	Heads of Families.	No. in Family.	Males.	Females.	Quantity of Land.	Yearly Rent.	Cause of Eviction.	Title.	Observations.
1	Michael White	5	3	2	Cabin	—	—	At will	White died since expulsion. Work-rent.
2	Michael Meade	5	2	3	,,	—	—	,,	Meade died from same cause. Work-rent.
3	James Mongovan	7	4	3	,,	—	—	,,	Work-rent.

Kilballyowen, E.D., the Lands of Fodra, the property of Mr. Westby; Thomas Fennell, Middleman.[2]

No.	Heads of Families.	No. in Family.	Males.	Females.	Quantity of Land.	Yearly Rent. £ s. d.	Cause of Eviction.	Title.	Observations.
13	Owen M'Enerney	9	5	4	House	0 5 0	—	At will	Fennell took advantage of this poor man's absence from his house, removed his family in a most inhuman manner, and locked the door. This case stands over for trial.

From List of Persons evicted and Houses levelled on the Lands of Drumelloty, in the Electoral Division of Kilmacduane, Kilrush Poor Law Union, County of Clare, on August 9, 1849, the Marquis of Conyngham's property; Marcus Keane, Agent.[3]

No.	Heads of Families.	No. in Family.	Males.	Females.	Quantity of Land.	Yearly Rent. £ s. d.	Cause of Eviction.	Title.	Observations.
	John O'Neill	5	3	2	1½ acres	1 10 0	Non-payment.	At will	Three more of this family died in the poorhouse.

[1] Blue-book No. 1089 : Reports and Returns relating to Evictions in the Kilrush Union, 1849, p. 52.   [2] *Ib.*, p. 35.   [3] *Ib.*, p. 21.

From List of the Number of Families ejected, and Houses thrown down, on the Lands of Querin, by the Messrs. Burroughs.

No.	Heads of Families.	No. in Family.	Males.	Females.	How dispossessed.	Cause.	Title.	Quantity of Land.	Yearly Rent. £ s. d.	Arrears.	Observations.
1	Pat Haugh	7	4	3	Ejected	Non-payment.	At will	11 acres	9 18 0	—	This case was tried by Record, with ruinous costs.

From List of the Number of Families driven from the Lands of Fromore, Mr. Vasey's property, parish of Kilmurry, and the Electoral Division of same, Barony of Hackauz.[1]

No.	Heads of Families.	No. in Family.	Males.	Females.	How dispossessed.	Cause.	Title.	Quantity of Land.	Yearly Rent. £ s. d.	Arrears.	Observations.
1	John Hearn	6	4	2	Not	Non-payment.	At will	1½ acres	3 10 0	—	All these families were turned off these lands by Mr. Michael Hearn, a middleman, since November, 1847, being obliged to surrender house and land after paying Mr. Hearn, three years ago, a fine of from £3 to £4 per acre. They owed no arrears; but surrendered under a promise of outdoor relief.
2	Michael Shanahan	5	2	3	,,	,,	,,	½ acre	1 0 0	—	
3	Anthony Shanahan	6	4	2	,,	,,	,,	,,	1 0 0	—	
4	Thomas Shanahan	3	1	2	,,	,,	,,	1 ,,	1 0 0	—	
5	Andy White	7	4	3	,,	,,	,,	,,	1 0 0	—	
6	Pat Meehan	2	1	1	,,	,,	,,	,,	0 10 0	—	
7	Bryan O'Connor	6	4	2	,,	,,	,,	,,	1 0 0	—	
8	Widow Falsey	7	2	5	,,	,,	,,	,,	0 10 0	—	
9	Michael King	6	4	2	,,	,,	,,	1 ,,	2 0 0	—	
10	Pat King	7	5	2	,,	,,	,,	,,	2 0 0	—	
11	John Shanahan	4	1	3	,,	,,	,,	,,	1 0 0	—	
12	Thomas Mungovan	6	5	1	,,	,,	,,	1 ,,	2 0 0	—	
13	Mary Shanahan	5	4	1	,,	,,	,,	,,	1 0 0	—	
14	Michael Akem	5	3	2	,,	,,	,,	,,	1 0 0	—	
15	Michael Boyle	4	2	2	,,	,,	,,	,,	1 0 0	—	
16	Norry Molloy	3	2	1	,,	,,	,,	1 ,,	1 0 0	—	
17	Scullane	5	3	2	,,	,,	,,	2 acres	1 0 0	—	

From List of the Number of Families turned out by the Summary Eviction on the Lands of Clongamane.[a]

No.	Heads of Families.	No. in Family.	Males.	Females.	How dispossessed.	Cause.	Title.	Quantity of Land.	Yearly Rent. £ s. d.	Arrears.	Observations.
27	James Downs	6	5	1	Ejected	Non-payment.	At will	2 acres	1 14 0	—	House thrown down. Dead.
28	Thos. McNamara	5	2	3	,,	,,	,,	2 ,,	1 14 0	—	Dead.
30	Wm. Stackpoole	5	4	1	,,	,,	,,	1 ,,	0 18 6	—	Dead.

[1] Blue-book No. 1089 : Reports and Returns relating to Evictions in the Kilrush Union, 1849, p. 13.   [a] Ib.

I have thought it necessary for several reasons to present this picture of a district in Ireland during the famine period with fulness of detail. A picture like this, drawn by an official hand, cannot be accused of partiality or over-colouring. The reports of Captain Kennedy, it is true, often make the blood run cold, and one's breath come faster; but there is not one in their hosts of appalling statements, of which Captain Kennedy does not give his proofs with all the neat precision of a statistician, and in lists of passionless figures. It will be remembered, of course, that I have described but one district in Ireland; and that what was going on in the Union of Kilrush was repeated—possibly even exceeded—in many other parts of Ireland.

The reader now has an opportunity of seeing Irish landlordism at work. I feel justified in summing up this part of the case by the statement that I have proved the Irish landlords to have used their powers—amid a national calamity of almost unprecedented extent—with a cruelty more atrocious than that of any other class of men in the modern history of civilized countries. Since the earlier editions of this work were published, England and the whole civilized world have been shocked by the story of Glenbeigh. In the midst of his gratitude for this outburst of human sympathy with his people, the Irishman could not help reflecting that in the Famine period there had been a hundred thousand evictions worse than Glenbeigh; and that England and the world heard nothing of them, or gave them but a passing thought. Of all the crimes an Irishman has to lay at the door of the Union, there is none more horrible and none more maddening than the deafness which the Union produced to the loudest cry of Irish agony.

I have given a picture of Irish landlordism in the days of Ireland's supreme agony; let us pass to the second part of the inquiry. What were the Government doing? They were not ignorant of what was going on in Ireland. If official reports could have spared the country any misery, there were enough reports to have defeated the worst efforts of famine; and Parliament, besides, was being constantly reminded by debates of what was going on. The great clearances were the subject of constant and persistent discussion, and Sir Robert Peel was far more energetic than Lord John Russell or any of the other Liberal Ministers in denouncing their cruelty. The reports of Captain Kennedy, from which extracts have just been given, supplied him with materials for making a strong speech upon these evictions. 'I must say,' he remarked, 'that I do not think that the records of any country, civil or barbarous, present materials for such a picture as is set forth in the statement of Captain Kennedy.' Then the Conservative leader takes up some of the instances which stand out in relief even in this catalogue of horrors. These are the cases of the two children lying asleep on the corpse of their dead father while their mother was dying fast of dysentery; the case of Ellen Lynch (Captain Kennedy's report, see *ante*, p. 61); and the case of the man who ran away from breaking stones when he saw the fire put to the hovel in which he had placed his wife and children (Captain Kennedy's report, see *ante*, p. 61). 'Three such tragical instances,' he went on, 'I do not believe were ever presented either in point of fact, or as conjured up even in the imagination of any human being.'[1]

It is in a speech of Sir Robert Peel, too, that one finds another of the worst cases of eviction in this period disinterred from the voluminous reports in the Blue-books. It is the case of an eviction by a man named

---

[1] Hansard, June 8, 1849.

Blake—a justice of the peace in Galway. Quoting the account given by Major McKie—an official employed like Captain Kennedy by the Poor Law Commissioners—Sir Robert Peel said :

'It would appear from the evidence recorded that the forcible ejectments were illegal, that previous notices had not been served, and that the ejectments were perpetrated under circumstances of great cruelty. The time chosen was for the greater part nightfall on the eve of the New Year. The occupiers were forced out of their houses with their helpless children, and left exposed to the cold on a bleak western shore in a stormy winter's night ; that some of the children were sick ; that the parents implored that they might not be exposed, and their houses left till morning ; that their prayers for mercy were in vain, and that many of them have since died. "I have visited the ruins of these huts (not at any great distance from Mr. Blake's residence) ; I found that many of the unfortunate people were still living within the ruins of these huts, endeavouring to shelter themselves under a few sticks and sods, all in the most wretched state of destitution ; many were so weak that they could scarcely stand when giving their evidence. The site of these ruins is a rocky wild spot fit for nothing but a sheep-walk." '[1]

It will be seen from these extracts that Parliament was perfectly familiar with the horrible intensity of the problem that demanded redress ; and again the story is that Parliament did nothing, or worse than nothing.

The expulsion of bankrupt landlords appeared for a time to commend itself to the minds of English statesmen as the one remedy required. This led to the passage of the Encumbered Estates Act in 1848. The object of this Act was to enable the estates of landlords to be sold, in spite of the elaborate machinery by which the feudal laws of the country guarded against alienation. Under the operation of this Act, some of the most ancient families of Ireland were driven from their properties. Here again the land legislation devised by the British Parliament proved once more a curse to the landlord as to the tenant. The landlords, forced to sell at a time of terrible depression, were unable to get anything like the true value of their lands. Then the new race of proprietors that were substituted for the old, were in rare cases an improvement. They came from the shopkeeper class who had amassed money in trade : the class of promoted *bourgeois* does not shine in the history of any race or country, and in Ireland it is made by the circumstances of the country, political and social, a peculiarly odious generation. The new landlords were more insolent than the old, looked on the land as purely an investment, almost always signalized their advent of possession by an increase of rent, and mercilessly evicted when the tenant at last found the struggle between hunger and rack-rent unequal. To the class of new proprietors, too, we owe many of the place-hunting generation of politicians—the meanest, most unscrupulous, and most pestilent race of politicians that ever shamed or cursed a race.

The Encumbered Estates Act was also an Act of gigantic plunder. As Mr. Gladstone has since, over and over again, told Parliament, no account was taken of the improvements of the tenants ; and the improvements of the tenants gave to the land all the difference between its actual and its prairie value. When the new landlord raised the rent, then, he created rent out of the labour of the tenantry : the industry of the robbed gave

[1] Hansard, June 8, 1849.

the ground and fixed the proportion of the robbery; the larger the property the tenant had created in the land, the higher the amount he paid to his plunderer. The amount of ransom was regulated by the wealth the tenant had added to the soil. It speaks eloquently of the difference between these days and ours—it is the most potent testimony to the helplessness of the tenant, and the profound demoralization of public opinion in Ireland at that period, that these acts of robbery were not concealed and were not largely resented. In the advertisements in which the coming sales of estates were announced, no statement was more regular than that the property was low-rented, and that the rents could be considerably raised.

Finally, the main object of the Encumbered Estates Act, and of much other legislation of the period, was the introduction into Ireland of a new element of proprietor. It was one of the chief dreams of that period that the Celtic race should be replaced by the sturdier and more self-reliant race that populated England and Scotland—the assumption being, of course, that it was Irish vice, laziness, and incapacity, and not English laws, that caused the hideous breakdown of the English land system in Ireland. The commencement was to be made with the landlords. This was one of the objects of the Encumbered Estates Act; and in March, 1850, as that Act did not seem to fulfil the purpose, another Bill was introduced for the purpose of establishing land debentures. 'They had devised a plan,' said the Solicitor-General, in introducing the measure, 'which he hoped would induce capitalists from England to take an interest in the sales.' And Sir Robert Peel himself took the trouble of elaborating, in several speeches before the House of Commons, a scheme for a new plantation of Ireland by the substitution of English and Scotch for Irish landlords.

But it was not the landlords of the Celtic race that were to be got rid of; these the country could very well afford to do without; and possibly a generation of English or Scotch landlords would have been incapable of the hideous cruelty depicted by Captain Kennedy and so many other writers of the time; it required the training in centuries of unchecked racial and religious ascendancy, through which the Irish landlords had passed, to inure their hearts to such revolting crimes. It was apparently the desire of the English statesmen of that period to get rid of as many of the peasantry of the Celtic race as possible. In these days, when emigration as a panacea for all evils is the creed of but a few featherbrained philanthropists, it will scarcely be believed that after all the ravages of hunger, the decimation through fever, the terrible emigration, it was deemed that the true remedy for Ireland was more emigration! Indeed, the unfitness of Ireland for the Irish race and the Irish race for Ireland, was a dogma preached with something like the fine frenzy of a new revelation in those days. 'Remove Irishmen,' wrote the *Times* (February 22, 1847), 'to the banks of the Ganges or the Indus, to Delhi, Benares, or Trincomalee, and they would be far more in their element there than in a country to which *an inexorable fate has confined them.*' A Select Committee of the House of Lords was equally catholic in its search for a better land for Irishmen than the land which had given them birth. They relate that they had taken evidence respecting the state of Ireland—Where? the reader will ask. 'In British North American colonies (including Canada, New Brunswick, Nova Scotia, Newfoundland), the West India Islands, New South Wales, Port Philip, South Australia, Van Diemen's Land, and New Zealand.' And not satisfied with this, they actually apologize for not having examined other countries as well. 'The committee,' says the Report sorrowfully, 'are fully aware that they have as yet examined into many points but superficially, and that some—as, for example, the state of the British possessions in Southern Africa, and in the territory of Natal—have not yet been considered at all.' 'The important discoveries of Sir T. Mitchell in Australia have also been but slightly noticed,' is added with a final sigh.

An Association, consisting of six peers and twelve commoners, styled 'The Irish Committee,' also devoted itself very earnestly to the question of emigration. In this Irish Committee were two Englishmen—Mr. Godley and Dr. Whately—the latter the well-known Archbishop of Dublin. Dr. Whately's name is still held in affectionate and respectful remembrance by many people in England. At this epoch, and, as will be seen, still more in a subsequent epoch of Irish history, his counsels were among the most fatal to the prosperity of Ireland. This body drew out an elaborate scheme under which a million and a half of the Irish people were to be sent to Canada at a cost of £9,000,000, which was to be levied in the shape of an income tax.

But all this time the idea never occurred to any of the English leaders that there should be the slightest interference with the power of the landlords. The power of the landlords had been the main cause of the horrors through which Ireland was passing; and yet the landlords were to be left that power. The mass of the people were to be exported to Canada or Australia, to Natal or Van Diemen's Land—and the country was to be delivered entirely to their lords and masters. The land of Ireland was to be laid waste of as many of six millions of people as ten thousand landlords chose to condemn to banishment. Such was the theory of the time.

At this point it will be instructive to pause for a moment, and consider the action of the Imperial Parliament. Lord John Russell, as has been seen, had got into office on the rejection of an Irish Coercion Bill. He had objected to the Coercion Bill of Sir Robert Peel, not merely on account of the harshness of its provisions, the weakness of the case in its favour, the sufficiency of the ordinary law; his chief ground of objection was that Ireland was in crying need of remedial legislation, and that no Coercion Bill ought to be considered by Parliament unless it was accompanied, and accompanied even stage by stage, by remedial proposals. His reference to the ills of Ireland were pitched in as high a key as even the most vehement of Irish Repealers could have wished. He had recapitulated the well-worn evidence before the multitudinous committees which in drear succession had inquired into the Irish problem, and then he went on:

'We have here the best evidence that can be procured—the evidence . . . of magistrates for many years, of farmers, of those who have been employed by the Crown—and all tell you that the possession of land is that which makes the difference between existing and starving amongst the peasantry; and that, therefore, ejections out of their holdings are the cause of violence and crime in Ireland. In fact, it is no other than the cause which the Great Master of human nature describes when he makes a tempter suggest it as a reason to violate the law.'

Then he quoted Romeo's address to the Apothecary; and went on:

'Such is the incentive which is given to the poor Irish peasant to break the law, which he considers deprives him of the means, not of being rich, but of the means of obtaining a subsistence. On this ground, I say, then, if you were right to introduce any measure to repress crime beyond the ordinary powers of the law, it would have been right at the same time to introduce other measures by which the means of subsistence might be increased, and by which the land, upon which alone the Irish peasant subsists, might be brought more within his reach, and other modes of occupation allowed to him more than he now possesses.'[1]

So strong was Lord John Russell in this demand for the accompaniment of coercive by remedial legislation, that he even wanted that the two classes of measures should go on side by side, stage by stage—either both or none should be accepted by Parliament.

'I know,' he said, 'indeed, the noble lord' (the Earl of Lincoln) 'has introduced within the last two or three days measures upon a very complicated subject—the law of landlord and tenant; but I think those measures *should have been introduced at the same time with the measure now before the House.* How is it possible for this House, upon such a subject, to be able to tell, from the noble lord's enumeration of them, whether upon such a delicate subject such measures are sufficient?'[2]

And shortly afterwards he declared that, while he opposed the measure, the state of crime did not supply 'sufficient ground for passing a measure of extraordinary severity.' The reason, 'above all,' of his hostility was that the Coercion Bill had 'not been accompanied . . . with such measures of relief, of remedy, and conciliation, affecting the great mass of the people of Ireland, who are in distress, *as ought to accompany any measure tending to increased rigour of the law.*'[3]

And then he sketched the measures by which the condition of the peasantry might be relieved. He proposed a grant for the reclamation of waste lands, and he proposed a Bill for 'securing at the same time the lives and properties of those who reside on the land;'[4] in other words, a scheme of tenant-right. If such measures were not proposed promptly, there might come 'a dreadful outbreak, when, indeed, you will hastily resort to measures of remedy and conciliation, but which measures will lose half their practical effect and almost all their moral effect.'[5]

And this remarkable speech wound up with an exhortation in favour of making the Union acceptable to Irishmen, by proving that the Imperial Legislature was as anxious as a native parliament could be to remedy the grievances of Ireland.[6]

Again, in 1847, while the stress of the famine made the neglect of Irish reform too shameful a thing for even the British Parliament to stomach, Lord John Russell was strongly in favour of reform. In the speech at the beginning of the session, in which he proposed the Soup Kitchen Act, he

---

[1] Hansard, lxxxvii., pp. 507-8.
[2] Ib., p. 508. [3] Ib., p. 510. [4] Ib. p. 514. [5] Ib
[6] 'If you wish to maintain the Union—if you wish to improve the Union, to make the Union a source of happiness, a source of increased rights, a source of blessing to Ireland as well as England, a source of increased strength to the United Empire, beware lest you in any way weaken the link which connects the two countries. Do not let the people of Ireland believe that you have no sympathy with their afflictions, no care for their wrongs, that you are intent only upon other measures in which they have no interest.'—Hansard, lxxxvii., p. 516.

declared that there was urgent necessity for some permanent alteration in the land laws. The miseries of Ireland, he laid down in the most emphatic language, were not due to the character of the soil.

'There is no doubt,' exclaimed Lord John Russell, 'of the fertility of the land; that fertility has been the theme of admiration with writers and travellers of all nations.'[1]

He was equally emphatic in denying that these miseries were due to the character of the people.

'There is no doubt either, I must say, of the strength and industry of the inhabitants. The man who is loitering idly by the mountain-side in Tipperary or in Derry, whose potato-plot has furnished him merely with occupation for a few days in the year, whose wages and whose pig have enabled him to pay his rent and eke out afterwards a miserable subsistence —that man, I say, may have a brother in Liverpool, or Glasgow, or London, who by the sweat of his brow, from morning to night, is competing with the strongest and steadiest labourer of England and Scotland, and is earning wages equal to any of them.

'I do not, sir, therefore think,' wound up Lord John Russell emphatically, 'that either the fertility of the soil of Ireland or the strength and industry of its inhabitants is at fault.'[2]

Earl Grey, another eminent Whig, was equally outspoken in his declarations. Like Lord John Russell, he had declared against coercion unaccompanied by remedial measures. He enumerated that long list of Coercion Acts which I have already set forth,[3] winding up with the Insurrection Act, passed in 1833, renewed in 1834, and but five years expired.

'And again,' he said, 'in 1846, we are called on to renew it. We must look further,' continued his lordship; 'we must look to the root of the evil; the state of the law and the habits of the people, *in respect to the occupation of the land*, are almost at the roots of the disorder. It was undeniable that the *clearance system* prevailed to a great extent in Ireland; and that such things could take place—he cared not how large a population might be suffered to grow up in a particular district—was a disgrace to a civilized country.'[4]

In 1848 the Famine had not passed away. As has been seen, the succeeding year was the very worst in the century, except 1847. But the British people and the Imperial Parliament had by this time grown accustomed to the deaths of thousands by starvation and to plague in Ireland as a thing of little meaning, though the sound was strong, and Lord John Russell entirely changed his tune. He met every demand for reform with an uncompromising negative. The Irish tenants had no grievances to speak of—self-reliance, industry, that is what they should rely on.

'While,' said Lord John Russell, 'I admit that, with respect to the franchise and other subjects, the people of Ireland may have just grounds of complaint, I, nevertheless, totally deny that their grievances are any sufficient reason why they should not make very great progress in wealth and prosperity, if, using the intelligence which they possess in a remark-

---

[1] Quoted in O'Rourke, p. 322.
[2] *Ib.*
[3] See *ante*.
[4] Quoted in Mitchel, ii., p. 228.

able degree, they would fix their minds on the advantages which they might enjoy rather than upon the evils which they suppose themselves to suffer under.'[1]

Then he made allusion to a Bill which had been brought in by Sir William Somerville, the Chief Secretary, for dealing with the Land question. Its proposals were indeed modest. It gave compensation to tenants for permanent improvements; but those improvements had to be made with the consent of the landlords, and it was not proposed that the Bill should be retrospective.

But modest as these proposals were, they did not gain the full approval of the Prime Minister, and did not secure the safety of the Bill. 'I have yielded my own conviction,' said Lord John Russell, 'to what appears to be the universal opinion. I think we have gone as far as we can with respect to that subject.' But whether the Premier had gone far enough or not did not much matter; for 'there will not,' said he, 'be time to pass it during the present session, and therefore it will be postponed.'[2]

To any such proposal as fixity of tenure the Liberal Prime Minister would offer his strongest hostility.

'The Tenant Right advocated by the honourable member'—Mr. Sharman Crawford, who had introduced a motion calling for the redress of the grievances of the Irish tenantry—'would amount to this, that the tenant in possession has a right to the occupation of the land provided he pay his rent punctually. *Can anything be more completely subversive of the rights of property . . . ? It is impossible for the Legislature, with any regard for justice, to pass such a law; and if such a law were passed for Ireland, it would strike at the root of property in the whole United Kingdom.*'

And, finally, he concluded with this proposal for the solution of the great Irish Land problem:

'But, after all' (said Lord John Russell), 'that which we should look to for improving the relations between landlord and tenant is a better mutual understanding between those who occupy those relative positions. Voluntary agreements between landlords and tenants, carried out for the benefit of both, are, after all, a better means of improving the land of Ireland than any legislative measure which can be passed.'[3]

The 'better mutual understanding' on which the Prime Minister relied for an improvement in the relations of landlord and tenant at this moment was hounding the landlords to carry on those wholesale clearances which have been described in the words of Sir Robert Peel and Captain Kennedy; which, in the opinion of Earl Grey, were 'a disgrace to a civilized country;' which had been denounced over and over again by Lord John Russell himself; and which, in the opinion of most men, remain as one of the blackest records in all history of man's inhumanity to man. In the year after the exhortation of the Prime Minister to voluntary agreements 'for the benefit of both,' the landlords evicted, according to some authorities, no less than half a million of tenants from their estates.

As the Ministers were opposed to any land legislation, no success naturally attended the efforts of private members to deal with the question.

Two other facts must also be recollected in connection with this period.

---

[1] Hansard, C., p. 943.   [2] Ib., p. 945.   [3] Ib., p. 945.

The final split between Young Ireland and O'Connell was precipitated, it will be remembered, by the attitude which O'Connell insisted on taking up towards the Whig Ministry. The Young Irelanders maintained that the Irish Party should hold towards Russell the same independent attitude as had been taken up towards the Tory Ministry of Peel; that the repeal agitation should be continued, and that the nominees of the Whig Ministry, like Sheil, should meet the same opposition as all other opponents of Repeal and all other British office-holders. O'Connell's main argument against these demands of the Young Irelanders was the good intentions and the promises of Lord John Russell; and he over and over again asserted that the Whig Ministry would pass measures of reform for Ireland,—among others, of course, a Bill of Tenant Right. The Young Irelanders would not place the same faith in Whig promises as O'Connell, the organization was broken up, O'Connell's power was destroyed, the Irish people were divided and impotent in face of the most awful crisis in their history, and O'Connell died of a broken heart. And here was Lord John Russell, on whom O'Connell had placed his reliance, to whose good faith O'Connell sacrificed his party and himself and his country, justifying the very worst predictions of the Young Irelanders, wrecking the hopes and blasting the lives of the Irish nation. It is the second great occasion, described in these pages, of an Irish leader placing confidence in a Whig Minister. In each case the result was exactly the same; the trust was betrayed, openly, shamelessly, heartlessly.

Furthermore, it will be remembered that the great point of dispute between the Young Irelanders and John O'Connell in the General Election of 1847 was whether or no the Irish Party should consist of men pledged to accept no office from a British Minister, and bound to a policy of independence alike of Whig and Tory. John O'Connell maintained that such a pledge was unnecessary, and succeeded in defeating the Young Irelanders hip and thigh. The fruit was now showing itself. The Whig Minister was able to answer every demand for justice with flouts and jibes and sneers, for he had nothing to fear from a party of beggars and adventurers who daily besieged his doors with petitions for themselves or their friends. This is the fact that explains the brutal and shameful tergiversation of the British Premier, and that really accounts for the rejection of all the Irish demands for a redress of the grievances. The nation was shorn of two millions and a half of her people, and in the next decade her population was reduced by still another million. Faith in Whig promises—a dependent Irish Party—these were the chief parents of these disasters.

Let us continue the dreary chapter of Land proposals in the House of Commons.

On February 25, 1847, Mr. Sharman Crawford brought in a Bill proposing to extend to the rest of Ireland the tenant-right custom which existed in Ulster. So little did the Ministers think of the importance of this proposal, that not a single member of the Cabinet was present when the Bill was proposed; and after the debate had been adjourned, it was rejected by the decisive majority of 112 to 25. In February, 1848, Sir William Somerville, Chief Secretary for Ireland, introduced a Bill dealing with the question. The fate of that measure has just been indicated. It was read a second time, it was referred to a Select Committee, and the Select Committee had not time to report before the close of the session. In the same year (1848) Mr. Sharman Crawford again brought in his Bill. It was denounced by Mr. Trelawney, an English member, as a measure of confiscation. Sir William Somerville demolished the suggestion of extending the tenure of Ulster to the rest of Ireland by the epigram that the Ulster custom was good custom, but bad law; and the Bill was defeated. On July 23, 1849, Mr. Horsman moved an address on the state of Ireland, pointing out that that country was now entering on its fourth year of famine, and that sixty per cent. of its population were in receipt of relief. 'What are the causes which have produced such results?' asked Mr. Horsman. 'Bad legislation, careless legislation, criminal legislation, has been the cause of all the disasters we are now deploring.' But bad legislation, careless legislation, criminal legislation remained untouched, for the debate was followed by no measure. In 1850 Sir William Somerville brought in another Bill. It was read a second time, it was sent into committee, and then it was no longer heard of. On June 10 in the same year Mr. Sharman Crawford again brought in his Bill, and again was defeated. On April 8, 1851, Sir Henry Barron moved for a committee 'to inquire into the state of Ireland, and more especially the best means for amending the relationships of landlord and tenant.' But Lord John Russell would hear nothing of such a resolution. If the law of landlord and tenant needed amendment, said the Liberal Prime Minister, the proper course to be taken was for some private member or for the Government to bring in a Bill on the subject, and not to raise the question by way of a resolution of a character so vague. And Lord John Russell from that day until he left office never brought in a Bill himself on the subject, nor supported a Bill brought in by a private member.

The neglect of all reform in the land tenure of Ireland at this epoch, as in previous epochs, is made the more remarkable by its contrast with the action of the Legislature in reference to demands upon its attention by the landlords. The frightful state of things in 1847 naturally produced a considerable amount of disturbance. Many of the tenants were indecent enough to object to being robbed of their own improvements, even with the sanction of an alien Parliament, and went the length of revolting against their wives and children being massacred wholesale, after the fashion described in Captain Kennedy's reports. In short, the Rent was in danger, and in favour of that sacred institution all the resources of British law and British force were promptly despatched. The Legislature had shown no hurry whatever to meet in '46 or '47 when the question at issue was whether hundreds of thousands of the Irish tenantry should perish of hunger or of the plague. Parliament came together at the usual time in 1846, and at the usual time in the beginning of 1847. When the Rent was threatened, Parliament could not be summoned too soon, and a Coercion Bill could not be carried with too much promptitude. The Coercion Bill of Lord John Russell and of 1847 was in all essentials the Coercion Bill of Sir Robert Peel and 1846. There were powers to proclaim districts by the Lord-Lieutenant, and when a district was proclaimed, everybody was obliged to stop within his house from dusk till morning under pain of transportation. There were orders for the delivery of arms, for the drafting of additional police into districts, and for the addition of the burdens thus imposed to the rates already payable by the starving tenants.

The reader will not fail to notice the abject inconsistency between the action of Lord John Russell and the other Whig leaders in opposition and in power. It will not be necessary to recall the quotations which have just been made from the speech of Lord John Russell in opposing the

Coercion Bill of 1846. Suffice it to say that while in 1846 he had objected to the Coercion Bill, 'above all' because it was not accompanied with measures 'of relief, of remedy, and conciliation,' and that he had gone so far as to pledge himself to the principle that some such proposals ought to accompany any measure which tended to 'increased rigour of the law,' Lord John Russell was now himself proposing a measure for greatly 'increased rigour of the law,' not only without accompanying it with any measure of 'relief, of remedy, of conciliation' on his own part, but vehemently opposing any such measure when brought in by any other person. Lord Grey has been quoted for his opinion on the clearance system; here was the clearance system going on worse than ever, and Lord Grey remained a member of the Ministry which through coercion gave that clearance system an enormous impetus.

The police at the same time were urged to unusual activity, and large bodies of the military even were pressed into the service of the landlords, seized the produce of the fields, carried them to Dublin for sale—acted in every respect as the collectors of the rent of the landlord, and thus shared with the landlord the honour of starving the tenants.

A second contrast between the acceptance of remedial and coercive legislation by the Imperial Parliament occurred in 1848. A number of Irishmen, as has been seen, driven to madness by the dreadful suffering they everywhere saw around, and by the neglect or incapacity of Parliament, had sought the desperate remedy of open revolt. The men who, for wrongs much less grievous, rose in the same year in Hungary or France or Italy were the idols of the British people, and were aided and encouraged by British statesmen. The action of the very same statesmen towards Ireland was to pass a brand-new Treason Felony Act, and to suspend the Habeas Corpus Act. The circumstances under which the Habeas Corpus Act was suspended are very instructive.

'The next day, although, being Saturday, it was out of course for the House of Commons to sit,' says the 'Annual Register'[1] of the Coercion Bill of 1848, Parliament came together. Lord John Russell brought forward his Bill. Sir Robert Peel at once 'gave his cordial support to the proposed measure.'[2] Mr. Disraeli 'declared his intention of giving the measure of Government his unvarying and unequivocal support.'[3] Mr. Hume was 'obliged, though reluctantly, to give his consent to the measure of the Government.'[4] And when the division came, there were for the amendment against the Bill proposed by Mr. Sharman Crawford eight votes, and for the first reading of the Bill 271.[5] But this was only the beginning of the good day's work. Lord John Russell said that, 'as the House had expressed so unequivocally its feeling in favour of the Bill, it would doubtless permit its further stages to be proceeded with *instanter*.' He moved the second reading.'[6] Of course the House permitted the further stages to be proceeded with *instanter*, and the Bill, having passed through committee, 'Lord Russell moved the third reading,' which was agreed to, 'and the Bill was forthwith taken up to the House of Lords.' 'On the next day but one, Monday, July 26,' goes on the 'Annual Register,' 'the Bill was proposed by the Marquis of Lansdowne, who concluded his speech in its favour by moving, "That the public safety requires that the Bill should be passed with all possible despatch."' Of

---

[1] 'Annual Register' for 1848, p. 100. [2] *Ib.*, p. 102.   [3] *Ib.*, p. 105.
[4] *Ib.*, p. 106.   [5] *Ib.*, p. 107. [6] *Ib.*, p. 108.

course the motion was accepted by their Lordships 'that the Bill should be passed with all possible despatch.' Lord Brougham 'cordially seconded the motion of Lord Lansdowne,' and, as the 'Register' winds up, 'the Bill passed *nem. dis.* through all its stages.'

Such was the action of the Imperial Parliament upon the Irish question. The agitation for Repeal, which had reached such mighty and apparently resistless proportions in 1843, had vanished amid dissensions, hunger, fever, emigration, and a vast multitude of corpses. The upholders of the Legislative Union were able to look abroad on the face of Ireland, and to rejoice that sedition, in the shape of the demand for Repeal, and treason, in the form of open insurrection, was gone. The Imperial Parliament was unchecked mistress of the destinies of Ireland; and this was how it was fulfilling its mission.

And now, having described the Famine, but two questions remain to be discussed. Was the Famine inevitable? or was it preventable evil—evil that was created by bad, and that could have been prevented by good, government?

I have sufficiently debated already the measures which were taken by the English Ministers to meet the calamity. I think most impartial men will see in the results which followed these measures a dread condemnation of these Ministers. Most persons will hold that a civilized, highly organized, and extremely wealthy government ought to be able to meet such a crisis as the Irish Famine so effectually as to prevent the loss of one single life by hunger. I have already alluded to the language in which some Irish writers are accustomed to speak of the actions and intentions of the Government. Their theory is that the terrors and horrors of the Famine were the result of a deliberate conspiracy to murder wholesale an inconvenient, troublesome, and hostile nation. Such a theory may be promptly rejected, and yet leave a heavy load of guilt on the Ministers. In political affairs we have to look not so much to the intentions as to the results of policies; and it is undeniable that in 1846 and in 1847 there were as many deaths as if the deliberate and wholesale murder of the Irish people had been the motive of English statesmanship. Statesmen, I say, must be judged by the results of their policy. The policy which created the Famine was the land legislation of the British Parliament. The refusal of the British Legislature to interfere with rack-rents; the refusal to protect the improvements of the tenants; the facilities and inducements to wholesale evictions—these were the things that produced the Famine of 1846; and such legislation, again, was the result of the government of Ireland by a Legislature independent of Irish votes, Irish constituencies, Irish opinion.

This must also be said, that the Act of Union, which produced the Famine, and then aggravated it to the unsurpassable maximum, had also the effect of increasing the existing hatred between the English and the Irish nations; and the strangest and saddest thing about it, is that the increase of hatred was undeserved by the one nation and by the other. The hatred of England for Ireland was caused by Ireland's political opinions; and Ireland's political opinions were right. The hatred of Ireland for England was caused by England's political action, and England's political action was conscientiously taken, and, above all, was the outcome of a good, and not of an evil, heart. The chief cause of the hatred of England for Ireland was the agitation for the Repeal of the Union, followed by the abortive rebellion. Peel says so in his 'Memoirs.'

'There will be no hope,' wrote Peel in the Memorandum he submitted to his Cabinet on November 1, 1845, 'of contributions from England for the mitigation of this calamity. Monster meetings, the ungrateful return for past kindness, the subscriptions in Ireland to repeal rent and O'Connell tribute, will have disinclined the charitable here to make any great exertions for Irish relief.'[1]

But what testimony could be so overwhelming, so tragic, in favour of Repeal of the Union as the Irish Famine, with all its attendant horrors of plague, emigration, eviction? And so the hatred of England for Ireland was hideously unjust. On the other hand, it is easy to understand how the Irish should have been embittered to frenzy when they saw the dominant nation, that claimed and had carried its superior right to govern, so performing its functions of government that roads throughout Ireland were impassable with the gaunt forms of the starving, or the corpses of the starved, and that every ship was freighted with thousands fleeing from their homes. To this day the traveller in America will meet Irishmen who were evicted from Ireland in the great clearances of the Famine time; there is a strange glitter in their eyes, and a savage coldness in their voice as they speak of these things, and their bitterness is as fresh as if the wrong were but of yesterday. It was these clearances, and the sight of wholesale starvation and plague, far more than racial feelings, that produced the hatred of English government which strikes the impartial Americans as something like frenzy. It was the events of '46 and '47, of '48 and '49, that sowed in Irish breasts the feelings that in due time produced eager subscribers to the dynamite funds.

And yet, I say again, while the hatred of the English institutions which produced these horrors was just, the hatred of the English people themselves was not deserved. The English people, indeed, did much to earn very different sentiments. 'No one,' writes Justin McCarthy, whose feelings in these days, as will be seen by-and-by, were keen enough to make him a rebel, 'could doubt the goodwill of the English people.'[2] Relief societies were formed almost everywhere. 'The British Association for the Relief of Extreme Distress in Ireland, and the Highlands and Islands of Scotland,' collected no less a sum than £263,251.[3] A Queen's letter was raised with the same object, and no less than £171,533 were collected. I have myself heard an Englishman say that he remembered the Famine because, being a child at the time, he was not permitted to take butter with his bread, in order that some money might be saved for the starving poor of Ireland. It was, then, not the English people that were to blame for the horrors of the Irish Famine, excepting so far as they were responsible for their choice of representatives, and for the maintenance of English institutions in Ireland. It was the British Parliament and the British Ministers that worked the wholesale slaughter of Irishmen, and that produced the murderous hatred of so many of the Irish race for England. In other words, the Act of Union is the great criminal. It is the government of Ireland by Englishmen and by English opinion that has the double result of ruining Ireland and endangering England—of producing much undeserved and preventable suffering to Irishmen, and much undeserved and preventable trouble and hatred to England.

[1] 'Memoirs,' by Sir R. Peel. Part III., p. 143.
[2] 'History of Our Own Times.'
[3] Census Commissioners, quoted from Trevelyan's 'Irish Crisis,' p. 288.

The second point that requires discussion is, whether the Famine was avoidable or unavoidable. John Mitchel speaks of the Famine as an 'artificial' famine, and other Irish writers maintain that, in spite of the loss of the potato, there was enough of food produced in Ireland during these very famine years to have prevented a single person in the country from dying of starvation. I have already made mention of the fact that ships were bearing away from the ports of Ireland wheat and cattle in abundance; and I have quoted the observation of Lord John Russell, pointing to the fact that in the year 1847 the wheat crop, instead of being under, was above the average.

We have no trustworthy statistics in reference to the live stock and agricultural produce of Ireland in the years 1845 and 1846—for it was not till 1847 that statistics on this head were collected in a regular manner. But we have fairly trustworthy statistics with regard to the export of produce in the first of those two years, and also to the export of produce and live stock in the second. First dealing with the year 1845, the following are the statistics of the export of produce for 1845 and the four preceding years :[1]

Year.	Wheat and wheaten flour.	Barley including bere or bigg.	Oats and oatmeal.	Rye.	Peas.	Beans.	Malt.	Total.
	qrs.	qrs.	qrs.	qrs.	qrs.	qrs.	qrs.	qrs.
1841	218,708	75,568	2,539,380	172	855	15,967	4,935	2,855,525
1842	201,998	50,297	2,261,435	76	1,551	19,831	3,046	2,538,234
1843	413,466	110,449	2,648,032	371	1,192	24,329	8,643	3,206,482
1844	440,152	90,656	2,242,308	264	1,091	18,580	8,155	2,801,204
1845	779,113	93,095	2,353,985	165	1,644	12,745	11,144	3,251,901

It will be seen from this that the export of wheat and wheaten flour, instead of being diminished in 1845 by the blight of the potato and the consequent famine, was enormously increased. The number of quarters exported in 1845, 779,113, is nearly double that exported in the two preceding years, and considerably more than treble that exported in the years 1841 and 1842. The export of barley, 93,095 quarters, is larger than any of the preceding years except 1843. In oats, the export is about the average. The grand total of exported produce is nearly 1,000,000 quarters beyond the exports of 1841, 1842, and 1844, and is higher than the export of 1843, which had the largest export of the preceding four years.[2]

The exports of articles of food in 1846 were :

	Quarters.
Wheat and wheat flour	393,462
Barley, etc.	92,854
Oats and oatmeal	1,311,592
Peas	2,227
Beans	14,668
Malt	11,329
Total	1,826,132[3]

[1] McCulloch, 'Dictionary of Commerce,' latest edition, by A. J. Wilson, p. 450.
[2] Thom's 'Almanack' for 1848 states that the total imports of Irish produce into Liverpool alone increased in value from £4,149,428 in 1842 to £6,383,498 in 1845.
[3] McCulloch, 'Dictionary of Commerce,' p. 450.

Here there is a considerable reduction as compared with the figures of the preceding years, but still there remains a total of 1,826,132 quarters of food exported from a starving nation. Coming now to the export of live cattle, here are the figures for 1846:

Oxen, bulls, and cows	186,483
Calves	6,363
Sheep and lambs	259,257
Swine	480,827[1]

These figures of exported cattle from Ireland in the midst of the horrors of 1846 make a very formidable total indeed.

Passing on to 1847, we find the exportation of food to be as follows:

	Quarters
Wheat and wheat flour	184,024
Barley, etc.	47,527
Oats and oatmeal	703,465
Rye	1,498
Peas	4,659
Beans	22,361
Malt	5,956
Total	969,490

This is the total quantity of produce, excluding potatoes:[2]

Description of Crops.	Extent under Crops.	Quantity of Produce.
	Statute acres.	Quarters.
Wheat	743,871	2,926,733
Oats	2,200,870	11,521,606
Barley	283,587	1,379,029
Bere	49,068	274,016
Rye	12,415	63,094
Beans	23,768	84,456
Total	3,313,579	16,248,934

The live stock of the year is estimated in the agricultural returns as being of the value of £24,820,547, and Thom calculates that the value of the stock and agricultural produce together amounted to £38,528,224.[3]

---

[1] McCulloch, 'Dictionary of Commerce,' p. 450.
[2] Census Commissioners' Report, 1851, p. 281.
[3] Thom's 'Almanack,' 1848.

In 1848 the agricultural returns of cereal crops were :[1]

Description of Crops.	Extent of land under Crops.	Quantity of Produce.
	Statute acres.	Quarters.
Wheat	565,746	1,555,500
Oats	1,922,406	9,050,490
Barley	243,235	1,135,120
Bere	53,058	263,415
Rye	21,502	105,375
Beans and peas	50,749	172,508

Exports of produce in 1848 are:

	Quarters.
Wheat and wheat flour	304,873
Barley	79,885
Oats and oatmeal	1,546,568
Rye	15
Peas	2,572
Beans	12,314
Malt	6,365
Total	1,952,592[2]

In the same year the value of the live stock is given in the official returns as £23,112,518.[3]

Official returns give the subjoined figures as to the cereal crops in 1849 :[4]

Description of Crops.	Extent under Crops.	Quantity of Produce.
	Statute acres.	Barrels.
Wheat	687,646	3,641,198
Oats	2,061,185	15,738,073
Barley	290,690	2,441,176
Bere	60,819	496,037
Rye	20,168	164,877
Beans and peas	59,916	1,436,262 bushels
Total cereal crops	3,174,424	2,182,514 tons

In the same year the value of the live stock was £25,692,617.[5] Food produce sent to Great Britain in 1849 amounted to :

---

[1] Census Commissioners' Report, 1851, p. 308.
[2] McCulloch, 'Dictionary of Commerce,' p. 450.
[3] The valuation of the live stock is founded on the same estimate of prices as in 1841. The returns for 1848 do not include Waterford, Tipperary, and the metropolitan district of Dublin, the inquiry in these parts of the country being abandoned on account of the disturbed state of the country.
[4] Census Commissioners' Report, 1851, p. 315. [5] Ib.

		Quarters
Wheat and wheat flour	... ...	234,680
Barley	... ...	46,400
Oats and oatmeal	... ...	1,123,469
Rye	... ...	414
Peas	... ...	3,369
Beans	... ...	22,450
Malt	... ...	5,181
Total	... ...	1,435,963[1]

These figures may well be left to tell their own tale. One thing necessary to bear in mind in considering the number of quarters of foods exported from Ireland is that one quarter of wheat is equal to 392 pounds of flour, or to 470 pounds of bread,[2] and this has been calculated as about the average annual consumption of an individual. It is a simple sum in multiplication to find how many daily rations of bread for starving peasants were exported in each of these years.

A second basis of calculation is a comparison between the value of the live stock and the agricultural produce in any of these years, and the amount of money which was required for meeting the distress. The Soup Kitchen Act (Relief Act, 10 Vict., c. 7) came into operation in March, 1847, and ceased on September 12, in the same year. Under this Act there were in July, 1847, three million twenty thousand seven hundred and twelve persons who received separate rations in one day. We have thus an easy means of calculating what the feeding of the people in distress in Ireland would cost for these months. The period of distress during which this Act operated was the very worst period of the whole cycle of years. The number requiring relief then reached the highest point, and therefore we have in this sum, spent under this Act, a maximum beyond which the numbers depending on Governmental or public aid, ought not to go. The sum, then, authorised under this Act was £2,200,000; the sum actually spent was £1,676,268:[3] in other words, about a million and a half. Put this sum of a million and a half beside some of the figures which have just been quoted. It is, for instance, one-sixteenth of the value of the live cattle in Ireland in this same year of 1847. Taking the value of the cattle, sheep, and swine on the figures of 1841, the value of the total exported was £1,988,492. Thus there was exported in cattle, sheep, and swine alone in this year—to say nothing whatever of the 969,490 quarters of cereals—nearly half a million more in money value than was required to feed three millions of starving people in the same year. Finally, a million and a half was the amount spent under the Soup Kitchen Act, and the absentee rents alone were five millions sterling.

The position, then, is this. The landlords took from the tenants all the produce, 'minus the potatoes necessary to keep them from famine'—to fall back upon the phrase of John Stuart Mill. When the potatoes failed, the remainder of the produce, instead of being divided between the landlords and the tenants, was sent to either home or foreign markets for the purpose of paying the rent of the landlords. In other words, it was the consumption of food by rent instead of by the people that produced the Famine. It was, as Mitchel calls it, an artificial Famine—starvation in the midst of food.

[1] McCulloch, 'Dictionary of Commerce,' p. 450.   [2] Thom's 'Almanack,' 1848.
[3] Census Commissioners' Report, pp. 287, 288.

Meantime a change had come over Ireland which has been noted by every writer, either during or since that time. Testimony is unanimous as to the sadness and the completeness of this change. 'Here are twenty miles of country, sir,' said a dispensary doctor to me, 'and before the Famine there was not a padlock from end to end of it. Under the pressure of hunger, ravenous creatures prowled around barn and store-house, stealing corn, potatoes, cabbage, turnips—anything, in a word, that might be eaten. Later on, the fields had to be watched, gun in hand, or the seed was rooted up and devoured raw. This state of things struck a fatal blow at some of the most beautiful traits of Irish life. It destroyed the simple confidence that bolted no door; it banished for ever a custom which throughout the island was of almost universal obligation—the housing for the night, with cheerful welcome, of any poor wayfarer who claimed hospitality. Fear of "the fever," even where no apprehension of robbery was entertained, closed every door, and the custom once killed off has not revived. A thousand kindly usages and neighbourly courtesies were swept away. When *sauve qui peut* has resounded throughout a country for three years of alarm and disaster, human nature becomes contracted in its sympathies, and "every one for himself" becomes a maxim of life and conduct long after. The open-handed, open-hearted ways of the rural population have been visibly affected by the "Forty-seven ordeal." Their ancient sports and pastimes everywhere disappeared, and in many parts of Ireland have never returned. The outdoor games, the hurling-match, and the village dance are seen no more.'[1]

'The Famine,' says Gavan Duffy, 'swallowed things more precious than money and money's worth, or even than human lives. The temperance reformation, the political training of a generation, the self-respect, the purity and generosity which distinguished Irish peasants, were sorely wasted. Out of the place of the damned, a sight of such piercing woe was never seen as a Munster workhouse, with hundreds of a once frank and gallant yeomanry turned into sullen beasts, wallowing on the floor as thick as human limbs could pack. Unless, indeed, it were that other spectacle of the women of a district waiting in pauper congregation around the same edifice for outdoor relief. New and terrible diseases sprang out of this violation of the laws of nature. There was soon a workhouse fever, a workhouse dysentery, a workhouse ophthalmia; and children, it was said, were growing up idiots from imperfect nourishment. In eight of the worst poor-law unions, the contract coffin left the workhouse seventy times a week with the corpse of a human being. The ophthalmia often carried with it consequences more painful than death, when it left the sufferer unfit to earn his bread any more in the world. There were upwards of 2,000 cases of this disease within ten months in the Tipperary Union, and as many in the Limerick Union. In Tipperary, Sir William Wilde, one of the Census Commissioners, saw eighty-seven patients whose sight was permanently damaged, eighteen incurably blind figures, thirty-two who had lost one eye. In Connaught, where poverty was long the chronic condition of the country, the famine had actually created a new race of beggars, bearing only a distant and hideous resemblance to humanity. Wherever the traveller went in Galway or Mayo, he met troops of wild, idle, lunatic-looking paupers wandering over the country. Gray-headed old men, with faces settled into a leer of hardened mendicancy, and women filthier and more frightful than harpies, who at the jingle of a coin on the pavement swarmed in myriads

---
[1] A. M. Sullivan's 'New Ireland,' pp. 67, 68.

from unseen places, struggling, screaming, shrieking for their prey like monstrous and unclean animals. Beggar-children, beggar-girls, with faces gray and shrivelled, met you everywhere; and women with the more touching and tragic aspect of lingering shame and self-respect not yet effaced. I saw these accursed sights, and they are burned into my memory for ever. Poor, mutilated, and debased scions of a tender, brave, and pious stock, they were martyrs in the battle of centuries for the right to live in their own land, and no Herculaneum or Pompeii covers ruins so memorable to me as those which lie buried under the fallen roof-trees of an "Irish extermination."'[1]

These two pictures from brilliant writers agree with hundreds of others drawn by Irish pens. It is certain that to-day Ireland is the saddest country in this world of many countries and many tears. With the Famine joy died in Ireland; the day of its resurrection has not yet come.

One word finally. The population of Ireland by March 30, 1851, at the same ratio of increase as held in England and Wales, would have been 9,018.799—it was 6,552,385.[2] It was the calculation of the Census Commissioners that the deficit, independently of the emigration, represented by the mortality in the five Famine years, was 985,366,[3] nearly a million of people. The greater proportion of this million of deaths must be set down to hunger, and the epidemics which hunger generated. To those who died at home must be added the large number of people who, embarking on vessels or landing in America or elsewhere with frames weakened by the Famine or diseases resulting from the Famine, perished in the manner already described. Father O'Rourke,[4] calculating these at 17 per cent. of the emigration of 1,180,409, arrives at the total of 200,668 persons who died either on the voyage from their country or on their arrival at their destination. This would raise the total of deaths caused through the Irish Famine to upwards of a million of people.

CHAPTER V.

THE GREAT BETRAYAL.

At last it seemed as if the very excess of the evil was about to produce its own remedy. The wholesale evictions filled the peasants of the south with a desperate resolve to make another attempt for the relief of their position; and the rack-renter in Ulster was gradually working up that province to a state of feeling as bitter as that of the southern counties. For the Ulster farmer was finding that the Ulster custom gave him no security against the increase of his rent, and that thus the large amount of capital he invested in the purchase of the tenant right of the farm was turning out a disastrous investment. In this way the north and south were ripe for a new movement in favour of tenant right. The movement, when started, was not long in gaining strength; the leaders in the different parts of the country saw and understood each other; and a combination was made between the tenant-right leaders of the north and of the south.

---

[1] Extract from Lecture on 'Why is Ireland poor and discontented?' delivered in the Polytechnic Hall, Melbourne, on February 23, 1870, by the Hon. Gavan Duffy, M.P. London: Burns, Oates & Co., and Dublin: James Duffy. Printed with 'Is Ireland irreconcilable?' an article, reprinted from the *Dublin Review*, by John Cashel Hoey.
[2] Census Commissioners' Report, 1851, p. 245.   [3] *Ib.*, p. 246.   [4] *Ib.*, p. 499.

This union had elements of hope for the future of Ireland beyond the mere chance of settling the Land Question. Everybody knows that religious dissensions have been the most fruitful cause of that division among the Irish people by which their oppressors have been able to conquer and to hold them. Here were the Presbyterians of the north standing on the same platform as the Catholics of the south—fighting against the same relentless enemy, and for the same sacred rights. The hopefulness of the spectacle is best proved by the fears and condemnation which it received. Religious bigots were in a terrible state of alarm, and prophesied woeful things. The leader of this odious feeling in the north was a clergyman named Dr. Cook, a man of great eloquence and of great force of character, who was for nearly half a century the most commanding force in the Presbyterian Church. He was a Conservative of the Conservatives, and hated his religious opponents with the fervour of the Middle Ages. But the demand for tenant right made itself heard even in the conventions where he was the most prominent and powerful figure. For such demands he had nothing but condemnation. They were Socialism, Communism, and the like, and it all came from the original abomination of Presbyterian clergymen associating with the servants of Baal in the shape of the Catholic clergymen.

Nevertheless, this unholy alliance went on, gathered strength as it proceeded, and might have led to a permanent alliance on the basis of common triumphs which would have been full of blessings for all the Irish race. The movement at last took shape, and a circular was sent around calling for a Tenant Right Convention. The circular itself was a proof of the change that was coming over the times. It was signed by three men, among others—all members of different creeds—by Dr. (afterwards Sir John) Gray, an Episcopalian Protestant; by Dr. MacKnight, a Presbyterian; and by Mr. Frederic Lucas, a Catholic. In obedience to this call an influential meeting was assembled on August 6, 1850, in the City Assembly House, William Street, Dublin.

'The sharp Scottish accent of Ulster,' writes A. M. Sullivan, describing the gathering, 'mingled with the broad Doric of Munster. Presbyterian ministers greeted Popish priests with fraternal fervour. Mr. James Godkin, editor of the staunch covenanting *Derry Standard* . . . . sat side by side with John Francis Maguire, of the ultramontane *Cork Examiner*. Magistrates and landlords were there; while of tenant delegates, every province sent up a great army.'[1]

It is curious to look back in this year on the proposals put forward at this convention. The resolutions practically demanded what have since come to be known as the three 'F's'—Fixity of Tenure, Free Sale, and Fair Rents. Another question which has since been made familiar also came before the convention. This was the question of the arrears of rent. It was represented that during the period of Famine it was perfectly impossible for the tenants to pay any rent, large or small; and that if the landlords chose to insist on their rights they could evict the greater part of the whole Irish population. Accordingly, a resolution was passed to the effect that the arrears should be subjected to inspection by a valuator; that he should estimate the amount due on consideration of the prices and other circumstances of the Famine period; that he should compare the actual amount paid in rent by the tenant to the landlord; and that if there were

---

[1] 'New Ireland,' p. 149.

any balance still due on such a comparison, it should be paid to the landlords in instalments spread over a certain period.

To any impartial reader who has read the pages in which the story of the Famine has been told, this proposal will not appear to be very unreasonable; but the times were not ripe for reason on the Irish Land Question. The arrears of the Famine period were allowed to continue; they came to form a dread feature of the Irish peasant's life under the name of the 'hanging gale;' and for thirty-four years the 'hanging gale' was allowed to realise its ill-omened name, leaving the fortunes and the lives of nearly a hundred thousand families at the absolute mercy of their landlords.

The movement which was thus initiated took the country by storm, and was the first break in the disastrous gloom that had overhung everything since the advent of the Famine and the downfall of O'Connell. Famine had now apparently done with the country—at least, for an interval; the cataclysm under which the wretched party returned in 1847 had been able everywhere to debauch or deceive constituencies and drive all public honesty out of the representation of the country was now in the past, and there seemed a chance once more for the country, for constitutional agitation, and for honest and unselfish public men. Gavan Duffy thought the season so promising that he consented to stand for a constituency; and his newspaper wrote of the movement and of the coming time in a strain of sanguine expectation, which, representing as it did the hopes of the country generally, makes darker the tragedy in which these hopes were eclipsed.

'On as solemn a summons,' writes the *Nation*, Duffy's paper, 'as ever drew men together in any nation of this earth, since the sun first reached her solstice over it, do the delegates of the Irish people assemble on next Tuesday. . . . In a people beggared, broken, brutalized in some sense, *they* have undertaken to inspire the vigour and the comeliness of independence. They gird their strength to redeem a fallen land to its true place in the zodiac of nations. And, before God and man, they are amenable for grievous ignorance of the opportunity, and a heavy dereliction of duty, if the next week pass unused or misused by them.'

The most promising feature of the new movement was that it put a definite, a single, a great and absorbing issue before the country. The farmers formed still the majority of the electorate: they were known to be ready to stand by the representatives of their interests, in spite of the omnipotence still exercised over them by the landlord; and of course they were united to a man in the demand for security for their industry and their homes. They had the will and they had the power to return a majority of the Irish representatives; and an Irish Party has since shown that a body of men, earnest and honest, resolute and united, can wring from a Ministry a great measure of land reform, without even being the majority of the Irish representatives. It is no exaggeration, then, to say that the Tenant Right movement of 1850 might have succeeded in all its purposes: might have won fixity of tenure and free sale and fair rent, might then have gone on successfully to the demand for Home Rule, and might thus have saved Ireland a quarter of a century of the darkest and most bitter events in her history.

But it was not to be. The movement that began in such hope and with so many promises of complete success ended in fiercer, completer, more enduring disaster than any of those which had preceded it. Two men were mainly responsible for this : the one was a weak and foolish Englishman, the other a strong and an evil Irishman. The two men were Lord John Russell and William Keogh.

The conference of the Tenant League took place, as has been seen, on August 6, 1850 ; in November 4 in the same year Lord John Russell published the 'Durham Letter.' This was the letter addressed to the Bishop of Durham in which he denounced the movement, howled at in that period and laughed at in this, as 'Papal aggression.' The Pope had changed the titles of the Catholic archbishops and bishops in England and Scotland from titles *in partibus* into titles borrowed from English places. Thus Cardinal Wiseman was created Archbishop of Westminster. This innocent step called forth a tempest of indignation among the ignorant and fanatical in the English population. There rose one of those periodical 'No Popery' storms, and there was a panic-stricken cry for legislation against the revival of the rule of the Pope. Lord John Russell was weak enough or mean enough to allow himself to be carried away by the ruling frenzy, wrote a letter in denunciation of the action of the Pope, and promised legislation.

In Ireland this new move on the part of the British Minister provoked a counter-storm of popular passion as wild and as widespread. As the English people were startled by the bugbear of the ever-hateful Pope, the Irish were roused to fury by the dread that their religion was once more, and in the nineteenth century, to be subjected to some renewal of the Penal Code, which is one of the worst and bitterest recollections in the history of English rule and Irish suffering. It was probable that in this feeling all other interests and passions would be swallowed up.

This was the danger which the really honest members of the Tenant League foresaw. The 'No Popery' agitation roused up again those passions between Irishmen of different creeds which had been submerged in the great movement for tenant right ; and the different creeds, forgetting their common wrongs and sufferings, might be drawn off by sectarian passion from the Land question. While, then, the southern tenant-righters sympathized with their countrymen in their hatred and contempt of the bigotry and the imbecility of Lord John Russell, they saw with considerable misgiving the prominence which the new and the sectarian agitation was taking in the popular mind.

There was another body of men, however, to which this new movement was a godsend. Of this party William Keogh and John Sadleir were the chief spokesmen—two of the most remarkable and most sinister figures in Irish history.

Physically and mentally, Keogh was intended for a leader of democracy. Though small of stature, he had a chest of enormous depth, had a muscular and powerful frame, and a courage that was arrogant, audacious, inflexible. The face bespoke the immense moral and mental force of the man. In his earlier years it bore a singular resemblance to that of the first Napoleon, and even when it had grown flaccid and flabby, it still wore an appearance of dignity and strength. His look was calculated to inspire respect and even awe. Though ignorant of law and generally illiterate, he had a marvellous command of fluent, striking, vigorous language. He was coarse and vulgar in taste, and there was a dash of commonplace in everything he said. The *Nation*, which was his chief assailant throughout his political career, described his 'invective' as a 'deluge of dirt,' and his 'most pretentious oratory' as 'a jumble of bog Latin and flatulent English.' But his words, set off by a sonorous voice, vivid gesture, and his expressive and commanding face, made him the idol of mobs and the most competent orator at popular meetings. At the time when he entered politics he embarked upon his new career as on a desperate chance that would lead on to great fortune or hopeless ruin. In one of the most exciting and critical moments of his career the bailiffs were said to be in his house, and even when he was fighting one of his hard electoral contests the House of Commons was wading through sheaves of his unpaid bills, in order to find whether he had the then necessary qualification of £300 a year over all his debts. But of this afterwards.

A judicial office in Ireland was then, as indeed it is now, the haven in which the hard-pressed lawyer discovered wealth, ease, and dignity. On the principle that runs uniform through all the veins and arteries of English administration in Ireland, the salaries of judicial office are fixed at a figure far beyond what even the most successful lawyer is in the habit of making at the Bar. In fact, a puisne judgeship in Ireland occupies towards the working lawyer an exactly reverse position to that which it holds in England. In England, the lawyer who accepts a puisne judgeship, or even a much higher office, usually does so at an immense sacrifice of income ; in Ireland, the judicial office usually gives to the lawyer the first opportunity in his life of making something like an equilibrium between income and expenditure. Then the number of judges being far in excess of the requirements of public business, the fortunate holders of the judicial office spend all the year in comparative, and nearly half the year in absolute, idleness. The judges in Ireland, too, are members of the Privy Council. They meet and discuss with the other great officers of the State questions of policy and of government, with a mixture of judicial and executive functions which in England would shock every accepted principle of sound administration. The Irish judge is, therefore, after his elevation to the Bench, at once an active and a combative politician—one of the rulers of the State. It was one of the worst features in a thoroughly unsound state of things that the puisne judge was often promoted to a higher office—the Chief Justiceship of his own Court, the Mastership of the Rolls, or the Lord Chancellorship. Sometimes he received a solace for being passed over in a great and highly-paid commission ; such as the Commissionership of the Irish Church Act, with a salary of £2,000 a year, that was conferred on Mr. Justice Lawson.

To such a man as Keogh such an office offered the highest prize of fortune. It conferred high pay, and he was dreadfully needy ; dignity, and he was notoriously disreputable ; security, and his life was a series of hairbreadth escapes in the tempestuous sea of Irish politics. It is now clear that, from the first moment he embarked on a political career, a judgeship was Keogh's single purpose.

For this end he was ready to don the livery of every political party in turn ; to pass through mud-baths of deception, lying and broken oaths ; to assume all the worst arts of the demagogue ; to be foul-mouthed, audacious, sometimes even murderous in advice ; and then to betray the mob as quickly and shamelessly as he had pandered to its worst passions.

His first entrance into public life was in 1847. At that time he was known as a barrister without clients and without law ; indeed, at no period of his professional career, until he became a law officer of the Crown, did he obtain as much professional business as would keep the bloodhound of insurmountable debt from the door; and never, to his dying day, did he master even the elementary principles of his profession.

It was for my native town of Athlone that Keogh stood. Tradition still retails many of his strange exploits. His courage, for instance, was over and over again proved by the absolute fearlessness with which he encountered mobs inflamed with drink and the violent passions that election contests excite. He was known to march through the streets when a perfect hailstorm of stones were flying against him and his supporters. On one occasion, when he was delivering a speech from a window to a noisy and violent crowd, somebody threw a soda-water bottle at his head. 'That's a mighty bad shot, ——,' said Keogh, mentioning the name of the person who had thrown the bottle—a well-known local politician. Equally are there stories of the desperate remedies to which men resort who are hard pressed for money and neither troubled by scruples nor abashed by shame. For instance, he is said to have raised money in several cases by the trick, not unknown to the London police courts, of borrowing five pounds on each half of a five-pound note. Then there is the dim recollection of a strange scene, which forecast the tragic end to his strange and evil career. One night he was expecting, as the tradition goes, some money from one of the political clubs of London in aid of his candidature. A near relative was to be the bearer of the much-needed treasure; and when he arrived he had to announce that his mission was a failure. Keogh fell prone on the floor, grovelled there with the contortions and groans of one demented, and finally, when the agony had passed, rose up, went out into the town, and harangued the mobs with a self-confidence as great, a wit as ready, a hopefulness as inflexible, as if his highest expectations had been realized. Another reason of his success was his conviviality. He was all through his life a heavy drinker, and loved all the pleasures of the table. However late the night or heavy the drinking, Keogh was always the first to rise in the morning; and with the 'terrible familiarity' with men's names and characteristics, which was one of his talents, he was at the bedside of the companions of his debauch the next morning with a brandy-and-soda in his hand and the Christian name of the scarcely recovered inebriate in his mouth.

In order to understand the history of the time, it is also necessary to know something of the constituency in which Keogh played these parts. In defence of my native town, I must premise that it was neither better nor worse than the majority of the Irish and the English constituencies of that period. Its eminence consisted in the fact that the number of the voters was small, and that, therefore, the amount of the bribe was high. It was generally computed that this bribe averaged £30 or £40 the vote; and there were tales of a vote having run up to even £100 in one of Keogh's most hotly contested elections. The town, finely situated on the Shannon, with a large barracks and a castle old in story, plays an important part in the history of Ireland, and was for many centuries the most prosperous centre in the midland counties; but the famine swept the country round, and for years before the period at which Keogh began to figure in its history, Athlone had been steadily deteriorating. A large number of its people were, therefore, engaged in a desperate struggle with hard fortune, and, though centuries old, the position of the town had some resemblance to one of the mushroom towns of the United States—say Virginia City—which, owing their rise to some accidental and transitory cause, like the discovery of a mine, have a season of extreme prosperity, and then for years continue the struggle with departing fortune. In such a town it is not surprising that the election played a prominent part. With many of the people the periodic bribe entered into the whole economy of their poor, shrivelled, squalid, weary lives. Men continued to live in houses that had better have lived in lodgings, because the house gave a vote. The very whisper of a dissolution sent a visible thrill through the town; the prospect of common gain swallowed up amid the people all other passions, religious and political, and united ordinarily discordant forces in amity and brotherhood. There was, as there is, a tolerably strong minority of Protestants in the town; between the Protestant and the Catholic there was in those days irreconcilable difference of political as well as of religious feeling; and, indeed, there was rarely any social intercourse between people of the two creeds. But at election time the Catholic and the Protestant forgot their rivalries, remembered the interests only of their town, and fought strenuously and side by side in loving union for the man who gave the highest bribe. There was a highly respected Protestant tradesman in the town when I was a boy who had a large repute for political wisdom, and was generally esteemed; and I remember hearing a well-known saying of his quoted which put the philosophy of Irish electioneering in these times in a compendious form. 'I am a Protestant,' Ned —— used to say, 'and my father was a Protestant, and his father before him; but the man I want to see returned for Athlone is the man that leaves the money in the town.'

Such was the constituency, the representation of which Keogh sought in 1847. The circumstances of his candidature sufficiently foreshadowed his subsequent career. In that year, as has been seen, the supreme struggle in Ireland was between Young Ireland and the Repeal Party. But Keogh had no part in this struggle between different sections of Irish Nationalists. He knew his own purpose and he knew his constituency. Attachment to either of these two sections might have been inconvenient in subsequent years to a seeker after English office, and the constituency cared for the money and not for the politics of its candidates. He stood, then, as a member of an English party; he called himself a Peelite. This political character had the additional advantage of being entirely indefinite; for this was the period of the schism between the Free Trade Conservatives under Sir Robert Peel and the Protectionist Conservatives under Mr. Disraeli; and it was still an undecided question whether the healing of the schism would turn the Peelites back into the Conservative fold or its continuance would transform them into Liberals. Another curious fact about the candidature of Keogh was that the expenses, or a portion of them, were paid by an Englishman. This was Mr. Attwood, the well-known banker.

Mr. Attwood had some doctrines on the currency question which he was anxious to have advocated in Parliament, and he thought that the expenses of a contest in Athlone would be compensated for by the assistance of the glib and brilliant tongue of Keogh. Keogh was opposed by a local gentleman named O'Beirne. Keogh was elected. The numbers at the poll tell their own tale of the state of the country and the character of the constituency. They were:

      Keogh, William 101
      O'Beirne, William 95

But this success did not for some years bring Keogh any change in his desperate fortunes. It rather aggravated his difficulties. Professional business did not come; the election for Athlone was an expensive luxury and cost more than Mr. Attwood had supplied, and Keogh was sunk in a profounder morass of debt than before.

At the same election of 1847 John Sadleir had been returned for Carlow. In every respect Sadleir was the antithesis of Keogh. Keogh was garrulous; Sadleir was taciturn: Keogh was the boisterous and familiar *bon vivant*, with exuberant health and spirits; Sadleir was reserved, unsocial, and had the sallow complexion of the man who neither cares for nor enjoys the pleasures of the table; finally, Keogh was hopelessly poor, and Sadleir had the reputation of boundless wealth. John Sadleir was trained as a solicitor, and was intended by his people probably for the quiet life of an Irish lawyer. But he was ambitious and self-confident, and made for London. Here he became a 'Parliamentary agent,' and gained an acquaintance with the financial state of Ireland which he afterwards turned to great use. He gradually drifted into a financier, seized with the idea of making a great fortune rapidly. He adopted an excellent plan to start with. The Irish farmer had not yet become to any large extent a depositor in banks; Sadleir established the Tipperary Joint-Stock Bank. He came of a family that had the reputation of being wealthy, his own claim to financial ability was everywhere admitted, and the people deposited their money with the confidence of unquestioning faith. 'From the Shannon to the Suir,' writes A. M. Sullivan,[1] '"Sadleir's bank" was regarded with as much confidence as "the old lady of Threadneedle Street" commands from her votaries.' The money which Sadleir thus obtained from the grimy pockets of the Irish farmers he invested in English speculations, became in this way intimate with the money market of London, and was made chairman of the London and County Joint-Stock Bank. Every day he was credited with greater schemes and with more fabulous success.

To such a man Parliament offered chances of still further increasing his wealth and satisfying his ambition. His large command of money gave him a great advantage in the political fortunes of Ireland, in that dread period of desolation and demoralization, and he conceived, and to a large extent carried out, the project of building up in the House of Commons a party bound to him by ties of blood or of financial aid. One cousin—Robert Keatinge—was returned at the same time as himself for County Waterford; Frank Scully, another cousin, was returned for Tipperary. This was at the 1847 election; subsequently, in 1852, Mr. Vincent Scully, his nephew, was returned for County Cork. The Sadleirite party consisted, besides, of two brothers named O'Flaherty (Anthony and Edmund), of a Doctor Maurice Power, of Mr. Monsell (now disguised under the name of Lord Emly), and of Mr. William Keogh. How far and how many of these men were indebted to Sadleir for pecuniary assistance it is impossible, of course, to say; but two of them were certainly in his pay—Edmund O'Flaherty and William Keogh. The desperate fortunes of Keogh craved for help wherever it might come from; Sadleir on one occasion, as will be seen, subscribed £100 for his election expenses; and subsequently the name of Keogh was to many of the bills which were put in circulation by Edmund O'Flaherty. Keogh said his name was forged; possibly the statement was true; but it would not be surprising if it were false. This is not an uncharitable or unwarrantable conclusion, as will be subsequently seen.

The object of Sadleir and his associates was, of course, personal advancement, and personal advancement alone. But personal advancement could only be obtained from an English Minister; and the rise of the new Tenant

[1] 'New Ireland,' p. 157.

Right movement, hostile to the principles of every English Ministry of that period, was, therefore, to the Sadleirites the omen of defeat, and not the augury of hope. It seemed probable that the movement would become—as every national movement before or since, that has ever got a chance in Ireland, has become—a great national force, impossible to resist ; and that no constituency would accept any man who did not fight in its ranks. Then an idea was being put forward which would be still more fatal to such purposes as those of Sadleir and Keogh. It will be remembered that the great point of controversy between Old and Young Ireland was as to the pledge against office-seeking. The break-up of the hideous party of 1847 gave terrible confirmation to the objections which the Young Irelanders had brought against the tribe of office-seekers, and all Ireland now agreed in the opinion that nothing was to be gained from any Ministry by any party but a party of independent men. Gavan Duffy, and the other survivors of Young Ireland who had joined in the new movement, insisted that the old pledge should be revived, pointing out that the Land Question could never be settled in any other way. Thus, then, the Tenant Right movement had two distinct principles—a principle as to the end to be attained, and a principle as to the policy for attaining it. The party not only believed that Tenant Right was essential for the prosperity of Ireland, but believed as firmly that Tenant Right could only be won by an Irish Party which would oppose every Ministry that did not make Tenant Right a policy by which to stand or fall. In other words, the policy of the Tenant Righters was the very opposite of that of the Sadleirites ; the one wanted Tenant Right, and did not care for Ministries ; the other wanted office, and did not care for Tenant Right. The struggle was visible in the very earliest days of the Tenant Right movement ; its break-out was inevitable ; and if a struggle had taken place while the country was united and enthusiastic about Tenant Right, it is probable that Sadleir and Keogh would have been driven from public life and the Tenant Right battle have been won.

But the Ecclesiastical Titles Bill produced the disastrous diversion that postponed this struggle. Sadleir and Keogh were not slow to see the use to which Lord John Russell's proposals could be turned. Of course, the Ecclesiastical Titles Bill was a question upon which certain sections of the English people felt strongly at that moment. But Keogh and Sadleir probably knew that such outbursts of passion are as transitory as they are violent. Then the Bill was not a favourite with any English party ; Mr. Disraeli gave it at first but a half-hearted support on the part of the Conservatives ; it had strong opponents in Mr. Gladstone, Sir James Graham, and the other Peelites ; and there was every reason to think that even Lord John Russell himself had no great joy in his legislative child. It was unlike Tenant Right, which menaced great interests, at that moment as supreme in the Lower as in the Upper House of Parliament, and which was equally unacceptable to all sections of Parliamentary opinion except the insignificant group of Radicals. On the Ecclesiastical Titles Bill, then, a politician could be as violent as he pleased, without making himself everlastingly objectionable to anybody except to Mr. Newdegate ; while a strong position on the Land Question might mean permanent exclusion from office. Finally, Sadleir and Keogh knew the passionate attachment of the Irish people to their religion, and shrewdly calculated that any politician who was able to pose as a defender of that religion would establish a claim to their confidence and affections which it would take much to shake.

Accordingly, in the House of Commons, Keogh and Sadleir opposed the Ecclesiastical Titles Bill with extraordinary vehemence of language and of tactics. They exhausted the forms of the House, they fought the Bill obstinately and clause by clause. A portion of the Irish people, looking on at this struggle, were easily led to believe that it was heroic ; and the Sadleirites, playing upon another weakness, endeared themselves still further to Irish hearts by styling themselves 'the Irish Brigade'—the name of those exiled Irish warriors who fought heroically on every battlefield of Europe, after unjust laws had exiled them from their own country. By the English the party were known by the less flattering title of the 'Pope's Brass Band.'

In Ireland, meantime, the two agitations went on side by side. Great Catholic demonstrations were everywhere held, and Sadleir was the organizer and Keogh the orator of these demonstrations. At these meetings the Bishops of the Catholic Church attended, and Keogh excelled everybody else in the extravagant fulsomeness of the eulogies which he poured upon their heads. It was a singular fatality that at this very period an Irish prelate was first getting into prominence who was destined to be a main though unconscious, and perhaps innocent, instrument in the game Keogh and Sadleir were playing. This was Paul Cullen, afterwards Cardinal Cullen and Archbishop of Dublin. At this period he had just been appointed Archbishop of Armagh. He had been for many years the head of the Irish College in Rome, and it was a favourite reproach against him that he was more of a Roman monk than an Irish patriot. So far as I can gather his policy, he regarded it as his main if not sole duty to look after the interest of his Church, rather than the purely secular interests of politics. For this reason his whole political influence was thrown in on the side of any politician who had anything to give the Church. In afterstruggles, Cardinal Cullen was always on the side of the 'Government' as against all struggles of Nationalists, on the principle that England could do more for the interests of the Church than any National Party. England could serve the Church in Ireland through concessions on the education question ; she could serve the Church generally and in a wider area by her influence as a great power in the Councils of Europe ; and she could tolerate or persecute millions of Catholics scattered through her world-wide empire. This policy—intelligible from the standpoint of the Churchman—Cardinal Cullen pursued for upwards of a quarter of a century with a purpose that never swerved, and with a devotion that belonged to a man whose life was swallowed up in his principles. At a period later than this, Cardinal Cullen had means for giving effect to his will so large as to make him the greatest standing force in Irish politics. The power of the Catholic clergyman was almost unshaken ; throughout every town and village in Ireland the Catholic priest, strong in the affection of his flock, and, in the majority of cases, the best educated man in his district, was almost a political autocrat ; and over the action of nearly every priest in Ireland Cardinal Cullen had control. He was the prelate whose voice was practically law at the Holy See in regard to all Irish ecclesiastical affairs ; a few clergymen who resisted his will were summarily crushed, and every vacancy in the episcopate was filled with his nominees. Archbishop MacHale, and a few of the elder generation of prelates who had shared in O'Connell's struggle for repeal of the Union, resisted his influence to the end ; but practically, for many years, Cardinal Cullen was the Catholic Church in Ireland, and had all that mighty organization under his word of command.

On August 19, 1851, a great meeting was held in the Rotunda, in Dublin, for the purpose of forming a 'Catholic Defence Association.' Over this meeting Archbishop Cullen presided. Mr. John Sadleir was one of the secretaries, and William Keogh was the chief speaker. To the chairman of the meeting Keogh was laboriously complimentary. 'I now,' he said, 'as one of her Majesty's Counsel, whether learned or unlearned in the law, holding the Act of Parliament in my hand, unhesitatingly give his proper title to the Lord Bishop of Armagh.' These words received further emphasis as he held the Act of Parliament thus defined in his outstretched hand. At a meeting of his constituents in Athlone he paid even higher court to Archbishop MacHale—who then, and for many years afterwards, exercised enormous influence. 'I see here,' said Keogh, 'the venerated prelates of my Church, first among them, "the observed of all observers," the illustrious Archbishop of Tuam, who, like that lofty tower which rises upon the banks of the yellow Tiber, the pride and protection of the city, is at once the glory and the guardian, the *decus et tutamen* of the Catholic religion.' John Sadleir was also one of the speakers at this meeting.

Meantime the Tenant Right movement had been growing, and Keogh and Sadleir found it necessary to affect devotion to its purposes and policy. Over and over again they pledged themselves not to accept office from any Ministry that did not make Tenant Right a Cabinet question. Nor was this all. Under the example of the Tenant League, the Catholic Association also formulated the policy of pledging the Irish members to accept no office from any Ministry which did not make the Repeal of the Ecclesiastical Titles Act a Cabinet question ; and to that pledge Keogh over and over again gave his adhesion.

But Gavan Duffy, the other writers in the *Nation* and *Freeman's Journal*, and all the earnest Tenant Righters, still disbelieved in the 'Irish Brigade,' and Keogh and Sadleir were more than once accused of being office-seekers. These charges, repeated over and over again, made wider a distinct line of cleavage in the Tenant League, as the Tenant Right organization was called. The two parties were watchful and distrustful of each other, and between the two there arose a fight for life. The position of Sadleir and Keogh at this period was desperate. The fight in which they were engaged meant dazzling success or shameful and abysmal ruin. Sadleir, as will be seen, was reaching the point where he had to make the awful choice between the life of the convict and the death of the suicide. The position of Keogh was equally desperate. He was deeper than ever in debt ; as has been seen, the waiters at some of the entertainments in his house in Dublin were bailiffs in disguise ; arrest dogged his fleeing footsteps wherever he went, and arrest meant social, professional, political death. The hungry army of his creditors watched the rise and fall of his chequered fortunes with the wolfish glare of peasant depositors in a shaky bank ; the least slip or mishap, and they were down upon him, and then chaos was come again. It was possible that fate had a darker future for him than even enforced exile. How far he was acquainted with the financial enterprises of John Sadleir is not known, nor how deeply he was involved in the embezzlements of Mr. Edmund O'Flaherty. But he was an intimate and a debtor of the two men, and might well be implicated in some of their misdeeds. In his darker hours he may have shuddered at the thought that he had brought himself within the reach of the criminal law. The judicial bench or the convict's dock—these were the dread stakes that awaited the result of the game.

And the game was one of the wildest chance. The whole national press of the country was against him. Sadleir had established a paper called the *Catholic Telegraph*. It was a journal of ultra-religious fervour, went into fits of lunacy over the Titles Bill, and while upholding Sadleir and Keogh as the spotless champions of the Church, shook its head sadly over the orthodoxy of Gavan Duffy and the other advocates of Tenant Right. But the *Catholic Telegraph* had not the power of the national journals, and day after day the *Freeman's Journal*, week after week the *Nation*, dogged the utterances, watched the shifts, exposed the devices of Sadleir and Keogh. The overwhelming majority of the country, too, believed in the Tenant Righters, and disbelieved in the Catholic champions. Against this mighty combination in front, Keogh had in his flank the few desperate shopkeepers of Athlone, whom his money had bought, and the money of another man could buy again. Thus attacked in front and behind, and from all sides, he had no weapons of defence but his tongue, his brazen audacity, his desperate courage, and the adhesion or neutrality of a certain number of Catholic bishops.

These facts will explain to the reader the strange manœuvres Keogh had to employ. The thing above all things he wanted was office; the thing he was called above all things to forswear was office. At all the meetings, then, whether of the Catholic Defence Association or the Tenant League, he was bound to be loud above all others in the pledge against taking office.

'As I said, Whigs or Tories, Peelites or Protectionists,' he said to his constituents at Athlone in the speech already alluded to, in which he paid Archbishop MacHale such fulsome compliments, 'are all the same to me. . . . I know that in the career in which we are engaged we will have to meet open hostility. That we can do. We had, and I know we will have again, treacherous friends. These also we can dispose of. I will fight for my religion and my country, scorning and defying calumny, meeting boldly honourable foes, seeking out treacherous friends; and, as long as I have the confidence of the people, I declare in the most solemn manner, before this august assembly, I shall not regard any party. *I know that the road I take does not lead to preferment.* I do not belong to the Whigs; *I never will belong to the Whigs.* I do not belong to the Tories; *I never will have anything to do with them.*'

Thus he had separated himself from the two great parties in the English Parliament. There was, however, a third party in the House of Commons, which was one of its most noticeable and important elements. This was the party of the Peelites—the party under whose banner Keogh had fought when first he stood for Athlone. From that party also the incorruptible patriot cut himself off.

'I have read in the newspapers this morning,' he said, 'that Mr. Frederick Peel has joined the Whig Government, and that it is likely men of whose acquaintance I am proud, will become component parts of the Administration. Here, in the presence of my constituents and my country —and I hope I am not so base a man as to make an avowal which could be contradicted to-morrow, if I was capable of doing that which is insinuated against me—I solemnly declare, if there was a Peelite Administration in office to-morrow it would be nothing to me. . . . If all the Peelites in the

House joined the Whig Administration, *I would be their unmitigated, their untiring, their indefatigable opponent, until we obtain full justice.*'[1]

And then, to be completely explicit, he went on to define what he meant by the 'full justice,' the attainment of which should precede any acceptance of office.

'And what is that justice? I can state the terms of it we'l. I will not support any party which will not make it the first ingredient of their political existence to repeal the Ecclesiastical Titles Bill. I will not join any party which does not go much farther than that. I will have nothing to do with any party which, without interfering with the religious belief of the Protestant population, will not consent to remove from off the Catholics of this county the intolerable burden of sustaining the Church Establishment with which they are not in communion. . . . And . . . *I will not support any political party which does not make it part of its political creed to do all justice to the tenant in Ireland. I will not support any party which will not place on a satisfactory footing the relations of landlord and tenant.*'[2]

Nothing could be more explicit than this language, nothing more binding than those pledges; the whole gospel of the Tenant League, and even something more, was subscribed to by Mr. Keogh. And yet—and yet the Tenant Leaguers were suspicious. The *Freeman's Journal* and the *Nation* still openly expressed their want of faith in even these solemn pledges of the champions of religion. An incident confirmed these doubts. In February, 1852, Lord John Russell was defeated by the combination of Lord Palmerston with the Conservatives on the Militia Bill, and the first Derby-Disraeli Administration came into office. Dr. Maurice Power, M.P. for Cork, was offered and accepted office as Governor of St. Lucia. Dr. Power was a foremost and active member of the 'Irish Brigade;' and at once the Tenant Leaguers foretold that as Power had gone, so also would go Sadleir and Keogh. These doubts were finally expressed to Keogh's face.

Immediately after the promotion of Power, Keogh and Sadleir started Mr. Vincent Scully, a nephew of Sadleir, as their candidate. On Monday, March 8, 1852, Keogh was present at a meeting in the city of Cork in support of Mr. Scully. He had been assailed with even more than its usual vigour in that week's issue of the *Nation*. Mr. McCarthy Downing, who long years afterwards was member for County Cork, belonged to the Tenant Righters, and at this meeting openly expressed his doubts of the honesty of Keogh and Sadleir and the 'Irish Brigade.'

'I will tell the meeting fairly and honestly,' said Mr. Downing, 'that I believe the Irish Brigade are not sincere advocates of the Tenant Right question. I state that, and I believe it is in the presence of two of them. I attended two great meetings in the Music Hall in Dublin, at the inauguration of the Tenant League, at my own expense, when a deputation waited upon the Brigade to attend the meeting, and I protest I never saw a beast drawn to the slaughter-house by the butcher to receive the knife with more difficulty than there was in bringing to that meeting the members of the Irish Brigade.'[3]

---

[1] 'A Record of Traitorism; or, The Political Life and Adventures of Mr. Justice Keogh,' by T. D. Sullivan, p. 5.
[2] *Ib.*, pp. 5, 6.   [3] *Ib.*, p. 7.

'Then up rose Mr. Keogh,' writes A. M. Sullivan,[1] 'and never, perhaps, were his marvellous gifts more requisite than at this critical moment. The future fate and fortunes of his leaders and party hung on the turn affairs might take at this meeting, an open challenge and public charge having been thus flung down against them. There were a few hostile cries when he stood up, but silence was after a while obtained. With flushed countenance and heaving breast he burst forth in these words:

'"Great God!" he exclaimed, "in this assemblage of Irishmen, have you found that those who are most ready to take every pledge have been the most sincere in perseverance to the end? or have you not rather seen that they who, like myself, went into Parliament perfectly unpledged, not supported by the popular voice, but in the face of popular acclaim, when the time for trial comes are not found wanting? I declare myself in the presence of the bishops of Ireland, and of my colleagues in Parliament, that let the Minister of the day be whom he may—let him be the Earl of Derby, let him be Sir James Graham, or Lord John Russell—it was all the same to us; and, so help me God, no matter who the Minister may be, no matter who the party in power may be, I will neither support that Minister nor that party, unless he comes into power prepared to carry the measures which universal popular Ireland demands. I have abandoned my own profession to join in cementing and forming an Irish Parliamentary Party. That has been my ambition. It may be a base one. I think it an honourable one. I have seconded the proposition of Mr. Sharman Crawford in the House of Commons. I have met the Minister upon it to the utmost extent of my limited abilities, at a moment when disunion was not expected. So help me God! upon that and every other question to which I have given my adhesion I will be—and I know I may say that every one of my friends is as determined as myself—an unflinching, undeviating, unalterable supporter of it."

'No wonder,' writes A. M. Sullivan, continuing his description of the scene, 'the assemblage, who had listened as if spellbound while he spoke, sprang to their feet, and with vociferous cheering atoned for their previous doubts of the man whose oath had now sealed his public principles.'[2]

In the midst of this struggle between the different sections of the Irish members, the Derby-Disraeli Ministry went to the country. At the General Election in Ireland there were four parties. Roughly, the candidates may be divided into Tories and Whigs, pledged to either of the two great English parties, the Tenant Leaguers, and what were known as the Catholic Defenders. The latter were the men who were pushing the sectarian questions to the front in order to drive the Land Question to the rear, and they were under the direction, secretly or openly, of the Keogh-Sadleir brigade. In some constituencies the two sections came into collision; but the final result was a drawn battle, in which both sides gained and lost something.

Some of the most important leaders of the Tenant Leaguers had been returned. Gavan Duffy was elected for New Ross, John Francis Maguire for Dungarvan, George Henry Moore for the county of Mayo, and Frederic Lucas for the county of Meath. Moore was a great addition to the strength of the Tenant Leaguers. A landlord, he yet sympathized vehemently with the demand of the tenants for security in their holdings.

[1] 'New Ireland,' p. 161.   [2] Ib., p. 102.

He had also oratorical gifts of a high order, and his political honesty was inflexible. Frederic Lucas, an Englishman and a Protestant by birth, had changed both his religious and political faith; he had become a Catholic and an Irish Nationalist. Connected by marriage with Mr. John Bright, a man of independent fortune, and of a pure and lofty character, he held high rank in his party, and his name still has its place in the affections of the Irish people. He was proprietor of the *Tablet*, a journal which still exists. The *Tablet* at this period was a strongly national journal, and was one of the constant assailants of Keogh and Sadleir. There was one important defeat. Dr. (afterwards Sir John) Gray, proprietor of the *Freeman's Journal*, was defeated at Monaghan. The Irish Brigade was entirely successful. Sadleir and his three relatives, Francis and Vincent Scully and Robert Keatinge, were re-elected; James, his brother—of whom more anon—was elected for Tipperary; Anthony O'Flaherty was re-elected for Galway; Mr. Monsell for Limerick; and Keogh for Athlone.

In the General Election Keogh took a prominent and active part. His tongue was at the service of everybody who fought under the flag of the Catholic Defence Association—that is, of John Sadleir and himself. His speeches were remarkable, even in that vituperative period, for the violence of their language, the brutality and criminality of his appeals to the mob. One of his speeches in particular became the object of notice. In Westmeath the struggle was between Captain Magan, a friend and associate of Keogh, and Sir R. Levinge, a local landlord. In the town of Moate, Keogh made a speech in favour of Captain Magan, and in the course of that speech he used these words:

'Boys, we are in the midst of a delightful summer, when the days are long and the nights are short; next comes autumn, when the days and nights are of equal length; but next comes dreary winter, when the days are short and the nights long: and woe be to those, during those long nights, who vote for Sir Richard Levinge at the present election.'[1]

These terrible words derived additional significance from the surroundings under which they were delivered. Westmeath is one of the counties where eviction has raged most fiercely, with most widespread desolation, with circumstances of tragic suffering. To-day, one driving through Westmeath passes for miles through a land bare of houses or human beings, and studded all around with the skeleton walls of ruined homes—silent memorials of the dread times through which the country has passed. The people of the county are a fierce and stalwart breed, and resisted doggedly, though impotently, their tyrants. In Westmeath, accordingly, the Ribbon and other societies, bound by oath to meet eviction with assassination, used to be particularly strong; and the county has been the scene of some of the most terrible murders, and occasionally of the most violent epidemics of crime. It was more than probable that, among the audience to which these words were addressed, there were many men goaded to blind fury by eviction, suffered or impending, and organized with the object of avenging their wrongs in blood.

The election of 1852 was at last over, and the Tenant Leaguers were the chief victors. They had not been able to exclude the Catholic Defenders, but they had compelled them to swallow the Tenant League pledge. The country instinctively felt the soundness of the doctrine, that to beg for

---

[1] 'New Ireland,' p. 167.

office from the Minister and to demand justice for the tenant were irreconcilable positions; and accordingly the pledge against taking office, except from a Government that made the settlement of the relations between landlord and tenant a Cabinet question, was enforced from every candidate for a popular constituency. When, accordingly, the Leaguers held a Tenant Right Conference on September 8, 1852, all the Irish members returned on popular principles—whether as Tenant Righters or as Catholic Defenders—were compelled to attend. There were forty Irish members present in all. A resolution was proposed which put into definite form the pledge already taken at the hustings. It was in these words:

'Resolved: That in the opinion of this conference it is essential to the proper management of this cause that the Members of Parliament who have been returned on Tenant Right principles should hold themselves perfectly independent of, and in opposition to, all Governments which do not make it part of their policy, and a Cabinet question, to give to the tenantry of Ireland a measure embodying the principles of Mr. Sharman Crawford's Bill.'

This resolution was proposed by Keogh himself; it was carried with but one dissentient—Mr. Burke Roche, M.P., afterwards Lord Fermoy—'amid great cheering.'[1]

The position of parties in the House of Commons at the moment rendered it perfectly possible to carry out this policy to a successful issue. There were then three parties: the Whigs, under Lord John Russell; the Protectionist Conservatives, under Mr. Disraeli; and the Peelites. No one of these three parties had come back from the election sufficiently powerful to govern by itself, and a Coalition Ministry was plainly the only one possible. The Irish Party, numbering between forty and fifty members, had it in their power, if they preserved their unity, to make or mar any Ministry that could be formed by either of these contending sections; they were absolute masters of the situation. The Peelites had, as has been seen, opposed the Ecclesiastical Titles Bill, and that gave them a place in the confidence of the Irish people. It was the universal expectation in Ireland that the Tenant Leaguers would form a coalition with the Peelites, based on the repeal of the Titles Act, and the grant of security of tenure to the tenants.

Parliament met on November 4, 1852; on Friday, December 17 following, the Budget of Mr. Disraeli was rejected by a combination of different parties, and the Ministry resigned. The words of A. M. Sullivan, who was an active politician at the period, best describe what followed:

'A shout went up from Ireland. A thrill of the wildest excitement shook the island from the centre to the sea. Now joy and triumph—now torturing doubt—now the very agony of suspense, prevailed. What would the Irish Party do? Here was the crisis which was to shame their oaths or prove them true. No Liberal or composite Administration was possible without them, and their demand was one no Minister had ever deemed to be just. What would the Irish members do? The fate of the new Ministry, the fate of Ireland, was in their hands.

'As terrible deeds are said to be sometimes preceded by a mysterious apprehension, so in the last week of that old year a vague gloom chilled every heart. The news from London was panted for, hour by hour. At length the blow fell. Tidings of treason and disaster came. The Brigade was sold to Lord Aberdeen! John Sadleir was Lord of the Treasury! William

[1] T. D. Sullivan's 'Record,' p. 7.

Keogh was Irish Solicitor-General ! Edmund O'Flaherty was Commissioner of Income-Tax ! And so on. The English people, fortunately accustomed for centuries to exercise the functions of political life, may well be unable to comprehend the paralysis which followed this blow in Ireland. The merchant of many ships may bear with composure the wreck of one. But here was an argosy, freighted with the last and most precious hopes of a people already on the verge of ruin and despair, scuttled before their eyes by the men who had called on the Most High God to witness their fidelity ! The Irish tenantry had played their last stake and lost. A despairing stupor like to that of the Famine time shrouded the land. Notices to quit fell "like snowflakes" all over the counties where the hapless farmers had "refused the landlord" and voted for a Brigadier. But the banker-politician had won. His accustomed success had attended him. He was not as yet a peer, but he was a Treasury Lord. From their seats on the Treasury bench he and his comrade, "the Solicitor-General," could smile calmly at the accusing countenances of Duffy and Moore and Lucas. The New Year's chimes rang in the triumph of John Sadleir's daring ambition. Did no dismal minor tone, like mournful funeral knell, presage the sequel that was now so near at hand ?'[1]

But all was not yet lost. The new officials had to go before their constituencies for re-election ; and, poor as was the opinion of Irish patriots of the political morality of the constituencies of that period, it was hoped that the people would not be ready to condone treason so flagrant and so disastrous. It was resolved by the Tenant League to oppose the return both of Keogh for Athlone and Sadleir for Carlow, and deputations were appointed to go to both places. But when the deputations arrived at the constituencies they were astounded and shocked to find that, while all the rest of the country was loud in its curses or desperate in its wail over the destruction of national hopes, the constituencies thought either that nothing particular had happened, or that the traitors were to be congratulated on having got at the money and the patronage of the Government, and their constituents to be equally congratulated on their prospect of obtaining a share of the spoil. The state of feeling in Athlone and Carlow at this crisis of Irish history is one of the saddest proofs of the degradation which poverty and alien rule can bring about, even in a country so undying as Ireland in the ardour of its struggle against oppression. In Athlone in particular had bribery, poverty, and despair done their work effectively. The desperately needy voters saw, in a Government official, a man the better able to bribe themselves, and to obtain situations for their sons. These were the days before open competition, and nomination to a Civil Service situation was the appanage of the Parliamentary representative, and one of his chief means of advancing his interests with his constituents. This was especially the case in Ireland. Who but an Irishman can know the full hopelessness of the youth of one born in the lower middle-class of an Irish country town ? At home he sees squalor, the saddened foreheads of his parents, consumed by mean cares, by the bitter struggle to keep up appearances, by climbing up the ever-climbing wave of pecuniary embarrassment, in towns where the years bring dwindling population, decreasing trade, more hopeless effort. To the youth himself the future is utter darkness and dread emptiness. The shops, advancing in many cases to bankruptcy, offer but small wages ; of manufactories, the young Irishman's only knowledge is through the

[1] 'New Ireland,' pp. 167, 168.

crumbling ruins of the wool-mill or the distillery; he can become a doctor only if he have the luck to live in a town with a Queen's College; the legal profession, with its dinners in London and fees, used to be as inaccessible as a throne; and so it is that in Ireland, perhaps alone of all countries, the limbs even of youth are shackled, and its ardent spirit caged. The one pursuit the Act of Union has left to the youth of Ireland is the Civil Service. Thus it has come to pass that in Somerset House, at St. Martin's-le-Grand, and at all the other great Civil Service establishments of London, so great a proportion of the clerks are Irishmen. Entrance to a clerkship in the Civil Service had thus come to be regarded by the Athlone boy as the first step on the golden ladder of fortune. Keogh used his power of nomination in the most lavish manner; it was a saying in Athlone in his day that every young fellow who could or could not write his name had obtained a place in the Customs, or some other of the public departments. It will be seen that the use which Keogh made of this 'appointing power' was one of the charges which were brought against him afterwards.

This was the state of feeling by which the ardent spirits of the Tenant League found themselves confronted when they reached Athlone, and a similar state of things awaited those who went to Carlow. But the corruption of the people proved less shocking than the attitude of the clergy; they also not only condoned but applauded the action of the traitors. An appeal was made by the Tenant Leaguers to the bishops. From Dr. MacHale, Archbishop of Tuam, from the Bishop of Meath, and from the Bishop of Killala, there came prompt and emphatic condemnation of the acts of Keogh and Sadleir. This was good; but there were other prelates whose disapproval was more urgently required, and would have been decisive.

Dr. Cullen had been elevated from the See of Armagh to the Archbishopric of Dublin, and had at the same time been appointed Papal Legate. The whole country waited for a word from the new prelate, but Dr. Cullen obstinately held his peace, and silence, at the period, meant approval. In Athlone the bishop took even stronger action in favour of Keogh. His name was Dr. Browne, and he had a reputation beyond that of any other bishop of the period for gentleness and piety. O'Connell had called him the 'Dove of Elphin,' and by this name he was familiar and dear to the people of his diocese. I can remember him as he used to sit in the parish chapel in Athlone; a man of venerable appearance, with a singular resemblance to the pictures of some of the saints whose looks the great painters have made immortal. The people of his diocese had for him a respect that amounted almost to worship, and in Athlone he was especially beloved. The people of the town had got it into their heads that Athlone really held the first place in his heart; and there was an understanding that, when he died, Athlone would be privileged to receive his sainted remains. The man who gained the support of the bishop was certain of election, and the bishop gave his support to Keogh. The result of this difference of attitude produced even among the priests and bishops themselves a bitterness of feeling that prevailed for many years, and between two of the bishops, Dr. MacHale and Cardinal Cullen, it led to an estrangement that closed only with the grave. In every class, in fact, the fight was fought out with the frenzy which leads an armed population from words to civil war.

Meantime, while the whole country was looking with such desperate tension to the result of the contest in Athlone, Keogh was faced by a difficulty that threatened to wreck all. The reader knows of the property qualification of this period; it was charged against Keogh that he had not this qualification, and a committee of the House of Commons had been appointed to investigate the charge. In Ireland, the investigation was watched with a feeling of suspense, not unmixed with amusement. The financial difficulties of Keogh were notorious; it was known that, instead of having £300 a year over and above all incumbrances, he was in a shoreless sea of debt, and was not the possessor of three hundred pence that he could call his own. But he swore bravely before the committee. The committee went through complicated rolls of bank bills, by which the briefless barrister had been able to keep himself afloat and live the life of the Member of Parliament; and in the end, after the easy fashion of those good old days, held that he had proved his qualification, and so he was free to stand for Athlone. The influence of the bishop,[1] the sums of money Keogh had at his disposal, with the prosperous turn in his fortunes, and a system of organized mob violence, were greatly in his favour. Mr. Thomas Norton, his opponent, was an able man—he was known many years afterwards as a man of some social and political prominence in London society, as Master of the Queen's Bench, and Chairman of the Political Committee of the Reform Club; but, owing to the desertion of his own committee, some of whom were the very first to vote for Keogh, Norton resigned during the polling-day, and Keogh was returned, the figures standing thus: Keogh, 79; Norton, 40.[2]

[1] In his speech on the hustings, Keogh made the following allusion to the attitude of the bishop: 'Since I came into town, no matter where I went, no matter by whom I was accompanied, whether in the town or around the town, upon the hill-side or the ditch-side, on the public road or the narrow by-way, or in any other imaginable place, I have been received as the man of the people. How many hundred women have said this morning, "May God bless you!" How many hundred pretty girls have wished me success!' (A female voice—'You have the bishop's blessing, which is better than all.') Mr. Keogh: 'Yes; and I am authorized to announce to you, and he does not shrink from the announcement—you all know it; you all saw it—that I have the support, the confidence, the kind wishes, and the anxious throbbing expectations for my success of my revered friend the Roman Catholic bishop of this diocese.'—Quoted in T. D. Sullivan's 'Record,' p. 20.

[2] It is hard to bring home to the mind of any but an Irish reader the gigantic consequences on the future of Ireland which the action of Keogh produced, and it is necessarily as hard to understand the fierce hatred which was then and ever afterwards felt for him by the Irish people. The following quotation from the *Nation* of the period will perhaps do something to bring home to the reader of to-day the ideas, and still more the temper, of the time. It appeared on April 23, 1853, and was in reply to Keogh's speech on the hustings at Athlone: 'Mr. William Keogh has given tongue at last. For five months he has kept the silence of conscious infamy, while the whole island has been ringing with his shame. For five months the highest and the holiest voices in the land have been raised to accuse and to curse him, and he has held his peace. Words that would have made an honest man's blood choke him have met his eyes in every paper he read, and he has swallowed them without retort. He knew at the time that he dare not appear in an assembly of honest Irishmen, or he would be hooted from their sight. And he felt still nearer the touch of his own ignominy. In the Hall of the Four Courts, at his swearing in, a little gang of political blacklegs replaced the crowded array of the bar which used to attend the inauguration of a law official of the Crown. As he has driven through the streets of Dublin his furtive eye seemed to dread the fall of a dead cat or a shower of rotten eggs. For five months of place and power and emolument he has seen hatred and contempt of him wherever he turned. To remain silent in such a storm of execrations must have been hard for one of his passionate and voluble temper. But at last he has uttered himself. At last all the bitterness and anger which had been fermenting for five months in his heart have broken loose. And it has been like lifting a sluice-gate from a sewer. For hours he spoke, and the words rolled in one long gush of impure filth from his lips. For hours he spoke, and spared neither truth nor decency in his course. Bullying abuse that would demean a fishwoman, false scandal, and braggadocio, and dastardly innuendo he used, and used without stay or scruple. . . . There is a disease which is the last to feed upon a debauchee's bad-tempered frame—when the consti-

In the meantime the same good fortune had not attended the other members of the 'Brass Band.' John Sadleir had stood again for Carlow. Like Keogh, he was supported by large sums of money and by violent mobs. He got a letter from the Bishop of Kildare and Leighlin 'expressing the most earnest anxiety' for his success;[1] he was backed by the priests. One of his mobsmen was requested by the Rev. Father Maher to keep quiet and not disgrace 'a good cause.'[2] In spite of all these influences he was beaten by Mr. Alexander, the Conservative candidate, by a majority of six.

Keogh, though he had won the election at Athlone, was not yet safe. The violence of his temper, the unscrupulous audacity of some of his acts, his terrible speeches, his desperate expedients, had all been made notorious by the utterances of the press, and his conduct was brought in various ways before Parliament. Gavan Duffy obtained the appointment of a committee, known as the 'Corruption Committee,' to investigate the charges against Keogh and others of having used their position to make corrupt promises to obtain situations through their influence as members of Parliament. Keogh, appointed originally a member of this committee, was obliged to resign; the evidence against him became so strong that he had to pass from the position of judge to that of accused. The facts were notorious in Athlone. As has been seen, his wholesale promises of situations were one of many reasons why he had been able to overcome all opposition against him in the town. Again he escaped by the sheer force of audacious lying. One of the charges against him was that he had induced a Colonel Smith, of Athlone, to lend him £500 on the promise that he would obtain for that gentleman a stipendiary magistracy, and that this promise he had failed to keep. He denied every one of these charges, declared that the money raised by Smith had been raised in the

---

tution, rotten to its very springs, is only strong enough to secrete vermin, and the unhappy victim lives crawling, sick, and ashamed of his own foul existence. By this disease Mr. Keogh has chosen to illustrate the way in which he has been recently afflicted. He has felt the *morbus pedicularis* of his own ignominy itching him to the bone, and he says that *we* infected him with it. In an episodical attack upon the *Nation*, meant, we suppose, to be the coarsest and the foulest passage of his harangue, he says that, "unable to slay, and afraid to stab," we have "tried to inflict upon him the *morbus pedicularis*." We thank him for the word. The metaphor is a nasty one. It is one we have been loth to apply. But he has invented it, and let it stick to him. It completely illustrates a sense of degradation, patent and foul, and set in a natural quarantine from all honest men. "Unable to slay"! What does the gentleman mean? His character is dead, decomposed—it stinks. We do not estimate how far *we* have helped to scotch it. Let it rest. But "afraid"! Afraid of *what*? Afraid of *whom*? We have never hesitated to express the greatest contempt for Mr. William Keogh's character when there was occasion. We have never put a tooth in anything we had to say about him. We have stigmatized his conduct in the very broadest and plainest terms we could find. To be "afraid" of him is something too absurd for us to conceive. Afraid of a charlatan, afraid of a cheat, afraid of a public profligate and liar upon his oath, afraid of the greatest political scamp of his country, and the type *par excellence* of Irish demagogue rascality! Why, there are some men whom it requires courage to differ from and daring to assail. And we believe we have not wanted either upon occasion. But this paltry adventurer, who would be nothing were it not for his readiness, his flippancy, his contempt of scruples, and his flow of animal spirits—whose invective is only a deluge of dirt—whose most pretentious oratory is a jumble of bog Latin and flatulent English—whose character has been the by-word of everybody in this city for years as a sort of political Barnum—and whose legal standing is on a level with his ancestral patrimony—the Lord deliver us from fear of such a creature as that!"—Quoted by T. D. Sullivan, 'Record,' pp. 21, 22.

[1] *Dublin Evening Post.* Quoted by T. D. Sullivan, 'Record,' p. 14.
[2] T. D. Sullivan, 'Record,' p. 15.

Conservative interest, and not in that of himself personally, and represented himself as having remained on terms of intimacy with Smith to the day of his death. As a matter of fact, Smith was driven to bankruptcy by the failure of Mr. Keogh to keep his engagements, bitterly complained of the foul treatment he had received, and in the end he had to fly from his liabilities to America.[1]

But this was not the most serious attack made upon him. The reader will remember the terrible speech in recommendation of assassination which he had delivered to the Ribbonmen of Westmeath. The Conservative press of Ireland had denounced the appointment to a law office of a man capable of such a speech, just as vehemently as the *Freeman's Journal* and the *Nation*. 'No Prime Minister,' wrote the *Evening Mail*, 'ever offered a more audacious insult to his sovereign than Lord Aberdeen has done in naming him to be one of her Majesty's law officers.'[2] Conservatives took up the same position in the House of Lords. On June 10, Lord Westmeath first drew attention to the assassination speech. He quoted the terrible words already mentioned, in which a contrast was drawn between the short nights of summer, the longer nights of autumn, and the still longer nights of winter, with the significant wind-up, 'and then let everyone remember who voted for Sir R. Levinge.' (There are several versions of the speech, but they singularly agree in essential points.) The Ministerial speakers had nothing to reply to this charge; Lord Aberdeen had heard nothing of them; and the Marquis of Clanricarde did not think this was language which the House of Lords should be called upon to pay any attention to![3]

But the Conservative Opposition was not willing to allow the Ministry to escape so easily. Lord Derby thought the matter did not deserve to be treated so 'lightly.' It was a serious matter if such language had been used by a man who had been appointed to 'an office of all others in the world which was connected with the maintenance of the law and the suppression of turbulence and violence in Ireland;'[4] and Lord Eglinton, who had just ceased to be Lord-Lieutenant of Ireland, described Keogh, if he used this language, as having 'openly recommended assassination.' The language 'could bear no other construction than that he was distinctly recommending the people whom he was addressing, when the long nights would admit of it, to commit, if not murder, the most violent outrages.'[5]

The matter again came up on June 17. The use of the words by Keogh was so notorious that even an attempt at denial filled everybody with surprise. Two magistrates, the rector of Moate, where the speech was made, and three others, wrote to emphatically declare that they had heard the words recommending assassination. A policeman had been sent to report the speeches at the meeting. 'I have no more doubt,' added the Marquis of Westmeath, 'that the report of that constable may be found on the table of the Lord-Lieutenant, if he likes to look for it, than that I have now the use of my right hand.'[6] But the Duke of Newcastle did not produce the report of the constable; his only defence was a letter from Mr. Keogh, in which he did not deny the use of the words. He confined himself to the bold statement that he had no recollection of having used them; his recollection was confused by a speech that 'did not occupy five minutes,' and he trusted to the evidence of friends. Then a letter was enclosed from a

---

[1] T. D. Sullivan's 'Record,' pp. 39, 40.   [2] *Ib.*, p. 24.   [3] *Ib.*, pp. 24, 25.
[4] *Ib.*, p. 26.   [5] *Ib.*   [6] *Ib.*, pp. 27, 28.

'friend,' declaring that Keogh had used no such language.[1] The 'friend' was a solicitor named R. C. Macnevin, whose timely testimony was afterwards rewarded by the Registrarship in the court of Judge Keogh. This was assuredly a very weak reply to so grave a charge. As the Conservative *Evening Mail* put it, 'Mr. Keogh and his friends virtually entered a plea of guilty.'[2] Lord Eglinton pressed home the charge to absolute conviction by further declarations. A letter from a magistrate declared that 'twenty gentlemen of independence and station,' who were present on the occasion, were ready to testify to the use of the words 'on oath;' and then Lord Eglinton summarized the case in these vigorous terms :

'Mr. Keogh's speech was only one amongst many others which were brought under my notice. I certainly little expected these words had fallen from a man who was to become Solicitor-General for Ireland; but, as I have said, they came before me along with hundreds of other such reports and speeches, urging incitements, not only to riot, but even to disloyalty. BUT I CONFESS THAT DURING THE WHOLE TIME I WAS IN IRELAND, NO WORDS WERE BROUGHT TO ME WHICH, IN MY OPINION, SO DISTINCTLY RECOMMENDED ASSASSINATION.'[3]

Several other charges were brought against the new law officer. In the assassination speech he was accused of also asking the Westmeath 'boys' to come to Athlone with their shillelaghs and to use them, and with having headed himself a charge upon the hotel of his opponent. The 'boys' obeyed the command, and the intimidation which the shillelaghs created was one of the forces which won the election. This charge also was boldly denied by Keogh; but it was proved beyond any possibility of doubt.[4] Finally, a controversy arose between him and Lord Naas (afterwards Earl of Mayo); Keogh affirming, and Lord Naas positively denying, that office had been offered to him by the Conservative leaders. When challenged for proof, he appealed again to the testimony of a friend of his, whom he described as 'a gentleman of honour, veracity, and high character.'[5] The gentleman so described was Mr. Edmund O'Flaherty, of whom we shall hear a little more presently.

Thus Keogh had surmounted all the difficulties that at every turn seemed certain of overwhelming him. Success for the moment seemed to attend the other members of the gang also. Sadleir, defeated for Carlow, cast about for some other constituency. The Sligo of those days was not unlike the Athlone; it had the reputation of being among the most corrupt boroughs of the country, and it has since been disfranchised. It had been won by an Englishman named Townley, but the means of corruption he had employed were so open that he had been unseated for bribery, and thus the vacancy had been created. Sadleir employed exactly the same means as previous aspirants for the representation of the place. It was proved afterwards that several of the voters received sums running up to £25 for their votes. Sadleir, besides, though he was bitterly opposed by some of the clergy, had the support of several of the priests, and was actually proposed by a parish priest; and he had also the advantage of the intimidation of those hired mobs which he and Keogh had introduced into the factors of Irish electioneering. He was returned by a majority of four votes. There was a petition; the bribery was clearly proved; but

---

[1] T. D. Sullivan's 'Record,' pp. 28, 29.   [2] *Ib.*, pp. 29, 30.
[3] *Ib.*, p. 30,   [4] *Ib.*, pp. 32, 33.   [5] *Ib.*, p. 45.

according to the loose and shameless customs of the times, the tools were convicted while Sadleir was declared innocent. He actually retained his seat, and was perhaps in the House at the very moment when the Attorney-General moved for leave to prosecute some of the men whose bought votes had obtained him admission into the House. In 1855, Lord Aberdeen was replaced by Lord Palmerston, and Keogh was raised to the Attorney-Generalship in place of Mr. Brewster, who, being a Peelite, did not think it consistent to accept the change to a completely Whig Administration. Keogh also had begun life as a Peelite; but, of course, he was not troubled by the subtle distinction between one Ministry and another, and gladly accepted promotion. He had to seek election once more; but so broken was the spirit of the country that no attempt was made to defeat him; and to add to the tragic completeness of the situation, Dr. Browne, the 'Dove of Elphin,' came to the hustings and proposed Keogh as a 'fit and proper person' to represent the constituency.

And thus the triumph of the Irish Brigade was complete. All the men who had opposed them were crushed; some of the priests who had taken the true view of the situation were harried by their ecclesiastical superiors, or compelled to abstain from all action or speech on political matters. Frederic Lucas, who brought to the Irish cause a rare spirit of self-abnegation, resolved to go to Rome to lay the case at the feet of the Pope, and to call for redress and freedom for the priests that had endeavoured to avert from Ireland one of the greatest disasters and blackest shames of her history. But the Pope had received other information, and the mission was a failure. Lucas returned to England in breaking health and with a broken heart. He never saw again the land of his adoption, which he loved so dearly; he was taken sick on his return journey, and died at Staines on October 22, 1855. His death was taken by the Irish people as a calamity in addition to all those already suffered. Shortly afterwards another of the band of Tenant Leaguers, who had fought so bravely against the traitors, gave up the fight. Gavan Duffy despaired of the time. In such a season 'there was,' he said, 'no more hope for Ireland than for a corpse on the dissecting-table.' On November 6, 1855, he sailed for Australia.

It was at the moment of their complete triumph that Nemesis began to fall on the men who had destroyed and sold the hopes and fortunes of their country. Sadleir was the first to meet disaster. At Carlow, one of the agencies he had employed most extensively and relentlessly to secure his return, were the accounts of the bankrupt shopkeepers with the Tipperary Bank. It was a favourite plan of his, as of other Parliamentary aspirants afterwards, to lend money to the voters in the intervals between the elections on renewable bills, and with this unpaid bill he always held his power over the hapless elector, and could count on his vote when election time came. A man named Dowling, an elector of Carlow, was suspected of intending to vote against Sadleir, and he was arrested for debt on the morning of the election. Dowling took an action for false imprisonment; there were many damaging revelations against Sadleir in the trial, and he had to go into the witness-box. He swore boldly and unflinchingly, and the jury had either to brand him or Dowling a perjurer; the jury gave the verdict for Dowling. The result was that Sadleir had, in January, 1854, to resign his office as a Lord of the Treasury.

This was the first turn of the tide. In March of the same year there began to be rumours that, instead of being a millionnaire, he was in financial difficulties, but the rumours were laughed out of existence. Public confidence had but been restored in the financier of the 'Brass Band' when another scandal shook its credit. People began to ask where was Mr. Edmund O'Flaherty, the Commissioner of Income Tax. This was the 'gentleman of honour, veracity, and high character' whom Keogh had called in proof of his statement that Lord Naas, and not he, had lied in reference to the offer of office from the Conservatives; this also was the gentleman who had sent round the hat for Keogh at the time when, desperate and driven, he was about to stand for Athlone after he had accepted the office of Solicitor-General. Before many days the whole world knew that the Commissioner of Income Tax had fled no one knew whither, and that he had left behind bills amounting to £15,000 in circulation, some of them bearing names—Keogh's among the rest—which were stated to be forged.

This flight spread a painful degree of uncertainty in the public mind, and people began to ask who would be the next to go. The situation was rendered more complicated and painful by the fact, which the Opposition papers took care to largely advertise, that the absconding O'Flaherty had been on terms of the closest intimacy with the Peelite leaders, and had been, beyond doubt, the go-between in the infamous bargain by which the Peelites gave office and the 'Irish Brigade' sold a country. It was proved that O'Flaherty was on visiting terms with the Duke of Newcastle; a letter of his was published addressed to Mr. Richard Swift, M.P., in which the subscription was suggested that paid the expenses of Keogh for his contest in Athlone; and in the list of persons who had already subscribed, the honoured name of Sidney Herbert with a subscription of £100 appears side by side with that of John Sadleir for the same amount. And finally, the fact was notorious that, when the Income Tax was extended to Ireland, Mr. O'Flaherty received a reward for his services from the Peelites by his appointment as Commissioner.

The thing blew over for a while, and Sadleir once more was sailing before the wind. The death of Lucas and the departure of Gavan Duffy seemed to complete his triumph, and he was everywhere—especially, of course, in England—congratulated on the dispersal of his enemies.

Meantime he was approaching the abyss. The rumours that he was in financial difficulties were true. The vast schemes in which he had embarked proved in many cases disastrous; and then he took to all kinds of expedients for raising money; and finally he resorted to the forgery of title-deeds, conveyances, and bills. In February, 1856, the crash came. Glyns dishonoured some of the bills of the Tipperary Bank. The news spread; a run took place on some of the branches; but next day it was announced that a mistake had been committed and the drafts were honoured. The crisis might be averted if only a little ready money could be obtained. 'All right,' telegraphed James Sadleir to 'John Sadleir, Esq., M.P., Reform Club, London,' 'at all the branches: only a few small things refused there. If from twenty to thirty thousand over here on Monday morning all is safe.' This was received on a Saturday. Sadleir went into the City to see a Mr. Wilkinson, with whom he had large transactions; proposed various plans for raising money; all were rejected. 'He then became very excited,' says Mr. Wilkinson, describing the scene afterwards, 'put his hand to his head, and said, "Good God! if the Tipperary Bank should fail the fault will be entirely mine, and I shall have been the ruin of hundreds and thousands." He walked about the office in a very excited state, and urged me to try and help him, because he said he could not live to see the pain and ruin inflicted on others by the cessation of the bank. The interview ended in this, that I was unable to assist him in his plans to raise money.'¹

As the day went on, Sadleir heard news more disastrous. Mr. Wilkinson had previously lent him large sums of money. The money had been lent on one of the many securities Sadleir had forged during the previous year, and the suspicions of Mr. Wilkinson having been aroused, he had sent over his partner, Mr. Stevens, to Dublin to inquire into the matter. This was probably a portion of the news which was brought to Sadleir at ten o'clock on the night of this eventful Saturday by Mr. Norris, solicitor, of Bedford Row, one of his intimate friends. The two talked over the situation. It was agreed that there was no help for it, and that on Monday the Tipperary Bank must stop payment. At half-past ten Mr. Norris left. Sadleir spent some time in writing letters. He then got up to go out. As he passed through the hall, and was taking his hat from the stand, he met his butler, told him not to stay up for him, and then shut the door with a firm hand. As he left it was just striking twelve; it was Sunday morning. The next morning, on a mound on Hampstead Heath, the passers-by observed a gentleman lying as if asleep. A silver tankard smelling strongly of prussic acid was at his side. It was the dead body of John Sadleir—dead by his own hand.

'On Monday,' writes A. M. Sullivan,² 'the news flashed through the kingdom. There was alarm in London; there was wild panic in Ireland. The Tipperary Bank closed its doors; the country people flocked into the towns. They surrounded and attacked the branches; the poor victims imagined their money must be within, and they got crowbars, picks, and spades to force the walls and "dig it out." The scenes of mad despair which the streets of Thurles and Tipperary saw that day would melt a heart of adamant. Old men went about like maniacs, confused and hysterical; widows knelt in the street, and aloud asked God was it true they were beggared for ever. Even the Poor-Law Unions, which had kept their accounts in the bank, lost all, and had not a shilling to buy the paupers' dinner the day the branch doors closed. . . . Banks, railways, assurance associations, land companies, every undertaking with which he had been connected, were flung into dismay; and for months fresh revelations of fraud, forgery, and robbery came daily and hourly to view. By the month of April the total of such discoveries had reached £1,250,000.'

'Considerably above the middle height,' Sadleir is described by one who knew him; 'his figure was youthful, but his face—that was indeed remarkable. Strongly marked, sallow, eyes and hair intensely black, and the lines of the mouth worn into deep channels.'³

O'Flaherty fled; Sadleir dead; how was it, meantime, with Keogh? His name had been coupled with Sadleir and with Edmund O'Flaherty in the most intimate political association for nearly six years; was he going to be exposed also, and to choose flight or death in preference to shame and exposure? There was no such fate in store for him. It was reported that he was going to be raised to the bench! At once the national press of Ireland protested against this last indignity upon the country.

'Mr. William Keogh a judge!' wrote the *Nation* at an earlier period, 'when the report was first circulated, 'with life and death on his hands;

---

¹ 'New Ireland,' p. 179.   ² *Ib.*, pp. 180, 181.   ³ *Ib.*, p. 180.

with the peace, and honour, and property of the community hanging on the breath of his lips; with the liberties and the safeguards of society under his direct control. Mr. William Keogh, with the antecedents of his unprincipled political career, his mediocre professional character, his false pledges, his disreputable associates; this gentleman a judge! And the youngest judge, and the judge of the least standing at the bar, who has mounted the Irish bench within the memory of living man. We hesitate to believe it can be possible.'[1]

Then it spoke of the other judges on the bench, condemning their political partisanship, but admitting their professional claims and their personal integrity.

'There is not a man among them,' it went on, ' who has solemnly called God to witness a pledge of public conduct—who has ratified that pledge after months of mature consideration with another equally solemn—and who has scandalously broken both. There is not a man among them who, within seven years of public life, has been a Tory, a Whig, a Catholic Conservative, an anti-Repealer, an Ultramontane Radical, and a Tenant Leaguer—who has written pamphlets and spoken speeches on every side of every question, and tried the cushions of every bench in the House of Commons. There is none of them who need fear, when he takes up an indictment for forgery, that he will find the name of his bosom friend at its head —the name of the man upon whose word of honour he relied, and sustained himself in a position compromising his own political character. There is none of them who, when the officer of justice administers the oath of evidence before him, need blush, as the words "So help me God" are uttered, to think how that most solemn of human adjurations could not bind even him, a judge of the land, to the truth.'[2]

When after the death of John Sadleir the rumours were again resumed:

'It is very generally supposed,' wrote the *Nation*, 'that, after the scandalous conduct of Mr. Edmund O'Flaherty, the hideous suicide of Mr. John Sadleir, Government may feel a difficulty in elevating to the ermine of a justice a gentleman who was so intimately identified with both in their political profligacies, and who had, indeed, rather a worse public character than either.'[3]

'Can such a profanation be possible?' asked the *Wexford People*. 'Can public decency be so outraged? ... We believe the Government of Lord Palmerston is capable of doing a large amount of iniquity; but there is a limit beyond which they dare not pass, or the whole world would cry shame on them, and this is one.'[4]

'It was in the month of March, 1856,' writes T. D. Sullivan,[5] 'that these protests, and scores of others such as these against the probable elevation of Mr. Keogh to the bench of justice, were being published, The papers at the time were being loaded with the details of the Sadleir forgeries and swindles; the law courts were glutted with trials, motions, and all sorts of proceedings arising out of them; the air was ringing with the cries of the unfortunate people who were reduced from a state of sol-

[1] T. D. Sullivan's 'Record,' pp. 46, 47. [2] *Ib.*, p. 47.
[3] *Ib.*, p. 53. [4] *Ib.* [5] *Ib.*, p. 54.

vency and comfort to one of pauperism by the Sadleirite plunder. It was little wonder that the bare idea of the advancement of Mr. Keogh to the bench at such a time should have caused in the minds of honest men almost a frenzy of pain and horror.'

The protests were in vain. The death of Judge Torrens was announced in the Dublin papers of the morning of Tuesday, April 1. On Wednesday, April 2—the day after—Keogh had obtained the vacancy, and was one of her Majesty's judges.

'The administration of justice in Ireland,' said the *Nation*, 'has sustained a most grievous disgrace—a disgrace which would not be tolerated by the bench, by the bar, or the people of any other country on the face of the earth. . . . Fancy the effect of Mr. William Keogh going judge of assize to try the Westmeath Ribbonmen whom he cited to midnight violence—trying perjury in Athlone or Cork, before whole communities who heard him swear the oath of whose breach his presence on the bench before them is the startling evidence! It is an example sufficient to disgust or to demoralize the whole profession, and shake faith in justice. . . . What a startling and a scandalous spectacle it is to see this man, yet young—every year of whose life has been marked by infamous political tergiversation, whose career has never had in it a day of that patient, arduous, and laborious effort which is the peculiar dignity of the forensic robe, but has been like the advance of the chamois-hunter, springing from peak to peak, and always on the point of toppling over—now, after having been everything by turns and nothing long, broken faith with every party and laughed at every principle, set in ermine over this city, a judge among the twelve judges of the land!'

'Well may it be asked,' continues the national journal in the same article, 'Has God's providence ceased to rule in Ireland?'[1]

There is one scene more in this episode of Irish history. One prominent member of the 'Irish Brigade' had not been made a judge or committed suicide. It was James Sadleir, brother of John. On February 16, 1857, Mr. J. D. Fitzgerald, then Attorney-General for Ireland, moved the expulsion of James Sadleir for having fled before charges of fraud, and the motion was carried, *nemine contradicente*.

An Englishman was lamenting, a short time ago, to a brilliant Irishman who had formerly sat in Parliament, the disagreeable contrast between the Irish members of former days and the unpleasant specimens of the present hour. The Irishman surprised his interlocutor by admitting the contrast, but not after the same fashion. Then he put thus tersely the story which has just been told: 'There were four members of Parliament, personal intimates and political associates. One was a forger, and committed suicide; the other was a forger, and was expelled from Parliament; the third was a swindler, and fled; and the fourth was made a judge.'

[1] T. D. Sullivan's 'Record,' pp. 56, 57.

CHAPTER VI.

RUIN AND RABAGAS.

THE years which followed the treason of Judge Keogh are among the darkest in Irish history. The British Government and the landlords saw their power once more unquestioned by popular leaders and unopposed by popular organization or popular hopes. The landlords took advantage of the situation after their usual fashion.

And here again I must pause in the narrative to add another chapter to the long and monotonous history of the Land Question. The oppression which the landlords practised on their tenants at this period knew no limit of age or sex or circumstance; it penetrated into the smallest as well as the largest affairs of the tenant's life. The rent was raised year by year, the landlord knowing no other limit to his exactions than those of his own appetites or caprice or wants. The building of a new mansion in London, a bad night at the card-table, the demands of generous and exacting beauty, or the loss of a great race, remote as they were from the concerns of the Irish farmer in his cabin and on his patch of land, influenced and darkened his destiny; and year after year his rent steadily kept rising. When at last successive generations of folly and vice swept the old landlord into the maëlstrom of debt, the change of landlord meant in nearly every case a rise of rent and a master—penurious, perhaps, where the old proprietor had been spendthrift, but as grinding and as greedy.

There was in connection with most of the properties a code for the regulation of the tenantry which went under the name of 'office rules.' These rules dogged every action of the tenant's life.

A minute system of fines existed. Take these, for instances: William Bewley, a tenant on one of the estates of Lord Leitrim, was fined £11 because he sold hay contrary to the rules of the estate; Lord Leitrim himself visited this man's house in order to find fault with him, and the sight of this dreaded landlord and his brutal language drove Bewley's daughter insane. The widowed mother of the Rev. Mr. Lavelle, a well-known Catholic priest, was evicted because, contrary to the rules of the estate, she took in her son-in-law and daughter for companionship. A tenant on Lord Lucan's estate was fined 10s. for being three days late in the payment of his rent, and another tenant was fined 14s. 8d. for receiving a tenant's daughter into his house while her husband was in England. On the Ormsby estate in County Mayo, this system of petty fining reached its highest development. Thus a woman named Ann Cassidy could recall the infliction of the following fines upon her husband: 5s. for being absent from duty work one day; 10s. for a similar offence; 2s. 6d. for being absent from duty work on the day of his child's burial; 2s. 6d. because a pig rooted part of his land; 2s. 6d. for allowing an ass to stray on the road; 10s. 6d. because the top stone of a gable was not rightly whitewashed. James Sheerin, formerly a tenant on the Ormsby estate, was fined 10s. for cutting a branch from an ash-tree which he himself had planted; 5s. because a pig strayed back into a house from which he had been evicted; and 1s. 6d. because a horse was allowed out on the road. Margaret Conlon describes how, on the same estate, her husband was fined 7s. 6d. for not making a drain at a time when he was engaged in mowing for the landlord; 12s. 6d. for changing a window from one side of the house to the other in order to get more light; and

2s. 6d. for being too late at his work. Charles Durkin, a tenant on the estate of Sir Robert Blosse, was fined for taking carts of bog-mud from one part of his land to manure another; and £2 17s. 6d. for cutting loads of turf from a bog for which he was paying £1 8s. per acre.[1]

Thus beggared and driven, the tenant naturally took refuge or found some consolation in the contemplation of his religion, which promised a future life in which the poverty and tyranny of this world would exist no more, and where hearts would find peace, and sorrow could dry its tears. But even the poor luxury of his intercourse with the Unseen the landlord would not permit the tenant to enjoy in peace. Lord Plunket, for instance, evicted a large number of his tenants because they refused to send their children to the proselytizing schools. This system of proselytizing was one of the worst portents of the time. A society was formed, and is still in existence, the nominal purpose of which is to wean the Catholic population from the errors of their religion by lectures. Under this organization, known as the Irish Church Mission, the Catholics of Ireland have the privilege of seeing in the streets on public placards the most flagrant reflections on the most sacred mysteries of their creed. In the poorer parts of the country, food was the bribe by which the starving parents were seduced into selling the creed of their children. During periods of very deep distress these missions enrolled some of the population, but the return of such prosperity as the Irish farmer was allowed to enjoy brought back the people to the observance of the faith in which they believed. In some parts of the country the small churches which at one time had congregations of Catholics converted by such means are now empty and in ruins. The parents who thus deserted their religion naturally became the objects of their neighbours' contempt. They and their tempters were called by a nickname which sufficiently indicated the reason of their change of faith. 'Souper' is one of the vilest epithets that one person in Ireland can hurl at another, even up to the present hour. In another way also the landlords substituted a penal code of their own for that abolished by statute. On several estates every effort was directed towards expelling the Catholic population so as to replace them by Protestant tenants.

It might have been expected that the tenant thus reduced to an ill-paid labourer, as absolutely dependent as a serf, would not be an object of any further misgiving or annoyance to his landlord. But the frenzy for the destruction of the people that set in towards the beginning of the century seemed still to rage like an unholy and accursed mania in the souls of the landlords; and the period is marked by wholesale clearances on a scale that is appalling, and amid circumstances of horror and cruelty that are scarcely credible.

The instances are so numerous of such wholesale clearances that one has to pick and choose. It will suffice to take out a few of the typical cases; they will indicate what landlordism meant in those days.

Five names stand out in bold relief among the wholesale evictors of this and other periods and that immediately preceding it. These are the Marquis of Sligo, the Earl of Lucan, Mr. Allan Pollock, Lord Leitrim, and Mr. John George Adair. The Marquis of Sligo cleared out at various

---

[1] These cases were supplied to the solicitors for the traversers in the case of the Queen v. Parnell and others, by persons who were prepared to swear to their occurrence. The briefs containing this evidence were placed at my disposal by the widow of A. M. Sullivan. It will be referred to as 'Evidence for Queen v. Parnell.'

periods no fewer than two thousand families, with the result that a single tenant of his, with a few herds, occupied an area of no less than two hundred square miles. The Earl of Lucan absolutely swept from the earth the town of Aughadrina. Mr. Pollock evicted one hundred families from one estate, fifty from another. He was a Scotchman, and one of the objects of these wholesale evictions was to replace the Irish population by men of another race, and the tenantry by sheep and bullocks. 'Before the face of this "stranger" no less than five thousand souls had to fly the bounds of their country and their sweet fields.'[1] In 1856 Mrs. James Blake evicted fifty families, not one of whom owed her a penny of rent, and the land was changed into grass land. 'Some of the tenants then evicted are beggars in Loughrea,' says Dr. Duggan.[2] In County Cavan, seven hundred tenants were turned out by Messrs. O'Connor and Malone in the course of two days. In County Meath, Mr. Nicholson cleared out from eighty to one hundred people in 1862, and about three hundred persons in 1869-70, and the land was entirely turned into pasture. In 1857, Mr. Rochford Boyd, a Westmeath landlord, evicted a large number of tenants, not one of them owing any rent.

Wholesale eviction of this kind could not be carried on, of course, without terrible hardship. Sometimes people were turned out on Christmas Eve. Here is a case described by Father Lavelle. 'A certain landlord in County Galway got a cheap decree at Quarter Sessions against a tenant on his property. This was early in October; October and November passed over, and a gleam of hope began to enter the poor man's soul that, at least, he would be permitted to pass the Christmas holidays in his old home. December was fast running out; the sun of Christmas Eve had actually risen, and with it the poor man and his wife and family, when, horror of horrors! whom does he see approaching his cabin door, followed by a *posse comitatus* of the Crowbar Brigade, but the sheriff surrounded by a detachment of the constabulary force! The family were flung out like vermin, and the work of demolition occupied but a few minutes. The evicted family passed that and the subsequent Christmas night with no other covering but that of the wide canopy of heaven, as strict prohibitions had been issued to all the other tenants to harbour him on pain of similar treatment.'[3]

Father White, of Milltown-Malbay, tells how, in the winter of 1864 or 1865, he was present at the eviction of five or six families on Mr. Westby's estate in the parish of Carrigaholt. It was late in the evening of a cold winter's day; the bailiffs were in the act of carrying out an old woman about eighty years of age, and apparently in a dying state. She had been, it seemed, taken from her bed, being wrapped in a sheet. They laid her on the dunghill. 'I was so shocked that I threatened to prosecute the sub-sheriff for murder if she died,' says Father White.[4] The eviction of each of these tenants was carried out in the most heartless manner. The houses were nearly all afterwards unroofed. These tenants, until the bad years of 1862-3-4, were all comfortable and well-to-do. They held from five to forty acres.

'Whilst in Newmarket parish,' says the same clergyman, 'about 1872, Lord Inchiquin raised the tenants' rents considerably—I believe added

[1] Lavelle's 'Irish Landlord since the Revolution,' p. 271.
[2] Evidence for Queen *v.* Parnell.
[3] Lavelle, pp. 271, 272.
[4] Evidence for Queen *v.* Parnell.

about £5,000 to his rental. He evicted a number of tenants, not owing a penny rent, for the purpose of adding to his demesne.'

At an eviction in 1854, on a property under the management of Marcus Keane, James O'Gorman, one of the tenants evicted, died on the roadside. His wife and ten children were sent to the workhouse, where they died shortly afterwards. John Corbet, a tenant on another townland, was evicted by the same agent. He died on the roadside; his wife had died previously to the eviction; his ten children were sent into the workhouse and there died. Michael McMahon, evicted at the same time, was dragged out of bed to the wallside, where he died of want next day. His wife died of want previously to the eviction, and his children, eight in number, died in a few weeks in the workhouse.[1]

---

[1] Though it does not belong to this period, it may be well to quote here a description of an eviction which has become historical. The eye-witness to it was the Most Rev. Dr. Nulty, Lord Bishop of Meath, and the event occurred in September, 1847, near Mount Nugent, Co. Cavan. The names of the owners of the property were O'Connor and Malone; that of the agent was Mr. Guiness, then M.P. for Kinsale, but shortly afterwards unseated for bribery. Dr. Nulty says:

'In the very first year of our ministry, as a missionary priest in this diocese, we were an eye-witness of a cruel and inhuman eviction, which even still makes our heart bleed as often as we allow ourselves to think of it.

'Seven hundred human beings were driven from their homes in one day and set adrift on the world, to gratify the caprice of one who, before God and man, probably deserved less consideration than the last and least of them. And we remember well that there was not a single shilling of rent due on the estate at the time, except by one man; and the character and acts of that man made it perfectly clear that the agent and himself quite understood each other.

'The Crowbar Brigade, employed on the occasion to extinguish the hearths and demolish the homes of honest, industrious men, worked away with a will at their awful calling until evening. At length an incident occurred that varied the monotony of the grim, ghastly ruin which they were spreading all around. They stopped suddenly, and recoiled panic-stricken with terror from two dwellings which they were directed to destroy with the rest. They had just learned that a frightful typhus fever held those houses in its grasp, and had already brought pestilence and death to their inmates. They therefore supplicated the agent to spare these houses a little longer; but the agent was inexorable, and insisted that the houses should come down. The ingenuity with which he extricated himself from the difficulties of the situation was characteristic alike of the heartlessness of the man and of the cruel necessities of the work in which he was engaged. He ordered a large winnowing-sheet to be secured over the beds in which the fever victims lay—fortunately they happened to be perfectly delirious at the time—and then directed the houses to be unroofed cautiously and slowly, "because," he said, "he very much disliked the bother and discomfort of a coroner's inquest." I administered the last sacrament of the Church to four of these fever victims next day; and, save the above-mentioned winnowing-sheet, there was not then a roof nearer to me than the canopy of heaven.

'The horrid scenes I then witnessed I must remember all my life long. The wailing of women—the screams, the terror, the consternation of children—the speechless agony of honest, industrious men—wrung tears of grief from all who saw them. I saw the officers and men of a large police force, who were obliged to attend on the occasion, cry like children at beholding the cruel sufferings of the very people whom they would be obliged to butcher had they offered the least resistance. The heavy rains that usually attend the autumnal equinoxes descended in cold, copious torrents throughout the night, and at once revealed to those houseless sufferers the awful realities of their condition. I visited them next morning, and rode from place to place administering to them all the comfort and consolation I could. The appearance of men, women, and children, as they emerged from the ruins of their former homes—saturated with rain, blackened and besmeared with soot, shivering in every member from cold and misery—presented positively the most appalling spectacle I ever looked at. The landed proprietors in a circle all around—and for many miles in every direction—warned their tenantry, with threats of their direst vengeance, against the humanity of extending to any of them the hospitality of a single night's shelter. Many of these poor people were unable to emigrate with their families; while, at home, the hand of every man was thus raised against them. They were driven from the land on which Providence had placed them; and, in the state of

In one estate at least an 'office rule' regulated even the marriage relations of the tenantry. One of the estates on which this practice was most rigidly carried out was that of the Marquis of Lansdowne. The late Sir John Gray, in a speech in the Free Trade Hall in Manchester (October 18, 1869), describes this episode of landlord life in these graphic terms :[1]

'In the book he had already quoted from—"Realities of Irish Life"— there was told a very pathetic story of "Mary Shea," the pretty black-eyed girl of seventeen, who lived with her parents on a mountain farm. Mr. Trench tells with touching pathos how, when the "hunger"—the name given by the people to the famine—came, Mary's mother died, and was buried in the garden, because Mary and her father had not strength to carry her to the churchyard. He tells how Mary smothered the bees she had reared herself, though they all knew her well, and sold their store of honey for 15s., and bought meal, and kept her father alive for a month, but how, when it was exhausted, her father died too, and how he, too, was buried in the garden by herself and "Eugene," and how, thus left an orphan and alone, the kind-hearted Eugene took home "Mary Shea" to his mother's house, and shared the scanty meal with her. Mr. Trench with great power described, in the book he held in his hand, this sad "reality," and told how, when walking one day through his pleasure-grounds, he saw two bright spots shining from behind a holly-tree, and coming nearer he saw that behind the tree something moved, and forth came Mary Shea, the graceful Irish maiden of seventeen, with Spanish face, and almost kneeling, she said with blushing confidence, "Please, your honour, will you put Eugene's name on the book instead of mine?" Then a beautiful tale was told of Mary's woes, of her modesty, of her beauty, and of her marriage, on perusing which no English matron or noble maiden with tender or womanly heart could restrain their tears, so sweetly was told the affecting story of Mary Shea. But alas! Mr. Trench did not tell the dismal truth of landlord tyranny that was concealed behind the rose-tinted romance of this "reality of Irish life." He did not tell why it was that this blushing maiden of seventeen, the black-eyed Mary Shea, came to him, a man she had never before seen, to tell of her innocent love, and to introduce Eugene; he did not tell that, by "the rule of the estate," had Mary Shea or any other tenant dared to get married without the leave of "his honour" the agent, she would be hurled from her farm, and the roof torn down about her bridal-bed.' (Cries of 'Shame on him!' and loud cheers.) 'He (Sir John Gray) would now read for them an extract from a petition to a noble marquis, whose name was given in the title-page of Mr. Trench's book as one of those nobles whose agent he is, which would tell some of the true realities of Irish life; for these were realities of Irish life of which no glimpse was given in Mr. Trench's book. In the title-page of that book it would be found that the author, Mr. Trench, was agent to a noble marquis and two other great estated persons in Ireland; and in M. Perraud's "Ireland in 1862," he found a copy of a petition presented no farther back than 1858, by the whole body of the tenantry of the noble marquis, who was, he believed, the landlord of black-eyed Mary Shea.' (Cries of 'Name,

---

society surrounding them, every other walk of life was rigidly closed against them. What was the result? After battling in vain with privation and pestilence, they at last graduated from the workhouse to the tomb; and in little more than three years, nearly a fourth of them lay quietly in their graves.'

[1] 'Authorised Report,' pp. 28–30.

name.') 'The name of the landlord was the Marquis of Lansdowne, the estate was in Kerry, and this was the petition :

'"We (the tenants) have been made keenly sensible of this abject dependence, by certain rules and regulations, which are now forced on this estate. By these rules no tenant can marry, or procure the marriage of his son or daughter, without permission from your lordship's agent, even when no change of tenancy would arise."' (Cheers, and loud cries of 'Shame.') 'That was the petition of the tenantry of Lord Lansdowne in April, 1858.'

The Lansdowne property brought another of the many 'rules' on estates over Ireland to its logical and tragic conclusion. Again the words of Sir John Gray will be quoted :

'He would now ask leave to read, not from the petition of the tenantry, but from the judgment of the Chief Baron of the Irish Court of Exchequer, another illustration of the "rule of the estate," which forbade a tenant to give shelter even to a relative in his most dire distress upon that very same property. Passing sentence upon some persons in the dock who were accused of the manslaughter of a boy of twelve years of age, Chief Baron Pigott said: 'The poor boy whose death you caused was between twelve and fourteen years of age.' Now mark the history of that boy, as told by the Chief Baron : "His mother at one time held a little dwelling from which *she was expelled*. His father was dead. His mother had left him, and he was alone and unprotected. He found refuge with his grandmother, who held a little farm, *from which she was removed* in consequence of *her harbouring this poor boy*, as the agent of the property had given public notice to the tenantry *that expulsion from their farms* would be the penalty inflicted upon them if they harboured any persons having no residence on the estate." These two cases, not of eviction, but cases where eviction did not occur, showed that the tenantry were, because of the extraordinary powers conferred by law on landlords, in such a state of serfdom, that the mother could not receive her daughter—that the grandmother could not receive her own grandchild unless that child was a tenant on the estate' ('Shame,' 'Inhuman')—'and the result in the case he was referring to . . . was this, that the poor boy, without a house to shelter him, was sought to be forced into the house of a relative in a terrible night of storm and rain. He was immediately pushed out again, he staggered on a little, fell to the ground, and the next morning was found cold, stiff, and dead.' (Sensation.) 'The persons who drove the poor boy out were tried for the offence of being accessories to his death, and their defence was, that what they did was done under the terror of "the rule of the estate," and that they meant no harm to the boy.' ('Shame.')[1]

Finally, on this point there were cases in which the landlord had made even harder claims. The *droit de seigneur* reigned as completely in Ireland as in France ; but while in the one case it ended with the French Revolution, it endured in Ireland—thanks to British rule—until our own times. Lord Leitrim in this way, as in many others, raged like a plague over the people, whom a hideous destiny and evil laws left entirely at his mercy. On his estates a comely girl was ordered to come nominally as a domestic servant inside his house. The house became a prison, and the service was the service of shame. In due time the lord of the seraligo sent the

[1] '"Authorised Report,' pp 30, 31.

distasteful mistress to America, and to some other hapless girl on his estate the dread choice was offered between entering the harem or exposing her parents and her family to eviction, *i.e.*, starvation.

Such are a few instances, selected out from hundreds, of what landlordism meant for Ireland during the years between the treason of Keogh and the year 1865. To complete the picture it is necessary to describe in some detail one other eviction scene, which, from its peculiar cruelty, attracted universal attention. The story of Glenveigh has been told often since, not merely in history, but in romance. Derryveigh is situate in the highlands of Donegal, and has some of the most beautiful scenery in Ireland. The beauty of its scenery attracted the attention of Mr. John George Adair, a Queen's County landlord, while on a sporting visit to the locality, and he resolved to buy the property. Up to this period the population enjoyed a universal reputation for the virtues associated usually with remote mountaineers. They were quiet, industrious, and on excellent terms with their landlords. The advent of Mr. Adair changed all this. The struggle between him and his tenants began in a small dispute about his right to shoot over some land formerly in the possession of one of their landlords. The farmers attempted to prevent Mr. Adair shooting; there was a scuffle; litigation ensued with varying success, and with increasing bitterness between Mr. Adair and one of the tenants. A further cause of dispute arose soon after. Mr. Adair had, like some other of the landlords, imported a number of Scotch black-faced sheep, which were supposed to be a very profitable investment. These sheep disappeared in considerable numbers; Mr. Adair charged his tenants with having maliciously destroyed them, and succeeded for a while in obtaining large sums in compensation from the grand jury. These taxes fell very heavily upon the tenantry, and tended to exasperate feeling still further. It was represented, too, that while the sheep only cost 7s. 6d. to 10s. a head, the amount claimed at the presentments was from 17s. 6d. to 25s. a head. The Judge of Assize—the late Chief Justice Monahan—indignantly refused to *fiat* these monstrous claims, and an impression began to prevail that the disappearance of many of the sheep at least was due, not to malice, but to the stress of weather.

This, however, was not the view taken by Mr. Adair. He had been exasperated so much by the quarrel over the rights of sporting and the disappearance of the sheep, that he came to regard himself as engaged in a fierce and merciless struggle with the tenantry. He had prepared for such a struggle by getting possession of the entire district by purchase at different but closely following dates, and he was in the end the absolute master of ninety square miles of country. Several small acts led up to a final cause of quarrel. Two of his dogs were poisoned, as he thought maliciously, although the grand jury refused him compensation, and an outhouse was set on fire. Finally, one of his herds was murdered. This fixed Mr. Adair's determination: the banishment of the whole population —nothing less would feed fat his big revenge.

The tenantry heard of this fell intention, but, removed from much contact with the outside world, and unable to face even in imagination such a terrible possibility, they went on without taking any particular notice. But they were the only persons who were undisturbed. The other landlords, alarmed at the transformation of the country from its normal tranquillity into all this tumult of conflict, passed a strong resolution in favour of the tenantry; the clergymen of all denominations were as vehemently on their side; the local authorites were loud in their anger. 'Is it my duty,' wrote Mr. Dillon, the resident magistrate, to Sir Thomas Larcom, then Under-Secretary at Dublin Castle, 'to stand by and give protection while the houses are being levelled ?' In Dublin Castle itself they were in a fever of apprehension, and they made preparations for assisting the landlord in this act of brutal and wholesale cruelty as extensive as if they were preparing for a small campaign. Mr. Adair's bailiffs were supplied with the services of a large number of soldiers and police. On the night of Sunday this body took possession quietly and without any warning of all the approaches to the valley in which the doomed people slept; on the following morning—Monday, April 8—the work of eviction began. The *Derry Standard*, a Presbyterian journal of the district, described through its special correspondent what followed :

'The first eviction was one peculiarly distressing, and the terrible reality of the law suddenly burst with surprise on the spectators. Having arrived at Lough Barra, the police were halted, and the sheriff, with a small escort, proceeded to the house of a widow named M'Award, aged sixty years, living with whom were six daughters and a son. Long before the house was reached loud cries were heard piercing the air, and soon the figures of the poor widow and her daughters were observed outside the house, where they gave vent to their grief in strains of touching agony. Forced to discharge an unpleasant duty, the sheriff entered the house and delivered up possession to Mr. Adair's steward, whereupon six men, who had been brought from a distance, immediately fell to to level the house to the ground. The scene then became indescribable. The bereaved widow and her daughters were frantic with despair. Throwing themselves on the ground, they became almost insensible, and, bursting out in the old Irish wail—then heard by many for the first time—their terrifying cries resounded along the mountain-side for many miles. They had been deprived of the little spot made dear to them by associations of the past—and with bleak poverty before them, and only the blue sky to shelter them, they naturally lost all hope, and those who witnessed their agony will never forget the sight. No one could stand by unmoved. Every heart was touched, and tears of sympathy flowed from many. In a short time we withdrew from the scene, leaving the widow and her orphans surrounded by a small group of neighbours who could only express their sympathy for the homeless, without possessing the power to relieve them. During that and the next two days the entire holdings in the land mentioned above were visited, and it was not until an advanced hour on Wednesday the evictions were finished. In all the evictions the distress of the poor people was equal to that depicted in the first case. Dearly did they cling to their homes till the last moment, and while the male population bestirred themselves in clearing the houses of what scanty furniture they contained, the women and children remained within till the sheriff's bailiff warned them out, and even then it was with difficulty they could tear themselves away from the scenes of happier days. In many cases they bade an affectionate adieu to their former peaceable but now desolate homes. *One old man, near the fourscore years and ten, on leaving his house for the last time, reverently kissed the doorposts, with all the impassioned tenderness of an emigrant leaving his native land.* His wife and children followed his example, and in agonised silence the afflicted family stood by and watched the destruction of their dwelling. In another case an old man, aged ninety, who was lying ill in bed, was brought out of the house in order that formal possession might be taken, but readmitted for a week to permit of his removal. In nearly every house there was some one far advanced in age—many of them tottering to the grave—while the sobs of helpless children took hold of every heart. When dispossessed, the families grouped themselves on the ground, beside the ruins of their late homes, having no place of refuge near. The dumb animals refused to leave the wallsteads, and in some cases were with difficulty rescued from the falling timbers. As night set in the scene became fearfully sad. Passing along the base of the mountain the spectator might have observed near to each house its former inmates crouching round a turf fire, close by a hedge; and as a drizzling rain poured upon them they found no cover, and were entirely exposed to it, but only sought to warm their famished bodies. Many of them were but miserably clad, and on all sides the greatest desolation was apparent. I learned afterwards that the great majority of them lay out all night, either behind the hedges or in a little wood which skirts the lake; they had no other alternative. I believe many of them intend resorting to the poorhouse. There these poor starving people remain on the cold bleak mountains, no one caring for them whether they live or die. 'Tis horrible to think of, but more horrible to behold.'[1]

This tragedy excited the attention of many people. An appeal was made for assistance, and the appeal was signed in a province unfortunately remarkable for religious dissension by the Catholic bishop, the Protestant rector, the Presbyterian minister, and the Catholic parish priest of the district, who united in warm defence of the people against their landlord. In Australia, meantime, one of their countrymen, who was a member of the Legislature—the late Hon. Michael O'Grady—had formed a relief committee, and offered to assist them to homes in a better and freer land than their own. The late Mr. A. M. Sullivan—from whose book I have quoted the details of the story—actively interested himself in their welfare. 'The poor people,' he writes, 'were sought out and collected. Some by this time had sunk under their sufferings. One man, named Bradley, had lost his reason under the shock; other cases were nearly as heartrending. There were old men who would keep wandering over the hills in view of their ruined homes, full of the idea that some day Mr. Adair might let them return; but who at last had to be borne to the distant workhouse hospital to die.'

'With a strange mixture of joy and sadness,' continues Mr. Sullivan, 'the survivors heard that their friends in Australia had paid their passage-money. On the day they were to set out for the railway station *en route* for Liverpool, a strange scene was witnessed. The cavalcade was accompanied by a concourse of neighbours and sympathisers. They had to pass within a short distance of the ancient burial-ground where the "rude forefathers" of the valley slept. They halted, turned aside, and proceeded to the grass-grown cemetery. Here in a body they knelt, flung themselves on the graves of their relatives, which they reverently kissed again and again, and raised for the last time the Irish *caoine*, or funeral wail. Then—some of them pulling tufts of the grass, which they placed in their bosoms—they resumed their way on the road to exile.'[2]

It was not alone to the tenants themselves and the country population generally that these wholesale clearances were disastrous. Agriculture is

---

[1] Quoted in 'New Ireland,' pp. 227, 228.   [2] *Ib.*, p. 229, 230.

practically the one industry of Ireland, and with the disappearance of the farmers around disappeared the customers and the trade of the towns. Nor was this the only way in which the towns suffered from the general exodus. The evicted farmers, in many cases, had not sufficient capital to pay their passage to America, and drifted into the towns. There but a comparatively small number of them could obtain employment, and they were transformed by due gradation into the vast army of beggars that infest the Irish towns, or into the paupers that rot in idleness within the workhouses. The towns thus suffered doubly in the decrease of the customers and the increase in the pauper population; and hence it is that to-day there is in the villages and the smaller towns of Ireland poverty more hopeless, chronic, and appalling than we can find even in the country. The agricultural labourers, the misery of whose condition has passed into a by-word even among Irish Chief Secretaries, and into the facts sadly acknowledged by even the most hostile and opposite sections of Irish opinion, are for the most part farmers whom eviction divorced from the soil.

On the decadence which the clearances brought to the Irish in towns, the evidence is overwhelming; indeed, any Irishman that has revisited after some years of absence his native place can give testimony on this point by recounting the painful impressions the terrible change he everywhere sees has left upon his mind. He finds a painfully large proportion of the people he has known gone in despair from the place—to America, or Australia, or England. Of those who remain behind, the majority are in the unrelaxing grip of unconquerable poverty. Take, out of the numberless instances, the case of two towns. Mr. John Hynes tells [1] how on Mr. Lahiff's estate, close to the town of Gort, there used in his young days to be two hundred families and a mile in tillage. Now—he was speaking of 1880—all was grazing land and the town of Gort had been changed for a lane, and prosperous town to a struggling village. Francis Nicholls tells [2] the effect of the clearances by Mr. Nicholson on the neighbouring town of Kells; the pauper population had been largely increased, and it was impossible to tell how many of them lived through the winter months. These people were in almost every case evicted families.

Ireland to-day bears the still fresh scars of the terrible sufferings of the years I am describing and the years which immediately preceded them. The most prominent, the most frequent, the ever-recurring feature of the Irish landscape is the unroofed cottage. There are many parts of the country where these skeleton walls stare at one with a persistency and a ghastly iteration that convey the idea of passing through a land which had been swept by rapidly successive and frequent waves of foreign invasion—by war, and slaughter, and the universal break-up of national life. Or shall I rather say that Ireland conveys the idea, not of a nation still young in hope and daily increasing in wealth and in possibilities, but rather the image of one of those Oriental nations whose history and empire, wealth and hopes, belong to the irrevocable past. There are several counties where one can pass for miles without ever catching sight of a house or of any human face but that of the shepherd, almost as isolated as his hapless brother in the stretching plains of California.

Meantime, while throughout Ireland this ghastly destruction of a nation was going on, the season was the most pleasant and profitable that the political adventurer has ever known in Ireland. The country had fallen

---

[1] Evidence for Queen v. Parnell. [2] Ib.

from rage to despair, and from despair to cynicism. The electoral contests of the time were conducted on a principle well understood though not publicly avowed. The political aspirant was to make profession of strong patriotic purpose, which the elector professed on his side to believe, and, as the candidate used Parliament solely for the purpose of personal advancement, the elector pocketed the bribe while professing to believe the candidate. A good deal of this corruption was the result of two other causes besides the daily increasing poverty of the country. First, there was no great or commanding personality; secondly, there was nothing like the unity of a national purpose. This latter fact is a most important factor in this as in several other periods of Irish history. Election contests turned on purely personal or local issues. This man was preferred in one place because he was a better speaker or a more genial fellow; and one constituency wanted a harbour and another a bridge. Thus, for instance, in Galway the chief desire of the people was that there should be some means of utilizing the splendid bay of the town and its geographical destiny as the *entrepôt* between the old and the new world. This aspiration of Galway was so notorious that it was utilized by all kinds of people. One of my boyish recollections is of a travelling show which added to the attractions of the then newly-discovered ghost of Professor Pepper a panorama of America—a country which at that time, in spite of the vast number of Irish emigrants, was a *terra incognita*. The lecturer who accompanied the show had taken the precaution to consult some of the knowing men of the town as to the local weaknesses, and turned the information thus received to excellent account. He was describing one night some bay in America, and after a eulogy of its beauties in language of Transatlantic fervour, he wound up with the statement that it was the most beautiful bay in the world with two exceptions—the bay of Naples and the bay of Galway. The election in Galway was fought throughout these years on the question of the bay and a Transatlantic mail service; and an English gentleman was returned more than once because he had succeeded in getting a subsidy from Lord Derby for a mail service between Galway and New York.

A third reason of the political corruption of the constituencies was that the people had a distrust so profound in the men who sought their representation. They regarded them, one and all, as adventurers who, assuming different names—Tory, Whig, Peelite, Patriot—had all the same common end—personal aggrandisement. When men in Athlone, for instance, were reproached for taking bribes, the retort was that whether it was one self-seeker or another got in made no difference, and that a poor man might be well excused if he made one or other of the rogues pay for his promotion.

The candidate of these days belonged, as a rule, to one of three classes. First, there were a certain number of Englishmen or of Irishmen settled in England who were anxious for a seat in Parliament, because of the advantages it gave them in floating companies and other financial operations in the city of London. Then there were the children of the *bourgeoisie*, who desired to gild the wealth gained by their parents in the sale of tea or of whisky. These men had become, as a rule, landed proprietors. The establishment of the Incumbered Estates Court had enabled a large number of the bankrupt gentry of Ireland to dispose of their estates, and a new generation of landlords grew up in the shape of successful tradesmen who had the Celtic passion for the acquisition of land

and the general desire to enter the county families which belongs to the successful men of trade in all parts of the three kingdoms. To make the transformation in such a case complete, a title was necessary; and many of the children of the *bourgeoisie* spent tens of thousands of pounds, and followed the Ministerial whip with the abject devotion of ten years, in the hope of receiving a baronetcy at the end of it all!

But the most common type of Irish politician in these days was the man who entered Parliamentary life solely for the purpose of selling himself for place and salary. This was the golden season when every Irishman who could scrape as much money together as would pay his election expenses was able, after a while, to obtain a governorship or some other of the many substantial rewards which English party leaders were able to give to their followers. The chief persons to benefit by this time of universal corruption were the Irish barristers. They had advantages over all other competitors. They were accustomed to speaking; their names were familiar to the public; in short, they were marked out for political life above all other classes in Ireland, as in every other country where there are Parliamentary institutions and a legal profession. Parliament was made during this whole period the sole avenue through which professional promotion could be obtained. It was one of the many things which helped to embitter Irish opinion against English rule, in those robust natures where national feeling still lived, that English Ministers at this period seemed to delight in increasing the chances of political adventurers, and sought to maintain the hated Act of Union by means as shameless as those by which it had been passed. For nearly a quarter of a century there were only two cases in which men were raised to the bench who had not in the first instance been members of Parliament. These two cases were, I may add, those of two Conservatives and Protestants—Mr. Christian and Baron Fitzgerald, who, according to universal acknowledgment, were two of the greatest judges that ever sat upon the Irish bench. In every other instance the judge passed first through a Parliamentary career. The man who was sure of a constituency was certain of a judgeship, even though he was ignorant of the very elements of law, and had rarely even received a brief.

The career of most of these politicians had a certain resemblance to that of Judge Keogh, though, of course, there were wanting the circumstances that gave such fatal results to his treachery, and were conceived in a minor key of lies and pledges. The barrister started as a patriot of rather a pronounced type, lamented the emigration, called for a Land Bill, and spoke disrespectfully of the Government. A typical case was that of the gentleman who is now known as Lord Fitzgerald. He was present, when a young barrister, at a banquet in Cork to the Lord-Lieutenant, and being called upon to make a speech, he astounded everybody and shocked the greater part of a servile audience by bursting into a violently national speech, and uttering things about the miseries and wrongs of Ireland which, though true, were not deemed such as Viceregal ears should hear or a rising and ambitious barrister should utter. But, in the midst of the interruptions of the loyal, Mr. Fitzgerald went on his way, and in the end became, or affected to become, so frenzied by his grief at his country's wrongs that he jumped on the table, and there continued his harangue. A young reporter who was present at this strange scene remarked to Serjeant Murphy—a cynical Irishman who had been a member of Parliament for many years, and had nothing in the shape of political corruption to learn—what a pity it was that a promising young barrister like Fitzgerald had ruined himself. 'Ruined,' said Murphy with a laugh; 'why, he has *made* himself!' And the prophecy was correct, for shortly afterwards Mr. Fitzgerald was a law officer of the Crown, then in due time was created a judge, and atoned for any patriotic passion, real or simulated, of his electioneering days by the fervour with which he has persecuted all national movements ever since. The reporter who had the conversation with Murphy just recorded reappears in these pages; he was Justin M'Carthy.

Another typical case is that of Mr. Justice Lawson. Mr. Lawson began life as a Conservative, and, as a Conservative, sought election for Trinity College—a Conservative stronghold. In his election address he made no mention of the Irish Church. When reproached with the omission, the nimble-tongued and unabashed lawyer was ready with an answer. He had made no mention of the Irish Church for the same reason that there was no mention of parricide in the Roman law. The attack on the Church by one of her sons was like the murder of a parent by a child—a crime too horrible to be contemplated, and, therefore, not to be mentioned. This was in 1857, when the Irish Church stood solid and unassailed. Four years passed away; the Disestablishment of the Irish Church became the cry of a great English party; and Mr. Lawson stood as an advocate of the destruction of the Church of his fathers. He was returned for Portarlington, and, as Attorney-General for Ireland, was one of the most prominent and active of the men who helped Mr. Gladstone in his great enterprise. Raised in time to the bench, he has never missed an opportunity of flouting and trampling on the people through whose votes he reached dignity and wealth. If still another example were required, there is the case of Mr. William (now Mr. Justice) O'Brien. Mr. O'Brien stood for Ennis in 1879 and 1880 as a Home Ruler. He was rejected; but he has since been elevated to the bench, and he has used all his strength and position to oppose the advent of Home Rule. Another point is worth noting in connection with these gentlemen. They were nearly all elected by small and therefore corrupt constituencies, and they obtained election by corruption. Judge Keogh bribed heavily and almost universally in Athlone. Judge Lawson was returned for Portarlington in 1865. The character of the constituency may be judged from the poll—Lawson, 46; Damer, 35. It is scarcely an exaggeration to say that every one of the 46 voters who gave Mr. Lawson Parliamentary existence and then judicial eminence was paid in Mr. Lawson's hard money for the service. Chief Justice Morris bribed heavily in Galway; the late Lord Chancellor of Ireland, Sir E. Sullivan, bribed heavily in Mallow. It is hard to say which of the two competitors in the old days for Dungarvan bribed the more heavily—Lord Justice Barry or Mr. Henry Mathews, her Majesty's Principal Secretary of State at the present moment.

I deem it necessary to bring out and to accentuate these facts for more than one reason. They are notorious in Ireland, but they are probably revelations to the people of England. Many of the judges whose names I have mentioned have been able to pass themselves off on English opinion as pure men of public spirit and patriotic purpose. They have nearly all of them distinguished themselves in times of trouble; for they have all been ready to deliver charges which can serve Irish Chief Secretaries with arguments and cases for coercion; and these charges have been taken by Englishmen as the pronouncements of calm, impartial, upright men. I have told enough to show that their utterances are those of violent partisans who hate the people they have betrayed and the principles they have abandoned with the characteristic hatred of the renegade. These facts will account for what might otherwise appear to be the unreasonable hatred of Irishmen for the Irish judges, and for attacks on these personages which often surprise and even shock Englishmen. The difference between the judicial benches of the two countries may be summed up as this : that in England the bench consists of the best of men, and in Ireland it is largely recruited from the worst.

This further reason I have for dwelling upon this painful topic. One of the points in the scheme of Mr. Gladstone which was most assailed—especially by Liberal Unionists—was the bestowal on the Irish Executive of the power to appoint the judges and the other persons entrusted with the administration of the law. Sir George Trevelyan, the most candid and the most courteous of the opponents of Mr. Gladstone's scheme, practically pledged himself to the acceptance of Home Rule, if this portion of Mr. Gladstone's plan were abandoned. The Irish members would probably have rejected the Bill if Sir George Trevelyan's support had been purchased by such a concession, and their rejection would have come from precisely the same reason as Sir George Trevelyan's acceptance ; that is to say, having exactly the same zeal for the maintenance of law and order as Sir George Trevelyan, they would regard that as the most potent instrument against law and order which Sir George Trevelyan thinks its most effective guarantee. Judges appointed by the imperial authority would be political judges, and political judges looking for approval to the politicians and public opinion, not of their own country, but of another. This would mean judges who would intrigue with English Ministers, and fight for English party, and appeal to the passions and the prejudices of the English people. We should have in Ireland a continuance of the pestilent race of Keoghs, and Lawsons, and O'Briens ; and this would mean the continuance of two of the worst features in the existing situation. It would mean that in all times of trouble we should have Irish judges making vehement political harangues to the order of English Ministers and English opinion, and such men would help, not to calm, but to infuriate the angry feelings between the two nations. And such judges would perpetuate that gulf between law and the Irish nation which at present exists, to the disturbance of Ireland and to the perplexity of England. In short, to have judges English-made would be to poison law at its source.

In the controversy, then, on this point we have two parties advocating two diametrically opposed plans for the same end. Whether native or foreign writers are the wisest and most trustworthy authorities in such a matter of domestic concern I leave the reader to decide, with this final word, that I vehemently deny that the Irish politicians have a desire less ardent, or an interest less keen, in proper safeguards, for the maintenance of law and order than the English politician of any school. Why should not the Irish politician want the maintenance of law and order under a Home Rule Administration ? The relations between landlord and tenant and the government of Irish local affairs by an Imperial Parliament are the only obstacles to the sympathy between the Irish nation and the law. Home Rule would remove the second obstacle ; the advent of Home Rule presupposes in most minds the settlement of the Land Question, and therefore the removal of the first obstacle. If Irish politicians wanted, therefore, to perpetuate the conflict between the law and the nation, it must be from an incurable love for crime, and in hostility to their own interests, to the best interests of the nation, and to the preservation of that self-government for which they are so ardently struggling. Some at least of the most prominent leaders of the Irish Party of to-day will have some share in the administration of a self-governed Ireland, and to put down disorder, to punish crime, to preserve peace, will be their business. That business well done will mean their political success; that business neglected will mean their political destruction.

Returning from this digression, though political profligacy was thus triumphant in this disastrous interval in the Irish struggle I am now describing, the struggle was not wholly abandoned. The old principle of the Tenant League, that the candidate should remain independent of both the English parties and fight for the cause of Ireland alone, was still preached. This principle was known as the policy of Independent Opposition. At every election Independent Opposition candidates were started, and occasionally they managed to get returned. But they were always few in number, and the number became smaller as time went on. As every army contains within its ranks a certain number who, being miserably base, become deserters, every Irish Party had its quota of corrupt or mean natures, that were in time transformed from Irish patriots into Liberal or Tory camp-followers. In this way many candidates, elected as members of an Independent Irish Opposition, became place-holders under some English Administration. The times were out of joint, and Independent Opposition never realized the proportions of a large and effective party.

There was one other influence which deserves to be mentioned. Throughout all these years of apparently hopeless struggle the *Nation* newspaper remained true to the principles of its founders. It preached in season and out of season the right of Ireland to national existence, of the tenant to protection, and Independent Opposition as the only means by which these great ends could be attained. In face of the British Government, unchecked by perfidious Parliamentarians, by omnipotent landlordism, by the narrow electorate sunk in open corruption, and of the masses buried in despair, A. M. Sullivan and his brother, T. D. Sullivan, worked on, hoped on. To these two brothers Ireland owes it that the lamp of national faith and hope was held aloft through this long and apparently endless night of eviction, hunger, emigration, triumphant tyranny, and political perfidy.

Meantime the moment has come again for surveying the position of Ireland from the standpoint of the Unionist Liberal and Tory. Ireland was now in the position which ought to appear the very ideal position to the Unionist and the Tory. As after the overthrow of O'Connell, so after the treason of Keogh, there was no party either of open violence or of a constitutional character seeking any change in the legislative relations between England and Ireland. On the contrary, the overwhelming majority of the representatives from Ireland were pledged and firm upholders of the Act of Union. Whiggery was in a position in Ireland equally ideal and equally prosperous. The Whigs had during all these years an almost undisputed monopoly of power. Lord Palmerston, in the period between 1855 and 1865, occupied a position of something like dictatorship in English politics; and Ireland supplied to his ranks a large majority of representatives whom no neglect of their country could madden into a patriotic outburst, and no insult could rouse to a moment of stalwart manhood. The National Party was extinct—murdered by Irish treason and Whig corruption : in its stead reigned the Whig Party, and to the Imperial Parliament the Irish people could alone look. It ought to follow, according to the conclusions which Unionist reasoning regards as inevitable, that this would be a period of halcyon and dazzling prosperity for the country. Proof has been given of how much prosperity there was, and now it is well to turn from the country advancing daily more rapidly to depopulation, with tyranny more and more aggressive, and see what the Imperial Assembly, with its Whig majority, was doing for the Irish people.

The tale of the Imperial Parliament may be summed up in a sentence. Every proposal for the reform of the land tenure, or of any other Irish abuse, met with steady and usually with contemptuous rejection.

In 1852 Mr. Sharman Crawford brought in a Tenant Right Bill once again; it was defeated on the second reading by 167 votes to 57. In November of the same year the Conservative Government were in power, and the first gleam of light broke the long eclipse of the question. It was an Irish Conservative that deserves the credit of making the attempt to settle the question. Mr. (afterwards Sir) Joseph Napier brought in a series of Bills ; three were in the interests of the landlords, one—the Tenant Compensation Bill—was in favour of the tenants. These Bills and a Bill by Mr. Sharman Crawford were referred to a committee. In February, 1853, the committee met, and, principally through the influence of Lord Palmerston, Sharman Crawford's Bill was rejected, and the Tenant Compensation Bill of the Conservative law officer was amended for the worse. This Bill passed the three stages in the House of Commons ; it was sent up to the House of Lords in August ; there was an immediate concourse of their lordships, and the Bill was hung up. In the following year (1854) their lordships resumed the consideration of the Bills. The three measures favourably changing the law for the landlords were accepted, the Tenants' Compensation Bill was rejected, and thus came to a final end the well-meant and bold effort of a Conservative statesman to give the tenant some compensation for the expenditure of his capital.

The Irish Tenant Righters still hoped on, and in 1855 the work of introducing Bills was again renewed, and again Irish demands met in each succeeding session the same reception. Serjeant Shee, who brought in a Bill, proposed that compensation should be given for improvements both retrospective and future. Lord Palmerston could not tolerate such an interference with the rights of property, and carried an amendment limiting the period to which compensation for improvement should be confined to twenty years. This destroyed the good that was in the Bill, and it was dropped. In 1856, again, Mr. George Henry Moore brought in a Bill ; its object was to extend the Ulster custom to all Ireland. It was read a second time on June 8. The next day Mr. Horsman, the Liberal Chief Secretary, announced that the Government intended to oppose it, and it was dropped. In 1857 Mr. Moore again brought forward a Bill, but he could not secure a day for its discussion, and it was dropped. In 1858 Mr. John Francis Maguire brought in a Bill ; it was defeated on the second reading, mainly through the influence of Lord Palmerston.

In 1860 the question was taken up by the Ministry, and they passed two Acts ; both were completely inoperative, one most fortunately so. Mr. Cardwell passed an Act giving limited owners a right to grant leases, but the terms were so severe and so unsuitable that nobody took advantage of it, and year after year returns showed the same result—in no single instance had anybody taken any advantage of the Act.[1]

The other Act passed in the same year, and known as Deasy's Act, was intended to make tenancies in Ireland entirely a matter of contract, and to deprive the tenants of all those rights which they had claimed from time immemorial, and which, though robbed of them by the landlord, they really were entitled to by the common law of England. It was doubtful whether, under that common law, the tenant was not entitled to compensation for his improvements.[2] Deasy's Act set all this at rest, for it declared that the tenant could lay no claim to any improvements, save such as had been made by express contract with the landlord. The meaning of this Act, if it had been carried out, would be that practically all the improvements made by the tenants throughout Ireland were by a stroke of the pen confiscated to the landlord. In successive sessions after this till 1868 the Land Question met with the same fortunes. All reform was steadily refused, and with the accompaniment of bitter insolence.

'It is indeed almost impossible,' justly remarks Mr. J. Cashel Hoey, 'to realize now the depth of imbecility and insolence which characterized the language of the Liberal statesmen of this period whenever they spoke of the affairs of Ireland.'

'Tenant right is landlord wrong!' exclaimed Lord Palmerston, when one Land Bill was brought before the House. 'It would be trifling with the House and an abuse of its forms, to read it a second time,' he said with regard to another. When Mr. Macguire obtained, in 1865, a Select Committee to inquire into the question, Mr. Roebuck was cheered from all parts of the House when he declared that the committee ought to be 'a committee composed of men of cross-examining powers, or, as I once heard a learned friend term it, eviscerating powers.' 'If a committee contained good cross-examiners,' replied Lord Palmerston, genially nodding to Mr. Roebuck, 'so much the better.' 'I am exceedingly glad,' exclaimed Mr. Cardwell, on June 23, 1865, 'that we are not about to separate under the imputation of having given an uncertain sound upon this subject. I wish,' he said, 'to express my individual opinion that, by whatever name it may be called, compulsory compensation for improvements effected against the will of the landlord is not a principle which is consistent with the rights of property. I am convinced,' he wound up in a final flourish, 'that it is more in accordance with the feeling of a high-spirited people that they should be spoken to in plain terms ; and I have that opinion of the Irish people that I do not think they would approve an insincere and uncertain course on an important subject like this, or that they would at all thank the committee for giving an ambiguous opinion upon it.'[3]

To the list of outbursts of insolent ignorance which Mr. Cashel Hoey has arrayed, many others could be added—some by the gentlemen whom he has quoted. Mr. Lowe, speaking in the debate on a small Tenant Right Bill in 1865, denounced any attempt to interfere between landlord and tenant in unmeasured terms :

[1] 'Is Ireland Irreconcilable?' (reprinted from the *Dublin Review*) by J. Cashel Hoey, p. 10.
[2] *See* Barry O'Brien, 'The Parliamentary History of the Irish Land Question,' 113.
[3] J. Cashel Hoey, 'Is Ireland Irreconcilable?' pp. 8-13.

'If the tenant chooses to improve the land, unless he takes the precaution to obtain the consent of the landlord—*whether he increases the value of the property or not*—he has no business to meddle with it. It is in the nature of a deposit on his hands, and he ought to return it as he received it. He receives it for a particular purpose, and for that purpose only ought he to use it. If he uses it for another purpose—to build a house on it, for instance—it may be a great improvement, but he has no right to do it ; it is beyond the contract he entered into.'[1]

'No attempt,' he again said, ' has been made to show that there is any case of practical grievance. . . . I do not believe that there is any really serious demand on the part of the tenantry of Ireland for this measure.' ('Oh ! oh !') ' I do not pretend to have any extensive knowledge of Ireland or its people. . . . I do not find, after hearing the evidence of a great number of gentlemen, that there was any such demand. . . .'[2]

But it was in Ireland itself that the Irish people were preached at in the most maddening form. While all around their country was being reduced to a desert, and the people were flying with curses from their shores, the English authorities kept proving that the country was never in a more prosperous position. Of this gospel there were three preachers prominent above all others—Archbishop Whately, Mr. Nassau Senior, and Lord Carlisle.

'If a piece of land is your property,' writes Archbishop Whately, 'you ought to be at liberty to dispose of it *like any other property* ; either to sell it, or to cultivate it yourself, or *to employ a bailiff and labourers to cultivate for you*, or to let it to a farmer.'

There the absolute claim of the landlord at this period to do what he liked with his own—to starve through rack-rent, to impoverish or even kill through eviction—was represented not as the greedy and heartless gospel of a dominant class, but as a great scientific truth.

' If you were to make a law for lowering rents,' writes Archbishop Whately, 'so that the land should still remain the property of those to whom it now belongs, but that they should not be allowed to receive more than so much an acre for it, *the only effect would be that the landlord would no longer let his land to a farmer, but would take it into his own hands, and employ a bailiff to look after it for him.*'

These words were written at a time when the Irish farmers were engaged in an effort to bring about the passing of a law that would lead to the ' lowering of rents,' and under which the landlords ' should not be allowed to receive more than so much an acre for it ' ; in other words, for the fair rent fixed by a Law Court which has been conferred by the Land Act of 1881. The children of these farmers were taught—and in the name of the Science of Political Economy—that the only effect of getting what they were demanding would be the utter ruin of their class. For it is a significant fact that the extracts I have quoted appear in one of the reading-books supplied by the Commissioners of National Education in the so-called National Schools of Ireland.[3]

The opinions of Mr. Senior are scattered over several volumes. His

---

[1] ' Hansard, vol. clxxxiii., p. 1079.   [2] *Ib.*, pp. 1082-1084.
[3] Fifth Reading Book, pp. 257, 262, Sixth Edition. These extracts were also, I believe, in the earlier editions.

'Journals, Conversations and Essays relating to Ireland' give the best insight into his own ideas and the ideas then dominant among English thinkers and statesmen. Mr. Senior spent the greater part of his time in Ireland among those landlords and agents who were remarkable above others for their ruthless persecution of the tenantry, and he quotes with much approval their nostrums for the cure of the Irish malady.

'Mr. Trench spoke highly of his cousin, Mr. Francis Trench,' writes Mr. Senior. 'His intelligence,' he said, 'may be estimated by what he has done. Soon after the Famine, the Duke of Leinster's tenants in Kildare threw up their holdings (amounting to about 2,000 acres in all), frightened by the potato failure and the poor-rates. Francis Trench had undertaken the agency a few years before. *He cleared the land by an extensive emigration, and advertised widely in the Scotch papers for tenants.* In time, the estate was relet. The rental, which had been £35,000 a year, was *by improved management, and by the falling in of very old leases,* raised to £45,000; *and the tenants (especially the Scotch) are doing well.*'

² Journals, vol. ii., pp. 85, 86. The italics are mine. This Mr. Trench, who found the conduct of his cousin so admirable, had acted on the same principle on more than one estate himself—in the district of Farney, for instance, in County Monaghan. This area, 70,000 acres in extent, was seized from the M'Mahon and given to the Earl of Essex. He relet it to Ever M'Mahon for £250 a year. The land became more valuable as time went on: in 1729 the estimated value was £2,000 a year; in 1769, the barony having been divided between two sisters, co-heiresses, the two estates were valued at £8,000 a year; and 'in the year 1843, and seventy-four years after the estimated value of the year 1769, I found, on my arrival at Carrickmacross, that the rent-roll of the two estates together amounted to upwards of £40,000 per annum, whilst the inhabitants had increased in such an extraordinary manner that by the census of 1841 the population amounted to something upwards of 44,107 souls.' ('Realities of Irish Life,' quoted in Sir John Gray's speech at Manchester, p. 25.) In 1867, the rent had increased still further to £54,833. 'No doubt,' said Mr. Trench in a Committee of the House of Commons, 1867 (quoted by Gray, p. 26), 'the rise in the price of produce and the value of land has done much in causing this increase. But the main cause, beyond all question, is that the barony had increased enormously and rapidly in population, and, as a consequent necessity, in cultivation. In 1633 there were only 38 tenants acknowledged in the barony, and though I believe there were a considerable number of undertenants, yet the population must have been very small. In 1841 there were upwards of 8,000 tenants, and the population amounted to 44,000 persons; in fact, a human being for every Irish acre of land. This vast population, driven to extremities to support themselves, gradually converted, *by their own labour*, the lands of the barony from being a waste unenclosed alder plain, into one of the most cultivated districts in Ireland, well enclosed arable land, while scarcely an acre of reclaimable land now lies unreclaimed.' 'Mr. Trench,' comments Sir John Gray (pp. 26, 27), 'admitted that 'the main cause, beyond all question,' of the conversion of the wild and waste alder plain into a tract of the richest and best cultivated land in Ireland, and the consequent increase of its value, was due to the energetic and unrelaxing toil of the tenant farmers who lived upon it, but who, when they had made the barren plain fruitful, and when there remained no more land to be reclaimed for the landlord's benefit, were felt to be an intolerable burden upon the landlord's hands, with whom they 'had to deal.' (Hear, hear, and cheers.) How these toiling industrious people were 'dealt with,' what became of these Celts who were permitted—'allowed,' was, he believed, the phrase—to increase and multiply in Farney, who, by their labour had changed the value of the estate from £250 a year to £40,000, increased, according to Mr Trench's sworn evidence, to £54,833 in 1867, he (Sir John Gray) could not tell, nor did he think it would be of much use now to inquire (hear, hear); but this he could tell, that the population of Farney, which was 44,107 in 1841, and Mr. Trench says it was 'something upwards' in 1843, when he came to rule over it, has in eight years of his rule been reduced to 31,519, and that in the same period 2,009 houses were levelled. (Cheers.) More than 12,588 of the 'surplus population' of that barony were moved out of it in eight years—some to America—some to Australia—some to the pauper's grave. (Hear, hear.) All were gone. As the sheep who had eaten down all the rape and trampled the refuse into the land could fertilize it no more and were sent to the shambles, so the Celts, at one time 'allowed to multiply' in Farney, could reclaim no more, and they, too, were sent off as useless incumberers of the ground. (Cheers.)

Again, Mr. Senior records a conversation with a gentleman disguised as 'Dr. G.' They are talking about the land question.

'Well,' said Dr. G., 'we have got our Poor Law, and it is a great instrument for giving the victory to the landlords. Another and a still more powerful instrument is emigration, and it is one never used on such a scale before. No friend of Ireland can wish the war to be prolonged—*still less, that it should end by the victory of the tenants; for that would plunge Ireland into barbarism worse than that of the last century. The sooner Ireland becomes a grazing country, with the comparatively thin population which a grazing country requires, the better for all classes.*'

Mr. Senior is naturally delighted with such sound opinions. 'Earnestly wishing, as you do,' he says to Dr. G., 'to see Ireland a grazing country, and, therefore, thinly populated as respects its agricultural population,' etc.[1]

The gospel that emigration was the real cure for Ireland had an even more potent advocate in the Lord-Lieutenant of the period. From 1855 to 1858 Lord Carlisle was Viceroy, and again from 1859 till 1864. Two extracts will suffice to show the crass gospel of this enlightened ruler.

'Nor can I be debarred,' said Lord Carlisle, speaking at the Annual Cattle Show of the Royal Agricultural Society in Athlone, on August 7, 1855, 'even by the golden promise of those harvests which now gladden our eyes, from urging you to bear in mind, what Nature in her wise economy seems specially to have fitted this island for, is to be the mother of flocks and herds; to be, if I may say so, the larder and dairy of the world; to send rations of beef and bales of bacon to our armies wherever they are; and to send firkins of butter to every sea and harbour of the habitable globe.'[2]

In a speech at the cattle show at Cork (July 5, 1860), and indeed in nearly every one of his speeches, the same gospel was laid down, that the more people left Ireland the more prosperous the country was, and that the great ideal of legislation was to change as much of the land as possible into pasture.

'Cattle,' he said, 'above all things, seem to be rendered, by the conditions of soil and climate, the most appropriate stock for Ireland.... Hence, the great hives of industry in England and Scotland across the Channel can draw their frequent shiploads of corn from more southern and drier climates, but they must have a constant dependence in Ireland for a supply of meat.... With reference to the general concerns of Ireland, I feel I am justified in speaking to you, upon the whole, in the terms of congratulation and hopefulness.... Then .... the mud-cabins of Ireland amounted in 1841, not twenty years ago, to 491,000; they have now diminished to 125,000.[3] The number of emigrants, which had been gradually decreasing for some years, has somewhat increased in the last and present years....

[1] Journal, vol. ii., pp. 282, 283. In justice to Mr. Senior, it should be said that he was perfectly impartial as to all nationalities in his doctrine, that the fewer people were on the land the better. In the same conversation he speaks of the 'absorption of the surplus population of the Highlands of Scotland, when black cattle and sheep took the place of men as 'one of the largest and most beneficent clearings on record' (*ib.*, p. 282).
[2] 'The Speeches, Lectures, and Poems, etc., of the Earl of Carlisle,' pp. 158, 159. By J. J. Gaskin.
[3] He does not say what had become of the occupants.

They now comprise many young people of both sexes who have been comparatively well educated, and who hope to find in a less crowded community a better market for their industry, and a more adequate demand for their natural and acquired intelligence ; but I conceive *this is not a symptom*, with whatever immediate and local inconvenience it may no doubt be attended, *at which, viewed at large, we ought to repine.*'[1]

A few statistics will bring clearly before the mind of the reader how the policy of expatriation was working :—

Emigration from Ireland.

1849-1860	1,551,000
1861-1870	867,000[2]

And another table will be still more instructive : it is the ratio of the ages of the emigrants[3] :—

Under 15 years	15 per cent.
15 to 35 ,,	75 ,,
Over 35 ,,	10 ,,

Thus it will be seen that only half the case is stated when it is said that emigration—with great assistance from hunger, plague and eviction—within the years 1845 and 1885 has reduced the population by nearly one-half : the half that emigrated was the better, the half that remained was the worse, half of the population. Seventy-five per cent. of the emigrants were between fifteen and thirty-five—the best years in the life of men or women. 'During the seven months of the year' (1863), wrote the *Times*,[4] '80,000 chiefly young men and women, have left Ireland, most of them for ever They have gone off with money in their pockets, and with strong limbs and stout hearts. *They have left behind the ailing, the weak, and the aged.*'

There is no passion like the suppressed passion of statistics ; and I leave these figures to tell their own moral. Meantime, there was one force further which must be reckoned among the factors that produced the temper of Ireland at this epoch.

The sight of a race rushing from its native land in millions might, it would be thought, have touched even enemies as marking the very height of tragic suffering. But such was not the effect upon the journalism of England. As the Irish peasants left their country in curses and tears, the English newspapers seized every opportunity of mocking at their sufferings and their demands for the reform of the laws by which their misery and their enforced exile were produced. The *Times* and other English journals over and over again pointed with exultation to the probability that the Irish race would be annihilated in Ireland, and that the country would then be entirely seized by the population of the stronger country.

'If this goes on long' (it wrote of the emigration in 1860), 'as it is continuing to go on, Ireland will become very English, and the United States very Irish. When an English agriculturist takes a farm in Galway or Kerry, he will take English labourers with him.'[5]

'The Irish will go' (it wrote in 1863). 'English and Scotch settlers must

---

[1] 'The Speeches, Lectures, and Poems, etc. of the Earl of Carlisle,' pp. 178-181.
[2] Mulhall's ' Dictionary of Statistics,' p. 168.
[3] *Ib.*   [4] Quoted in *Nation*, Oct. 24, 1863.
[5] Quoted in *Irishman*, May 12, 1860.

be speedily got in their places, for Great Britain will suffer, the British markets will go.'[1]

'The Celt' (it wrote again in 1865) 'goes to yield to the Saxon. This island of 160 harbours, with its fertile soil, with noble rivers and beautiful lakes, with fertile mines and riches of every kind, is being cleared quietly for the interests and luxury of humanity.'[2]

This extract, finally, from the leading English journal:

'Curran used to say that his countrymen made very bad subjects, but much worse rebels. The *mot* was a good one in its own day, but it has not lost its point. . . . Comparative anatomists of political societies might, by a close study of it, perhaps make a complete sketch of the social monstrosity which such a phrase would fit—a discontented, hungry, empty-bellied community, begging for alms; too idle to work, too shrewd to fight, too profoundly convinced of the dishonesty of its own members to do aught but shout and roar and threaten and beg.'[3]

An Irish priest, lamenting the wrongs of Ireland, was described in the *Daily Telegraph* as 'a surpliced ruffian;' a Catholic Archbishop, mourning over the emigration, was described by the *Saturday Review* as regretting the departure 'of the demons of assassination and murder.'

'The Lion of St. Jarlath's' (said the article of the *Saturday Review*, November 28, 1863) 'has growled in grievous dudgeon that bucolic tastes are prevailing in Ireland. Archbishop John of Tuam surveys with an envious eye what, in a Churchman, it seems rather profane to style the Irish Exodus; and in a letter addressed to Mr. Gladstone . . . *he sighs over the departing demons of assassination and murder*. Like his friend Mr. Smith O'Brien, he regrets the loss of the raw materials of treason and sedition. Ireland, he says, is relapsing into a desert, tenanted by lowing herds instead of howling assassins. So complete is the rush of departing marauders, whose lives were profitably employed in shooting Protestants from behind a hedge, that silence reigns over the vast solitude of Ireland. . . . Ireland has long been seething in the flames of misrule and agitation and sedition. Ireland is boiling over, and the scum flows across the Atlantic; and the more the Archbishop and the like of him blow at the fire, the more the scum will boil over. It can be spared, and the many excellencies of the Irish people will only become the more excellent by the present process of defecation.'

The people who were thus described were as like the pictures drawn of them as real human beings usually are to the portraits of political opponents. They were attached to the country in which they were not permitted to live with a patriotism remarkable for its fervour even among the many passionate patriotisms of the world; and their family ties were peculiarly close and strong. A look at the railway-stations, and then at the fields, of Ireland would have brought to any sympathetic eye the inner meaning of the terrible and widespread tragedy that was there being enacted. At every railway-station crowds of people were to be seen locked in each other's arms, shouting aloud in their grief, and exchanging everlasting farewells. What these partings meant could only be understood by those who know and sympathize with the home-life of the Irish poor. There is perhaps no

---

[1] Quoted in *Nation*, Nov. 4, 1863.   [2] *Ib.*, Aug. 26, 1865.
[3] *Ib.*, Nov. 6, 1858.

country in the world where the sense of the duty of the members of a family to each other is held more sacred. How sacred the feeling is receives yearly proof in the vast sums which are sent over out of hardly-earned wages by the Irish in America to the Irish at home. Then, too, the authority of the head of the house is carried in Ireland still to extremes that in most countries are as dead and ancient as the other ways and ideas of the patriarchal period. As a result, the child has less self-confidence at years comparatively mature than is acquired in other countries at a much earlier age ; and the parent looks at a grown young man or woman as having all the innocence and helplessness of childhood. The sense of separation was, accordingly, terribly embittered by the awful apprehension for the future of those children cast on the unknown and terrible temptations of the great world. The latent sense that was in the mind of the father or mother who followed, panting and sobbing, the train, was that the engine with its accursed haste was carrying off the loved ones to want or vice, to early and painful, or perchance shameful death amid strange faces. It was this factor in the separation that gave to it much of its poignant grief and tragic import. To many a cabin in Ireland emigration meant that the light of a life had gone out, and that aged parents never more knew a bright or happy hour.

Over the country is to be seen to this day the marks of this dreadful and terrible time. There are many parts of Ireland to-day that still look as if they had just been passed over by an invading army led by a commander with the spirit of Attila. The traveller can pass for miles through some of the best land in the County Meath, and see a country on which not a single human being remains ; the frequent ruin speaks of a vanished population as effectually scattered as the populations of those entombed cities in Italy, the ruins of which to-day with such compelling silence tell the tale of tumultuous life reduced to stillness and death.

Such, then, was the condition of Ireland in the interval between 1855 and 1865. It is one of the saddest and most dreadful stories in all history. It is the spectacle, under the semblance of law, and without any particular noise, and certainly without attracting any particular attention, of an ancient and brave nation being slowly but surely wiped out of existence. Not a section, or a class, or a percentage, but the whole people were being swept away, their land was yearly becoming more desolate, and all the probabilities pointed to the near advent of the period when the country would be one great sheep and cattle farm, with the vast desert broken only at long intervals by the herd.

Meantime the Imperial Parliament looked on and did nothing ; the rulers declared that the hellish work was good ; the press of the dominant country hissed out triumphant hate ; and popular representation had fallen into the hands of self-seekers, heartless, lying, and base. It is in such periods that a desperate spirit is evoked and is necessary. The masses of the people were still sound, and there were among the population chosen spirits who were resolved to show that the struggle, which had been maintained through so many centuries, was not even yet at an end ; that, if the Irish nation were to be murdered, at least her people would try to make one final and desperate stand ; and that her political life would find other types than the pestilent race of Rabagas.

CHAPTER VII.

REVOLUTION.

I HAVE written very clumsily if the reader, whatever be his nationality, does not now understand the forces which produced Fenianism. This movement, like many other movements before and since, took its rise in America, where the men evicted under such circumstances as I have described, daily brooded over the means whereby they might avenge their personal and political wrongs. Meagher and Mitchel, after escaping from the penal settlements to which they had been condemned after the failure of 1848, supplied the Irish of America with names and ability to keep alive and to inspire the movement for the rescue of Ireland. To America, too, had gone James Stephens, who as a young man had stood by Smith O'Brien at Ballingarry. Stephens was in Ireland in 1858, and he visited, among other places, the town of Skibbereen, in which had been recently established a society half literary, half political, and the chief spirit of which was a man whose name was destined to be long afterwards a name of horror and of fear. This was Jeremiah O'Donovan, as he was originally called, and Jeremiah O'Donovan (Rossa) as he is now better known. Between O'Donovan and Stephens an interview took place, at which Stephens informed O'Donovan that the Irish in America were willing and anxious to supply arms for insurrection to so many Irishmen as would be enrolled in a revolutionary conspiracy in Ireland. The bargain was sealed, and the movement made some way, but was confined in its operations to the south-west districts of the country. Finally the Government were informed of the position of matters, and the conspirators were put on their trial. Many of them were convicted, among others O'Donovan (Rossa), but the Crown, despising the movement as futile, did not insist on heavy punishments being inflicted on any of the conspirators.

The Irish-American revolutionaries now set to work again, and the business of propagandism continued to go on actively. No particular progress was made, however, and probably the movement would not have assumed formidable proportions but for the outbreak of the Civil War in America. This portentous event brought into actual warfare many thousands of the exiled Irish, made them familiar with the use of arms, and thereby gave a stimulus to the idea of liberating Ireland through insurrection. An accidental occurrence gave the propagandists of the revolution an immense start. Terence Bellew McManus, one of the '48 leaders, having, like the others, escaped from Australia, settled and died in San Francisco in 1861. It was resolved that his remains should be buried in his native country. The body was conveyed across America with every circumstance of pomp and solemnity. To Ireland at last came the funeral procession that had thus swept solemnly across the vast continent and the wide expanse of ocean. Such a spectacle was well calculated to inspire the imagination and to stimulate the patriotic passions of the people. The coffin was landed at Queenstown on October 30, 1861, and the funeral took place in Dublin on Sunday, November 10. Fifty thousand people followed the remains; at least as many lined the streets; and the procession solemnly paused, with uncovered heads, at every spot sacred to the memory of those who had fought and died in the good fight against English tyranny. Finally, as night closed in, the body was deposited in Glasnevin Cemetery.

From this time forward the advance of Fenianism was extraordinarily rapid. Organizers went all over the island, swearing in men by the dozen, sometimes by the score, every night. In one quarter the conspiracy met with unexpected and almost inexplicable success. This was in the army. At that time there were in Ireland a large number of Irish regiments. Several of the ablest of the Fenians became soldiers for the purpose of gaining recruits to their ranks. The calculations of the Fenians themselves, even in these days of cool reflection, is that by 1865 they had enrolled in their ranks, amongst the British army alone, 15,000 men.

With the close of the American war hundreds of Irish-American officers were released from their duties. They poured into Ireland, and the air became thick with rumours of the impending rising. Meantime, the Government were kept well informed of everything that was going forward by their spies in the enemy's camp. The *Irish People*, the organ of the revolutionaries, was seized on September 15, 1865. Mr. Luby, Mr. John O'Leary, and O'Donovan (Rossa) were arrested, and in the following November Mr. Stephens. Before the latter was brought to trial he succeeded, by the aid of two prison officials, in escaping from Richmond Gaol. Parliament promptly suspended the Habeas Corpus Act, and throughout the country the leaders of the movement were seized and imprisoned.

When these prisoners were brought to trial, there occurred the spectacle of such ghastly familiarity to the student of Irish history. The criminal courts at Green Street and throughout the country were for months employed in the trial of prisoners, and man after man was convicted and sentenced to penal servitude.

It was one of the many scandals in these trials that the most prominent judge in trying them was Judge Keogh. Of all men and forces that created Fenianism, Judge Keogh was the most potent. It was his treason that broke down all faith in constitutional agitation, and it was the want of faith in constitutional agitation that drove men to the desperate risks to life and liberty of a physical-force movement. It was the treason of Judge Keogh that, destroying the Tenant Right movement of 1852, brought the dread epoch of rack-renting, eviction, and widespread emigration, and it was the horrors of these things that produced the frenzied temper of which revolutionary movements are born. The columns of the *Irish People*, the organ of Fenianism, supply abundant testimony of this. Whenever a voice was raised in favour of constitutional agitation and constitutional agitators, the *Irish People* mentioned the names of Keogh and Sadleir, and there was no reply. The original scandal of appointing such a man to preside over the Fenian trials was aggravated by his conduct of the cases. He bullied the prisoners so flagrantly that at last some even of the English press cried shame. And occasionally he poured upon some unhappy creature he was about to send to penal servitude for several years the plenteous vials of his abundant Billingsgate.

But the conspiracy was not yet dead. The men in America still cherished the idea that an armed rising was necessary and possible, and sent encouraging messages home. Stephens publicly pledged himself that there would be a rising in 1866. 1866 went by, and no insurrection came. At last the conductors of the movement at home became desperate, and it was resolved that, whether assistance came from America or not, the insurrection should be attempted. Sporadic efforts occurred all over the country; men assembled to the word of command, and met at the trysting-place, but they found no arms there, and were easily dispersed.

Another series of State trials followed, at which the chief spirits of the movement were again sentenced in batches to penal servitude. The movement was now apparently extinct, but before its conclusion it was marked by two incidents that have exercised a deep influence on succeeding events. Much of the strength of Fenianism lay among the Irish population of England, and emissaries were constantly passing between the two countries. It thus came to pass that some of the leaders were arrested and lodged in English gaols. One of these, General Burke, was incarcerated in Clerkenwell prison. It was resolved that he should be rescued. The task was entrusted to ignorant hands. A barrel of gunpowder was placed in a narrow street by the side of the wall in that part of the prison where General Burke was supposed to be exercising. The wall was blown down. The prisoner, fortunately for himself, was not in that portion of the prison at all; if he had been, his death would have been certain. A number of unfortunate people of the poorer classes, living in tenement houses opposite the prison, were the victims. Twelve were killed, and a hundred and twenty maimed. This occurred on December 13, 1867. A man named Barrett was tried and convicted, and was hanged in front of Newgate prison.

The second event brought out with equal emphasis the hold which the insurrectionary movement had taken upon the Irish in England, and the reality and proportions of the danger to the empire. The conduct of the movement had passed, after the arrest of Stephens, and during his absence in America, into the hands of Colonel Kelly. In the autumn of 1867 Colonel Kelly was in Manchester, at a Fenian meeting. As he was returning home with a companion, Captain Deasy, the two were arrested on suspicion of loitering for a burglarious purpose. They gave false names, but were soon discovered to be the formidable leader of the conspiracy and one of his chief lieutenants. The Fenian organization was at the time extremely strong in Manchester, and a rescue was resolved upon. On Wednesday, September 18, 1867, the prison van, while being driven to the county gaol at Salford, was attacked at the railway arch which spans Hyde Road at Bellevue. A party of thirty rushed forward with revolvers, shot one of the horses, and the police, being unarmed, fled. An attempt was made to open the door of the van with hatchets, hammers, and crowbars, but this failed; and meantime the police came back, accompanied by a large crowd. Sergeant Brett, the policeman inside, had the keys, which some of the party, opening the ventilator, asked him to give up. He refused; a pistol was placed to the keyhole for the purpose of blowing open the lock; the bullet passed through Brett's body, and he fell mortally wounded. The keys were taken out of his pocket and handed out by one of the female prisoners; Kelly and Deasy were released, and hurried off into concealment, and were never recaptured. Meantime, a crowd had gathered, several of the rescuing party were seized and almost lynched; one of them, William Philip Allen, was almost stoned to death. Soon after William Philip Allen, Michael Larkin, Thomas Maguire, Michael O'Brien (alias Gould), and Edward O'Meara Condon (alias Shore) were tried for the wilful murder of Sergeant Brett. They were convicted, and all sentenced to be hanged. The trial took place amid a hurricane of public passion and panic. The evidence was tainted, and was soon unexpectedly proved to be utterly untrustworthy. Thomas Maguire, tried on the same evidence, identified by the same witnesses, convicted and sentenced by the same judges, was proved so conclusively innocent that he was released a few days after his trial. Allen and the others declared solemnly that they had not intended to hurt Sergeant Brett. Condon, in speaking, used a phrase that has become historic: 'I have nothing,' he said, in concluding his speech, 'to regret or to take back. I can only say, "God save Ireland."' His companions advanced to the front of the dock, and, raising their hands, repeated the cry, 'God save Ireland.' Maguire was released, and Condon was reprieved. For some time there was a hope that the breakdown of the trial in the case of Maguire would result in a reprieve in the cases of the other three. But the authorities ultimately decided that the three men should be hanged, and on the morning of November 23, 1867, Allen, Larkin, and O'Brien were executed in front of Salford gaol. A short time afterwards their bodies were buried in quick-lime, in unconsecrated ground, within the precincts of the prison.

It is impossible, even after the considerable interval that has elapsed, to forget the impression which this event produced upon the Irish people. In most of the towns in Ireland vast multitudes walked in funeral processions through the streets to testify the terrible depths of their grief. A few days after the execution, Mr. T. D. Sullivan wrote the poem with the refrain uttered from the dock, 'God save Ireland !' and wherever in any part of the globe there is now an assembly of Irishmen, social or political—a concert in Dublin, a convention at Chicago, or a Parliamentary dinner in London—the proceedings regularly close with the singing of 'God save Ireland.'

To one Irishman, then a youth, living in the country-house of his fathers, and deeply immersed in the small concerns of a squire's daily life, the execution of the Manchester martyrs was a new birth of political convictions. To him, brooding from his early days over the history of his country, this catastrophe came to crystallize impressions into conviction, and to pave the way from dreams to action. It was the execution of Allen, Larkin, and O'Brien that gave Mr. Parnell to the service of Ireland.

An indirect effect of all these startling occurrences was to force the attention of the English people and their Parliament upon the Irish Question. In other words, the evils that had been allowed to eat out the vitals of Ireland for so long a period amid apathy tempered by scoffs, began to attract attention when Irishmen abandoned the paths of constitutional and tranquil agitation, and sought remedy in conspiracy and force. By several circumstances the Irish Church was pushed to the front, the Irish Members began to actively discuss it in Parliament, and finally, as everybody knows, after a fierce struggle and a General Election, the Church was disendowed and disestablished.

This great reform turned attention once more to Parliamentary methods; the spirit of apathy, which had given the fruits of electoral contests without care or regret to the first adventurer, was broken, and people began to think again that it was of some importance whether an honest man or a rogue should be sent to Westminster to represent Ireland. The awakening of Ireland from the long slumber since 1845 had begun, and the awakening of Ireland means the revival of an agitation for self-government. Another movement was destined to add a new and even more potent force to the growing cause of Home Rule. Though the Church Question had been pushed to the front, the Land Question still retained its place as the supreme issue to the majority of the population. Throughout the country mass meetings were held, and the demand of the farmers was put forward with thunderous emphasis. The demand was for the 'Three F's'—

fixity of tenure, free sale, and fair rent; and the farmers had heard this demand advocated so often, had shouted themselves hoarse by so many hillsides in uttering it, had been so stimulated and encouraged by the sight of their battalions in regular array, Sunday after Sunday, and in county after county, that by the time Parliament met they regarded the 'Three F's' as having already passed from the region of popular platforms to that of Parliamentary debates and of statute law.

The introduction of Mr. Gladstone's Bill was the mournful awakening that came to all these splendid dreams, for the measure of the Prime Minister stopped far short indeed of the 'Three F's.' The sentimental forces which had been gathering in such might in favour of self-government were now materially increased by the accession of the mighty battalions of the disillusioned and disappointed farmers of the country.

But the foundation of the Home Rule movement, curiously enough, was laid, not in obedience to the impulse of the masses of the people, but in the rancour of a small and a defeated minority of the population. The Disestablishment of the Church had brought back a certain proportion of the Protestant population to that spirit of nationality which had found its most eloquent advocates in the exclusively Protestant Parliament of the ante-Union days. A certain number of very moderate gentlemen of the Catholic faith saw in a movement which Protestant Conservatives were able to support elements which need not alarm the most milk-and-water adherents of the doctrine of Nationality. There were more stable elements in constitutional agitators who had fought doggedly on for a Native Parliament through the long eclipse of national faith between 1855 and that hour, like Mr. A. M. Sullivan; and in some men—such as Mr. O'Kelly, M.P. for Roscommon—who, appearing under disguised names, sought, after the breakdown of their efforts to free Ireland by force, whether there was any chance of success through Parliamentary action. The latter element took up this attitude at that period with a certain amount of trepidation, and at some personal risk; for the distrust of constitutional agitation, and the hatred of constitutional agitators, still survived among the relics of Fenianism, and the new movement was looked upon by them with the same latent and perilous distrust as all its predecessors. The meeting was held on May 19, 1870, in the Bilton Hotel, Sackville Street, Dublin.

At this meeting were present Conservatives as well known as Mr. Purdon, then Conservative Lord Mayor of Dublin; Mr. Kinahan, who had been High Sheriff; and Major Knox, proprietor of the *Irish Times*, a Conservative organ; nor should the name be omitted of a gentleman who was for a considerable time to play a prominent part in the new movement— Colonel, then Captain, Edward R. King-Harman. Mr. Butt was the chief speaker, and on his proposition, and without a dissentient voice, the resolution was passed,

'That it is the opinion of this meeting that the true remedy for the evils of Ireland is the establishment of an Irish Parliament with full control over our domestic affairs.'

A new organization was founded under the name of 'The Home Government Association of Ireland.' Before long, the movement spread with the rapidity which always comes to movements founded on indestructible aspirations. Now, just as in 1843, the people had only to see a movement in favour of self-government to flock enthusiastically to its ranks. Then the

Prime Minister had passed another measure which transcended in importance any other of the great Acts which made his first Premiership so momentous an epoch in the resurrection of Ireland. This was the Ballot Act. For the first time in his history the Irish tenant could vote without the fear of eviction, with the attendant risks of hunger, exile, or death. The Ballot Act as an act of emancipation to the Irish tenant in a sense far more real than the Emancipation Act of 1829. From the passage of that Ballot Act is to be dated the era when, for the first time in her history, the real voice of Ireland had some opportunity of making itself heard. The new force advanced against all opponents, and every constituency that had its choice declared with unfaltering fidelity in favour of the National candidate.

In four bye-elections the Home Rule candidates triumphed over every obstacle. The struggle between Whiggery and Home Rule was now over. Ireland had definitely declared for the new movement. This will be the place to tell the end of Judge Keogh. In the year 1878 the sensational rumour reached Dublin that he had developed symptoms of insanity in Belgium, whither he had been removed for the benefit of his health, and that he had attempted to kill his attendant and himself. The rumour proved correct. From this period forth he seems never to have recovered full possession of his senses, and gradually sank. He was removed to Bingen, and there died on September 30, 1878. An Englishman, with characteristic appreciation of Irish character, is said to have placed a stone over his remains with the inscription, '*Justum et tenacem propositi virum.*' The country which he had betrayed and ruined, on the other hand, congratulated itself in not having received his remains. Indeed, some desperate spirits had resolved that the remains should never rest in hallowed Irish ground; a plot was complete for seizing the body during the funeral and throwing it into the Liffey.

CHAPTER VIII.

ISAAC BUTT.

ISAAC BUTT, the leader of the new movement, was the son of a Protestant clergyman of the North of Ireland. The place of his birth was near the Gap of Barnesmore, a line of hills which is rarely, if ever, without shadow —not unlike Butt's own life. It was one of his theories that people born amid mountain scenery are more imaginative than the children of the plains. His own nature was certainly imaginative in the highest degree, with the breadth and height of imaginative men, and also with the doubtings, despondency, and the dread of the Unseen.

For many years he stood firmly by the principles of Orange Toryism, and he had the career which then belonged to every young Irish Protestant of ability. He went to Trinity College, which at the time presented large prizes, and presented them to those only who had the good luck to belong to the favoured faith. Butt's advancement was rapid. He was not many years a student when he was raised to a Professorship of Political Economy.

When he went to the Bar his success came with the same ease and rapidity. He was but thirty-one years of age, and had been only six years at the Bar, when he was made a Queen's Counsel. In politics, however, he had made his chief distinction. It will be remembered that when O'Connell sought to obtain a declaration in favour of Repeal of the Union from the newly emancipated Corporation of Dublin, Butt was selected by his co-religionists, young as he was, to meet the Great Liberator, and his speech was as good a one as could be made on the side of the maintenance of the Union; and many a year after, when he had become the leader of a Home Rule Party, was quoted against him by Sir Michael Hicks-Beach, the Irish Chief Secretary of the period.

Of great though irregular industry, deeply devoted to study, with a mind of large grasp and a singularly retentive memory, he was intimately acquainted with all the secrets of his profession; and throughout his life was acknowledged to be a fine lawyer. He represented in Parliament both Youghal in his native county, and Harwich in England. His entrance into Parliament aggravated many of his weaknesses. It separated him from his profession in Dublin, and thereby increased his already great pecuniary liabilities. His character in many respects was singularly feeble. Some of his weaknesses leaned to virtue's side, and many of the stories told of him suggest a resemblance to the character of Alexandre Dumas père. He borrowed largely and lent largely, and often in the midst of his sorest straits lavished on others the money which he required himself, and which often did not belong to him. Throughout his life he was, as a consequence, pursued by the bloodhound of vast and insurmountable debt. At least once he was for several months in a debtors' prison, and there used to be terrible stories—even in the days when he was an English member of Parliament—of unpaid cabmen and appearances at the police-courts.

But he was a man of supreme political genius; one of those whose right to intellectual eminence is never questioned, but willingly conceded without effort on his side, without opposition on the part of others. The irregularities of his life shut him out from official employment, and he saw a long series of inferiors reach to position and wealth while he remained poor and neglected. There is a considerable period of his life which is almost total eclipse. There came an Indian summer when he returned to the practice of his profession in Ireland, and once more joined in the political struggles of his countrymen.

Mr. Gladstone's dissolution of 1874 came upon Butt with the same bewildering surprise as upon so many other people. That election found him in a cruel difficulty. On the one hand, the country was beyond all question with him; he knew that he could count on the masses to vote in favour of self-government as securely as every other popular leader who has ever been able to make the appeal. The majority of the constituencies were ready, he knew, to return Home Rule candidates; and thus the General Election afforded him the opportunity of creating a greater Home Rule Party. But, on the other hand, elections cannot be fought without money; elections were dearer then even than they are now, and Butt wanted to fight, not a seat here and there, but a whole national campaign; for three-fourths of the constituencies could be won by a Home Rule candidate if a Home Rule candidate could be brought forward. For so immense a work he had nothing to fall back on but a few hundreds of pounds in the funds of the Home Rule Association, and he himself was at one of his recurrent periods of desperate need. He was arrested for debt on the very morning of the day when, learning of the dissolution, he was making his plan of campaign, though the matter was arranged in some way or other, he had to fly to England, and this prevented him from exercising that personal supervision over the General Election which is absolutely required from the leader of a movement.

Butt could only adopt, under the circumstances, a policy of compromise, and make the best out of bad but inevitable material. Where there was a real and genuine Home Rule candidate ready to come forward, and able to bear the expenses of an election contest, Butt fought the seat. In this way he was able to bring into public life many earnest men who had for years found it impossible to take any Parliamentary part in rescuing the country. His party contained A. M. Sullivan, Mr. Biggar, Mr. Richard Power, Mr. Sheil, and several others, who were really devoted to the National cause. On the other hand, he had to accept, in constituencies where he had not the men or the money to fight, the 'deathbed repentance,' as it was called, of men who had grown gray in the service of one or other of the English parties. These time-worn Whigs or Tories—such as Sir Patrick O'Brien and Sir George Bowyer—of course swallowed the Home Rule pledge. Some of the new men were little better. The race of Rabagas had been scotched but not killed, and among Butt's recruits was a certain proportion of lawyers, who were as ready as any of their predecessors to sell themselves and their principles to the highest bidder. Many of them have since received office; all of the tribe have expected and asked it. It was, then, a very mixed party Butt had gathered around him—a party of patriots and of place-hunters, of men young, earnest, and fresh for struggle, and of men physically exhausted and morally dead, a party of life-long Nationalists and of veteran lacqueys. There was a tragic contrast between such a party and the renewed and sublime and noble hopes of the nation. Of the 103 Irish members, sixty were returned pledged to vote for the entire rearrangement of the legislative relations between the two countries.

Such was the party; and now how was it with the leader? His weakness with regard to pecuniary matters has been already touched upon; he had, besides, all the other foibles, as well as the charms, of an easy-going, good-natured, pliant temperament. Though his faults were grossly exaggerated—for instance, many intimates declare that they never saw him, even during the acquaintance of years, once under the influence of drink—he had, unquestionably, made many sacrifices on the altars of the gods of indulgence. It may be that with him, as with so many others, the pursuit of pleasure was but the misnomer for the flight from despair. He was all his life troubled by an unusually slow circulation, and it may be that the central note of his character was melancholy. In his early days he was a constant contributor to the *Dublin University Magazine*, and his tales have a vein of the morbid melancholy that runs through the youthful letters of Alfred de Musset. Allusion has been already made to his imaginativeness: this imaginativeness did much to weaken his resolve. Curious stories are told of the superstitions that ran through his nature. Though a Protestant, he used to carry some of the religious symbols—medals, for instance—which Catholics use, and he would not go into a law court without his medals. There are still more ludicrous stories of his standing appalled or delighted before such accidents as putting on his clothes the wrong way, and other trivialities. Then, the demon of debt, which had haunted him all his life, now stood menacing behind him. He had just re-established himself in a considerable practice when he again entered Parliament, and membership of Parliament is entirely incompatible with the retention of his entire practice by an Irish barrister. He was, throughout his leadership, divided between a dread dilemma : either he had to neglect Parliament, and then his party was endangered ; or neglect his practice, and then bring ruin on himself and a family entirely unprovided for, deeply loving and deeply loved. There is no Nemesis so relentless as that which dogs pecuniary recklessness ; the spendthrift is also the drudge ; and in his days of old age, weakness, and terrible political responsibilities, Butt had to fly between London and Dublin, to stop up o' nights, alternately reading briefs and drafting Acts of Parliament : to make his worn and somewhat unwieldy frame do the double work, which would try the nerves and strength of a giant with the limber joints and freshness of early youth. And at this period Butt's frame was worn, though to outward appearances he was still vigorous. The hand of incurable disease already held him tight, and the dark death, of which he had so great a horror, was not many years off ; finally, in 1874, he was sixty-one years of age. On the other hand, he had great qualities of leadership. He was unquestionably a head and shoulders above all his followers, able though so many of them were, and was, next to Mr. Gladstone, the greatest Parliamentarian of his day. Then he had the large toleration and the easy temper that make leadership a light burden to followers ; and the burden of leadership must be light when—as in an Irish Party—the leader has no offices or salaries to bestow. And, above all, he had the modesty and the simplicity of real greatness. Every man had his ear, every man his kindly word and smile, and some his strong affection. Thus it was that Butt was to many the most lovable of men ; and more than one political opponent, impelled by principle to regard him as the most serious danger to the Irish cause, struck him hard, but wept as he dealt the blow.

This sketch of the character of Butt will show the points in which he was unsuitable for the work before him. He was the leader of a small party in an assembly to which it was hateful in opinion, and feeling, and temperament. A party in such circumstances can only make its way by audacious aggressiveness, dogged resistance, relentless purpose ; and for such Parliamentary forlorn hopes the least suited of leaders was a man whom a single groan of impatience could hurt, and one word of compliment delight.

The history of Butt's attempts to obtain land or any other reform in Ireland from the Imperial Parliament was the same as that of so many of his predecessors. Year after year, session after session, there was the same tale of Irish demands mocked at, denounced with equal vigour by the leaders of both the English parties alike, and then rejected in the division lobbies by overwhelming English majorities.

The following is the list of the Land Bills proposed by Parliament between 1871 and 1880 :[1]

---

[1] Healy, p. 67.

DATE.	BILL.	INTRODUCED BY	FATE.
1871	Landed Property, Ireland, Act, 1847, Amendment Bill	Serjeant Sherlock	Withdrawn
1872	Ulster Tenant Right Bill	Mr. Butt	Dropped
1873	Ulster Tenant Right Bill	Mr. Butt	Dropped
1873	Landlord and Tenant Act, 1870, Amendment Bill	Mr. Butt	Dropped
1873	Landlord and Tenant Act, 1870, Amendment Bill, No. 2	Mr. Heron	Dropped
1874	Landlord and Tenant Act, 1870, Amendment Bill	Mr. Butt	Dropped
1874	Landlord and Tenant Act, 1870, Amendment Bill, No. 2	Sir J. Gray	Dropped
1874	Ulster Tenant Right Bill	Mr. Butt	Dropped
1874	Irish Land Act Extension Bill	The O'Donoghue	Dropped
1875	Landed Proprietors, Ireland, Bill	Mr. Smyth	Dropped
1875	Landlord and Tenant, Ireland, Act, 1870, Amendment Bill	Mr. Crawford	Rejected
1876	Landlord and Tenant, Ireland, Act, 1870, Amendment Bill	Mr. Crawford	Withdrawn
1876	Tenant Right on Expiration of Leases Bill	Mr. Mulholland	Dropped
1876	Land Tenure, Ireland, Bill	Mr. Butt	Rejected
1877	Land Tenure, Ireland, Bill	Mr. Butt	Rejected
1877	Landlord and Tenant, Ireland, Act, 1870, Amendment Bill	Mr. Crawford	Withdrawn
1878	Landlord and Tenant, Ireland, Act, 1870, Amendment Bill	Mr. Herbert	Dropped
1878	Tenant Right Bill	Lord A. Hill	Rejected by Lords
1878	Tenant Right, Ulster, Bill	Mr. Macartney	Withdrawn
1878	Tenants' Improvements, Ireland, Bill	Mr. Martin	Rejected
1878	Tenants' Protection, Ireland, Bill	Mr. Moore	Dropped
1879	Ulster Tenant Right Bill	Mr. Macartney	Rejected
1879	Ulster Tenant Right Bill, No. 2	Lord A. Hill	Withdrawn
1879	Landlord and Tenant, Ireland, Bill	Mr. Herbert	Dropped
1879	Landlord and Tenant, Ireland, Act, 1870, Amendment Bill	Mr. Taylor	Dropped
1879	Landlord and Tenant, Ireland, Act, 1870, Amendment Bill, No. 2	Mr. Downing	Rejected
1880 (1st Session)	Landlord and Tenant, Ireland, Act, 1870, Amendment Bill	Mr. Taylor	Dropped
1880 (1st Session)	Ulster Tenant Right Bill	Mr. Macartney	Dropped

The English journals at the same time gave equally abundant testimony of the invincible ignorance of English opinion upon Irish questions. While in every part of Ireland the tenants were being crushed under a yearly increasing load of rack-rents into a deeper abyss of hopeless poverty, and the whole country was drifting once again to the periodic famine, an influential London journal was gaily declaring that Mr. Butt's whole case rested on an agreeable romance. Of the squalid lives of Irish farmers in their miserable patches of over-rented land; of the crushing of hearts and the break-up of homes through eviction and emigration; of the swift and inevitable advance of the spectre of famine—of all the cruel and intolerable suffering and wrong that provoked the cyclone of the Land League, the *Daily Telegraph* could write this airily and pleasantly:

'A large allowance must be made for the vivid fancy of Irishmen. But for that reflection the sad story which Mr. Butt told the House of Commons last night about the effects of the Irish Land Act (of 1870) would be disheartening indeed. . . . Mr. Butt warns us that the old "land war" is breaking out again; not through any fault of the farmers, he is careful to explain, but through the infatuation of those landlords who have used their wits to make the Act a dead letter. Were all this true, we should not wonder at Mr. Butt's demand for a Royal Commission to see how the Act works. But then, we repeat, allowance must be made for the vivid imagination of Irishmen. . . . It might have been contended that Mr. Butt had made a fair case for a small inquiry, if he had not betrayed at every turn of his speech his real aim, which is, not to amend the Land Act, but to secure the Irish farmers fixity of tenure at a rent arranged on some general ground. . . . Mr. Butt could scarcely have expected the Government to treat such a project seriously, and he must have been prepared for its decisive rejection by the House.'[1]

Butt was very much pained and disappointed by this universal rejection of all his proposals, and began to have gloomy forebodings as to the success of his policy. Intimately acquainted as Butt was with the working of the Land Act of 1870, he probably knew very well that a crisis was inevitable—such as came upon Ireland in 1879. And possibly, in one of those moments of gloom and depression with which he was too familiar, he may have anticipated an hour when there would come the same tragic and terrible close to his agitation which had wound up the career of O'Connell—a country not freed and prosperous, but once more tight in the grip of hunger, and more helpless than ever against oppression.. To preach patience to a people under such conditions was to mock a starving man with honeyed words.

There was, however, another and a graver danger to the success of Butt's movement. Butt knew very well that, as time went on, he was bound to lose a certain proportion of such a party. When there is on the one side a certain number of men willing to sell themselves, and on the other a Government with vast resources and occasional need for the services of corrupt Irishmen, the moment when the two will come to a bargain is a matter of mutual arrangement. The Home Rule Party had not been many years in existence when two or three of its members had accepted place, and there was not the least doubt that several others were willing. Then, apart from the want of pence, which was driving several of Butt's followers into office-seeking, the party was suffering from that hope deferred which depresses and then disintegrates political bodies. Session passed after session, motion after motion, Bill after Bill, and still no advance was made. Then the party, drawn from elements so heterogeneous as Colonel King-Harman and Mr. Gray, Sir Patrick O'Brien and Mr. Richard Power, could not be held in any strict bonds of discipline. Butt was exceedingly anxious to get the party to act together as a party on the great questions which divided the two English parties; all his efforts in this direction failed. In the Parliament of 1874, it gave Sir Stafford Northcote very little concern if Colonel King-Harman voted in favour of Home Rule, after the annual and academic discussion, when the Irish were put down by a combination of all the English parties in the House; for in all English party divisions he was secure of Colonel King-Harman's vote, as though he had not corrupted the general purity of his Conservatism by the heresy of Home Rule. And, similarly, even Lord Hartington might excuse the occasional

---

[1] Quoted in 'New Ireland,' pp. 398, 399.

error of an expectant Whig like Mr. Meldon, when Mr. Meldon's vote against the Tories was as certain as his desire for a place.

Butt fully grasped this truth of Parliamentary tactics, but, of course, was unable to get men to act as an Irish Party who were bound by corrupt hopes or party predilections to give their first allegiance to an English Party and an English Leader. Thus his whole policy was founded on sand. All these various causes, working together, had produced in the Irish Party of 1874 disorganization, depression, the breakdown of the barriers of shame among the corrupt, the sealing up of the fountains of hope among the pure. The period of dry-rot had set in.

In the light of subsequent events, it is now easy to see the dread abyss to which the Home Rule Party was once more bringing Ireland. The accession of a Liberal Ministry would have immediately completed the disaster which the defeat of Butt's proposals had begun. At least half the party would at once have become applicants for office, and probably a considerable number would have realized their wishes. The remainder would gradually have sunk deeper and deeper into a position of obedience to the English whips, and Irish national interests would once more have been made absolutely subservient to the interests of a single English party, to the convenience of Ministers, and to the opportunities of an overworked, listless, and generally hostile House of Commons. The first result of this state of things would have been to break down once more all faith in Parliamentary agitation. A portion of the people would have found some hope for the redress of intolerable grievances in another resort to revolutionary methods. The majority, following the precedent of the period immediately subsequent to Keogh's betrayal, would, in the cynicism begotten of blighted hope, once more have chosen bad or good men, honest patriots or self-seeking knaves, in the spirit of chance and of caprice. This downfall of constitutional agitation would have been made the more disastrous by events which at this moment were hurrying upon Ireland. The year 1879, as will presently be seen, brought one of those crises which were bound to recur in Ireland as long as its land system remained unreformed. Famine would have followed the distress of 1879, as it followed the blight of 1846. The country, without an honest and energetic Parliamentary representation, would have been left at the mercy of the ignorance, and the flippant levity of English Ministers, and Ireland, once more on the threshold of a successful movement, would have been dragged back for another generation into the slough of hunger, eviction, dishonest representatives, and futile insurrection.

The men and the methods that warded off this catastrophe were chosen with the ironical capriciousness of destiny. The one was a man already advanced in years, without the smallest trace of oratorical ability, without culture, with no political experience wider than that to be acquired on a water board or a town council. The other, at this time at least, was a young and obscure country gentleman, who had given no pledges to the political future save those of a very unsuccessful election contest, and two or three stumbling and very ineffective attempts at public speech.

On the night of April 22, 1875, the House of Commons was engaged in the not unaccustomed task of passing a Coercion Bill for Ireland. Mr. Butt, for some reason or other, thought it desirable that the progress of the measure on this evening should be slow, and he asked a member of his party, who was still young to the House, to speak against time. 'How long,' asked the member of his leader, 'would you wish me to speak?' 'A pretty

10

good while,' was Mr. Butt's reply. Mr. Biggar, who was the member appealed to, gave an interpretation to this *mot d'ordre* far larger than probably Mr. Butt had ever imagined or intended. It was five o'clock when Mr. Biggar rose, it was five minutes to nine when he sat down.

Let us quote Hansard for a description of the scene; its unconscious humour and significance will be interesting:

> The hon. member proceeded to read extracts from the evidence before the Westmeath Committee—as was understood—but in a manner which rendered him totally unintelligible. At length——
>
> 'The Speaker, interrupting, reminded the hon. gentleman that the rules required that an hon. member, when speaking, should address himself to the Chair. This rule the hon. gentleman was at present neglecting.
>
> 'Mr. Biggar said that his non-observance of the rule was partly because he found it difficult to make his voice heard after speaking for so long a time, and partly because his position in the House made it very inconvenient for him to read his extracts directly towards the Chair; he would, however, with permission, take a more favourable position.
>
> 'The hon. member accordingly, who had been speaking from below the gangway, removed to a bench nearer to the Speaker's chair, taking with him a large mass of papers, from which he continued to read long extracts, with comments.
>
> 'At length the hon. member said he was unwilling to detain the House at further length, and would conclude by stating his conviction that he had proved to every impartial mind that the Government had made out no case for the maintenance of this monstrous system of coercion, and that their proposal was perfectly unreasonable. The hon. gentleman, who had been speaking nearly four hours, then moved his amendment.'[1]

Neither Mr. Butt, nor the House of Commons, nor Mr. Biggar himself, could possibly have foreseen the momentous place which this night's work was destined to hold in all the subsequent history of the relations between England and Ireland. It was on this night that the policy was born which has since become known to all the world—the policy known as 'obstruction' by its enemies and as the 'active policy' by its friends.

There are few men of whom friends and enemies form so different an estimate as Mr. Biggar. The feelings of his friends and intimates is affectionate almost to fanaticism. When there are private and convivial meetings of the Irish Party, the effort is always made to limit the toasts to the irreducible minimum, for talking has naturally ceased to be much of an amusement to men who have to do so much of it in the performance of public duties. There is one toast, however, which is never set down and is always proposed: this toast is the 'Health of Mr. Biggar.' Then there occurs a scene which is pleasant to look upon. There arises from all the party one long, spontaneous, universal cheer, a cheer straight from every man's heart; the usually frigid speech of Mr. Parnell grows warm and even tender; everything shows that, whoever stands highest in the respect, Mr. Biggar holds first place in the affections of his comrades. There is another and not uninteresting phenomenon of these occasions. To the outside world there is no man presents a sterner, a more prosaic, and harder front than Mr. Biggar. On such occasions the other side of his character stands revealed. His breast heaves, his face flushes, he dashes his hand with nervous haste to his eyes; but the tears have already risen and are rushing down his face.

[1] Hansard, vol. ccxxiii., p. 1458.

To his intimates, then, Mr. Biggar is known as a man overflowing with kindness; of an almost absolute unselfishness. A man once bitterly hated Mr. Biggar until he had a conversation with one of Mr. Biggar's sisters, and found that she was unable to speak of all her brother's kindness with an unbroken voice. In the House of Commons, with all his fifty-seven years, he is at the beck and call of men who could be almost his grandchildren. Mr. Healy is preparing an onslaught on the Treasury Bench: 'Joe,' he cries to Mr. Biggar, 'get me return so-and-so.' Mr. Biggar is off to the library. He has scarcely got back when the relentless member for Monaghan requires to add to his armoury the division list in which the perfidious Minister has recorded his infamy, and away goes Mr. Biggar to the library again. Then Mr. Sexton, busily engaged in the study of an official report, approaches the member for Cavan with a card and an insinuating smile, and Mr. Biggar sets forth on an expedition to see some of the importunate visitants by whom Members of Parliament are dogged. As a quarter to six is approaching on a Wednesday evening, and Mr. Parnell thinks it just as well that the work of Government should not go on too fast, he calls on Mr. Biggar, and Mr. Biggar is on his legs, filling in the horrid interval—Heaven knows how! The desolate stranger, who knows no Member of Parliament, and yearns to see the House of Commons at work, thinks fondly of Mr. Biggar, and obtains a ticket of admission. He is seen almost every night surrounded by successive bevies of ladies—young and old, native and foreign—whom he is escorting to the Ladies' Gallery. Nobody asks any favour of Mr. Biggar without getting it. The man who to the outside public appears the most odious type of Irish fractiousness is adored by the policemen, worshipped by the attendants of the House; and there is good ground for the suspicion that there was a secret treaty between him and the late Serjeant-at-Arms, the genial and universally popular Captain Gossett, founded on their common desire to bring sittings to the abrupt and inglorious end of a 'count out.'

But this is only one side of his character. His hate is as fierce and unquestioning as his love, and he hates all his political opponents. He has the true Ulster nature: uncompromising, downright, self-controlled, narrow. The subtleties by which men of wider minds, more complex natures, less stable purpose and conviction, are apt to palliate their changes are entirely incomprehensible to Mr. Biggar, and the self-justifications of moral weakness arouse only his scorn. His purpose, too, when once resolved upon, is inflexible. It is this inflexibility of purpose that has made him so great a political force. Finally, he is as fearless as he is single-minded. The worst tempest in the House of Commons, the sternest decree that English law could enforce against an Irish patriot, and equally the disapproval of his own people, are incapable of causing him a moment of trepidation. He has said many terrible things in the House of Commons: the instance has got to occur of his having retracted one syllable of anything he has ever said. There is a scene in 'Père Goriot' in which the pangs of the dying and deserted father are depicted with terrible force. He is speaking of his daughters and of their husbands: of the one he speaks with the tenderness of a woman's heart; of the other, with the ferocity of an enraged tiger. The passage suggests the two so contrary sides of Mr. Biggar's nature: in the depth of his love, in the fierceness of his hate, he is the 'Père Goriot' of Irish politics.

A great difficulty meets the biographer of Mr. Biggar at the outset. He is not uncommunicative about himself, but he does not understand himself, and he much underrates himself. Asked by a friend to write his autobiography, his answer was: 'I am a very commonplace character.' In his early days, when he used to be asked to make a speech, he cheerfully started out on the attempt, having made the preliminary statement, 'I can't speak a d——d bit.' He was born in Belfast on August 1, 1828, and was educated at the Belfast Academy, where he remained from 1832 to 1844. The record of his school-days is far from satisfactory. He was very indolent —at least, he says so himself—he showed no great love of reading—in this regard the boy, indeed, was father to the man—he was poor at composition, and, of course, abjectly hopeless at elocution. The one talent he did exhibit was a talent for figures. It was, perhaps, this want of any particular success in learning, as well as delicacy of health, which made Mr. Biggar's parents conclude that he had better be removed from school and placed at business. He was taken into his father's office, who—as is known—was engaged in the provision trade, and he continued as assistant until 1861, when he became the head of the firm. This part of his career may be here dismissed with the remark that he retired from trade in 1880, and is now entirely out of business.

Mr. Biggar always took an interest in politics, and it will not surprise those acquainted with his subsequent career to know that he was always on the side which was in a hopeless minority, and which opposed the reigning clique and the established *régime*. For instance, when the late Mr. McMechan sought on one occasion the representation of Belfast, he had only fourteen supporters in all, and Mr. Biggar was one of the fourteen. In 1868, Mr. Biggar had a share in creating the curious combination by which Mr. William Johnston, of Ballykilbeg, was elected by Orange Democrats and Catholic Nationalists.

In 1870 Mr. Biggar made an attempt to get into the Town Council, standing for his native ward, which had always been regarded as a Tory stronghold. He was well beaten. Mr. Biggar received his defeat with the declaration that he would fight the ward on every occasion until he became its member. In the following year he again stood, with the result that he was returned at the head of the poll. He had previously to this obtained a seat on the Water Board, and he was chairman of that body from August, 1869, to March, 1872. Some stormy scenes occurred during Mr. Biggar's tenure of office; for the future member for Cavan gave his colleagues some specimens of that absolutely irreverent freedom of speech which has since alternately shocked and amused a higher assembly. There was a meeting in county Antrim for the purpose of expressing sympathy with the Queen on the recovery of the Prince of Wales; and, whether it was because of his disbelief in princes generally, or because he was disgusted with the fulsomeness of some of the language employed, Mr. Biggar wrote to the newspapers to say that the attendance at the meeting did not exceed fifty. When his year of office closed he was superseded, and was even refused the customary vote of thanks.

Mr. Biggar's first attempt to enter Parliament was made at Londonderry in 1872. He had not the least idea of being successful; but he had at this time mentally formulated the policy which he has since carried out with inflexible purpose—he preferred the triumph of an open enemy to that of a half-hearted friend. The candidates were Mr. (now Sir Charles) Lewis, Mr. (now Chief Baron) Palles, and Mr. Biggar. At that moment Mr. Palles, as Attorney-General, was prosecuting Dr. Duggan and other Catholic bishops for the part they had taken in a famous Galway election, and Mr. Biggar made it a first and indispensable condition of his withdrawing from the contest that these prosecutions should be dropped. Mr. Palles refused ; Mr. Biggar received only 89 votes, but the Castle official was defeated, and he was satisfied. The bold fight he had made marked out Mr. Biggar as the man to lead one of the assaults which at this time the rising Home Rule Party was beginning to make on the seats of Whig and Tory. When the General Election of 1874 came, it was represented to Mr. Biggar that he would better serve the cause by standing for Cavan. He was nominated, and returned, and member for Cavan he has since remained.

It was not long after the night of Mr. Biggar's four hours' speech that a young Irish member took his seat for the first time. This was Mr. Parnell, elected for the county of Meath in succession to John Martin—a veteran and incorruptible patriot who had died a few days before the opening of this new chapter in the Irish struggle.

When the dissolution of February, 1874, came, Mr. Parnell wished to stand for Wicklow ; but he was then high sheriff of the county, and the Government would not allow him to qualify himself by resigning. Shortly after, Colonel Taylor's acceptance of office as Chancellor of the Duchy in the new Disraeli Administration made a vacancy for the county Dublin, and it was deemed advisable to fight the seat. The contest was regarded as a forlorn hope, and was known at the same time to be necessarily an expensive one. The offer of Mr. Parnell to fight the seat at his own expense came at a time when there was scarcely a penny in the exchequer of the National Party, and the mere fact alone of his willingness to bear the burden in such a contest was enough to secure him a hearing ; but there were many doubts and fears, and the first impression was that, if a young landlord, hitherto entirely unknown in the national struggle—for the outer, and still more, the inner history of this shy, reserved young man, buried in his Wicklow estate, was a closed book to everybody in the world—if such a man wished to represent a constituency, it was from no higher motive than social ambition ; and men who had become Members of Parliament for such reasons have left a long record of half-hearted adherence, ending in violent hostility to the national cause. At last it was agreed that the young aspirant should at least get the privilege of a hearing, and he had a personal interview with the Council of the Home Rule League. John Martin and Mr. A. M. Sullivan were favourably impressed ; the latter undertook to propose his adoption at a meeting in the Rotunda, and here is his account of what followed and of Mr. Parnell's *début* in public life :

'The resolution which I had moved in his favour having been adopted with acclamation, he came forward to address the assemblage. To our dismay he broke down utterly. He faltered, he paused, went on, got confused, and, pale with intense but subdued nervous anxiety, caused everyone to feel deep sympathy for him. The audience saw it all, and cheered him kindly and heartily ; but many on the platform shook their heads, sagely prophesying that if ever he got to Westminster, no matter how long he stayed there, he would either be a "Silent Member," or be known as "Single-speech Parnell." '[1]

Nobody was surprised when, as the result of the election, Colonel Taylor was returned by an overwhelming majority. If anything were needed to account for the expected result, and to encourage hope for a better chance

[1] 'New Ireland,' p. 409.

next time, it was found in the universal sentiment that the Nationalists had been represented by an extremely poor candidate. Then, as now, Mr. Parnell had none of the qualities which had hitherto been associated with the idea of a successful Irish leader. He has now become one of the most potent of Parliamentary debaters in the House of Commons, through his power of saying exactly what he means and his thorough grasp of his own ideas and wants.[1] But Mr. Parnell has become this in spite of himself. He retains to this day an almost invincible repugnance to speaking; if he can, through any excuse, be silent, he remains silent, and the want of all training before his entrance into political life made him a speaker more than usually stumbling. Then his manner was cold and reserved; he seemed entirely devoid of enthusiasm, and he spoke with that strong English accent which in Ireland has come to be inevitably associated with the adherents of the English garrison and the enemies of the national cause.

But, if the truth were known, Mr. Parnell, in entering upon political life, was reaching the natural sequel of his own descent, of his early training, of the strongest tendencies of his own nature. It is not easy to describe the mental life of a man who is neither expansive nor introspective. It is one of the strongest and most curious peculiarities of Mr. Parnell, not merely that he rarely, if ever, speaks of himself, but that he rarely, if ever, gives any indication of having studied himself. His mind, if one may use the jargon of the Germans, is purely objective. There are few men who, after a certain length of acquaintance, do not familiarize you with the state of their hearts, or their stomachs, or their finances; with their fears, their hopes, their aims. But no man has ever been a confidant of Mr. Parnell. Any allusion to himself by another, either in the exuberance of friendship or the design of flattery, is passed by unheeded; and it is a joke among his intimates that to Mr. Parnell the being Parnell does not exist. But from various casual and unintentioned hints the following may be taken as a fair summary of his life and its influences.

The history of his own family was well calculated to make him a strong Nationalist. The family comes from Congleton, in Cheshire, and it is from this town that one branch, raised to the peerage, has taken its title. Thomas Parnell, the poet, was one of the race. The Parliamentary distinction dates, in the Parnell family, from the early part of the last century. John Parnell was member for Maryborough, in the Irish House of Commons, one hundred and fifty years ago. He was son of a judge of the Queen's Bench. He died in 1782, and he was immediately succeeded by his son John, afterwards Sir John. In 1787 Sir John was made Chancellor of the Exchequer. In the 'Red List,' in which Sir Jonah Barrington sums up his impressions of the Irish politicians of his time, he writes opposite the name of Sir John Parnell the one word 'Incorruptible.' He proved his claim to the title by giving up the office he had held for seventeen years, and voting steadily against the Union.

Henry Parnell, the son of Sir John, was a member of the Irish House of Commons at the same time, and, like his father, stood steadily by Grattan and the other advocates of Irish nationality to the last. Sir John was elected to the United Parliament, but died in the first year of his new posi-

---

[1] 'No man, as far as I can judge, is more successful than the hon. member in doing that which it is commonly supposed that all speakers do, but which in my opinion few really do—and I do not include myself among those few—namely, in saying what he means to say.'—Mr. GLADSTONE, Hansard, vol. cclxxvii., p. 482.

tion, and was immediately succeeded by Henry. Sir Henry Parnell was for many years a strong advocate of the rights of his fellow-countrymen, and was in favour of the abolition of the Corn Laws, short Parliaments, extension of the franchise, vote by ballot, and, curiously enough, the abolition of flogging in the army and navy, at a period when such doctrines were associated with advanced Radicalism. He was Secretary for War in Lord Grey's Ministry for 1832, and Paymaster of the Forces in the Administration of Lord Melbourne, and in 1841 he was created first Baron Congleton.

John Henry Parnell, of Avondale, was grandson of Sir John Parnell, and nephew of the first Lord Congleton. Making a tour through America while still a young man, he met, at Washington, Miss Stewart. Miss Stewart was the daughter of Commodore Charles Stewart, who played an important part in the history of America. It was he who, in his ship the *Constitution*, in the war between England and America in 1815, met, fought, beat and captured the two English vessels—the *Cyane* and the *Lerant*—with the loss of seventy-seven killed and wounded among the British, and only three killed and ten wounded in his own vessel. It is, perhaps, characteristic of the love for legality in his race that he did not enter upon this engagement until the British vessels first attacked, for he had received from a British vessel, three days before the engagement, a copy of the London *Times*, containing the heads of the Treaty of Ghent, as signed by the Ministers of the United States and Great Britain, and said to have been ratified by the Prince Regent.[1] After a series of striking adventures, Stewart reached home with his vessel. His victory excited extreme enthusiasm among the Americans, and every form of public honour was bestowed upon him. In Boston there was a triumphal procession; in New York the City Council presented him with the freedom of the city and a gold snuff-box, and he and his officers were entertained at a dinner; at Pennsylvania he was voted the thanks of the Commonwealth, and presented with a gold-hilted sword. Congress passed a vote of thanks to him and his officers, and struck a gold medal and presented it to him in honour of the event.

Afterwards Commodore Stewart was sent to the Mediterranean, where there was something approaching a mutiny amongst the officers under a different commodore. He soon came to a definite issue with his subordinates. He ordered a court-martial on a marine to be held on board one of his vessels. The officers preferred to discuss the case at their leisure in a hotel in Naples, and there tried and convicted the marine. The commodore promptly quashed the conviction, and, when the Court passed a series of resolutions, put all the commanding officers of the squadron under arrest. The result was the complete restoration of order, and the approval of Commodore Stewart's conduct by the President and the Cabinet.

Admiral Stewart, as he became, lived to a great age, and in time had taken a place in the affections of his countrymen somewhat similar to that of old Field-marshal Wrangel among the Germans of our day. He used to be known as 'Old Ironsides,' and the residence which he purchased in Bordentown was baptized 'Ironsides Park.' He was once prominently spoken of as a candidate for the Presidency, and, in less than four months, sixty-seven papers pronounced in his favour. He was eighty-three years of age when Fort Sumter was fired upon. At once he wrote asking to be put into active service: 'I am as young as ever,' he

---

[1] 'The Life of Charles Stewart Parnell,' by Thomas Sherlock, p. 23.

declared, 'to fight for my country.'[1] But of course the offer had to be refused. He survived nine years.

The following is a description of his appearance and character:

'Commodore Stewart was about five feet nine inches high, and of a dignified and engaging presence. His complexion was fair, his hair chestnut, eyes blue, large, penetrating, and intelligent. The cast of his countenance was Roman, bold, strong, and commanding, and his head finely formed. His control over his passions was truly surprising, and under the most irritating circumstance his oldest seaman never saw a ray of anger flash from his eye. His kindness, benevolence, and humanity were proverbial, but his sense of justice and the requisitions of duty were as unbending as fate. In the moment of greatest stress and danger he was as cool and quick in judgment as he was utterly ignorant of fear. His mind was acute and powerful, grasping the greatest or smallest subjects with the intuitive mastery of genius.'[2]

It is said that, in many respects, Mr. Parnell bears a strong resemblance to the characteristics of his grandfather, whose name he bears. In physique he is much less English or Irish than American. The delicacy of his features, the pallor of complexion, the strong nervous and muscular system, concealed under an exterior of fragility, are characteristics of the American type of man. Mentally, also, his evenness of temper and coolness of judgment suggest an American temperament.

Mr. Parnell was born in Avondale, county Wicklow, in June, 1846. Curiously enough, nearly the whole of his early life was passed in England, and in entirely English surroundings. When he was six years of age he was placed at school in Yeovil, Somersetshire. Next, he was under the charge of the Rev. Mr. Barton at Kirk-Langley, Derbyshire; next, under the Rev. Mr. Wishaw, in Oxfordshire; and, finally, he went to Cambridge University—the *alma mater* of his father. He did not graduate, and probably did not pay any very great attention to the study of the curriculum of the university.

He is not a man of large literary reading, but he is a severe and constant student of scientific subjects, and is especially devoted to mechanics. It is said to be one of his amusements to isolate himself from the enthusiastic crowds that meet him everywhere in Ireland, and, in a room by himself, to find delight in mathematical books. He is a constant reader of *Engineering* and other mechanical papers, and he takes the keenest interest in all machinery.

The surroundings of the house in which he was born and still lives were well calculated to arouse in young Parnell the hereditary disposition to strong national opinions. Wicklow, on the whole, is the most beautiful and the most historic county in Ireland, and Avondale is in the centre of its greatest beauties and its most historic spots.

Many of the lessons which these historic spots were calculated to teach were reinforced by the servants around the family mansion. I have made the remark that it is particularly difficult to follow the mental history of a man who is neither introspective nor expansive; and it is not from the lips of Mr. Parnell himself that one could learn much of his internal history. But one day, sitting in his house at Avondale, he happened to mention the name of Hugh Gaffney, a gate-keeper in Avondale, and retold

---

[1] 'The Life of Charles Stewart Parnell,' by Thomas Sherlock, p. 28.
[2] *Ib.*, p. 28.

a story which the gate-keeper used to tell him when he was a youth. Gaffney was old enough to have seen some of the scenes of the Rebellion; and one of his stories was of a man who was taken by the English troops in the neighbourhood. The sentence upon him was that he was to be flogged to death at the end of a cart. The interpretation of the sentence by Colonel Yeo—such was the name of the commander—was that the flogging was to be inflicted on the man's belly instead of on his back. Gaffney saw the rebel flogged from the mill to the old sentry-box in Rathdrum—the town near which Avondale is situate—and heard the man call out in his agony, 'Colonel Yeo! Colonel Yeo!' and appeal for respite from this torture; and also heard Colonel Yeo reject the prayer with savage words; and finally saw the man, as he fell at last, with his bowels protruding. When Mr. Parnell told the story, in his usual tranquil manner, the thought suggested itself to my mind that, at last, I had reached one of the great influences that made Mr. Parnell the man he is, and that in this poor gate-keeper was to be found the early instructor whose lessons on British rule and its meaning imbued the young and impressionable heir of the Parnell name and traditions with that love and admiration for British domination in Ireland which have characterized his public career.

Such stories appeal to what is, beyond doubt, the strongest feeling, the most positive instinct of Mr. Parnell's nature—his hatred of injustice. He has the loathing of masculine natures for cruelty in all forms. This feeling, though never expressed in words, finds strong manifestation often in acts. One of his acts while still the unknown squire was to prosecute a man for cruelty to a donkey. Recently, while a very important and vital resolution was under discussion at a meeting of the Irish Party called to arrange the plan of the electoral campaign, the meeting was amused, and a little disconcerted, to see Mr. Parnell rise with *naïf* unconsciousness, leave the chair, and disappear from the room. He was followed by a handsome dog, which had been presented to him by his friend and colleague, Mr. Corbet; and the meeting had to tranquilly suspend its discussions until the leader of the Irish people had seen after the dinner of a retriever. It was characteristic of the modesty and, at the same time, scornfulness of his nature, that all through the many attacks made upon him by Mr. Forster, and other gentlemen who wear their hearts upon their sleeves, he never once made allusion to his own strong love of animals; but to his friends he often expressed his disgust for the outrages that, during a portion of the agitation, were occasionally committed upon them.

In 1867, the ideas that had been sown in his mind in childhood first began to mature. His mother was then, as throughout her life, a strong Nationalist, and so was, at least, one of his sisters. There is a tradition among the survivors of the literary staff of the *Irish People* newspaper of a young lady, closely veiled, coming with a contribution to the office of the journal during its troubled career. This was Miss Fanny Parnell. Many of the Fenian refugees found shelter and protection in the house of Mrs. Parnell, and were in this way enabled to escape from the pursuing bloodhounds of the law. It was at this epoch that the execution of Allen, Larkin, and O'Brien took place in Manchester; and this, as has already been mentioned, was the turning-point in the mental history of Mr. Parnell, and set him irrevocably in favour of Nationalist principles.

However, it was a considerable time before he even thought of entering political life. Like his father, he spent some time in travel in America.

While there he met with a railway accident in company with his brother John. 'The best nurse I ever had,' said Mr. John Parnell to me in America, ' was my brother Charlie.' And then he told me how, for weeks, his brother had remained night and day by his side.

In 1871, Mr. Parnell returned to Avondale, and began the life of a country squire. His American blood showed itself in a keener sense of the possibilities of his property and of his own duties than are usually associated with the Irish landlord. Then, though he cannot be described as a joyous man, he takes a keen interest in life and everything going on around him, and could not, under any circumstances, keep from being actively occupied in some pursuit. He hunted and he shot like those around him; but, besides this, he set up saw-mill and brush factory, and sunk shafts in search of the mineral ore in which Wicklow was said to abound. He was a kind and generous landlord, and enjoyed the affection of all around him. His subsequent history has been told; and now the narrative returns to an account of his Parliamentary career.

Mr. Biggar and Mr. Parnell brooded for some time over the strange spectacle of the impotence that had fallen upon the Irish Party. Both were men eager for practical results; and debates, however ornate and eloquent, which resulted in no benefit, appeared to them the sheerest waste of time, and a mockery of their country's hopes and demands. Probably they drifted into the policy of 'obstruction,' so called, rather than pursued it in accordance with a definite plan originally thought out. When one now looks back upon the task which these two men set themselves, it will appear one of the boldest, most difficult, and most hopeless that two individuals ever proposed to themselves to work out.

They set out, two of them, to do battle against 656; they had before them enemies who, in the ferocity of a common hate and a common terror, forgot old quarrels and obliterated old party lines; while among their own party there were false men who hated their honesty and many true men who doubted their sagacity. In this work of theirs they had to meet a perfect hurricane of hate and abuse; they had to stand face to face with the practical omnipotence of the mightiest of modern empires; they were accused of seeking to trample on the power of the English House of Commons, and six centuries of Parliamentary government looked down upon them in menace and in reproach. In carrying out their mighty enterprise, Mr. Parnell and Mr. Biggar had to undergo labours and sacrifices that only those acquainted with the inside life of Parliament can fully appreciate. Those who undertook to conquer the House of Commons had first to conquer much of the natural man in themselves. The House of Commons is the arena which gives the choicest food to the intellectual vanity of the British subject, and the House of Commons loves and respects only those who love and respect it. But the first principle of the active policy was that there should be absolute indifference to the opinions of the House of Commons, and so vanity had first to be crushed out. Then the active policy demanded incessant attendance in the House, and incessant attendance in the House amounts almost to a punishment. And the active policy required, in addition to incessant attendance, considerable preparation; and so the idleness, which is the most potent of all human passions, had to be gripped and strangled with a merciless hand. And finally, there was to be no shrinking from speech or act because it disobliged one man or offended another; and therefore, kindliness of feeling was to be watched and guarded by remorseless purpose. The years of fierce conflict, of labour by day and by night, and of iron resistance to menace, or entreaty, or blandishment, must have left many a deep mark in mind and in body. 'Parnell,' remarked one of his followers in the House of Commons one day, as the Irish leader entered with pallid and worn face, 'Parnell has done mighty things, but he had to go through fire and water to do them.'

Mr. Biggar was heard of before Mr. Parnell had made himself known; and to estimate the character of the member for Cavan—and it is a character worth study—one must read carefully, and by the light of the present day, the events of the period at which he first started on his enterprise. In the session of 1875 he was constantly heard of; on April 27 in that session he 'espied strangers'; and, in accordance with the then existing rules of the House of Commons, all the occupants of the different galleries, excepting those of the Ladies' Gallery, had to retire. The Prince of Wales was among the distinguished visitors to the assembly on this particular evening, a fact which added considerable effect to the proceeding of the member for Cavan. At once a storm burst upon him, beneath which even a very strong man might have bent. Mr. Disraeli, the Prime Minister, got up, amid cheers from all parts of the House, to denounce this outrage upon its dignity; and to mark the complete union of the two parties against the daring offender, Lord Hartington rose immediately afterwards. Nor were these the only quarters from which attack came. Members of his own party joined in the general assault upon the audacious violator of the tone of the House. Mr. Biggar was, above all other things, held to be wanting in the instincts of a gentleman. 'I think,' said the late Mr. George Bryan, another member of Mr. Butt's party, 'that a man should be a gentleman first and a patriot afterwards,' a statement which was of course received with wild cheers. Finally, the case was summed up by Mr. Chaplin. 'The hon. member for Cavan,' said he, 'appears to forget that he is now admitted to the society of gentlemen.'[1] This was one of the many allusions, fashionable at the time—among genteel journalists especially—to Mr. Biggar's occupation. It was his heinous offence to have made his money in the wholesale pork trade.

'Heaven knows' (said a writer in the *World*) 'that I do not scorn a man because his path in life has led him amongst provisions. But though I may unaffectedly honour a provision-dealer who is a Member of Parliament, it is with quite another feeling that I behold a Member of Parliament who is a provision-dealer. Mr. Biggar brings the manner of his store into this illustrious assembly, and his manner, even for a Belfast store, is very bad. When he rises to address the House, which he did at least ten times to-night, a whiff of salt pork seems to float upon the gale, and the air is heavy with the odour of the kippered herring. One unacquainted with the actual

---

[1] Mr. Biggar's action on this occasion had a secret history, which may here be told. It was the desire of the Liberals to bring the relations of the press with Parliament into a more satisfactory position. Especially it was felt to be a grievance that the press could be excluded by a single member. Mr. Disraeli favoured leaving things as they were: and it was thought that he should be brought to his senses by such patent proof of his mistake as the ordering out of the reporters by the words, 'I espy strangers.' Mr. Biggar's intrepidity suggested him as a proper person to take so audacious a step. A few nights afterwards, when Lord Hartington was demanding a reform, and Mr. Disraeli was advocating the old state of things, Mr. A. M. Sullivan cleared the House; and the whole Liberal Party cheered him to the echo. Mr. Biggar was deserted and denounced, though he acted on the suggestion of others, because he happened to interfere with the convenience of Royalty.

condition of affairs might be forgiven if he thought there had been a large failure in the bacon trade, and that the House of Commons was a meeting of creditors and the right hon. gentlemen sitting on the Treasury Bench were members of the defaulting firm, who, having confessed their inability to pay ninepence in the pound, were suitable and safe subjects for the abuse of an ungenerous creditor.[1]

These things are mentioned by way of illustrating the marks and symptoms of the time through which Mr. Biggar had to live, rather than because of any influence they had upon him. On this self-reliant, firm, and masculine nature a world of enemies could make no impress. He did not even take the trouble to read most of the attacks upon him. Those that were made in the House of Commons in his own hearing neither touched him nor angered him. The only rancour he ever feels against individuals is for the evil they attempt to do to the cause of his country. This little man, calmly and placidly accepting every humiliation and insult that hundreds of foes could heap upon him, in the relentless and untiring pursuit of a great purpose, may by-and-by appear, even to Englishmen, to merit all the affectionate respect with which he is regarded by men of his own country and principles.

The Irish people have long since decided between Mr. Biggar and the members of his own party with whom he was at war. If anyone desire to see how far that party is removed from the party of to-day, he has but to read the descriptions of some of the encounters between the member for Cavan and some of his colleagues upon the Coercion struggles of those days. Thus, on one occasion, Mr. McCarthy Downing, a so-called Nationalist, went out of his way to compliment Sir Michael Hicks-Beach on the courtesy with which he treated the Irish members when carrying through the House a Bill destructive of the liberties of their country. This was the speech which drew from Mr. Ronayne the grim remark that such compliments to the Minister in charge of a Coercion Bill reminded him of the shake-hands of the murderer with his executioner. On another occasion, when Dr. O'Leary proposed an adjournment of a stage of a debate on a Coercion Bill to another day, his own colleagues rose in revolt against the unreasonable proposal; and Dr. O'Leary, scared and overwhelmed, had to consult the convenience of the Government to accelerate the destruction of his country's liberties, and to withdraw his motion for adjournment. More interesting than these collisions with small and now forgotten men was Mr. Biggar's conflict with the leader of his party. The contest between these two men is one of the most picturesque in Parliamentary history. Rarely has a struggle appeared more unequal. The House of Commons never had an opportunity of seeing Butt at his best, but with an audience before him sympathetic with his views, he was a speaker of a persuasiveness as great as that of Mr. Gladstone himself. There was not a resource of the orator, a trick of the lawyer, a device of the Parliamentary tactician's art unknown to him. He was, indeed, marked out as a leader of men in Parliamentary struggles.

Mr. Biggar, on the other hand, had not one of the gifts that make a great Parliamentarian. He spoke haltingly, and with difficulty; his sparse education was not improved by reading; he was absolutely new to Parliamentary and, practically, to political life. But the moral chasm between Biggar and Butt was as wide as the intellectual chasm between Butt and

[1] March 5, 1875.

Biggar. The relentless self-control of Biggar, the subordination of all his wants to his means,[1] his inflexible courage, and his unshakable persistence, made him a dangerous competitor for a man of the loose habits, of the easy self-indulgent nature, of the weak will and capricious purpose of Butt. Biggar was ultimately conqueror in this struggle. Sheer strength of character broke down sheer intellectual superiority.

The new policy, which had been inaugurated by Mr. Biggar in the session of 1875, was developed rather than formulated. It began simply in the practice of blocking a number of Bills in order to bring them under the half-past twelve rule, which forbids opposed measures to be taken after that hour. It also became the custom of either the member for Cavan or the member for Meath to propose motions of adjournment in various forms when half-past twelve was reached, on the ground that proper discussion could not take place at so late an hour. Then, interstices of time which the Government would gladly employ for advancing some stage of their measures were filled in by the Irish members. Thus, for instance, a Bill standing for second reading would be approaching that stage at twenty minutes past twelve at an ordinary sitting, or half-past five on a Wednesday. To the horror and disgust of everybody else, Mr. Biggar or Mr. Parnell would rise and occupy the time between that hour and half-past twelve or a quarter to six, when contentious business could be no longer discussed, and further consideration of the measure had to be postponed to another day. In this manner the two members gradually felt their way, became more practised in speaking, and obtained an intimate acquaintance with the rules of the House. Throughout all this time, of course, they were harassed by interruptions, shouts of 'Divide,' groans, and calls to order; and for a time, at least, Mr. Parnell used occasionally to lay himself open to effective interruption by his yet immature acquaintance with the laws of the assembly. 'How,' said a young follower of his to the Irish leader, 'are you to learn the rules of the House?' 'By breaking them,' was Mr. Parnell's reply; and this was the method by which he himself gained his information.

It was not till the session of 1877 that Mr. Parnell and Mr. Biggar became engaged in the passionate and exciting scenes which made their names known all over the world, and brought the House of Commons definitely face to face with the new and portentous force which had unmasked itself within the Parliamentary citadel. Anyone who has been a member of the House of Commons will know how tremendous is its reserve power. There had been 'obstructives,' of course, before the time of Parnell and Biggar. During the great Ministry of Mr. Gladstone, between 1868 and 1874, obstruction had been developed to a fine art by several of the gentlemen who at this moment held official positions under Lord Beaconsfield. Everybody remembers how the Church Bill and the Land Bill, the Ballot Bill, and the Bill for the abolition of purchase in the army, had been dogged at every step of their progress by endless and silly amendments, by speeches against time, and by countless motions for adjournment.

It was part of the skilful tactics of Parnell and Biggar that their intervention in the debates of the House was always rational. They did not indulge in any wild declamation, nor make speeches full of empty and purposeless talk. Their plan was to propose amendments to the different

---

[1] Mr. Biggar lost heavily in his business for a couple of years while he was a Member of Parliament. He so rigidly economised that, instead of dining in the House, he trotted off to a cheap restaurant outside.

measures before the House; and their amendments were rarely, if ever, open to the charge of irrelevance or frivolity. On March 26, 1877, there was a lengthy discussion on some new clauses of the Prison Bill for the better treatment of prisoners. At a little after one o'clock Mr. Biggar proposed to report progress. Some eight members, who had acted with the 'obstructives' up to this time, now deserted; and, when the division was called, there were in favour of the adjournment but 10, while 138 voted against it. Motions for adjournment followed each other in rapid succession, and, at three o'clock in the morning, the Government gave way. Mr. Butt had watched these proceedings with no friendly eye. There was no doubt about his genuineness as a Home Ruler, but he had been a Conservative for many years, and a friend and associate of the party in power, and he was certainly considerably under the influence of its leaders. Curiously enough, one of the men who was supposed to have the most influence over him was the then Chief Secretary, Sir Michael Hicks-Beach, though there had never been a Chief Secretary who met all demands for Irish reform with rejection more uncompromising and more insolent. It is characteristic of the natures of the two men that it was the attitude of Hicks-Beach towards Mr. Butt which drove Mr. Biggar, as much as anything else, forward into the policy he had now adopted. He was asked by Sir Michael to chide his supporters, and he consented. It showed a strange want of any appreciation of the real facts of the case that the Irish leader should have thus interpreted the request addressed to him. The recognition of his power came only when it was employed in meeting the views of the Ministry and in yielding to the temper of Parliament; it had received no recognition so long as it was used in pressing forward against the Ministry, and against the House—demands for the redress of the intolerable wrongs of his country. Where was his memory gone of the contemptuous rejection for the past three years of every one of the proposals that he made with the assent of the overwhelming majority of his countrymen? A leader who, with such recollections, and such incontestable proof of the futility of soft methods, of appeals to the sense of justice in English Ministries, and to the reason of Parliament, could think of the 'dignity of Parliament,' and not the wrongs of Ireland, 'lacked gall to make oppression bitter.' Mr. Butt, however, threw in his lot with the enemies of his country, and attacked his two subordinates with fierce anger and reproach.

Condemned by their own leader, and by the majority of their own party, Mr. Parnell and Mr. Biggar were naturally the more hated by the House of Commons, and their conduct the more bitterly resented; and the resolve to put them down grew more vehement and more passionate. It was on the South African Bill that the long-pent-up storm burst forth with tempestuous violence. On July 25, 1877, the House was in committee on the Bill. Mr. Jenkins had rendered himself obnoxious to some of the members of his own party by his opposition to the measure, and Mr. Monk accused him of abusing the forms of the House. Mr. Jenkins rose to order, vehemently denied the charge, and then moved that those words be taken down. Mr. Parnell at once rose. 'I second that motion,' he said; 'I think the limits of forbearance have been passed. I say that I think the limits of forbearance have been passed in regard to the language which hon. members opposite have thought proper to address to me and to those who act with me.' At once Sir Stafford Northcote, who was then Chancellor of the Exchequer and leader of the House, rose and moved that the latter words of Mr. Parnell be taken down. The motion of Mr. Jenkins was irregularly got rid of by the intervention of the Chairman of Committees—Mr. Raikes—who declared that the words of Mr. Monk were not a breach of order. The chairman, however, proceeded to raise another subject of dispute by calling upon Mr. Parnell to withdraw his statement, 'accusing hon. members of this House of intimidation.' 'The hon. member must withdraw that expression,' said Mr. Raikes, amidst the cheers and intense excitement of the House. Mr. Parnell rose to explain; he was constantly interrupted by 'conversation, coughs, exclamations, cries, and groans.' He denounced the Bill as mischievous both to the colonists and to the native races, and instituted a comparison between Ireland and the South African colonies; 'therefore,' he went on, 'as an Irishman, coming from a country which had experienced to its fullest extent the result of English interference in its affairs, and the consequence of English cruelty and tyranny, he felt a special satisfaction in preventing and thwarting the intentions of the Government in respect to this Bill.'

The moment these words had been uttered, the House thought that it had at last caught the cool, wary, and dexterous Irish member in a moment of forgetfulness and passion, and that he had given the long-sought opportunity for bringing him to account. Amid loud shouts, Sir Stafford Northcote rose and moved that the words of Mr. Parnell be taken down; and this having been done, he proposed that all further business should be stopped, and that the Speaker should be sent for. The Speaker was brought in, the House filled with an excited crowd, and Sir Stafford Northcote moved that Mr. Parnell 'be suspended till Friday next.' Mr. Parnell was called upon to explain. While the House was storming around him, and he was brought face to face with the prospect of undergoing Parliamentary censure after a manner unprecedented, and thus viewed with horror by all the men around him, he began by a technical objection. He pointed out that another motion had been proposed to the House before that of Sir Stafford Northcote's, and that, therefore, the motion of the leader of the House was out of order. But the Speaker ruled this objection as untenable; and Mr. Parnell had to proceed with his own defence. He addressed to the House a speech full of the boldest defiance and of stinging suggestion. The House was now beside itself with rage, and there were loud shouts that Mr. Parnell should withdraw, as is the custom when the conduct of a member is under consideration. Mr. Parnell left his seat and calmly proceeded to a place in the Speaker's Gallery, and from this point of vantage looked down on the proceedings in which he himself was the subject of debate.

Sir Stafford Northcote now moved that 'Mr. Parnell having wilfully and persistently obstructed the public business, is guilty of contempt of the House, and that Mr. Parnell for his said offence be suspended from the service of the House till Friday next.' A fatal flaw was discovered in the proposal of Sir Stafford Northcote. Mr. Parnell had certainly declared his interest in 'thwarting and preventing the designs,' not of the House, which, of course, would be obstruction, but 'of the Government,' which is the object and the legitimate pursuit of every opponent of a Ministerial measure. Sir Stafford Northcote had evidently lost his head in his eagerness to throw a Christian to the lions, and he was obliged to postpone further debate upon the question until the following Friday. Mr. Parnell, escorted by Mr. Biggar, re-entered the House, stood up again, and resumed his speech exactly at the point at which he had been interrupted two hours before by the impulsive motion of Sir Stafford Northcote.

On the Friday following Sir Stafford Northcote proposed two new rules. The first was, that any member called to order twice by the Speaker or the

---

¹ 'New Ireland,' p. 424.

Chairman of Committees could be suspended for the remainder of the sitting; and the second, that no member be allowed to propose more than once in the same sitting a motion for reporting progress or the adjournment of the debate. The resolutions met with some criticism from the Liberal benches, but the Irish members offered no opposition, and the two rules were adopted for the session. On Wednesday, July 31, occurred the first of those prolonged sittings which have since become so familiar. The Government, owing to the dogged and persistent opposition of Mr. Parnell and Mr. Biggar, and to some extent of the Radicals below the gangway, were very far behind with their legislative proposals, and especially with the South African Bill. At last it was resolved that the measure should be pushed through on the night of Tuesday, the 31st; and on that night, for the first time, the expedient of relays which has since become so familiar was employed. The Irish members, aware of the arrangement that had been made against them, accepted the challenge, and determined to carry on the contest as long as their strength would hold out. There were but a few of them to make the fight—seven in all. They were supported for some time by Mr. Courtney, who was as hostile as they to the principle of the South African Bill, and who has since been justified, as well as Mr. Parnell and Mr. Biggar, by the disastrous termination to the measures of which the South African Bill was the starting-point. But Mr. Courtney gave up the struggle in the small hours of the night. The fight still went on. At a quarter-past eight in the morning, after he had been fifteen hours at work, Mr. Parnell retired to rest; he came back at a quarter-past twelve, four hours later, and resumed his share in the debates. At two o'clock the last amendment on the South African Bill was disposed of, and the Bill was through. When the House rose it had been sitting for twenty-six hours. One other little incident is worth recording. Throughout the long watches of the night the Ladies' Gallery was occupied by one solitary and patient figure; this was Miss Fanny Parnell, who shared and inspired the convictions of her brother, and who afterwards gave to the Irish cause some of its most stirring lyrics and its ablest argumentative defences, and an incessant labour amid daily increasing weakness and fast-approaching death.

This unprecedented sitting in the House of Commons produced in England a tempestuous burst of anger and excitement, and for some days Mr. Parnell, Mr. Biggar, and their associates were denounced with a wealth of invective that would not have been unequal to the merits of Guy Fawkes or Titus Oates. In their own party, too, the dissent from their tactics was reaching a climax; Mr. Butt seemed resolved to throw down the final gage of battle, and call upon the party to make their choice between the continuance of his leadership and the suppression of the two mutineers. But all efforts to get the party to take decisive action proved abortive. Time-servers and office-seekers, they wanted to survive till the advent of the blessed hour when the return of the Liberals to power would give them the long-desired chance of throwing off the temporary mask of national views, to assume the permanent livery of English officials. Before that period could arrive, they well knew that a General Election had to intervene, and who knew what control over that election might be exercised by such extremists as Mr. Parnell and Mr. Biggar? This fact adds another element of tragedy to the woeful eclipse in which the last days of Butt ended. His opponents were honest and resolute; his friends, self-seeking, treacherous and half-hearted, ready to turn without a blush or a pause from the worship of the setting to that of the rising sun.

There was another portent of the time which still more disquieted Butt, and brought the peril of the situation more clearly and unmistakably before his eyes. The policy of Mr. Parnell and Mr. Biggar might not as yet have won the intelligence of Ireland, but it had beyond all question gained its heart. The session of 1877 had ended on August 13; on the 21st of the same month there was a meeting in the Rotunda in Dublin in honour of Mr. Parnell and Mr. Biggar; the meeting was crowded; the reception was enthusiastic; the verdict of Dublin was given, and it was in favour of the new men and the new policy.

The reader, to understand the success of the active policy, has to recall the fact which I have endeavoured all through this narrative to imprint upon his mind as a central fact of Irish politics. This was that, since the betrayal of the national cause by Keogh and Sadleir in 1855, the heart of the Irish people had never been won for Parliamentary agitation; there was ever the tendency to the cynic doubtfulness of those who have once been greatly deceived. This had a bad effect in several ways. In the first place, it was a steady obstacle to that infectious enthusiasm by the aid of which alone the scattered interests and forces and tendencies of a nation can be moulded into the unity of a great national movement. It left the constituencies to make the fight on local or capricious or non-essential issues instead of a common national platform; above all things, it left the Parliamentary Party without that force of national passion behind them without which, in a struggle in an assembly alien, ignorant and generally hostile like the House of Commons, the words of Irish national representatives were but as sounding brass and tinkling cymbal. To give the people faith—that was the first necessity of a great movement in Ireland; that was the object, and that is the chief justification, of the policy of the active party.

Meantime the struggle was going on inside the bosom of the Home Rule Party itself. On Monday and Tuesday, January 14 and 15, 1878, a conference was held in Dublin. There had been reports that the two parties would come into serious collision at this meeting. A notice appeared in the name of Mr. Butt, recapitulating resolutions which had been passed after the election of the party in 1874—resolutions pledging the party to act independently of both the English parties, and at the same time in unity with each other, and containing the suggestion that 'no Irish member ought to persevere in any course of action which shall be declared by a resolution adopted at a meeting of the Home Rule members to be calculated to be injurious to the National cause.'[1]

On the other hand, Mr. O'Connor Power had given notice of a resolution which declared that, in consequence of the hostility with which the just and constitutional demands for self-government made by a majority of the Irish representatives had been met 'by both English parties in the House of Commons, it was essential to the success of the Irish cause that more determined and vigorous action should be taken by the Parliamentary Party.'[2]

As the time for the conference approached, however, Butt again found that he was fighting without his army. A private meeting of the Irish members, held on the Saturday before the conference, arrived at a compromise. The rival resolutions were withdrawn, and a set of resolutions proposed by a Mr. P. McCabe Fay were accepted, which, if anything, were more favourable to Mr. Parnell than to Mr. Butt.

[1] *Nation*, January 19, 1878.   [2] *Ib*.

So the conference ended in a drawn battle; but the session of 1878 was soon to show how impossible it was to do anything with the existing party, or with Mr. Butt himself. A more regular attendance on the part of members was requested, and the only result was that often when an important Irish Bill was proposed there were not half a dozen Irish members in their places. Joint action had been recommended on the Eastern Question, and when the great party division came the members took different sides. There was even a graver scandal, for Mr. Butt, the leader of the party, not only voted with the Ministry, and thereby swelled the majority of a party that had up to that time refused every single demand of the Irish people, but he spoke in a tone far more worthy of an Imperialist 'Jingo' than of an Irish Nationalist.

The victory of Mr. Parnell at the conference had been immediately preceded by another important gain. There are no Irishmen more fierce or resolute in the national faith than the Irishmen settled in England and Scotland. They are, though this is not generally thought, far more extreme in their views than the majority of the Irish in America, and they have an unbroken unity and a clear-sighted appreciation of the essential truth in grave national controversies that might well put to the blush the half-heartedness, the wavering purposes, and the divided counsels of the Irish who have remained in Ireland. The Irish in England were from the very first on the side of Mr. Parnell. They were enrolled in an organization known as the Home Rule Confederation, and Mr. Butt was its president. At the annual convention of the Confederation at the close of 1877, Mr. Butt was deposed, and Mr. Parnell was elected in his place. The man who proposed the change bore to Butt that extraordinary affection with which this weak, kindly, unassuming, and childishly simple old man was accustomed to inspire nearly every man, and could with difficulty maintain his composure as he gave the tottering Cæsar the fatal stab.

Mr. Butt now virtually retired from the leadership of the Home Rule Party. His resignation of his position was not accepted, and he was induced to remain on the condition that his attendance should not be regular; this condition was for the purpose of allowing him to devote his attention to his practice. Like O'Connell, he had virtually to abandon his profession when he undertook the duties of Parliamentary leadership. In this way his already vast load of debt had been increased, and his hours of waking and sleeping were tortured by duns, threats of proceedings, and all the other shifts and worries of the impecunious. His quarrel with the 'obstructives' had now come to interfere with his financial as well as with his political position. A national subscription had been started. In Ireland the response of the people to the needs of their leaders has often been bountifully generous, more often than perhaps in any other country; but those who depend on the assistance of the public are subject to the chances of fortune that always dog the dependents in any degree on the popular mood. There are times and seasons when even the most popular leader will not receive one-tenth the support which will be given in more favourable circumstances, and the popular leader dependent for his living on the pence of the people has the life of the gambler or the theatrical speculator. The support of the people had been definitely transferred from Mr. Butt to Mr. Parnell, and financial support followed the tide of popular favour. The subscription was a miserable failure, and Butt was now without any resource but his profession.

But the time had passed when he could do anything there. The weakness of the heart's action, which had pursued him from his early years, was rapidly becoming worse, and in 1878 there were many warnings of the approaching end. In that year he made the remark to a friend, speaking of some troublesome symptoms from his heart, 'Is not this the curfew bell, warning us that the light must be put out and the fire extinguished?' Still he fought on, attending the law courts daily, and now and then joining in a desperate attempt to meet his daily triumphant opponents. His last appearance was at a meeting in Molesworth Hall, on February 4, 1879. He was at this time engaged in the *cause célèbre* of Bagot v. Bagot. The appearance of the old man at this meeting has left a deep and a sad impression on the minds of all those who were present. When he came in the look of death was on his face; the death of his hopes and his spirits had already come. There were many faces among those around that once had lighted at his look, and that now turned away in estrangement. 'Won't you speak to me?' he said in trembling tones to one man who had been his associate in many fights and amid many stirring scenes. But his old persuasive eloquence was still as fresh as ever, and he defended his whole policy with a vigour, plausibility, and closeness of reasoning that were worthy of his best days. This was the last meeting he ever attended. The next day he fell sick. The heart had at last refused to do its work; the brain could no longer be supplied; he lingered for nearly a month with his great intellect obscured, and on May 5, 1879, he died.

The people retained a kindly feeling for him to the end, but he had unquestionably outlived his usefulness; and his triumph over Mr. Parnell at this period of Irish history would have been a national calamity that might have brought hideous disasters. Sufficient time has elapsed since his death to pronounce a calm estimate of his career. The unwisdom of his policy was largely due undoubtedly to the difficulties of his circumstances. He had a wretched party—with one honest and unselfish man to five self-seekers—but he laid the foundations of a great party in the future, and, more than any other man, he prepared the people for the new struggle for self-government. It was his misfortune to come at the unhappy interval of transition from the bad and old and hopeless order of things to a new and a better and brighter epoch. Between the era of 1865 and the era of 1878 Ireland was, so far as constitutional movements were concerned, in a political morass. It was Butt that carried the country over that dangerous ground. His foot was light, and slippery, and timid; but the ground over which he had to pass was treacherous, perilous, and full of invisible and bottomless pools.

But all the same, it was well for Ireland that Butt died at this moment. The country was again approaching one of those crises the outcome of which was to mean either a re-plunge into the Slough of Despond, such as she had been immersed in from 1845 to 1865, or the start of a new era of hope, effort, and prosperity. If Butt had survived, and had retained the leadership, there is little doubt that he would have been incapable of rising to the height of the argument, and would have counselled shilly-shallying where shilly-shallying meant death, and moderation where extreme courses were required to avert a national disaster, wholesale, violent, and perhaps fatal; or, if he had not retained the full leadership by the destruction of the rising efforts of Mr. Parnell and Mr. Biggar, and if he and they still remained in political existence, and to some extent in political alliance, then there would have been divided counsels; and the time was one for unity.

All the meanness and servility and half-heartedness of the country would have found in Butt a rallying-point, and the crisis was one that demanded all the energy and courage and concentrated purpose of the country. For the year of 1879 was at hand.

CHAPTER IX.

FAMINE AGAIN!

BEFORE coming to 1879, a few words more on the progress of Mr. Parnell. The arrangement in the Home Rule Party was to elect, not a leader by that name, but a sessional chairman. Mr. Shaw was elected as the successor of Mr. Butt. Meantime the Ministry was about to supply Mr. Parnell with the best of all justifications for his policy. It has been seen with what contemptuous scorn the Government rejected all Mr. Butt's proposed reforms. Mr. Butt and his methods had thus been flouted for three years; within one year of the growth of 'obstruction,' the Government proceeded to bring forward concessions to Ireland. In the session of 1878 they introduced an Intermediate Education Bill. This was especially satisfactory to Mr. Parnell; his practical mind judges every policy by its results, and he was now able to show to the Irish people a practical result from his policy.

In the session of 1879 Mr. Parnell succeeded, after his dexterous fashion, in catching hold of a subject upon which it was possible to address the House with great frequency and at great length. The Army Regulation Bill, among other things, regulated the question of flogging. In the previous session, Mr. Parnell and Mr. Biggar had been left to fight the question of flogging alone. Now the curious spectacle was presented of the Irish 'obstructives' being supported by Mr. Chamberlain and by several other prominent and promising members of the Radical section. In the end, Parnell and Biggar, seeing how well their purpose was being served by the Liberal Opposition, drew slightly into the background, and allowed the question to be practically taken out of their hands; and this brought curious developments. As Mr. Parnell had been left fighting alone the battle against flogging when he began the struggle, so Mr. Chamberlain was left alone by the orthodox Liberals when he took it up. In the same way, too, as Mr. Parnell had been vehemently attacked by the whole force of the two parties combined in his early days of assault upon the lash, the persistence of Mr. Chamberlain's agitation of the question in the House drew down upon him a rebuke from the Marquis of Hartington, and there was a sharp scene between the two. But in the end the agitation against the lash became strong enough to be taken up by the orthodox Liberals, and in the same way as Parnell was succeeded by Chamberlain, Chamberlain was succeeded by Lord Hartington and the Liberal leaders. The result of this was that the lash became one of the prominent subjects of debate between the two parties, and in more than one constituency a Conservative member was hounded out of public life by the vehement speeches of Liberals upon the question.

It is needless to say that Mr. Parnell was not allowed to go through the sessions of 1878 and 1879 without occasionally passing through storms of the most tempestuous violence. 'Mr. Parnell,' wrote the *World* (March 29, 1876), 'is always at a white heat of rage, and makes with savage earnestness fancifully ridiculous statements, such as you may hear from your partner in the quadrille if you have the good fortune to be a guest at the annual ball at Colney Hatch.' 'The writer,' said the same journal (same date), 'who cherishes a real affection for Ireland, and who has an unaffected admiration for the genius of her sons, bitterly reproaches Meath that it should have wronged Ireland by making such scenes possible under the eye of the House.' And finally, the sapient writer said (same date), 'Mr. Biggar, though occasionally endurable, is invariably grotesque. . . . But Mr. Parnell has no redeeming qualities, unless we regard it as an advantage to have in the House a man who unites in his own person all the childish unreasonableness, all the ill-regulated suspicion, and all the childish credulity, of the Irish peasant, without any of the humour, the courtliness, or dash of the Irish gentleman.'

Meantime events were developing in Ireland which were destined to mould his future and to meet his career at the true psychological moment. What had been the state of Ireland since 1870? The Land Act of 1870 made no provision against rack-rent; rack-renting went on in many parts of Ireland, especially in the province of Ulster, more relentlessly and continuously than perhaps ever before. Eviction was but partly provided against by an arrangement that compelled the landlord to give compensation for disturbance. It was supposed, and perhaps intended by Mr. Gladstone, that this compensation should bear some relation to the loss of the tenant; but in a country where the land supplied a man with the only means of livelihood, it was plain that the only compensation which would really supply the place of his lost farm would be a compensation that would give him an income for the remainder of his days. Thus compensation for disturbance was, in Ireland, practically a contradiction in terms; to talk of a man being compensated for disturbance was the same thing as to talk of the compensating of an ocean waif for the loss of the raft which alone gives him a hope of safety. In the next place, the courts to which the question of disturbance was referred had prejudices and conceptions on the relations between landlord and tenant which rendered it absolutely impossible for them to administer justice. It must be remembered, as one of the leading facts of this whole controversy, that the whole bent of the land law in Ireland, not for years or for generations, but for centuries, was to make the landlord omnipotent: that the lawyers dealing with the question, whether Protestant or Catholic, Conservative or Liberal, were saturated with the principles of a law founded on this basis; and that, therefore, the rights of the tenants were often honestly held to be legally infinitesimal. Finally, there was no provision—at least no adequate provision—in the Land Act of 1870 for compensation for disturbance in cases where the tenant was unable to pay the rent. This also was contrary to the spirit of the Act, because Mr. Gladstone plainly laid down, in discussing the Bill, that over and above his right for any improvements he might have made upon the soil, the tenant was entitled to compensation from the mere fact of being disturbed or evicted; and it was plainly the spirit of the Land Act of 1870, that, even when the tenant was unable to pay his rent, eviction should not necessarily deprive him of compensation for his own property in the shape of improvements added to the land. But as the law stood, or was interpreted, the way the Act of 1870 worked was that the landlord was enabled, on the one hand, to raise the rent to the highest point he thought fit; that the tenant could only obtain compensation for eviction; and finally, that when either through the rack-rent or bad seasons the tenant was unable to pay his rent, all his improvements could be confiscated by the landlord, and he himself be thrown upon the world without house, without resources, without mercy.

It was obvious to anybody who considered the Irish Land Question with an impartial mind that legislation of this kind could only be endured as long as the people were utterly incapable of having it mended. Another fact was equally obvious, that it only required the strain of a few bad seasons to reduce the greater portion of the tenantry of Ireland to a state of bankruptcy. And, finally, with the farmers dependent for the most part on a crop whose fickleness had been proved by such tragic testimony in the previous history of Ireland, it was plain that such stress was bound at some period to come. It is an instructive commentary on the effect of the Government of Ireland from Westminster that, seventy-nine years after the Act of Union, the farmers remained in practically the same position as at the beginning of the century; that in these seventy-nine years there had been two famines, one among the most tragic in the awful depths of its horrors and sufferings of all human events; and that, after two famines, the country was approaching a third. In 1879, too, as in 1846, the potato crop could without exaggeration be described as the thin partition which stood between famine and a vast number of the Irish tenantry. Let us take this fact in connection with the following figures showing the depreciation in the potato crop for the years 1876, 1877, and 1878.

VALUE.[1]

1876	...	...	...	£12,464,382
1877	...	...	...	5,271,822
1878	...	...	...	7,579,512

There was hope, of course, that 1879 would repair the loss which had been inflicted by the two previous years; but 1879, instead of bringing relief, aggravated the disaster, and brought a supreme national crisis. The state of the weather and the reports from the country showed clearly to any observer of the time that a disaster was impending that might, unless properly met, plunge Ireland into the odious and tragic horrors of 1846 and 1847. Another circumstance tended very much to aggravate the distress in the poorer parts of the country. It is the habit of a considerable section of the farmers of Mayo, Galway, and Donegal to migrate to England and Scotland for the harvest season every year. The sums which they thus earned by the migration, calculated at about £100,000, went, not to their wives and families, but to the landlord. Labour for English and Scotch farmers was part of the tribute they had yearly to pay to their oppressors. It was, indeed, a peculiarity of the Irish land system that it pursued the Irish race wherever that race went. The son or daughter of the Irish farmer who had emigrated to America, or Australia or New Zealand did not leave behind in Ireland the curse of his race. The wages earned as a labourer, or a servant-maid, or a miner, or a sheep-farmer in any of these places of exile went home to help their parents in their yearly deepening poverty, through their yearly increasing rent. It has been calculated that between the years 1848 and 1864 no less a sum than £13,000,000 was sent by the Irish in America to their people at home.[2] The people at home, in the meantime, remained either in the same con-

[1] Thom's Directory.
[2] Lord Dufferin, quoted by Healy, p. 49.

dition or usually sank deeper into the mire of inextricable poverty. In other words, the money sent from the Irish in America did the farmer no good: it was all swallowed up by the Irish landlord; it was part of the world-wide tribute this caste was able to extort. This incontestable fact adds another element of humour to the complaint of the landlord class that the subscriptions which were brought into the Irish National League by the Irish race in America and Australia came mostly from servant-girls, and much rhetoric was expended from the same quarter in denunciation of the agitators who lived on their hard-won wages. These denunciations, which, as a matter of fact, were not founded upon truth, would have been more becoming if they had not proceeded from a class which had been for a generation the greatest tax and the most prominent burden of the servant-girls of New York, Chicago, Melbourne, and every other city where exiled Irish labour seeks the market it has been refused at home.

The loss of the migratory labourers in 1877 is calculated by Dr. Nelson Hancock at £250,000.[1] The amount of value of the potato in 1879[2] was £3,341,028. In other words, two-thirds of the entire potato crop was gone, and in some parts of the country the crop was entirely gone. 'The potato crop,' said the Registrar-General, 'will be deficient in every province, county, and union.' 'The salient point is,' says the same authority, 'that in 1878 the estimated produce of potatoes in Ireland was 50,530,080 cwt. the average for ten years being 60,752,910 cwt., whereas the estimated yield for 1879 is only 22,273,520 cwt., a most alarming decrease.'[3] The meaning of these figures was unmistakable. Famine was coming again!

The next factor in the situation was the action of the landlords. The action of the landlords in 1879 justified their whole traditions. The deeper grew the distress of the farmers, the more exacting became the demands and the more merciless became the attitude of the landlords. Here are the official figures upon the subject, and they may be left to tell their own tale:

EVICTIONS.

1876	...	...	...	... 1,269
1877	...	...	...	... 1,323
1878	...	...	...	... 1,749
1879	...	...	...	... 2,667

It was at first sight apparently one of the tragic facts of the case that the Chief Secretaryship of Ireland at this period of impending and awful disaster was held by such a man as Mr. James Lowther. The appointment of such a person, with his illiterate mind, his mediæval and impenetrable ignorance, his bold but perilous stubbornness, was universally regarded as one of the jokes by which Lord Beaconsfield occasionally gratified the wanton caprice of great power. As if to deepen the contrast between the condition of Ireland and the tenure of the Chief Secretary's office by such a man, Mr. Lowther was accustomed to clothe his thoughts in a brusque humour that smacked somewhat of the stable, but at the same time was not unamusing. But the Irish people were not in the condition to relish jokes, especially at their own expense; and to them it seemed an almost intolerable aggravation of their lot that this hopelessly ignorant and densely obstinate man should grin, buffoon-like, as the succession of scenes in the national tragedy unveiled themselves before his eyes.

[1] Healy, p. 72.   [2] Ib.   [3] Ib., p. 71.

During the earlier months of 1879 the attention of the Chief Secretary had been called more than once to the calamity that was impending over Ireland. He received all these statements with easy and jaunty denials. At last, on May 27, when the House was adjourning for the Whitsuntide recess, the Irish members made a final attempt to force the condition of the country upon the attention of the Chief Secretary. Entreaty, argument, intimate acquaintance with the facts of the case—graphic pictures of the dire distress of the country—all were lost on Mr. Lowther. He was ready to go so far as to acknowledge that there was 'some' depression in the agriculture of Ireland ; but he went on to say he was glad to think that that depression, although undoubted, was 'neither so prevalent nor so acute as the depression existing in other parts of the United Kingdom.'[1] 'Seldom,' justly remarks Mr. A. M. Sullivan, 'did an English Minister speak a sentence destined to have more memorable results. In that moment Mr. James Lowther sealed the doom of Irish landlordism ;'[2] for Mr. Lowther's answer drove Mr. Parnell into the ranks of the Land League. The agrarian movement in Ireland meantime had been greatly stimulated by Mr. Davitt—a remarkable man with a remarkable history.

Michael Davitt was born in 1846, near the small village of Straid, in the county of Mayo. His father was a farmer who was among the many thousand victims of those wholesale evictions in that dread period which have been fully described in previous pages of this book. Mr. Davitt was but four years of age when he saw his home destroyed. His father and mother came to England, 'and had to beg through the streets of England for bread.' The family settled in the little town of Haslingden in Lancashire. His mother was in the habit of frequently repeating the details of this cruel and memorable episode in his earliest years ; and, undoubtedly, it was this eviction scene which influenced the fortunes of his entire family, and has been the fiercest incentive of Davitt's attitude towards landlordism ever since. Over and over again references to this incident occur in his speeches. Replying once to an ungenerous attack made upon him, which appeared under the name of the late Archbishop MacHale, though probably never written by him, he wrote :

'Some twenty-five years ago my father was ejected from a small holding near the parish of Straid, in Mayo, because unable to pay a rent which the crippled state of his resources, after struggling through the famine years, rendered impossible. Trials and sufferings in exile for a quarter of a century, in which I became physically disabled for life, a father's grave dug beneath American soil, myself the only member ever destined to live or die in Ireland, and this privilege existing only by virtue of "ticket-of-leave," are the consequences which followed that eviction.'[3]

When he was still a child he was sent to a mill to work, and there he was by an accident deprived of his right arm. At this time he had received but the merest rudiments of education, and this accident obtained for him the advantage of another instalment of instruction. At eleven years of age he secured employment in the local post-office ; and as the postmaster had also a business in printing and stationery, Mr. Davitt had an opportunity of taking an occasional peep at books.[4]

[1] Hansard, vol. ccxlvi., p. 246.   [2] 'New Ireland,' p. 438.
[3] D. B. Cashman's 'Life of Michael Davitt,' p. 96.
[4] 'Land of Eire,' by John Devoy, p. 38.

In this way he had already attained some prominence among the Irishmen of his district; but up to this time he had not formed strong national opinions; or, if there were the germs of such opinions in his mind, they had not assumed definite shape. One night he went to hear an address on an Irish subject. The wrongs of Ireland were narrated by an eloquent tongue. All the latent forces and unformed notions in Mr. Davitt's nature were at once crystallized; and from that hour forward he was an ardent Irish Nationalist. He soon became an active member of the Fenian organization, and he took part in the attempted seizure of Chester Castle. 'Unable to shoulder a rifle with his single arm, he carried a small store of cartridges in a bag made from a pocket-handkerchief.'[1]

After the failure of the enterprise, he managed to escape arrest and return to Haslingden; but he soon entered on active operations again in connection with the movement, and was employed in the work of purchasing arms and forwarding them to Ireland. On May 14, 1870, he was arrested in London along with an Englishman named John Wilson, a gunsmith of Birmingham, and he was convicted mainly on the evidence of an informer named Corydon, and sentenced to fifteen years' penal servitude. He was often subjected, like the other Irish political prisoners, to that brutality of punishment which England and Russia are alone among European countries in inflicting upon political prisoners. It is impossible for a man of any nationality to read his own account of the sufferings and indignities through which he had to pass without feelings of burning anger. A rebel against laws which had broken up his home, impoverished and exiled those dearest to him, he had resorted to the only weapons which then seemed capable of arresting the attention of that country whose apathy to Irish ruin Mr. Gladstone has so well described, and he was but ante-dating reforms, most of which have since passed into law; but he was sent to herd with murderers, pickpockets, and burglars, passed through solitary confinement, and was overworked, underfed, and exposed to all changes of the seasons.

At last, on Wednesday morning, December 19, 1877—after seven years and seven months of this dread suffering—he was released. A series of enthusiastic receptions awaited him and the three other Fenian prisoners who had been released about the same time, namely, Colour-Sergeant McCarthy, Corporal Thomas Chambers, and Private John P. Bryan. It had been constantly denied that Sergeant McCarthy had been ill-treated in prison, and asserted that his health had in no way suffered. Two days after his arrival in Dublin, however, McCarthy gave testimony that could no longer be denied. Mr. Davitt, McCarthy, and the two other released prisoners had been invited by Mr. Parnell to breakfast with him in Morrison's Hotel. While they were awaiting breakfast, McCarthy was observed to grow pale and totter across the room, and, having been laid on the sofa, in a few moments he was dead. The twelve years of penal servitude had at last done their work.

Mr. Davitt then proceeded on a lecturing tour throughout England and Scotland. Later on, he determined to go to America to see his mother and other relatives who had settled in the town of Manayunk in Pennsylvania. He landed in New York about the beginning of August, 1878. At this time he had very few acquaintances in America; he soon, however, came in contact with some leading Irishmen settled in that country, and made

[1] 'Land of Eire,' by John Devoy, p. 38.

a favourable impression upon them. After various consultations, Mr. Davitt formed an outline of a land movement; but his ideas were still in a crude and indefinite shape.

When he returned to Ireland, time and the seasons fought upon his side. Widespread distress threatened to be most severe in the West, and, curiously enough, there already existed in that region the germs of a land movement. The tenants had kept up some form of association from the moment at which the worthlessness of the Land Act of 1870 was discovered. In Dublin, for instance, there was an organization known as 'The Central Tenants' Defence Association,' the object of which was the attainment of what afterwards became known as the 'Three F's.' There was also a local organization which subsequently, perhaps, did more than any other to beget the Land League; this was the Tenants' Defence Association of Ballinasloe. The foremost figure of this association was a man named Matthew Harris. Matthew Harris is one of the most interesting and striking figures of the Irish movements of the last thirty years. During all this period he has devoted himself with self-sacrificing and unremitting zeal to the attainment of complete redress of his country's grievances. In this respect politics are with him an absorbing passion, almost a religion. In pursuit of this high and noble end he has risked death, lost liberty, ruined his business prospects. Eager, enthusiastic, vehement, he has at the same time that grim tenacity of purpose by which forlorn hopes are changed into triumphant fruitions. He has fought the battle against landlordism in the dark as well as in the brightest hour with unshaken resolution. Reared in the country, from an early age he saw landlordism in its worst shape and aspect; his childish recollections are of cruel and heartless evictions. Thus it is that in every movement for the liberation of the farmer or of Ireland during the last thirty years he has been a conspicuous figure, as hopeful, energetic, laborious in the hour of despair, apathy, and lassitude, as in times of universal vigour, exultation, and activity.

But it was not in the county of Galway that this movement took its birth. Mr. Davitt, as has been seen, was a native of the neighbouring county of Mayo, and there he determined to make the first start. The Land League may be dated from one of these meetings. This was a gathering which assembled on April 20, 1879, at Irishtown, in the county of Mayo. This meeting was convened for the purpose of protesting against some acts of oppression on the part of the landlords of the district. The promoters of the meeting were Mr. Davitt and Mr. Brennan, the latter afterwards secretary of the Land League. Mr. Davitt did not attend the meeting, and the chief speaker at it was Mr. O'Connor Power, M.P. Several other meetings followed. The deepening distress among the farmers and the increase of evictions by the landlords supplied an impetus which had the effect of advancing the movement with extraordinary rapidity. The times, in fact, were ripe for an agrarian revolt. But, as yet, the movement was local and obscure. Scarcely any reports found their way into the metropolitan newspapers, and the country was generally unconscious of the portentous new birth. Deservedly great as was the influence of Mr. Davitt, and immense as were his exertions, the movement could not be said yet to have reached its pinnacle until the leader came to whom, at this moment, the eyes and hopes and affections of all Irish Nationalists were gradually turning. One of the great forces which had inspired the hope and strength that made the new movement possible was the spirit excited throughout Ireland by the attitude of Mr. Parnell and Mr. Biggar in the House of Commons. The scenes—vexatious, indecorous, wanton, or boorish, as they appeared to the English public—were to the people of Ireland the electric messages of new hopes. Every word of these scenes was read with fierce and breathless eagerness. The representatives of a country trodden under foot for centuries were seen in the citadel of the enemy, aggressive and defiant. The Parliament that trampled upon every Irish demand for so many generations was seen raging in hysteric and impotent fury against the growing omnipotence of two determined men. The movement that starts from 1879 will not be understood unless the fact is grasped that Ireland at that moment was living under the burning glow of Parliamentary 'obstruction.' The temper which this fact produced was the original impulse in preventing the farmers of 1879 from lying down, dumb, helpless, and cowering, under eviction, famine, and plague, as was done by their fathers in 1846-47.

The position Mr. Parnell had already attained marked him out as a man who, if he undertook the leadership of a movement, would carry it through every defile of difficulty and danger to the end. He was rapidly becoming the idol of the people, who could fuse their passions and their affections into a united and mighty effort. For a considerable time Mr. Parnell hesitated before taking a step beyond the 'Three F's,' but at last he crossed the Rubicon and joined the ranks of those who declared that the struggle on the Land Question should only end with the transfer of the proprietorship of the soil from the landlord to the tiller. This was to be the final settlement of the question; but, meanwhile, the wolf was at the door. How was the emergency of deepening distress, of ever-advancing famine and ever-increasing eviction to be met? This was the terrible problem which Mr. Parnell had now to face.

And now I have come to one of the cross-roads in my story. All that I have written will have failed in its purpose if the reader do not see the road to take at this crisis, clearly marked out as with an iron finger. My chief reason in bringing into this chapter of Irish history an account of 1846 and 1847 and the years immediately after, was because 1846 and 1847 are the background of 1879 and 1880. The second epoch is entirely unintelligible without a knowledge and true appreciation of the first. 1846 and 1847 left two memories: the memory of the terrible suffering, and the memory of how that suffering was submitted to. Ever since there has been no feeling so bitter in the hearts of Irishmen—especially the hearts of young Irishmen—as the feeling that much of the awful suffering could have been prevented if the people only had had the courage to act in their own defence; to refuse to allow food to be exported from a starving nation; to refuse the payment of impossible rents that one man might luxuriate in an hour of national cataclysm and tens of thousands perish in the agonies of hunger and of typhus fever; to refuse submission to decrees of eviction, and, through eviction, of death or exile from lands brought to fertility by their toil, from houses built in their own sweat and blood and tears. And this is something more than a mere feeling. The idea will stand the test of the severest examination, that in a moment of national crisis, such as the Irish famine, the safety of the nation demanded some sacrifice on the part of the landlords—a sacrifice best if willingly made, as by the landlords in England and in Scotland; in any case, a sacrifice, whether willing or unwilling.

Mr. Parnell found the majority of the farmers face to face with either of these two dilemmas: If they had all the rent, they might give every penny to the landlord, and allow themselves, their wives, and their children to perish. If they had not the rent, and the landlord insisted on his 'rights,' they were subject to eviction on a scale as wholesale as the clearances that followed 1846 and 1847. To call upon the people, under circumstances like these, to pay all their rent, was to recommend them to follow the example of 1846 with the sequels of 1847—wholesale starvation and wholesale eviction. This was not the policy that recommended itself to Mr. Parnell; such a policy would have been that of a coward and a traitor. The first Land meeting attended by Mr. Parnell took place at Westport on June 8, 1879. Mr. Parnell, in his speech, laid down on clear and distinct lines the Land policy of the future and the policy of the hour. He declared in favour, not of the 'Three F's,' but of Peasant Proprietary.

'In Belgium,' said Mr. Parnell, 'in Prussia, in France, and in Russia the land has been given to the people—to the occupiers of the land. In some cases the landlords have been deprived of their property in the soil by the iron hand of revolution; in other cases, as in Prussia, the landlords have been purchased out. If such an arrangement could be made without injuring the landlord, so as to enable the tenant to have his land as his own, and to cultivate it as it ought to be cultivated, it would be for the benefit and prosperity of the country.'

But this, as he said immediately, was to be regarded as the final settlement of the question; the immediate point was what the people were to do in order to avert the calamity which was at that moment at their very doors.

'Now,' he said, 'what must we do in order to induce the landlords to see the position? You must show the landlords that you intend to hold a firm grip of your homesteads and land.'[1]

The phrase had such appropriateness to the situation and to the time that it at once passed into men's mouths. While in the train which brought him to this meeting, Mr. Parnell was passing over in memory some of the scenes in which Mr. Biggar and himself had taken part in Parliament. He was musing over the deadly tenacity with which the member for Cavan always stuck to his purpose. Tenacity was translated into the shorter word 'grip,' and thus was born the memorable and potent phrase 'hold,' or, as it was afterwards expressed, 'keep a firm grip of your homesteads and land.'

From the moment Mr. Parnell put himself at the head of the Land movement it spread with enormous rapidity, and soon reached startling proportions. Meeting after meeting was held in many parts of Ireland, and before long it was evident that Mr. Parnell was at the head of the mightiest popular movement since the days of O'Connell and 1845. Meantime, the Government and the London press looked on with sinister eye. A central organization was formed in September, 1879. On October 21, 1879, a meeting was held by circular in the Imperial Hotel, Lower O'Connell (then Sackville) Street; Mr. A. J. Kettle presided. The Land League was then and there founded. The following resolutions set forth the principles of the new organization:—

I. That the objects of the League are, first, to bring about a reduction

[1] *Freeman's Journal*, June 8, 1879.

of rack-rents ; second, to facilitate the obtaining of the ownership of the soil by the occupiers.

II. That the objects of the League can be best attained (1) by promoting organization among the tenant farmers ; (2) by defending those who may be threatened with eviction for refusing to pay unjust rents ; (3) by facilitating the working of the Bright Clauses of the Land Act during the winter ; and (4) by obtaining such reform in the laws relating to land as will enable every tenant to become the owner of his holding by paying a fair rent for a limited number of years.

Mr. Parnell was elected president, and Mr. Kettle, Mr. Davitt, and Mr. Brennan were appointed honorary secretaries. Mr. J. G. Biggar, M.P., Mr. W. H. O'Sullivan, M.P., and Mr. Patrick Egan were appointed treasurers, and a resolution was passed calling upon Mr. Parnell to go to America and obtain assistance. Mr. John Dillon was to accompany Mr. Parnell to America.

This was the first time that the leader of a constitutional movement had gone among the Irish in America for the purpose of obtaining assistance for the people at home. Mr. Parnell's tour was a series of enthusiastic receptions. Wherever he went, and in nearly every town through which he passed, he addressed thousands of people. Officials of the United States attended and presided over his meetings, and at last he was paid the compliment of which only two other men—Kossuth and Dr. England—had been the recipients in the whole course of American history : he was permitted to address the House of Representatives at Washington. The financial results of this tour were extraordinarily large. The Land League, owing to the severity of the distress throughout the country, had resolved to devote a portion of their funds to the relief of the distress. The funds raised by Mr. Parnell were divided into two parts—one for the purpose of organization, the other for the relief of distress. For both, about £72,000 had been subscribed.

The indirect effects of this tour were, perhaps, even more important. The reality of Irish distress could no longer be denied, and there grew up a competition between different sections as to which should most liberally contribute towards the movement for preventing famine. Thus, although Mr. Lowther as Chief Secretary had denied the existence of distress, the fact had been brought so clearly home to the mind of the Lord-Lieutenant, that his wife, the Duchess of Marlborough, issued an appeal, giving a dark picture of the state of the country, and formed a relief committee. The Lord Mayor of Dublin for 1880 happened to be a man of great energy and ability—Mr. E. Dwyer Gray—and he also formed a committee of relief ; and thus, by the beginning of 1880, no fewer than three committees were working to prevent the occurrence of famine. Thus the action of Mr. Parnell and the Land League had brought the condition of the country from the region of debate into that of admitted fact, notorious to all the nations of the world.

Even Mr. Lowther and the Parliament were compelled at last to listen. Acknowledging the distress, they adopted a method for meeting it which is perhaps unexampled even in the history of the legislation of the House of Commons on the Irish Land Question. While the landlords were scattering notices of eviction over the country wholesale, the Government conceived the felicitous idea that the landlords formed the most suitable agency for supplying relief to the tenants. Accordingly, a Bill was introduced, the effect of which was to lend to the landlords the sum of £1,092,985 without interest for two years, and one per cent. at interest afterwards. This money was to be used by the landlords in giving employment to their tenants, and in thus preventing the spread of famine. With unconscious humour this extraordinary measure was called 'The Relief of Distress Act.'

In March, 1880, Lord Beaconsfield decided to dissolve Parliament. The cry he chose was an anti-Irish manifesto. I will not stop in this place to examine into the morality of the statesman who, at the moment when Ireland was in the very agony of famine, did not scruple to arouse the fierce racial passions of the more powerful against the weaker nation.

The news of the impending Dissolution reached Mr. Parnell on March 8, when he was speaking at Montreal. At once he saw that it was necessary for him to proceed to Ireland without one moment's delay. His lecture delivered, he started for New York. On the very morning of his departure he laid the foundation of a Land League in America, and on March 10 he sailed for home. He reached Queenstown on March 21; the Dissolution took place on March 24, and the first election in Ireland was on April 1. The interval for a general electoral campaign was small indeed. However, the moment he landed in Ireland he proceeded to fight the election with an energy that seemed diabolic. He rushed from one part of the country to another, made innumerable speeches, had interviews with most of the Parliamentary candidates, himself stood for three constituencies. Throughout all this feverish struggle there was ever by his side, sharing, and often doing most of his work, the bright, fiercely industrious, sleeplessly active young secretary whom he had summoned to him in America.

Mr. Parnell fought the entire election with the sum of £1,250—£1,000 which he obtained as a personal loan, £100 sent from Liverpool, and £150 which was obtained by his astute secretary from political opponents after a fashion not unamusing.[1] He was thus unable to put forward candidates for several constituencies in which his name would have ensured success, and he was obliged to put up with the wrecks of broken faith and falsified pledges which previous Parliaments had laid high and dry on the political shore. In some other constituencies he did not find time or opportunity to interfere at all. And in this way he and the constituencies and the Irish cause were deprived of many a man who might have swelled the ranks of those who fought throughout the memorable years between 1880 and 1885. His toughest contest was in the city of Cork, which he won from Mr. Nicholas D. Murphy, a characteristic specimen of the class of Catholic Whigs whose timidity and treachery have been one of the most potent agencies in the hands of English Ministers for prolonging the reign of Irish misery and of Irish servitude. The result of the whole election was that there were sixty-eight men returned as Home Rulers. The deceptiveness of this total will be judged from the fact that among the Home Rulers were reckoned such men as Mr. J. Orrell Lever, returned as one of the members for Galway, and Mr. Whitworth, returned for Drogheda. Of the other Home Rulers the majority were reckoned supporters of Mr. Shaw, and but a small minority were openly pledged to follow Mr. Parnell; a considerable number had not made a definite choice between the policies of the rival leaders.

---

[1] T. M. Healy in *United Ireland*, August 20, 1883.

CHAPTER X.

THE LAND LEAGUE.

THE struggle between the two sections of the Home Rule Party soon began. Without any consultation with Mr. Parnell a meeting of the new party was called for. Several of the new members refused to attend. A second meeting had to be convened, and this took place at the City Hall, Dublin, on May 17. On this occasion nearly every one of the new men who had been returned to support Mr. Parnell was present. To the general world they were unknown, obscure, and to some extent despised; and many of them were young. But there was scarcely one of them whose previous career had not been a preparation for the position which he now held, and who had not been living a life either of action or of thought to which membership of a party led by such a leader as Mr. Parnell was an appropriate climax. Amid their varied characters they all possessed something alike in a certain dash of fanaticism. Mr. Justin McCarthy had been elected before. Almost from his entry into the House of Commons he had drifted towards the side of Mr. Parnell. Some surprise was felt when he consented to stand and be elected as an Irish member; probably there was more than one city in England or Scotland that would have felt honoured by such a representative as the author of the 'History of Our Own Times,' and there certainly would in time have been a Liberal Administration that would have been glad to have counted him among its members. Even many Irishmen at the start of Justin McCarthy's career may have felt that he would have taken his place in the ranks of an English Liberal Government as appropriately as in those of an Irish National Party. And yet Justin McCarthy had a past of which but few people knew; but to those who knew that past, its most complete and fitting sequel was that Mr. McCarthy should be one of the leaders of the first really independent party in the British Parliament.

Justin McCarthy was born in Cork in 1830. When he was a boy the capital of Munster could lay claim to really deserve the traditional reputation of the province for learning. Mr. McCarthy's father was one of the best classical scholars of the day, and there was at that time a schoolmaster named Goulding—the name is familiar to many a Corkman still—who was a really fine scholar. Justin McCarthy was one of Goulding's pupils, and when he left school he had the not common power even among hard students of being able to read Greek fluently, and to write as well as translate Latin with complete ease. He had taught himself shorthand, and his first employment was that of a reporter on the *Cork Examiner*. It may be an interesting fact to note that his hand still retains its cunning, and that he may often be observed taking down on the margin of the Parliamentary Order Paper the exact words of some important Ministerial statement for quotation in his leading article. There are two other important reminiscences of Mr. McCarthy's reporting days. He was present at the meeting in Cork at which the late Judge Keogh swore that oath which played so tragic a part in Irish history; and he was also present, as has been seen, at the famous dinner at which the present Lord Fitzgerald, then a rising young lawyer, in the ardour and virulence of his patriotism, bearded a Lord-Lieutenant, and scandalized an audience of Cork's choicest Whigs. It was in 1847 that Mr. McCarthy started his professional life, and everybody knows that all that was young, enthusiastic, and earnest in Cork shared the political aspirations of that stormy time. There had been in existence for many years a debating society known as the 'Scientific and Literary Society,' and one of the many forms in which the new spirit roused by Young Ireland showed itself was the starting of a body known as the Cork Historical Society, as a rival to the older and tamer association. Among the members of this body were many young fellows who afterwards rose to importance. Sir John Pope Hennessy, lately Governor of the Mauritius, and Justin McCarthy himself, were among its first recruits. The Historical Society became a recruiting ground for Young Ireland; nearly all its members joined the party of combat, and they founded one of the many Confederate Clubs that were started to prepare for the coming struggle.

President Grévy in his sober age remembers the day when he mounted a barricade. Similarly Justin McCarthy, in his maturity of philosophic calm, can look back to a time when he dreamed of rifles and bayonet charges, and death in the midst of fierce fight for the cause of Ireland. To those who know him there is no difference in the man of to-day and the man of '48. He has still the same unflinching courage as then. In this respect, indeed, Justin McCarthy is a singular mixture of incompatibilities. There is no man who enjoys the hour more keenly. He has the capacity of M. Renan for finding the life around him amusing; enjoys society and solitude, work and play, a choice dinner or an all-night sitting. But he has eminently 'a two o'clock in the morning courage'—a readiness to face the worst without notice. With his fifty-seven years he is still a man of sanguine temperament; but in '48 he was only eighteen. He naturally, therefore, belonged to the section which had Mitchel for its apostle, and open and immediate insurrection for its gospel. Mitchel was arrested, and no attempt was made to rescue him; and there were many among the companions of McCarthy who saw in this failure the death of their hopes, the end of their efforts for the Irish cause. Justin McCarthy was not one of those.

Even after Mitchel's arrest, and the miserable *fiasco* in which the rebellion of 1848 had ended, there were still some young and unconquerable men who thought that all hopes of resurrection through revolution should not be allowed to die. Probably they did not hope to win in the struggle against the might of England; but the awful tragedy thus being enacted in Ireland made acquiescence a crime, and they resolved to do something which would get the world to stop and listen, and perhaps pity and help. If they could not win, they would show at least that there were some Irishmen who knew how to die, and, perchance, out of their graves might come some hope for the awful despair of the Irish nation in this epoch of famine, plague and eviction. They enrolled members, gathered arms, drilled, settled a scheme of simultaneous revolt in various parts of the country. In all these things Justin McCarthy took his part, and in the region where the Cork Park now stands, the future historian swore in the members of a revolutionary organization. The effort ended as so many before and since: there was a mistake about the signal; the simultaneous outbreak did not take place, and the few sporadic risings which did break out were crushed.

With this episode ended for the moment Justin McCarthy's political history, and from this period, for many years, his story is that of the literary man. In the year 1851 Mr. McCarthy first tried his fortunes in London. The attempt ended in failure, and he had to return to the reporter's place in Cork. Not long after this he met with his first piece of luck. There was at that time a Royal Commission for inquiring into the fairs and markets of Ireland, and the secretary having broken down, Justin McCarthy was taken on as the official shorthand writer. His aptitude was such that some member of the Commission urged him to again go to London, and armed him with letters of introduction to persons of influence. This was in 1852. McCarthy again tried his chance, and went to the *Times* and other offices, but without success. Before he could continue this fruitless labour he heard of the *Northern Times*, the first provincial daily of England, which was just about to be started in Liverpool, applied for a situation, and was accepted.

But he was still only a reporter, and even he himself did not yet very well know whether he was fitted for better things. He worked on, gave literary lectures, and in the end was allowed the privilege of contributing to the editorial columns. He remained in Liverpool till 1860; in that year the *Northern Times*, pressed hard by more daring rivals, failed. McCarthy was contended for by several Liverpool journals, but he declined all, fixed in the resolve to make or mar his fortune in London. At this time the young journalist had a counsellor who for many years was the chief arbiter of his destiny. Before he had left Cork he had seen, but he had never spoken to, Miss Charlotte Allman, a member of the well-known Munster family, and, in the meantime, Miss Allman had come to reside with her brother in Liverpool. The two young people resolved to marry, in spite of the strong opposition of relatives and in face of the frowning fortunes of a young, a badly paid, and as yet unknown journalist; and in 1855 they were married in the town of Macclesfield. To those who knew Mrs. McCarthy there is no need to dilate on the resistless charm of her truly beautiful nature. She never wrote a line; she did not even pretend to any literary power; but she had the keen intelligence of sympathy, she had faith in her husband, and she had indomitable courage. It was she that induced Mr. McCarthy to refuse all the Liverpool offers, and that turned his face steadily to the larger hopes of London. The joint capital of the young couple when they landed in London was £10. Of that they spent more than £1 in buying an olive or some other sprout, which was planted with lofty hopes in the garden of their new house in Battersea, and which, of course, perished after a short and sickly existence.

Mr. McCarthy's first engagement in London was as a Parliamentary reporter on the *Morning Star*. He found time to do other work in the intervals of this hard occupation, and, mainly through the persuasions of his wife, tried his hand at an essay for one of the big magazines. He had taught himself French, German, and Italian; was familiar with the three literatures; and his first attempt at essay-writing had Schiller for its subject. He next tried the *Westminster Review*, and two articles of his in that periodical suggested views so novel, and at the same time so correct, that they attracted the attention of John Stuart Mill. The philosopher was introduced to the young writer, showed a friendly interest in his welfare, and helped to advance his fortunes. Promotion at last began to come rapidly. In the autumn of 1860 he was appointed foreign editor of the *Morning Star*, and in 1865 he became editor-in-chief. Those who remember the journal and the times when it lived will know what splendid service it did to the cause of Ireland, which at that period seemed terribly hopeless indeed; and its tone of energetic and even fierce advocacy of Irish national claims was, of course, largely due to the inspiration of the ardent Irishman who was then at its head. It was while he was in this position that Mr. McCarthy became intimately acquainted with Mr. John Bright. The great tribune was fond of spending some hours in the office of the *Star*, in which his sister—the widow of Samuel Lucas, who was brother of the Frederick Lucas of Irish history—had some shares; and many an hour did the editor and the politician spend together in discussing the oratorical exploits of Mr. Gladstone, the thing that did duty for a conscience in Mr. Disraeli, or the comparative merits of Shakespeare and Milton. It is one of the unpleasant consequences of the fierce struggles of the last few years that those two old friends have ceased even to speak to one another. But in 1868, when it became clear that Mr. Bright was going to become a Minister, and when he sold out his share in the *Morning Star*, Mr. McCarthy lost all desire to be further connected with the journal, and resigned his position.

He then went to America. His reputation had gone before him, and he found an embarrassing choice of offers awaiting him. He had, while still editor of the *Star*, published his first novel, 'Paul Massey' (this appeared in 1866)—a story written after the sensational fashion of that hour, which Mr. McCarthy has since suppressed. This had been followed, in 1867, by the 'Waterdale Neighbours'—a charming story. One of Mr. McCarthy's first engagements was to write a series of stories for the *Galaxy*, then perhaps the chief literary magazine in America. He was also asked to lecture, and partly because the terms were extremely remunerative, and partly out of a desire to see the country, he consented. He was an extremely successful lecturer, and between his pen and his tongue found the United States the El Dorado it has proved to so many from the old world. He paid a brief visit to London in the middle of 1870, returned again in the autumn of that year, and finally in the autumn of 1871 came back to England for good. His name meantime had been kept steadily before the English reading public. In 1869 'My Enemy's Daughter,' which had been written nearly ten years before, ran through *Belgravia*, then under the management of Miss Braddon. Immediately after his return Mr. McCarthy was offered, and accepted, an engagement on the *Daily News* as Parliamentary leader writer. For years he was one of the best-known figures in the Reporters' Gallery, and was looked up to by most of his editorial colleagues, as the man who took the most rapid and the most accurate view of a Parliamentary situation, and as having the most sagacious head of the political writers of his time. His literary fortunes, meantime, steadily advanced; and in 'Dear Lady Disdain' he wrote a novel which everybody talked about, and upon which there was a real run. With the versatility which is so singular he soon after devoted himself to another and a very different kind of work, undertaking a contemporary chronicle, under the title 'The History of Our Own Times,' the first two volumes of which were published in 1878. Everybody knows the result. The book—to quote the hackneyed expression—took the town by storm. It was praised with equal fervour by Conservative and by Liberal critics; its style was as much an object of eulogy as its tone and its temper. It was, indeed, a model of what contemporary history should be. Equal justice was dealt out to all parties; the portraits of men were clear-cut and sympathetic, and the style was evenly melodious without one single attempt at rhetoric, without one phrase or one passage that could be called pretentious. The book sold with enormous rapidity, and edition followed edition in rapid succession. Great as was its success on this side of the water, it had a success still greater in America. Rival publishers brought out rival editions, and the present writer never remembers to have gone on any journey in America without seeing a copy of the 'History of Our Own Times' in the hands of several of the passengers. But the hapless author gained little from this enormous American sale, for as yet there is no copyright between England and America. His old publishers, the Messrs. Harper and Brothers, with that fair dealing which characterises all their transactions, did send him voluntarily an occasional instalment of a hundred pounds or so, but they at the same time told him that if there had been an international copyright they could have well afforded to have given him £10,000 for his rights. It may be interesting to note that Mr. McCarthy's profits from the book up to the present have been £6,000.

Little has been said of Mr. McCarthy's modern political career. The member for Longford is one of the men who does not owe Mr. Parnell anything—as the Irish leader would himself be the first to acknowledge—but Mr. McCarthy soon saw that in Mr. Parnell there was the real chief of that honest and independent Parliamentary Party for which, like so many of the old '48 men, he had been vainly looking upwards of thirty years; to Mr. Parnell, then, he unreservedly gave his confidence and his support. Sagacious, tranquil, and experienced, he was thrown into a prominent position at an epoch of fierce and tempestuous passions; but nobody was readier to see, when the time came, the necessity for strong action. He has been ready on every emergency to take his share of the unspeakable drudgery to which Irish members have been subjected during the last few years; and it imposed a greater sacrifice on him than on any other member of the Irish party to face the odium and the loss of personal and professional *prestige* which a part in these unpopular labours involved. If the delivery of Mr. McCarthy were equal to his intellectual and rhetorical powers, he would be amongst the foremost speakers of the House. He is ready; he has eminently clearness of head and calmness of temper; and his ideas clothe themselves in language of beauty, smoothness, and appropriateness with an unerring regularity which belongs to but two other speakers in the House—Mr. Gladstone and Mr. Sexton. He has in more than one debate delivered the best speech in point of matter and of form. His was the best speech in the strange debate which occurred on Mr. O'Donnell's suspension for his attacks on M. Challemel-Lacour, and his was the most effective of the many effective replies given to Mr. Forster's historic attack on Mr. Parnell. Mr. McCarthy in one style of speech is far and away superior to any of his party, and probably to any man in the House—that is, as an after-dinner speaker. He bubbles over with wit of the most delicate and playful kind, and can keep the table in a roar.

Finally, let this sketch of Mr. McCarthy's career be closed with the mention of the saddest and darkest page of his life. Just as his long struggle was crowned with success, and as he became from the poor and obscure reporter the popular novelist, the successful historian, and the member of Parliament, the woman without whom he would have remained, in all probability, poor and obscure to the end, was seized with a lingering illness and died. It would be unbecoming to even attempt a description of what this loss meant to Mr. McCarthy.

Few can paint a character completely, and it is acquaintance only with the member for Longford that can make intelligible the peculiarly strong hold he has over the affections and admiration of his intimates. It is not often that there are found united in the same man modesty and literary genius, a toleration of others with a power of absolute self-abnegation, a sane enjoyment of every hour, with the courage of calmly facing, for the sake of the right cause, Fortune's worst blows, Destiny's most cruel decrees

Moderate in advice, when the fortunes of his country are at stake, he is always boldest when acts involve only personal risk to himself. It is this curious mixture of tenderness, shyness, and almost feminine romanticism with a thoroughly masculine and fearless spirit, that make him so beloved. There is something incomplete, says the French epigram, in the noble life that does not end on the scaffold, in the prison, or on the field of battle. May Justin McCarthy have many and prosperous days, and a tranquil and honourable end! But it is almost a pity that he cannot be hanged for high treason, to show how calmly a quiet man could die for Ireland.

In the debates of the meeting in the City Hall, Mr. Thomas Sexton broke silence for only a few minutes. Nobody could help remarking that his voice was peculiarly melodious; but few had any conception of the great things that were in this thin, delicate, rather retiring man.

Thomas Sexton was born in Waterford in 1848. He had not yet reached his thirteenth birthday when he entered a competition for a clerkship in the secretary's office of the Waterford and Limerick Company. The post was naturally unimportant; the salary, of course, small; but that did not prevent thirty youths entering the lists. Of these Sexton was the youngest, but he obtained the first place. He remained in the secretary's office till he was between twenty and twenty-one years of age, when, as will be seen, he left his native town, drawn to Dublin, like most young men of ability and enterprise.

The influence of his many years of dry toil in an office is visible in Sexton to-day. It has often been remarked that he has what is considered an un-Irish talent of dealing readily, clearly, and accurately with figures. This is no new talent. When he was in the railway office in Waterford his friends used to amuse themselves by giving him a long sum in compound addition, which most people would find it hard to calculate rapidly even with the aid of pen and ink. Sexton would close his eyes, and in a few minutes would give the answer with invariable accuracy. He used to say that the figures were 'written on his brain.' Sir George Trevelyan once brought in a Bill to increase official pay; and, speaking within a few minutes after the Chief Secretary had concluded, Sexton was able to tell, almost to a penny, what the sum-total meant to each individual, and was complimented by Sir George on his accuracy. But Sexton had another life beside that of the railway official. In his boyhood's days there was still a good deal of literary and social activity in the Irish provincial towns. The Mechanics' Institute and the Catholic Young Men's Society were both flourishing institutions in Waterford, and Sexton soon became the most prominent figure in both. He established a debating society; lectured when he was but sixteen on Oliver Goldsmith and John Banim, and on one occasion did duel in the Town Law with a delegation from the Portland Debating Society—a neighbouring rival —on the still vexed question of emigration. It speaks well for their instinctive appreciation of genius that the people of Waterford did not allow Sexton to leave their town, though he was but twenty-one years of age, altogether unnoticed. A public dinner was held in his honour, and he received addresses from the societies in which he had figured so largely.

This was the end of Sexton as a public speaker for a long series of years. In Dublin, where he arrived in 1869, he at once became a leader-writer on the *Nation*, then, as so long before, the most outspoken advocate of Nationalist principles. Sexton also in time became editor of the *Weekly News* and of *Young Ireland*, two publications also issued from the *Nation* office. Immersed in these things, and of a temperament shy and easy-going, Sexton never sought or even accepted any opportunity of displaying his great oratorical powers. He took his share in all the National movements, but it was as a silent and unknown member of those committees which do the practical work and leave the speech-making to others. Probably there was not one even of his intimates who suspected that this retiring *littérateur*, fond of his cigar, of pleasant company, and of prolonged vigils, would ever have the courage to face an audience larger than the *petit comité* which his wit—sly, delicate, slightly cynic—used to delight. But in 1879—the year of the Land League and of revolutionary upheaval—Sexton was brought at last, and almost in spite of himself, into the stormy arena of public life. In 1879 he was sent by the Council of the Land League to address a meeting in Dromore West, County Sligo. To the credit of the people there be it said that his speech made a profound impression, and that his great gifts received immediate recognition. But Dublin still did not know him; and when the General Election came he went very near being excluded from the ranks of the new Parliamentarians. He was proposed for his native county, but he was withdrawn; and when he was sent to Sligo he had to overcome many difficulties, and even friends thought an attack by so young and so obscure a man on a great magnate like Colonel King-Harman was a hopeless enterprise. But Sexton stumped the county, roused enthusiasm everywhere, and drove Colonel King-Harman from the seat.

In Parliament, Sexton again showed no anxiety to push himself prematurely forward. During his first session of Parliament he remained, comparatively speaking, unnoticed. He was phenomenally constant in attendance, and he was in the habit of putting what, in these early days of the new Irish Party, was considered a very large number of questions. But nobody yet had any idea that there was anything in him above very earnest and very respectable mediocrity, nor during the recess which followed did he advance his position to any appreciable degree. He was certainly one of the most constant among the speakers at the Land League meetings throughout the country; but this fact, while it procured him the notice of the Government so far that he was included in the famous trial of the traversers, did not have any very perceptible effect upon his own political fortunes. It was on an evening when Mr. Forster's Coercion Bill was under discussion that Sexton broke upon the House for the first time as a great orator. The House was, when he rose, but ill-prepared, indeed, for a patient acceptance of any speech from an Irish member; for of the subject it was already sick to death; and the final outcome was as predestined as the procession of the earth through the regions of the air. The physical circumstances of the moment tended to increase the prevalent depression, for it was a dull, dark, dismal evening. The House was, therefore, listless, sombre, and but thinly filled when Sexton rose. He spoke for two hours, not amid the enthusiastic plaudits which greet a powerful exponent of a great party's principles, but amid chilling silence, interrupted occasionally by the thin cheers of the small group of Irishmen around him—and yet when he sat down the whole House instinctively felt that a great orator had appeared among them. In the London newspapers the speech was reported in but a few lines. But members talked of it in the lobby and the smoke-room; Sir Stafford Northcote was reported to have praised it highly, and, among members of the House of Commons at least, Sexton's reputation was established.

In the councils of his party, the voice of Sexton has always been for good sense. Sagacity is, indeed, the very soul of his oratory. To think of him merely as the eloquent speaker is to forget the still greater claim to respect he holds as a man of remarkably well-balanced mind, of keen and almost faultless judgment. To describe the characteristics of Sexton's oratory is a task of extreme difficulty. He can marshal facts; he can discuss figures with the driest statistician, and can balance arguments with the most logic-chopping member of the House; and he can at the same time invest every subject with the glory of splendid language.

For the rest, Sexton is a keen observer, and his reading of men's motives is helped by a slight dash of cynicism. In ordinary affairs *blasé* and physically lethargic, his political industry is marvellous. He enters the House of Commons when the Speaker takes the chair, and never leaves it until the door-keeper's cry of 'Who goes home?' is heard. He sits in his place during all those long hours, grudging the time he spends at a hasty dinner—practically the one meal he takes in the day—or the few minutes he gives to the smoking of the dearly-loved cigar. Before he goes down to the House he has mastered all the business of the day, and his breakfast is of Blue Books. Orderly in many of his habits, he rarely approaches the discussion of any question without full knowledge of all the facts carefully arranged and abundantly illustrated by letters or other documents. He has great mastery of detail. Probably he was the only one except Sir Charles Dilke who knew all the figures connected with the Redistribution Bill. With every measure that in the least degree concerns Ireland he is acquainted down to the last clause, and thus it is that he enters on all debates with a singularly complete equipment. Finally, his mind is extraordinarily alert. His opponent has scarcely sat down when he is on his feet with counter-arguments to meet even the plausible case that has been made against him. It seems impossible to take him unawares, and words come without hesitation to express every shade of meaning. This gift, aided by *sangfroid*, makes him a most formidable opponent, and even the Speaker, backed by all the new rules of the House, and his own large and generous interpretation of his powers, has had more than once to succumb before the ready answer and the cool temper of Mr. Sexton.

Not one man in a hundred would ever guess when he heard Mr. Arthur O'Connor addressing the House of Commons that he had a drop of Irish blood in his veins. The whole air of the member for Queen's County is rigid, serious, icy. He drops his words with calculated slowness, and the subjects he selects for treatment are dry and formal and statistical—the subjects, in short, which are supposed to attract the plodding mind of the typical Englishman. The physique of Arthur O'Connor, too, suggests the same idea of a calmness and unemotional self-control which an Irishman is rarely supposed to possess; he is tall, thin, with a sombre air, and a cold, dark-blue eye. But to those who have learned to know him, all these outward presentments are but a mask; in the whole Irish Party—with all its fierce and strange spirits—there is not one whose heart beats with emotion so profound, with a hatred so fierce, a holy rage so lethal. The keen analysis of the French mind has divided enthusiasm into two kinds—the enthusiasm that is warm, and the enthusiasm that is cold. The enthusiasm of Arthur O'Connor is of the cold, that is, of the perilous, type.

Arthur O'Connor was born in London on October 1, 1844. His father was a county Kerry man, and was for many years one of the most eminent physicians, and at the same time one of the best-known figures in the social life of London. Arthur was educated at Ushaw; and in the year 1863 began life for himself by competing for a clerkship in the War Office. There was but one vacancy, and there were thirty competitors; O'Connor got the place, obtaining a higher average of marks than any Civil Service competitor for many years. For the space of sixteen years the young Irishman led the dull, sombre, monotonous life of the Civil Servant in the gloomy building in Pall Mall. He was a model clerk in being always accurate, attentive, hardworking; there never was, and there never could be, a charge of a single act of neglect or stupidity during the entire period. But outside his office Arthur O'Connor was the most unclerklike of men. He had political opinions—and political opinions of the most unpopular, the most unfashionable, above all of the most unprofitable, character. An effusive and unmeaning address to some monarchical personage was once being hawked around the War Office; it came in the end to Arthur O'Connor's desk. 'If you don't take that away,' said O'Connor to the gentleman who was collecting signatures, 'before I count twenty, I will put it into the fire.' Then he not only professed Irish National principles, but he joined an Irish organization, and in time became one of its rulers; for he was elected a member of the executive of the Home Rule Confederation. Finally, he began to be seen in the lobby in the House of Commons in earnest and frequent colloquy with Mr. Parnell, and the whisper went abroad that the statistical clerk was priming the Irish agitator with obstructive powder and shot. In this connection it may just be as well to make the passing observation that O'Connor never on a single occasion told Mr. Parnell even one word in reference to matters which official honour called upon him to keep private. Arthur O'Connor was by no means anxious to remain in his dingy rooms in Pall Mall. Under a scheme of reorganization, an offer was made to him, as well as to other clerks, to retire if he chose. He did so choose, and shook the dust of the War Office from off his feet.

He had already given a taste of his quality as a political gladiator in minor theatres, and the poor-law guardian in his case was veritably the father of the member of Parliament. In 1879 he was elected member of the Chelsea Board of Guardians, and the main purpose which he and his friends had in getting this place was that he might look after Catholic interests. These interests did, indeed, stand in sad need of some advocate. For six months, not one of the Catholic inmates of the workhouse had been allowed to go out to Mass, either on a Sunday or on a holiday; nor was a Catholic priest permitted to enter the place; no Catholic prayer-books were given to be read, and the Catholic children were sent to Protestant schools; and, finally, the institution was not stained by having a single 'Romanist'—as the phrase went in the vocabulary of the Board—among its officials. On the very first day on which O'Connor took his seat, the most eligible of all the applicants for the humble position of 'scrubber' was rejected on the sole ground that he was a Catholic. This was the large and complete penal code which the new member set out to destroy, and the task seemed certainly audacious and desperate enough. The Board consisted of twenty members. O'Connor was the single Catholic in the whole number —it was one man against nineteen. O'Connor started on his enterprise in a characteristic fashion. He was not aggressive in manner, nor violent in language; he made no speeches, either strong or long, nor did he, on the other hand, intrigue, or smile or coax. He relied on two weapons alone

—the weapons of knowledge and of hard work. He first mastered the whole complicated system of the poor-law code: after a while he had become such an expert in the law of the workhouse, and was withal so calm and so composed, that his fellow-guardians abandoned any attempt to trip him up.

But this was only a small part of O'Connor's work. He had been elected a member of the General Purposes Committee—this was when he was still an unknown quantity to his fellow-guardians—and the General Purposes was the committee which had the contracts to give and to examine, which dealt with accounts and other matters of high import in the economy of the workhouse. O'Connor devoted days and weeks to the study of all these accounts, with the result that he knew every item as intimately as if he had to pay it out of his own pocket. This was of all forms of knowledge the one which made O'Connor most formidable. It became impossible for a penny to pass muster for which full and satisfactory explanation was not given—jobbery trembled beneath the pitiless eye of this cold and calm inquisitor, and rogues fled abashed. All this could not be accomplished without terribly hard work. The meeting of the General Purposes Committee and of the Board was on the same day—Wednesday—and every Wednesday, as inevitable as night or death, O'Connor was in his place on the Committee and at the Board; and though this work often extended continuously from ten o'clock in the morning till eight at night, with the exception of half an hour for lunch, in his place he remained all the time. The Board was shocked at this indecent scrupulousness, this shocking conscientiousness, this rude industry, and disappointed jobbers began to ask how it was that a man could at the same time perform efficiently the duties of a Civil Servant and a poor-law guardian. 'How,' asked a guardian, 'could Mr. O'Connor attend every Wednesday, without exception, from ten to eight, without neglecting his official duties for at least one day in the week?' This guardian resolved to have the matter out, and proposed a resolution calling the attention of the Secretary for War to the conduct of the War Office clerk. The gentleman's disgust may be imagined when Mr. O'Connor himself stood up to second the resolution; and so had it laughed out of court. O'Connor had nothing to fear from any investigation by the War Secretary, or anybody else, for he had not neglected his official duties: he had not lost one single day, and the manner in which he carried out this programme will indicate the kind of man he is. In the War Office, as in the other Civil Service departments, each clerk is entitled to a month's vacation, and this vacation he is generally allowed to take at such times as he may wish. He may take it in a continuous month, or in a week now and a week again, or even by days if he like. Now the year of the War Office began in January; that of the Board of Guardians some months subsequently; the poor-law year, therefore, overlapped the year of the War Office. Thus O'Connor was able to take the War Office vacation of two years within the single year of the Board; and his two years' vacation were the Wednesdays which he spent at the Board of Guardians! The men are not many who would seek recreation, rest, enjoyment, in ten hours' work every Wednesday of every week, and in work without pay, without glory, and entirely for the benefit of the poorest and lowliest of mankind. Never was reformer so completely and so rapidly successful. He was but one year a member of the Board of Guardians—the combined forces of bigotry and jobbery took care that he should not be elected a second time. As has been said, he was one Catholic against nineteen

Protestants, most of them bigoted Protestants, too; and at the end of that year every Catholic could go to church on Sunday or holiday; the Catholic priest was admitted to the workhouse once a week to instruct the inmates; Catholic prayer-books were distributed in the same way as Protestant; Catholic children were sent to Catholic schools: in short, of the vast multitude of Catholic grievances not one remained unredressed. And yet all this had been accomplished without a departure, perhaps, for one second, on the part of O'Connor, from his cold, calm delivery: without one violent word, with that exterior of perfect and, on occasion, almost genial courtesy, under which lay concealed fierce passion and relentless purpose.

Arthur O'Connor's part in Parliament has been such as one might have anticipated from his previous career. He at once devoted himself to the work which was sorest and most uninviting; had acquired in a short time a knowledge so intimate of the rules of the House as to be a terror to all Speakers, and was a more potent, more dangerous, a more detailed critic of the Estimates than Parnell or Biggar in their palmiest and most 'active' days. It is curious to see O'Connor enter the House with a bundle of notes, which apparently must have consumed days in their preparation; to hear him put Mr. Courtney to shame as he describes the extravagant wages of a charwoman in the Foreign Office; and to bring confusion to the mind of the First Commissioner of Works as he dilates on the bad quality of the mortar in the last repairs of a Royal Palace. All this is done with an air of unbroken severity, but, at the same time, of unruffled temper and of inflexible courtesy. O'Connor is the calm, patient, lofty spirit of economy that chides, but pities, and that speaks in the accents of sorrow rather than of anger. At some moments it is an explanation which O'Connor prays for with his inimitable air of sad deference. A small speech is required, of course, to preface the inquiry. The Minister having answered, a second speech is necessary in order to have a further word on just a trifling little difficulty that still remains to disturb O'Connor's mind. Then the Minister again explains, and O'Connor, now fully satisfied, has to express his gratitude and content; and the expression of his gratitude and content requires a third speech. And thus it goes on hour after hour—O'Connor calm, deferential, appallingly inquisitive, miraculously omniscient—the Minister restless, apologetic, divided between the desire to swear and the dread of its consequences—with the result that, when the night is over, the Treasury has got about one out of every fifteen votes it had hoped to carry. Work of this kind, which is constantly done by such men as O'Connor and Biggar —and in former days by gallant Lysaght Finigan—is and can never be reported, is rarely even described, is rarely even heard of; but it is in willingly, patiently, relentlessly, continuously going through the hideous drudgery of unrecognised toil like this that such men show the depths of their self-devotion, the reality and earnestness of their self-forgetfulness. With the doubtful exception of Mr. Parnell, Arthur O'Connor has the most thoroughly and the best House-of-Commons style of any man in the party. Clear, deliberate, passionless in language, gesture, delivery, he is the very best model of an official speaker. The narrow limits within which he confines himself do injustice to his powers. The only occasion on which he did prominently enter into general debate was on the Bradlaugh question; and his answer to Mr. Bright on that occasion suggested possibilities of sober, but lofty eloquence.

Finally, the sternness of Mr. O'Connor's faith does not prevent him from being one of the kindliest of companions, one of the most tolerant and even-tempered of counsellors; though he has much of the antique Roman, he has much also of the social charms of the modern Irishman.

'Few sights,' wrote the late A. M. Sullivan of Bantry Bay, by whose shores he and his brother T. D. Sullivan were born, 'could be more picturesque than the ceremony by which in our bay the fishing season was formally opened. Selecting an auspicious day, unusually calm and fine, the boats, from every creek and inlet for miles around, assembled at a given point, and then, in solemn procession, rowed out to sea, the leading boat carrying the priest of the district. Arrived at the distant fishing-ground, the clergyman vested himself, an altar was improvised on the stern-sheets, the attendant fleet drew around, and every head was bared and bowed while the Mass was said. I have seen this "Mass on the ocean" when not a breeze stirred, and the tinkle of the little bell or the murmur of the priest's voice was the only sound that reached the ear; the blue hills of Bantry faint on the horizon behind us, and nothing nearer beyond than the American shore. Where are all these now? The "Mass on the ocean" is a thing of the past, heard of and seen no more; one of the old customs gone apparently for ever. The fishermen—the fine big-framed fellows, of tarry hands and storm-stained faces? The workhouse or the grave holds all who are not docksidemen on the Thames or the Mersey, on the Hudson or the Mississippi. The boats? I saw nearly all that remains of them when I last visited the little cove that in my early days scarce sufficed to hold the fleet at low water; skeleton ribs protruding here and there from the sand, or the shattered hulks helplessly mouldering under the trees that dropped into the tide when at full.'

Timothy Daniel Sullivan was born in 1827. The home of the Sullivans was thoroughly National, and amid the stirring times of 1848, and the hideous disasters of the two preceding years, there were all the circumstances to make the National faith of the family bitter and robust. The father was carried away, like the majority of the earnest and energetic Irishmen of that time, by the Gospel which the Young Ireland leaders were preaching with such fascination of voice and pen, became one of the leaders of the local '48 club, and, as a reward, was dismissed from his employment by one of the local magistrates. T. D. Sullivan, like the rest of his brothers, though brought up in a small and remote town, had an opportunity of receiving a good education in the best sense of the word, and the family was essentially literary as well as National in its tendencies. The Sullivans were closely associated with another Bantry household, which was destined by-and-by to give a prominent figure to the Irish history of the present day. The chief and the best schoolmaster of the town was Mr. Healy, the grandfather of the two members of the present House of Commons of the same name. It was from Mr. Healy that Mr. Sullivan learned probably the most of what he knows. The ties between the two families were afterwards drawn still closer when T. D. Sullivan married Miss Kate Healy, the daughter of his teacher. Though A. M. Sullivan was younger than T. D., he was the first to leave home and seek fortune abroad. After trying his hand as an artist, A. M. ultimately adopted journalism as a profession, and became connected with the Dublin *Nation*. T. D. meantime had also allowed his mind to run into dreams of a literary future, and had filled a whole volume with his compositions; but, with the secrecy which youth loves, he had not confided his transgression to anyone. Two or three of the pieces had appeared in print, but it was not till he came to Dublin and began to write in the *Nation* that the poetical genius of T. D. Sullivan sought recognition. Into the columns of that journal he began at once to pour the verses which he had hitherto so religiously kept secret, and from the first his songs attracted attention. From this time forward the name of T. D. Sullivan is inextricably associated with the *Nation*.

Though T. D. Sullivan has written love-poems and tender elegies, his preference has always been for the muse that stirs and cheers. Many of his poems became popular immediately on their appearance, and spread over that vast world of the Irish race which now extends through so many of the nations of the earth. A well-known story with regard to the 'Song from the Backwoods' will illustrate the influence of T. D. Sullivan's muse. Most Irishmen know that splendid little poem, with its bold opening, and its splendid refrain:

> Deep in Canadian woods we've met,
> From one bright island flown;
> Great is the land we tread, but yet
> Our hearts are with our own.
> And ere we leave this shanty small,
> While fades the autumn day,
> We'll toast old Ireland!
> Dear Old Ireland!
> Ireland, boys, hurrah!

The song, which was published in the *Nation* in 1857, first became popular among the members of the Phœnix Society—who, it will be remembered, were at work in 1858—and was carried to America by Captain D. J. Downing, one of the association. It rapidly became popular, both among the Fenians, who were beginning to be organized, and among the Irish soldiers who were fighting in the American army. Every man of the Irish Brigade knew it, and it was often sung at the bivouac fire after a hard day's fighting. An extraordinary instance of its popularity was given by a writer, signing himself 'Romeo,' in the *New York Irish People* of March 9th, 1867. 'On the night,' he writes, 'of the bloody battle of Fredericksburg, the Federal army lay sleepless and watchful on their arms, with spirits damped by the loss of so many gallant comrades. To cheer h brother officer, Captain Downing sang his favourite song. The chorus of the first stanza was taken up by his dashing regiment, next by the brigade, next by the division, then by the entire line of the army for six miles along the river; and when the captain ceased, it was but to listen with indefinable feelings to the chant that came like an echo from the Confederate lines on the opposite shore of

> Dear Old Ireland,
> Brave Old Ireland,
> Ireland, boys, hurrah!

The song 'God save Ireland' became popular with even greater rapidity. It was issued at an hour when all Ireland was stirred to intenser depths of anger and of sorrow than perhaps at any single moment in the last quarter of a century, and this profound and immense feeling longed for a voice. When 'God save Ireland' was produced the people at once took it up, and so instantaneously that the author himself heard it sung and chorussed in a railway carriage *on the very day after its publication* in the *Nation*.

On several other occasions the pen of T. D. Sullivan has given popular expression to popular sentiment. It has been his invariable rule in composing these songs to make them 'ballads' in the true sense of the word—

songs, that is to say, that expressed popular sentiment in the language of everyday life, that had good catching rhymes, and that could be easily sung.

It will not be necessary to write at any great length of the Parliamentary career of T. D. Sullivan. He was elected, as is known, along with Mr. H. J. Gill, for county Westmeath, at the General Election of 1880; and, in spite of the absorbing nature of his journalistic duties, he has been one of the most active and one of the most attentive members of the party. He has been perhaps still more prominent on the platform: and it is at large Irish popular gatherings that his speech is most effective. He is Irish of the Irish, and expresses the deep and simple gospel of the people in language that goes home; and then his keen sense of humour enables him to supply that element of amusement which is always looked forward to with eagerness by the crowd. He often lights up his Parliamentary, like his conversational efforts, with bright flashes of wit. Speaking of special clauses in the Crimes Act for the protection of certain humble agents of the law one night, he declared, 'There's a divinity doth hedge a bailiff *rough h'use* him how we will.' 'Punctuality,' he said once to a colleague who turned up at a meeting with characteristic lateness, 'punctuality, in the opinion of the Irish Party, is the thief of time.'

It is when the county meeting is over, and T. D. Sullivan sits amid a genial crowd of sympathetic friends, that his best—certainly his most attractive—talents are seen. Like all the Sullivan family, he has plenty of musical ability, and, like poor A. M., has a splendid voice. A song by T. D. Sullivan has never been really understood until it has been heard sung by T. D. himself. His voice—loud, clear, penetrating—easily leads the chorus, no matter how many voices join in, and he throws himself into the spirit of the thing with all his heart and soul. His singing of 'Murty Hynes' is worth going many miles to hear.

Such has been the career of T. D. Sullivan—honourable, consistent, and tranquil. He has to-day the same convictions which guided his pen when he wrote surreptitious verses; he has stood by these convictions through years of trial and failure; he is as fresh and as vigorous in pushing them forward at this hour, when his hairs are gray, as he was when he sailed in boyhood's auroral days over Bantry Bay. His verses have marked the epochs which they have helped to produce, have won for him the affection of millions of Irish hearts, and form one of the many potent chains of memory and love that bind the scattered children of the Celtic mother to their race and to their cradle-land.

James O'Kelly was born in Dublin in the year 1845. He made acquaintance at an early age with the passions which make the Irish patriot. Among his companions in the Irish metropolis were a number of young men who, even in the dark hours between '55 and '65, worked and hoped for the elevation of the country: and, on the other hand, he learned in a school in London, in which he spent a part of his boyhood, the scorn that belongs to the child of a conquered race. O'Kelly accordingly entered upon political work at an unusually precocious age, and certainly had not reached his legal majority when political aims had become the lode-star of his dreams. This was the dark period when the treason of Sadleir and Keogh had broken all faith in Parliamentary activity and constitutional agitation; and when Youth—especially if it had the mental and physical robustness of O'Kelly—was not inclined to listen to statistical comparisons between the resources of England and Ireland. The 'set' to which O'Kelly belonged were certainly arch-heretics against the orthodox creed of constitutionalism, and had made up their minds to set about the liberation of Ireland in quite a different kind of style. The companions with whom O'Kelly then mixed lived to try, and many of them to suffer for, their experiment. Many of them are dead. Some of them survived, and are to-day as active and as hopeful as if they had not passed through hideous suffering and abysmal disaster.

In 1863 O'Kelly was enrolled in the Foreign Legion in Paris, and was immediately called upon to enter into active service. The Arabs in the province of Oran were in rebellion, and here O'Kelly had an opportunity of learning all the wiles as well as all the dangers of Arabian warfare. The rebellion had scarcely been suppressed when the French army was called to another and a very different scene of operations. Everybody remembers that when Maximilian was made Emperor of Mexico, French forces were sent by the Emperor Napoleon to win for his nominee his new dominion, and O'Kelly's regiment was one of those which were detailed for this service. In all the fighting which went on O'Kelly had his share. O'Kelly was made prisoner by the forces of General Canales in June, 1866. O'Kelly had now a period of restraint, discomfort, possibly of danger to look forward to; but an attempt to escape, unless successful, meant death. O'Kelly decided to make a dash for liberty; his guards proved careless, and in the darkness of the night he eluded their vigilance, and rushed out into the Unknown. For days he had to wander about in hourly peril of his life. At one time he took to the river, hoping to float down to the point where Mexican territory joined the United States. The inducement to attempt this mode of escape was his discovery by the banks of the river of what is called a 'dug-out'—a rude boat made from a hollowed-out tree—and in this primitive craft he floated with the stream for a day. He had at last to come to land, owing to the attentions of some Mexicans on the shore. They proved, however, not unfriendly, and finally O'Kelly made his way into Texas. On American soil he was once more a free man; but that was the end of his blessings. He had not a cent; his clothes, after his many days of wandering, were ragged; and who looks so disreputable as the soldier in a travel-stained uniform? However, O'Kelly managed to 'strike' a fellow-countryman, and was by him given a job. The job—historical accuracy is especially desirable in the biography of a soldier—was that of removing some lumber. He managed finally to make his way to New York, and when he got there he was confronted with stirring news that led him for a while to the hope that the next time he went a-soldiering it would be for his own land.

The stories which were current in these days of the possibilities and the resources for rebellion in Ireland have been described long since by many pens, and have produced a bitterness of controversy that warns off any writer. Suffice it to say that O'Kelly did not find things as he expected, that he had seen too much of real warfare to have any faith in unarmed crowds, and that he was one of those who most fiercely opposed any attempt at insurrection. Everybody knows that these counsels did not then prevail, and that in 1867 there came some sporadic risings with their sad sequel of wholesale arrests, imprisonments, and long terms of penal servitude. For years O'Kelly had to pass through the daily and nightly risks, the never-ceasing strain, the strange underground life, of the revolutionary. O'Kelly passed through it all with that calm courage and that cool-headedness which everybody recognises, and, through determination, vigilance, and prudence combined, succeeded in coming out unscathed.

Again the French cause drew him from politics, and during the Franco-Prussian war he rejoined the French army; when Paris surrendered, he once more left the French service.

He then went to New York. Up to this time he had not seriously contemplated adopting journalism as a profession, and his efforts had been confined to occasional correspondence in the National weeklies. He applied for a situation on the *New York Herald*, and his application, like that of most beginners in all manners of life, was received coolly enough. At last, through the absence of all the regular employés of the journal on a special Sunday morning, O'Kelly got his opportunity. General Sheridan was to arrive from Europe on that morning, and there was a general anxiety to know what the American Napoleon had to say about the military resources and the military strategy of the old world. The task of interviewing so distinguished a soldier was a highly honourable one, but it had one great drawback—General Sheridan was a man who was known to hold the 'interviewer' in mortal hate. There was a whole host of reporters on board the steamer which went out to meet the General. The competition, therefore, was keen with a keenness which nobody who has not been in America can completely understand. Each reporter, in his turn, tried his hand on the General, and each went back disappointed. At length O'Kelly made the attempt. He began his attack altogether out of the ordinary: mentioned places in France which the General, as well as he, had recently seen, gave a military estimate or two, and in this way conveyed the impression to the General that he was something of a kindred spirit, and knew what he was talking about. The General unbent, and O'Kelly, who was the 'greenhorn,' as newcomers are scornfully called, of the journalistic host, was the one who was able to give the best account of General Sheridan's views on his European tour.

O'Kelly, starting thus well, was gradually advanced, until he became one of the leader-writers—or 'editors,' as they are called in America—of the *New York Herald*. In 1873 there arose an opportunity of making or marring his fortune—an opportunity which O'Kelly gladly embraced, but which ninety-nine out of every hundred men would have absolutely and unhesitatingly rejected. The rebellion in Cuba was going on, and it was a movement in which the people of the United States took a keen interest, these being the days when the annexation of Cuba was one of the political possibilities and aspirations of the hour. But what was the nature, and what were the methods, of the rebels? These were points upon which no trustworthy information could apparently by any possibility be obtained. The Spaniards had the ear of the world, and the story they told was that there was no such a thing as a rebellion at all. If there had ever been anything of the kind, it was entirely crushed, and Cespedes, its leader, was dead. What now remained was simply a few scores of scattered marauders, who were nothing but itinerant robbers and murderers. There was a strong conviction in the United States that these representations were not altogether to be relied on, and there were plenty of Cuban refugees and insurrectionary committees in the United States who circulated reports of quite a different character. It was said, for instance, that the Spanish troops were guilty of horrible cruelties—that they gave no quarter to men, and foully abused women; and the rebellion, instead of being repressed, was represented as fiercer and more determined than ever. But how were these statements to be confirmed? The rebels, whether few or many, were hidden behind the impenetrable forests of the Mambi Land (as the country frequented by them was called) as completely as if they had ceased to exist. To reach these rebels, survey their forces—in short, attest their existence—was the duty which O'Kelly volunteered to perform.

He knew when he set out for Cuba that his task was difficult enough, but it was not until he arrived in Cuba that he realized to the full the meaning of his enterprise. He imagined that he might have been able to accompany the Spanish troops, then to pass through their lines to the rebels, and, investigations among the latter being completed, to return to the Spanish lines again. He therefore asked a safe-conduct from the Captain-General; but that functionary soon made it apparent that nothing would induce him to facilitate O'Kelly's task in any way; and he plainly told him that, if he persisted in trying to get to the rebels, he would do so at his own risk. O'Kelly soon realized the true meaning of these words. Throughout all Cuba there was a perfect reign of terror. Tribunals hastily tried even those suspected of treason, and within a few hours after his arrest the 'suspect' was a riddled corpse. Any person who, therefore, was under the frown of the authorities was avoided as if he had the plague. Thus O'Kelly was invited to dinner in the heartiest manner by a descendant of an Irishman; but when this gentleman heard of O'Kelly's mission, he begged him not to pay the visit, and promptly went to the Spanish authorities to explain the unlucky invitation. 'It was not possible,' writes O'Kelly in 'The Mambi Land,' the interesting volume in which he afterwards recounted his adventures—'it was not possible to turn back without dishonour, and, though it cost even life itself, I would have to visit the Cuban camp.' 'My word,' he says in another place, 'had been given to accomplish this, and at whatever cost it should be done'—language that in the mouth of a man like O'Kelly really means the resolve to meet the worst that fortune could inflict.

He made various efforts to accompany expeditions of the Spanish troops which were supposed to be marching against the insurgents; but these expeditions either were postponed, or, after they had been started, turned back without coming even within sight of the rebel lines. Then O'Kelly thought that his purpose might be carried out if he got into communication with some of the secret sympathizers with the rebellion who remained in the towns; but they, carrying their lives every hour in their hands, would not trust a stranger. At last he formed the desperate resolve to set out for the rebel lines alone, with the chances of being shot by the Spaniards as a rebel, by the rebels as a Spaniard, through a country which in parts was supposed to be overrun by robbers, quite ready to murder, with impartial ferocity, Spaniard or rebel; and into the midst of almost impenetrable forest, where the loss of the trail meant death. But he had not proceeded far on his way when he was placed under arrest by the Spanish authorities. Then came an order which made the situation still more hopeless: the order was that under no circumstances should O'Kelly be permitted to penetrate to the rebel lines, and the penalty was affixed in no obscure language. Brought before General Morales, one of the Spanish authorities, O'Kelly made the remark, 'I should regret very much if one of these days you should be obliged to shoot me.' 'I would regret it very much also,' was the reply of the Spaniard; 'but if you are found in the insurgent lines, or coming from them, you will be treated as a spy or as one of the insurgents'—in other words, shot.

And still O'Kelly persevered. His plan now was to trust to the sympathizers with the rebellion; and at last he found a letter on the floor of his room in his hotel one night, telling him that if he would proceed to a certain point alone on the following day, he would be conducted to the rebel lines. O'Kelly, armed with a couple of revolvers, set out the next day, reached the trysting-place, and after hours of waiting in the blackness of a dark night, was conducted into the rebel lines, saw General Cespedes, President of the Republic, and spent a month in marching and countermarching, and in generally studying the resources, the customs, and the prospects of the rebels. His task he had now succeeded in accomplishing, though every other person attempting it had failed. He had ascertained the existence and estimated the chances of the rebels, and the only thing now left for him was to return to America. Cespedes offered to send him home by Jamaica, but O'Kelly thought it necessary to go into the Spanish lines, in order that there might be no possibility of a denial that he had actually entered into the rebel camp. He had scarcely returned to the settlements of the Spaniards when he was thrown into a dungeon in a fortress, where the stench was terrible, his only companion a forger; and he was convinced that the object of his captors was, if they could not shoot him, to kill him through scarlet fever. For weeks he was daily tortured while in this terrible den by inquisitions and threats of immediate execution, alternating with tempting offers of large bribes and immediate release if he would betray the men who had helped him to reach the Cuban lines. In time he was removed to another prison, bound with ropes as he was conveyed there. In this guise he reached Havana, and there again he was incarcerated in a cell—this time of such sickening odour that he had to fly continually to the grated door in the hope of breathing a little fresh air. It was evident that the Spanish authorities were thoroughly bent on inducing his death from yellow fever. He escaped all these perils, however, was sent to Spain, and then, through the united efforts of General Sickles, Señor Castelar, and Isaac Butt, was set at liberty.

Later on, in the war with 'Sitting Bull' and the Sioux Indians, an expedition of considerable peril, O'Kelly remained throughout the business, until 'Sitting Bull' was driven to take refuge in Canada. More recently O'Kelly conceived the bold idea of reaching the Mahdi. The continued obstacles which were placed in his way frustrated his object, but he did not abandon his purpose until he had adopted many expedients of characteristic daring and adroitness. The letters which he contributed to the *Daily News* excited much attention, and were the first to throw any light upon the character and strength of the movement under the Mahdi. With singular accuracy he pointed out the future of the movement, and some time later, in a series of articles in the *Freeman's Journal*, on the strategy of Lord Wolseley, he forecast the perils and the final failure of the campaign with striking truth. He writes with the bold, slightly rugged, realistic pen of the special correspondent diverted to journalism from his true avocation as a soldier. Though he has given proof so abundant of a courage that dares all, O'Kelly's advice has always been on the side of well-calculated rather than rash courses; he has, in fact, the true soldier's instinct in favour of the adaptation of ways and means to ends, of mathematical severity in estimating the strength of the forces for, and of the forces against, his own side. He is, like so many men, a bundle of contradictions. His whole temperament is revolutionary; he chafes under the restraints of Parliamentary life, and hates the weary contests of words; and, on the other hand, he insists on every step being measured, every move calculated. A friend jokingly described him once as the 'Whig-rebel.' Again, his large experience of life and the ruggedness of his sense, give to his thoughts the mould of almost cynic realism, and yet he is an idealist of the first water; for throughout his whole life he has held to the idea of his country's resurrection with a fanatical faith which no danger could terrify, no disaster depress, no labour fatigue. And it is as a steady though silent labourer for the elevation of his people that O'Kelly would himself wish to be remembered. 'My best work,' he wrote to a friend, 'was not the showy pages which have caught the general eye, but rather the quiet political work which I have done for the last twenty years. To the mere *sabreur's* part of my life I attach no importance whatever, except that within certain limits it has furnished me with the opportunity of observing men, and acquainting myself with the motive forces which induce men to do or not to do.'

One figure was absent from this gathering which was destined to play a prominent part in subsequent struggles. This was Mr. John Dillon. Mr. Dillon at this moment was absent in America completing the organization of the Land League movement that had been started by Mr. Parnell before his departure from that country. Mr. Dillon, as so often happens, is the very opposite in appearance and manner from what the readers of his speeches, especially the hostile readers, would expect. He came in the course of time to be regarded by large sections of the English people as the embodiment of everything that was brutal and sanguinary in the Irish nature. He was accustomed during the fiercer days of the Land League to the most violent denunciation, and he was daily in receipt of letters of menace or of insult. To those who know him this popular image was grotesquely inaccurate. Tall, thin, frail, his *physique* is that of a man who has periodically to seek flight from death in change of scene and of air. His face is long and narrow; the features singularly delicate and refined. Coal-black hair and large, dark, tranquil eyes, make up a face that immediately arrests attention, and that can never be forgotten. A stranger would guess that Mr. Dillon was an artist of the school that found delight in painting Madonnas, that spoke of the pursuit of art for art's sake alone, with a sublime unconcern for the struggles and aims and welfare of the workaday world. A tranquil voice and a gentle manner would further combat the idea that this was one of the protagonists in one of the fiercest struggles of modern days. The speeches of Mr. Dillon are violent in their conclusions only. The propositions which startled or shocked unsympathetic hearers are reached by him through calculations of apparently mathematical frigidity, and are delivered in an unimpassioned monotone.

John Dillon is the son of Mr. John Blake Dillon, one of the bravest and purest spirits in the Young Ireland movement. His father was one of those who opposed the rising to the last moment as imprudent and hopeless, and then was among the first to risk liberty and life when it was finally resolved upon. John was born in Blackrock, county Dublin, in the year 1851. He never went to a boarding-school, and probably he owes more of his education to home than to other influences. He was mainly instructed in the institutions connected with the Catholic University: first in the University school in Harcourt Street, Dublin, and afterwards in the University buildings in Stephen's Green. He was intended for the medical profession, passed through his course of lectures, and took the degree of Licentiate in the College of Surgeons. His entrance into the political struggle was not precocious. It was not until after the arrival of John Mitchel in Ireland to fight the Tipperary struggle after his many years of exile that Dillon first appeared in the political arena. Mitchel had been one of the oldest friends, as he had been one of the earliest companions, of his father; and John Dillon was among those who went down to Queenstown to bid a welcome to Ireland to the returning and still unrepentant rebel. He then took an active part in the electoral contest, and helped to get Mitchel returned. The rise of Mr. Parnell and the active policy brought Mr. Dillon more prominently to the front. He was one of the first to appreciate correctly the new policy, and to see the road to salvation to which it pointed the way. At once he became an eager advocate of Mr. Parnell and his policy. This brought him into direct collision with Mr. Isaac Butt, and his was the fiercest and most damaging speech made against the old leader in the Molesworth Hall meeting, at which Butt made his last political speech. When the Land League movement was started, Dillon at once threw himself into the agitation, and was appointed to accompany Mr. Parnell upon his historic visit to America.

There were many other members at the meeting in the City Hall whose history would throw light upon the circumstances and tendencies of Irish life, social and political, but I have not space to give them more than a few passing words. Richard Power, who was elected in 1874, when he was barely of age, is a member of a Waterford family which has played a prominent and often a romantic part in Irish history for centuries. Richard Lalor, one of the members for Queen's County, represented a family ancient in Irish struggle. His father was one of the fierce spirits that led the movement against the tithes, and for many years was the foremost man in every political effort in the Queen's County. James Finton Lalor, his brother, was perhaps the most truly revolutionary temperament of '48. He lives again in the pages of Duffy,[1] and he it was who suggested to Mitchel the No Rent movement, which Mitchel is alleged to have spoiled, and which for the first time was carried into effect more than a quarter of a century after Finton Lalor's fiery and restless spirit had passed to rest. Another brother, who sought a home in Australia, was the leader in a small insurrection at Ballarat, and there lost an arm. When the reforms he fought for were granted, he became one of the rulers of the country, and is now Speaker of the Victorian Parliament. Richard Lalor is of the same stern spirit as all his stock. To-day he is a feeble and bent man with wearied eyes and a thin voice, and a constant prey to ill-health, but his spirit is exactly the same as in his hot youth. In 1848 he had his pike and his thousands of pikemen ready for action; to-day, as then, he is the unconquerable and irreclaimable rebel—the Blanqui of Irish politics.

The O'Gorman Mahon, to whom was entrusted the duty of proposing the name of Mr. Parnell, belonged to even an older agitation. Tall, erect as a pine, with huge masses of perfectly white hair and a leonine face, he is the majestic relic of a stormy and glorious youth. He is the last survivor of the once multitudinous race of the Irish gentleman, as ready with his pistol as with his tongue. Nobody can enumerate the number of times he has been 'out,' and the still larger number of occasions in which he despatched or received the *cartel*. A man of the spirit of The O'Gorman Mahon was necessary in such times as those of his youth. The Irish Catholic was still an unemancipated serf, and the Lords of Ascendency looked down upon him with the contempt of centuries of unbroken sway. It was at such a time that the swaggering adherent of English domination

---

[1] See 'Four Years of Irish History' (A new Tribune, a new Policy), pp. 464-532.

had to be met by a representative of the ancient faith and of the hidden longings of the oppressed majority, before whose eagle-eye privilege had to quail. O'Connell was the tongue, but The O'Gorman Mahon was the sword, of the Irish Democracy rising against its oppressors after its centuries of bondage; and so he did his own useful work in his own day. There was something strangely picturesque in the appearance in that group of young men engaged in a still infant movement of a man who had stood by the side of O'Connell at the Clare election which won Catholic emancipation. It was almost as if Thomas Jefferson were to rise, and with the same pen that had written the 'Declaration of Independence' to join in the composition of Abraham Lincoln's proclamation against slavery. In the years that had passed since that day, The O'Gorman Mahon had gone through a life of strange and varied adventure. When, in the whirligig of time, he was thrust from Irish politics, he had gone to South America, and there had taken part in the struggles of the young Republics for emancipation. Returning to his native land, he found Isaac Butt starting the new movement for Home Rule. Several constituencies competed for him, but he had chosen the historic county in whose history he had played so prominent a part.

Garrett Byrne, member for Wicklow, is in direct descent from Garrett Byrne, who was hanged in the Rebellion of '48. John Barry, his colleague, beginning life at almost its humblest rung, had become an important member in a Scotch manufacturing firm, and shortly afterwards was in business for himself. He had also taken a share in political struggles the history of which has yet to be told. Mr. Corbet was a member of an ancient Irish family, and a man himself of culture and of considerable literary power.

One more figure requires description. On the first day of the meeting of the Irish Party the chair was occupied by the Lord Mayor of Dublin, Mr. E. Dwyer Gray, M.P. for the county Carlow. Mr. Gray is the son of the late Sir John Gray, whose name has figured so frequently in preceding pages. He was born in the year 1846. Brought up from his earliest youth in the opinions of his father, whose favourite son he was, he attained at an early age a correct judgment of political affairs. His father had received many bitter lessons during a long political career. One story he was never tired of repeating to his son. It was of a man who offered to him, during the Young Ireland excitement, a plan of the defences of Dublin Castle. Gray treated the offer of the surrender of the Lord-Lieutenant's citadel with suspicion, and a few days afterwards was not surprised to find that the would-be traitor was a police-spy in disguise. The mind of the son is even clearer than that of his father, and refuses steadily to accept any doctrine or course until it has been fully thought out. In this way Gray has sometimes been regarded as backward when he was simply demanding the full reason for the proffered policy, and had not yet been able to see its eventual outlet. He succeeded his father in the management of the *Freeman's Journal*, the chief newspaper of Ireland, and soon raised it to double its previous circulation. Becoming a member of the Dublin Corporation, of which his father had been the guiding star for many years, he soon attained to the position of its leading figure, and took a keen interest in advancing the hygienic improvements of the city. At this period he was Lord Mayor, and had under his control vast sums which had been subscribed to the Mansion House for the relief of distress. Anticipating a little, Gray subsequently came into fierce collision with James Carey, whom he exposed for an attempted fraud upon the Corporation; and Carey from that day was his bitter and relentless enemy. Gray had been returned to the House of Commons shortly after the death of his father, and, though not a frequent, was already, as he is still, one of its most influential debaters. There is no man in the Irish Party, and few outside it, who can state a case with such pellucid clearness. When Gray has completed his statement, the whole facts are as clear to the minds of his hearers as they have already been to his own searching intellect.

The great question to be decided at this meeting was the future leadership of the party. Up to a few days before the meeting there was practically no intention even of proposing Mr. Parnell as a leader. The idea never even assumed shape until the night before the meeting in the City Hall. There happened to be stopping at the Imperial Hotel several gentlemen who had been returned or had resolved to support Mr. Parnell's policy. Among them they discussed the question of leadership. The gentlemen who took part in this informal and accidental conference were Mr. John Barry, Mr. Richard Lalor, Mr. O'Kelly, Dr. Commins, Mr. Biggar, Mr. T. P. O'Connor, and, strangely enough, Mr. McCoan; Mr. Healy, who had not yet been elected a member of Parliament, was also present.

There was an understanding rather than a formal resolution among these gentlemen that they would propose Mr. Parnell as leader. He himself did not come to Dublin until next morning; some gentlemen went to his hotel and others met him on his way to the City Hall. In his bedroom, and afterwards as he passed through the streets, mention was made to him of the suggestion that had been made at the informal meeting of the previous night. He neither rejected nor encouraged the idea, but seemed, on the whole, rather inclined to the notion, in case Mr. Shaw were displaced, of proposing that the office should be held by Mr. Justin McCarthy. This was the state of things when the meeting assembled. Finally the vote was: for Mr. Parnell, 23; for Mr. Shaw, 18.[1] Mr. Shaw apparently received his defeat at the moment with good humour, but when, the next day, the party formulated its policy and declared in favour of Peasant Proprietary as the final solution of the Land Question, Mr. Shaw already indicated a certain difference from Mr. Parnell and his friends.

When the party came over to London the first occasion arose for the two sections taking opposite sides. It was on a seemingly trivial question. The point at issue was the part of the House in which the Irish members should take their seats. In the view of Mr. Shaw and his friends, the existing Ministry was so friendly to Ireland that the Irish Party should signify their general adherence by sitting on the same side of the House. The supporters of Mr. Parnell maintained that even between a friendly Liberal Ministry and an Irish National Party there might arise irreconcilable difference on the Irish National Question and on several others. They held that the only hope of a satisfactory solution of the Irish Question was that Irish members should maintain a position of absolute independence of the English parties, that therefore the attitude of Irish Nationalists was

---

[1] The members on both sides were: For Mr. Parnell—Sexton, Arthur O'Connor, O'Kelly, Byrne, Barry, McCarthy, Biggar, T. P. O'Connor, Lalor, T. D. Sullivan, Commins, Gill, Dawson, Leamy, Corbet, McCoan, Finigan, Daly, Marum, W. H. O'Sullivan, J. Leahy, O'Gorman Mahon, and O'Shea. For Mr. Shaw—Macfarlane, Brooks, Colthurst, Synan, Sir P. O'Brien, Foley, Smithwick, Fay, Errington, Gabbett, Smyth, R. Power, Blake, McKenna, P. Martin, Meldon, Callan, and Gray.

one of permanent opposition to all English Administrations, and that this political attitude should be signified by their continuing to keep their seats on the Opposition side of the House.

Meantime, in Ireland, the Land Question was reaching a crisis. The increase of evictions, which had begun with 1877—the first year of the distress—showed still further signs of increase: the number of tenantry unable to meet their rents was reaching daily larger proportions, and the Relief Committee had on their rolls something like 500,000 recipients of charity. Side by side with all this the Land League was daily advancing with gigantic strides, and every week was receiving a vast impetus through the immense subscriptions sent from America. It was clear that the time had come when Ireland must make a tremendous step either of advance or retrogression. Either distress was to develop into famine, and famine to lead to wholesale eviction, and another lease of landlord power and oppression, or the Irish people were to throw off the chains of centuries, to revolt against the perpetuation of their miseries and of their servitude, and to dash forward in an effort for a new and a better era.

Such was the state of Ireland, and such the position of the Irish Party, when Parliament met in 1880. But how was it with the Ministry? They did not know the existence of the distress; they did not know the strength of the agitation; they were far more ignorant of the condition of the island than of countries separated by thousands of miles on land or by sea; above all things, they had no idea whatever of making an attempt to deal with the Land Question.

The first witness of the state of feeling among the Ministry is the Duke of Argyll, who, speaking in 1881, said:

'The present Government was formed with no expressed intention of bringing in another great Irish Land Bill . . . it formed no part of the programme upon which the Government was formed. Perhaps no Government was ever formed on a greater or wider programme, if we are to take the speeches of my right hon. friend the Prime Minister in the course of the Midlothian campaign as the programme of the Government; but, so far as I recollect and am concerned, it was not intimated in those speeches that it was the intention of the Government to unsettle the settlement of the Land Act of 1870.'[1]

In the Session of 1880 the Marquis of Hartington showed that his mind was not only not made up in favour of Land Reform in Ireland, but that he was, on the whole, rather antagonistic to any such reform.

He was speaking in reply to a motion of Mr. Justin McCarthy that a tenant farmer should be added to the Commission of Inquiry into the Land Question. Several of the Irish members had spoken of the Land Act of 1870 as an absolute failure, and had taken it for granted that the Ministry had made up their minds that another and a larger Land Act was required. Thus Lord Hartington rebuked them:

'The Marquis of Hartington said he was not surprised that the hon. member for Tralee (The O'Donoghue) objected to the composition of the Commission, seeing that with him the failure of the Land Act was a foregone conclusion. To some minds the conclusion was not so absolutely certain that the Land Act had failed, or that it had not, and it was in solving that question that the Commission was expected to be useful. The

[1] Hansard, vol. cclxii., pp. 1754, 1755.

speeches attacking the Commission had all been pervaded by a fallacious supposition, namely, that the Government looked to Baron Dowse and the other members of the Commission for a comprehensive scheme of land reform. . . . What they wanted was facts. In the last four years there had been almost continuous debates on the Irish Land Question. . . . The result was that neither the House nor the Government could arrive at any certain conclusion on the matter. What could be more advisable under these circumstances than to ask a set of honest and impartial men to make inquiry on the spot, and to report the facts brought under their notice? That was the object of the Commission, and not, as the hon. member for Longford (Mr. Justin M'Carthy) seemed to suppose, the elaboration of a comprehensive scheme of land reform.'[1]

The chief and most significant testimony of the mind of the Ministry at this period is that given by Mr. Gladstone himself. During his visit to Midlothian in the autumn of 1884, he said :

'I must say one word more upon, I might say, a still more important subject—the subject of Ireland. It did not enter into my address to you, for what reason I know not ; but the Government that was then in power, rather, I think, kept back from Parliament, certainly were not forward to lay before Parliament, what was going on in Ireland until the day of the Dissolution came, and the address of Lord Beaconsfield was published in undoubtedly very imposing terms. . . . I frankly admit that I had had much upon my hands connected with the doings of that Government in almost every quarter of the world, and I did not know—no one knew—the severity of the crisis that was already swelling upon the horizon, and that shortly after rushed upon us like a flood.'[2]

Such, then, was the condition of the problem presented to Mr. Parnell and his followers. In their own country thousands of people face to face with starvation ; land tenure still in such a position that the tenant had no protection from rack-rent and from eviction, and therefore from periodic famine ; an agitation rising daily in passion and in strength ; the hour demanding revolutionary land reform ; and the mind of even an honest Ministry either blank or hostile.

This contradiction between the demands of the Irish Question and the resolves of the Government is a central fact in all that follows. It will justify to any candid man measures which at the time appeared uncalled for and extreme ; and, above all things, it will explain how it was that the Parnellites were driven at the very outset of the Session of 1880 into an attitude of hostility to a Ministry that was Liberal and inclined to be friendly.

The Queen's Speech was soon to give evidence of the unmistakable ignorance and unreadiness of the Government. It was of considerable length ; it dealt with Turkey, and Afghanistan, and India, and South Africa ; but it contained not one word about the Irish Land Question. Immediately after the reading of the Royal Address the Irish members retired to the dingy rooms in King Street, Westminster, which were then their offices. The omission of all mention of the Irish Land Question was pointed out with indignant surprise, and it was immediately resolved that the moment the House reassembled, the Irish members should take action by at once giving notice of an amendment to the Queen's Speech. The

---

[1] Hansard, vol. cclv., pp. 1415-16.
[2] Times, September 2, 1884.

amendment to the Queen's Speech in 1880 was the germ which afterwards was transformed into the Land Act of 1881.

The section led by Mr. Shaw had much to say in favour of the difficulties of the Government, and could urge with some justice that it was unfair to demand immediate treatment from the Ministry of a question of such vast importance and such extraordinary complexity as the Irish Land Question. The section led by Mr. Parnell, on the other hand, pointed out that the Irish Land Question had already reached a stage when further delay meant wholesale destruction; showed how long and patient had already been the endurance of the postponement of the land settlement by their constituents; and, above all, urged that the primary consideration of a National Party was the need of the Irish people, and not the fortunes of an English Ministry. If the Irish demand were allowed to occupy a second and subsidiary place; if that demand were made dependent upon the convenience of the Ministry, it was held by Mr. Parnell and his followers that the cause would be lost.

The amendment was brought forward on the reassembling of the House after the interval which follows the reading of the Queen's Speech. It was in these words:

'And to humbly assure her Majesty that the important and pressing question of the occupiers and cultivators of the land in Ireland deserves the most serious and immediate attention of her Majesty's Government, with a view to the introduction of such legislation as will secure to these classes the legitimate fruits of their industry.'

It was on the night when this amendment was brought forward that Mr. Parnell spoke for the first time in Parliament since he had reached his new position. He rose about eleven o'clock; the House was crowded and eager; and when the Speaker called out the name of the member for Cork, there was a movement of keen interest, and in the galleries reserved to strangers almost everybody got up to have a look at the new Irish leader. Mr. Parnell spoke briefly, but with vehemence and force. He drew a rapid picture of the state of things in Ireland, which was listened to with more curiosity than sympathy, and the general result was that Mr. Parnell was estimated as a very violent and rather irrational man, who represented nothing but a small and irresponsible knot of senseless irreconcilables. The attitude of the House to Mr. Shaw was very different. He himself seemed to challenge comparison with his successor, for the moment Mr. Parnell sat down, Mr. Shaw rose. The first and most significant fact was that the two men spoke from different parts of the House. Mr. Parnell had risen from a seat below the gangway on the Opposition side. Mr. Shaw spoke from the very bosom of the Radical section, and when he rose he was rewarded with a burst of hearty cheers from all the Liberal benches. He spoke in the style that is now so well known; his speech gave a great deal of satisfaction, and the opinion was freely expressed by the English members that his remarks were in welcome contrast to the heat and exaggeration of Mr. Parnell. The contest between the two men was still held to be undecided. There was much contempt for the group of young men who formed Mr. Parnell's chief support, and the expectation was universal that Mr. Parnell's tenure of office would be brief and inglorious. The appearance of the two men in the debate strengthened this conviction in the English mind, and English members might be heard to comment with cheerfulness that Parnell might be a dashing *guerillero*, but Shaw was the sagacious statesman and the real leader.

But the Ministry and the House of Commons were soon to find that, however much Mr. Shaw's methods might be more agreeable than those of Mr. Parnell, it was with Parnell and his colleagues that they had to count. The new Ministers, confident in the magnificence of their recent victory, in the still verdant and unbroken strength of their party, and in the loftiness of their hopes, could not understand their path being crossed by this then insignificant section of the House. Between them and the Irish Party open war had not been declared, and its possibility would not be even contemplated, especially by men who had given such repeated assurances of their sympathy for Ireland as Mr. Gladstone and Mr. Bright. The Liberal Ministers and the followers of Mr. Parnell were at that stage in which it was yet undecided whether doubting affection would end in closer bonds or in permanent estrangement; but, meantime, Mr. Parnell and his friends contemplated a second move. The great object at that time was to stay the hand of the landlord, made omnipotent over the tenantry by the failure of the crops; and to meet this emergency the Irish Party brought in the Suspension of Evictions Bill. The second reading of the Suspension of Evictions Bill came on at two o'clock one fine morning, to the horror and surprise of the Treasury bench. Mr. Gladstone looked up from the paper on which he was writing his nightly report of Parliamentary proceedings to the Queen, with a gaze first of pained amazement and then of pathetic appeal to the serried and resolute ranks opposite him. But the Irishmen, who had to think of hundreds of thousands of other faces that looked to their inner minds with hungry hope from cabin and field, had their advantage, were determined to hold fast, and declared that the discussion of the Bill must go on. The Premier yielded to the inevitable, made the important announcement that the Government themselves would consider the subject raised by Mr. Parnell's measure, and so the Irish Land Question, which but a few days before had been scouted out of court, which had never been mentioned at the first Cabinet Council, of whose existence the Queen's Speech knew absolutely nothing, had already within a couple of weeks after the meeting of Parliament been taken up by the Government as one of the chief and primary questions of the Session; and the starving tenants, just emerging from famine, might hope that the landlords would not be allowed to work unchecked their wicked will. This, in fact, was the first Parliamentary victory that the Land League gained.

The Disturbance Bill of Mr. Forster was the Suspension of Evictions Bill of Mr. Parnell under another name. The Parnellites, so far, had gained their point, but they were to reap still further advantage. The speakers for the Government had, of course, to array the terrible figures of eviction increasing with distress,[1] to make strong speeches and urge powerful reasons in favour of a measure which went counter to so many of the prejudices of the House of Commons. Irish distress thus became the cry of an English as well as of an Irish party, and striking statements and valuable admissions were made which justified the whole position of the Land League. For instance, it was during a debate on the Disturbance Bill that Mr. Gladstone committed himself to the famous doctrine that, in

[1] 'If we look to the total numbers we find that in 1878 there were 1,749 evictions; in 1879, 2,667; and as was shown by my right hon. and learned friend, 1,690 in the five and a half months of this year—showing a further increase upon the enormous increase of last year, and showing, in fact, unless it be checked, that 15,000 individuals will be ejected from their homes, without hope, without remedy, in the course of the present year.'—MR. GLADSTONE, Hansard, vol. ccliii., p. 1666.

the circumstances of distress in which Ireland then was, a sentence of eviction might be regarded as equivalent to a sentence of death;[1] and it was this and such like expressions of opinion that long paralyzed the hand of the Government against the Land League agitation. Everybody knows that the Disturbance Bill was fiercely opposed stage after stage by the Tories in the House of Commons, that it was finally carried by overwhelming majorities, and that, when it went to the House of Lords, it was thrown out with every circumstance of ignominy and contempt.

This ending to the business placed both the Government and the Irish Party in a strange and difficult position. It had been stated by Mr. Gladstone that a sentence of eviction was equivalent to a sentence of death, and the equally significant and appalling statement had been added by him that, according to the statistics supplied by the Irish authorities, 15,000 persons were to receive the sentence of eviction within that single year. The reality of the dangers to the peace of Ireland Mr. Forster was himself foremost in acknowledging; and were they then to allow Ireland to drift unhelmed—or, to use Mr. Gladstone's own words, 'without hope and without remedy'—to the abyss of wholesale eviction, tempered by wholesale assassination, towards which the action of the House of Lords had pushed it? It is hard at this moment to say what the Government could have done. They had just come from the country with a triumphant majority. Was it in political human nature that they should risk this majority by another appeal to the country within a few months, and before they had fulfilled a single item in the vast programme they had set before them? The Ministry might have been greatly weakened, and the mighty weapon for the repair of past Conservative errors and for future Liberal conquest might have been returned to the hand of Mr. Gladstone, pointless and broken. The truth is, the difficulty of the situation was the permanent and incurable difficulty of the present Parliamentary relations of England and of Ireland; it was the difficulty of having to govern one country through the public opinion of another. An Irish Minister face to face with such a crisis could with confidence have appealed against a verdict so plainly hostile to the interests of Ireland as the rejection of the Suspension of Evictions Bill, with the full knowledge that the public opinion of his own people, at once sympathetic and informed, would have redoubled his power of meeting so portentous an emergency. But the English Minister had to appeal to a public almost entirely ignorant of the merits of the controversy, and fickle in its sympathies because of ignorance.

But there was one step which might have been taken, and which might have resulted in some good. On August 24th Mr. Forster made an important statement:

'He had always said they must carry out the law; but he must also repeat that, if they found, as they had not within the last two or three weeks found, and as they hoped they would not find, that the landlords of Ireland were to any great extent making use of their powers so as to force

[1] 'In the failure of the crops, crowned by the year 1879, the act of God had replaced the Irish occupier in the condition in which he stood before the Land Act. Because what had he to contemplate? He had to contemplate eviction for his non-payment of rent; and as a consequence of eviction, starvation. And ... it is no exaggeration to say, in a country where the agricultural pursuit is the only pursuit, and where the means of the payment of rent are entirely destroyed for a time by the visitation of Providence, that the poor occupier may under these circumstances regard a sentence of eviction as coming, for him, very near to a sentence of death.'—Hansard, vol. cclii., p. 1663.

the Government to support them in the exercise of injustice, the Government should accompany any request for special powers with a Bill which would prevent the Government from being obliged to support injustice. He would go further and say, under any circumstances if it was found that injustice and tyranny were largely committed—although he did not believe that such would be the case—it would then be their serious duty to consider what their action should be, and he did not think that any man in the House would expect him to remain any longer the instrument of that injustice.'[1]

Here was some promise of a break in the run of disaster which now menaced Ireland. The landlords might evict on a wholesale scale, and all their history down to that very year pointed to their making full and savage use of every power which the law and the seasons had placed in their hands; but if a Minister of the Crown, rather than carry on this law, were to resign his office, the public opinion of the country would necessarily be fixed upon the difficulties and the horrors of the problem; and the Ministry, with such a force behind them, would have been able to dictate to the House of Lords a prompt and complete remedy. But many days had not elapsed when this hope disappeared. A cold fit had supervened with extraordinary rapidity upon the outburst of angry and worthy resolve, and Mr. Forster, catechised by the Opposition, explained his words until his great purpose vanished into thin air and meaningless talk. The final result of the Session then was this: A Relief of Distress Bill had been passed, through which money was to reach distressed tenants, having first passed through the hands of the landlords; and a Commission of Inquiry had been added to the long and dreary inquisitions that had investigated the Land Question.

The situation which Mr. Parnell had now to consider was one of extreme difficulty. The composition of the Land Commission, the words of Lord Hartington, and the silence of the other Ministers, gave but too much reason to believe that the mind of the Government was not even yet made up for anything like a large measure of land reform. The refusal for so many years of any measure of relief, followed by the miserable insufficiency of the Land Act of 1870, were too much calculated to make Mr. Parnell draw pessimist conclusions from such facts. The great evil he had to avoid was that the mighty agitation of 1880 should not end, as did that of 1869-70, in an abortive and halting measure. Meantime there was the country before him, organizing itself, as it had rarely ever been organized before, with mightier forces making in the direction of complete reform than had ever, perhaps, stood behind any movement. The nature of Mr. Parnell impels him to drive in political matters the hardest of hard bargains within his power; his grip of a political advantage for his countrymen is as relentless as the grip of death. His course in the months that followed was dictated mainly by the sense that through no word or act of his should the chance of the people for a full and final settlement of all their claims be jeopardized or diminished.

It is another essential evil of the present relations between England and Ireland that no great reform can be carried out—especially on the Land Question—without bringing the people of Ireland, as Mr. Chamberlain said, to a state bordering on revolution; and to a state bordering upon revolution the Irish people were now fast approaching. Mr. Parnell natur-

[1] Hansard, vol. cclv., pp. 2022, 2023.

ally gave no encouragement to the idea that the position of the Irish Land Question had not yet passed beyond the stage of inquiry. The movement in its new phase received its first word of real guidance from Mr. Parnell at a meeting held in Ennis on September 19, 1880, and the speech he then delivered gave the keynote of the situation. First, he told the people to place no confidence in the Government Commission; and, while he did not positively advise the farmers against giving evidence, he warned them against the danger of the acceptance of any responsibility for the proceedings of that body. Then he passed on to the declaration which after-events did so much to prove correct—that it was to themselves and their own organization the farmers were mainly to look for redress.

'Depend upon it (he said) that the measure of the Land Bill of next session will be the measure of your activity and energy this winter; it will be the measure of your determination not to pay unjust rents; it will be the measure of your determination to keep a firm grip of your homesteads; it will be the measure of your determination not to bid for farms from which others have been evicted, and to use the strong force of public opinion to deter any unjust men amongst yourselves—and there are many such—from bidding for such farms. If you refuse to pay unjust rents, if you refuse to take farms from which others have been evicted, the Land Question must be settled, and settled in a way that will be satisfactory to you. It depends, therefore, upon yourselves, and not upon any Commission or any Government. When you have made this question ripe for settlement, then, and not till then, will it be settled.'[1]

And, finally, he gave the advice with regard to 'boycotting' which was afterwards quoted hundreds of times against him.

'Now what are you to do (he said) to a tenant who bids for a farm from which another tenant has been evicted?

'Several voices: Shoot him!

'Mr. Parnell: I think I heard somebody say "Shoot him!" I wish to point out to you a very much better way—a more Christian and charitable way, which will give the lost man an opportunity of repenting. When a man takes a farm from which another has been unjustly evicted, you must show him on the roadside when you meet him; you must show him in the streets of the town; you must show him in the shop; you must show him in the fair-green and in the market-place, and even in the place of worship, by leaving him alone; by putting him into a moral Coventry; by isolating him from the rest of his country as if he were the leper of old—you must show him your detestation of the crime he has committed.'[2]

There have been few things that Mr. Parnell has said throughout his career which have been more bitterly criticised than the counsel given in these words. Barristers have assailed him in the House of Commons who would have mercilessly boycotted the counsel that held direct intercourse with a client without the mediation of a solicitor; doctors who would mercilessly boycott a professional brother who advertised or compounded medicines, or violated any other article of a complex professional code; politicians who had mercilessly driven out of their organizations the back-sliders from political principles; members of clubs who had ostracized offenders against the laws of honour or of conventionality; representatives of working classes who had wrung from a Conservative Ministry the right

[1] *Freeman's Journal*, September 20, 1880.   [2] *Ibid.*

of workmen to boycott avaricious employers. The principles of boycotting have thus been applied in ordinary times, and in ordinary occupations, by some of those who most loudly denounced it. One of the most fertile sources of landlord wrong and tenant suffering was the fierce competition for the possession of land. It had induced tenants to offer a rent measured not by the capacities of the land, but by their own despair; and it is perfectly clear that as long as eviction produced, through this unchecked competition, an increase of rent, eviction was a temptation and not a horror to the landlord. At this moment the Irish tenants were engaged in a great effort to break, once and for ever, the thraldom of centuries. Against this effort were arrayed the mighty forces of the empire. By a strict combination alone among themselves could the Irish tenantry hope for success; and the boycotting of any man who lent, by land-grabbing, assistance to the landlord was essential to success. Boycotting was abused; it was occasionally used for private purposes; it sometimes led to crime; but it was at least a far less savage mode of warfare than assassination, which it largely replaced. Until coercion brought homicidal frenzy, it did much to keep down the number of outrages; and, as Mr. John Dillon said in reply to an attack, it kept the roof over the heads of many a thousand men and women who, without it, would have been thrown on the roadside to perish.

The meeting at Ennis was followed by several other demonstrations, at most of which there were the same array of numbers, which had been unparalleled since the days of the Liberator. At all of these meetings Mr. Parnell practically preached the same principles. It would be well worth while for anybody who wishes to study the strange career of this Irish leader to read over again those speeches; for he will find in them that foresight, and that grasp of the central and essential facts of the situation and the real necessities of the time, which justify Mr. Parnell's extraordinary reputation. He had to fight at this period not merely the halting purpose of the Ministry, but also the feeble resolves of some men within the National ranks. They solemnly recommended moderation to the farmers, when the real danger was not in the extravagance of the demands made by the Irish people, but in the grudging bestowal of minimized concession by the House of Commons and the House of Lords. They amused themselves with elaborate schemes, instead of leaving the responsibility to the Ministers. They had much to say of the difficulties of Mr. Forster, and little of the difficulties of the peasants who, with their backs to the walls, fought a life-and-death struggle with hunger and eviction. Mr. Parnell, while personally courteous and tolerant to a degree that looks almost weakness, at this time, to these gentlemen and their proposals, steadily pursued his own path.

He used to point out the objection to the 'three F's' as either a practical or a final solution to the question. The settlement which he proposed was Peasant Proprietary.

'We seek as Irish Nationalists (he said at New Ross on September 25, 1880) for a settlement of the Land Question which shall be permanent—which shall for ever put an end to the war of classes which unhappily has existed in this country . . . a war which supplies, in the words of the resolution, the strongest inducement to the Irish landlords to uphold the system of English misrule which has placed these landlords in Ireland. And looking forward to the future of our country, we wish to avoid all elements of antagonism between classes. I am willing to have a struggle between classes in Ireland—a struggle that should be short, sharp, and decisive—once for all ; but I am not willing that this struggle should be perpetuated at intervals, when these periodic revaluations of the holdings of the tenants would come under the system of what is called fixity of tenure at valued rents.'[1]

It is well to add that, in every one of the speeches in which he spoke of peasant proprietary, he definitely laid down the doctrine that peasant proprietary was to be obtained not by violence, but by the payment of reasonable compensation to the landlords.

'Now, then, is the time for the Irish tenantry to show their determination—to show the Government of England that they will be satisfied with nothing less than the ownership of the land of Ireland . . . And I see no difficulty in arriving at such a solution, and in arriving at it in this way : by the payment of a fair rent, and a fair and fixed rent not liable to recurrent and perhaps near periods of revision, but by the payment of a fair rent for the space of, say, thirty-five years, after which time there would be nothing further to pay, and in the meantime the tenant would have fixity of tenure.'[2]

One sentence, finally, from his speeches of this period. Mr. Parnell's mode, means, and end were impulsively described once by Mr. Gladstone as passing through rapine to dismemberment. I have already quoted the sentence which will effectually dispose of the charge of rapine, and now for one on which the seeking of dismemberment was mainly founded. Speaking at Galway on October 24, 1880, Mr. Parnell said :

'I expressed my belief at the beginning of last session that the present Chief Secretary, who was then all smiles and promises, should not have proceeded very far in the duties of his office before he would have found that he had undertaken an impossible task to govern Ireland, and that the only way to govern Ireland is to allow her to govern herself . . . And if they prosecute the leaders of this movement . . . it is not because they wish to preserve the lives of one or two landlords . . . but it will be because they see that behind this movement lies a more dangerous movement to their hold over Ireland ; because they know that if they fail in upholding landlordism here—and they will fail—they have no chance of maintaining it over Ireland ; it will be because they know that if they fail in upholding landlordism in Ireland, their power to misrule Ireland will go too. I wish to see the tenant farmers prosperous ; but large and important as is the class of tenant farmers, constituting as they do, with their wives and families, the majority of the people of this country, I would not have taken off my coat and gone to this work if I had not known that we were laying the foundation in this movement for the regeneration of our legislative independence.'[3]

This sentence, which was often quoted, as it will be seen, simply demands the restoration of the Irish Parliament ; and that is not dismemberment. It was almost enough to make an Irishman frenzied to hear this sentence of Mr. Parnell quoted over and over again as the sudden revelation of some new, diabolical, unheard-of policy. Mr. Parnell announced himself a Home Ruler. Was there anything new, or diabolical, or unheard-of in that ? Mr. Butt was a Home Ruler, so were all his followers ; Mr. Parnell himself had been elected as a Home Ruler five years before the Galway

[1] *Freeman's Journal*, September 26 1880.   [2] *Ibid.*   [3] *Ibid.*, October 25, 1880.

speech. To say that he could not have entered into the Land agitation if he did not believe that it would help towards Home Rule, was to make the not very unnatural declaration that the reform of the Land system would tend towards the restoration of an Irish Parliament.

In the meantime, while thus the movement in Ireland was reaching its spring-tide, how was it with the Chief Secretary? From this period forward Mr. Forster disappears from history as an advocate of reform, and becomes the chief, the fiercest, and the main champion of coercion. As the days went on, instead of resignation came symptoms of the most stringent resolution to carry out the unjust law to its bitterest end. Extra police were drafted into the counties of Mayo and Galway, thus raising the burden of taxation upon the two counties that had suffered the most bitterly and escaped the most narrowly from the bitterest horrors of famine. The Orange writers in the North of Ireland adopted their usual policy of representing as a vast conspiracy against Protestantism a movement the unsectarian character of which was universally acknowledged, and sought to prevent an alliance of Protestant and Catholic farmers against their common enemy by the characteristic effort to rouse the dying embers of religious hate. The landlord organs began to cry out for repression; and the London papers played their characteristic part of blackening events in Ireland and of exasperating the growing resentment between the two countries.

Towards the beginning of October the cry for coercion had swollen to a tempest, but for a moment it was laid by two remarkable speeches from Mr. Bright and Mr. Chamberlain.

'I saw,' said Mr. Bright, 'the statement the other day that about 100 of them (the Irish landlords), equal nearly to the number of the Irish members, had assembled in Dublin and discussed the state of things, and they had nothing but their old remedy—force, the English Government, armed police, increased military assistance and protection, and it might be measures of restriction and coercion which they were anxious to urge upon the Government. The question for us to ask ourselves is, Is there any remedy for this state of things? Force is no remedy' (loud cheers). 'There are times when it may be necessary, and when its employment may be absolutely unavoidable, but for my part I should rather regard, and rather discuss, measures of relief as measures of remedy, than measures of force, whose influence is only temporary, and in the long-run, I believe, is disastrous.'[1]

A conflict then arose within the Cabinet itself. I cannot pretend to tell the story of this internal struggle, and I can only repeat what was the gossip of the period. It was said that Mr. Chamberlain, Sir Charles Dilke, and Mr. Bright held out steadily, and for a considerable time, against the demand for coercion made by Mr. Forster. But Mr. Forster put forward this demand with daily increasing vehemence. For some days, according to the remark of the time, the Cabinet was within short distance of being broken up. The main argument before which the hesitations of the Ministry broke down was the enormous increase which Mr. Forster was able to show in the outrages in October and November. And the increase which appeared in the figures he laid before his colleagues was enormous indeed. By-and-by these figures will be examined, and it will be seen what the merits of the case were upon which Mr. Forster based his de-

[1] *Times*, November 17, 1880.

mands. For the present, suffice it to say that Mr. Forster carried his point; the opponents of coercion resolved to remain in the Cabinet, and it was announced that the next session of Parliament would open with a proposal for the enactment of coercive legislation. Meantime a blow was made at the leaders of the movement. On November 2, 1880, an information was filed at the suit of the Right Hon. Hugh Law, then the Attorney-General, against Mr. Parnell and four of his Parliamentary colleagues, Mr. T. D. Sullivan, Mr. Sexton, Mr. John Dillon, and Mr. Biggar; and also against Mr. Patrick Egan, treasurer, and Mr. Brennan, secretary, of the organization. In the indictment were also bundled several persons who held subordinate places in the organization, or were entirely unconnected with it.

There were nineteen counts in the indictment against the traversers. The main charges were—conspiring to incite the tenantry not to pay their rents; deterring tenants from buying land from which other tenants had been evicted; conspiring for the purpose of injuring the landlords; and forming combinations for the purpose of carrying out these unlawful ends. This, then, was the proceeding of the Government! There is scarcely one of these charges which was not the glory instead of the shame of Mr. Parnell and his fellow-traversers. Mr. Parnell had found the people face to face with famine and groaning under the oppression of centuries. He had brought them to such assertion of their rights, to such a potent combination, that, instead of being swept away, as in all previous crises, by wholesale hunger and plague and eviction, and thereafter reduced to deeper wretchedness and more hopeless slavery, not one man among them died from hunger or from disaster, and that, rising up from their misery and impotence, they gradually reached the position of practical omnipotence over their oppressors. The events and calamities which seemed to drive the tenantry back into the doom of hunger and of servitude had brought to them a new birth of political hope and power; and an hour of apparently darkest misery had been changed into the dawn of a new and a better day. A man of any other nationality who had accomplished such things—if he had been an Italian or a Pole; still more, at this epoch, if he had been a Bulgarian or a Montenegrin—would have taken an imperishable place in the adoration of Englishmen; and his reward, being an Irishman, was that a Liberal Administration dragged him through the mire of a criminal court. The trial was opened by a startling episode. With their usual mistake in regarding things in Ireland as necessarily the same as in England, because called by the same names, the English public were and are accustomed to look upon an Irish judge as raised above the passions of political partisanship. They were strangely shocked in the course of the preliminary proceedings of the trial to read a judgment of the Chief Justice of the Queen's Bench, in which the trial was to take place—a judgment in which the traversers were denounced with vehement passion. The times had been so changed since the elevation of a man like Judge Keogh to the Bench, that the Lord Chief Justice found that even the English people could not stomach such conduct, and he retired at the opening of the trial.

The trial was one of the solemn mockeries of the time. It was known by the Crown that no impartial jury would convict the saviour of the nation of treason to the nation; and after a trial extending over twenty days, the jury were discharged without agreeing to a verdict, ten, according to universal rumour, being in favour of acquittal and two for conviction. Another event of importance occurred during this recess. Shortly after his arrival in America on his memorable mission, Mr. Parnell found the services of a secretary absolutely necessary. He had previously made the acquaintance of a young Irishman who at that period was secretary in a London house of business and the London correspondent of the *Nation* newspaper. The young man had made a strong impression upon the Irish leader, had gained his confidence, and had taken part with some others in many of the important consultations at critical moments. This was Mr. T. M. Healy. To Mr. Healy Mr. Parnell's thoughts turned when he found himself immersed in a hopeless sea of correspondence. He requested Mr. Healy's presence in America by telegraph. On the day he received this telegram Mr. Healy threw up his situation, and on that same evening he was on his way to the vessel which took him to America.

Timothy Michael Healy was born in Bantry, county Cork, in the year 1855. Bantry, as has been seen, is also the birthplace of the Sullivans, and here Healy had beheld all the scenes of quick decay which have been already described. He had peculiar opportunities, indeed, for becoming familiar with the awful horrors of the famine, for his father, at seventeen years of age, had been appointed Clerk of the Union at Bantry, and his occupation brought him into contact with all the dread realities of that terrible time. He has told his son that for the three famine years he never once saw a single smile. Outside the abbey in which the forefathers of Healy and the other men of Bantry are buried, are pits in which many hundreds of the victims of the famine found a coffinless grave ; and Mr. Healy will tell you, with a strange blaze in his eyes, that even to-day the Earl of Bantry, the lord of the soil, will not allow these few yards of land to be taken into the graveyard, preferring that they should be trodden by his cattle. Reared in scenes like these, it is no wonder that Healy, whose nature is vehement and excitable, should have grown up with a burning hatred of English rule in Ireland.

He went to school to the Christian Brothers at Fermoy ; but fortune did not permit him to waste any unnecessary time in what are called the seats of learning ; for at thirteen he had to set out on the difficult business of making a livelihood. It is characteristic of his nature that, though he has thus had fewer opportunities than almost any other member of the House of Commons of obtaining education—except such as his father, an educated man, may have imparted to him as a child—he is really one of the very best informed men in the place. He is intimately acquainted with not only English but also with French and with German literature, and the 'rude barbarian' of the imagination of English journalists is keenly alive to the most delicate beauties of Alfred de Musset or Heinrich Heine, and could give his critics lessons in what constitutes literary merit and literary grace. Another of the accomplishments which Mr. Healy taught himself was Pitman's shorthand ; and shorthand in his case—as in that of Justin McCarthy and several other of his colleagues—was the sword with which he had in life's beginning to open the oyster of the world. At sixteen years of age he went to England and obtained a situation as a shorthand clerk in the office of the superintendent of the North-Eastern Railway at Newcastle. Newcastle-on-Tyne has a very large and a very sturdy Irish population, who take an active part in all political movements that are going on, and when Healy went there he found himself at once surrounded by countrymen who, if anything, held to the National faith more sturdily than their brethren at home. Probably he himself, if he were to trace the mental history of his political progress, would declare that in his case, as in that of so many other Irishmen, it was an English atmosphere that first gave form and intensity to his political convictions. At all events, the newcomer was not long at Newcastle when he was a persistent and an active participator in all the political strivings of his fellow-countrymen, and it speaks strongly of his force of character and their discrimination that, though yet but a stripling, he was chosen for several positions of authority. Newcastle is one of the few towns in England that can boast of having a society exclusively devoted to Irish purposes, and of the Irish Literary Institute Mr. Healy was for a considerable time the secretary. He was also, as far back as 1873, secretary to the local Home Rule Association. Of Mr. Healy's habits in Newcastle a characteristic account is given by one of his friends. He lodged in the house of an excellent Irish family—known to every Irish visitor to Newcastle—and in the family there was a Celtic abundance of children. It will relieve many friends of Mr. Healy to be informed that this man, before whom Ministers tremble, and even potent officials grow pale, is the delight and the darling of children, whose foibles, tastes, and pleasures he can minister to with the unteachable instinct of genius. The moment the young clerk put his foot inside his lodgings there came a shout of welcome from the young world upstairs; the next minute he was romping with them all; and, during the whole period of his stay within doors, he was the gayest and the youngest in the house. But when the time came for starting into the outside world of Newcastle and of Englishmen, Healy at once put on his suit of mail; his hat was tightened down on his head, his face assumed a frown of a most forbidding aspect, and even his teeth were set. And so he went out to encounter the world of strangers among whom he lived.

In March, 1878, he removed to London. He is distantly related to Mr. John Barry, M.P. for Wexford, and at that period Mr. Barry was associated with a large Scotch floor-cloth factory. Mr. Healy was employed as confidential clerk in this firm. He began at the same time to contribute a weekly letter to the *Nation* on Parliamentary proceedings, which had just begun to get lively. From this time forward his face accordingly became familiar in the lobby of the House of Commons. He had previously made the acquaintance of Mr. Parnell and the other prominent Irish figures of the last Parliament at Home Rule meetings and elsewhere; and his connection with the Sullivan family had made him more or less familiar with the 'inside' of Irish political movements. He at once threw all his force on the side of the 'active' section of the old Home Rule Party, and Mr. Parnell has several times remarked that it was to Mr. Healy's advocacy and explanation of his policy in the columns of the *Nation* that the active party owed much of its success in those early days, when its objects and tactics were misunderstood and actively misrepresented. The London correspondence of Mr. Healy was, indeed, a rare journalistic treat. In the opinion of many, his pen is even more effective than his tongue; mordant, happy illustration, trenchant argument—all this was to be found in those London letters, and is still, happily, at the service of Irish national journalism. The style of Mr. Healy is founded palpably on that of John Mitchel, and he has many of the excellences, and a few also of the faults, of that writer; but these very faults only make him the more readable; for liveliness, after all, is the first attraction of journalistic prose.

Anticipating a little, Mr. Healy had scarcely taken his place in the House when he set to work, and his first speech was in reply to the

Marquis of Hartington. It was late at night when the young member rose; the deputy-leader of the Ministerialists had made an effective address, and most of Mr. Healy's friends felt rather anxious as to the result. Mr. Healy can now bear to be told that there were very divided opinions as to the merits of his first appearance. His speech was delivered in a hard, dogged style, and gave evidence rather of fierce conviction than of debating power. It was some time, indeed, before the House would acknowledge that there was anything in Mr. Healy; and there has scarcely ever been an Irish member who had in his early days to face the fire of such brutal, mean, and cowardly attack. Gentlemen of the Press professed to be shocked at the intelligence that the new member was poor—that he actually, like themselves, wrote for a living; and even the cut of his clothes afforded proof of the ignobility of his character. But Mr. Healy took no notice of all this ribaldry, except, perhaps, to become fiercer in his wrath and more persistent in his activity. In the nine weeks' struggle against coercion he was, though a novice, one of the three or four men who did the largest amount of talking, and one has to go to the records of Biggar's best days and Sexton's longest speech to find any approach to the performances of Healy. When at last the Coercion Bills were done with, in 1881, Mr. Healy found more profitable employment in discussing the details of the Land Bill. While ninety-nine out of every hundred of the members of Parliament were floundering in the mazes of that extraordinary measure, Mr. Healy had found the key of the labyrinth, and was perfectly familiar with its details. He worked, as is known, night and day at the Bill, obtained several concessions, and finally succeeded, under circumstances to be presently described, in having the 'Healy Clause' adopted. These various successes at last made the House begin to change its opinion of its latest recruit. It was observed that Mr. Gladstone and Mr. Law used to listen with the utmost attention to anything Mr. Healy had to say. The Premier was even one night beheld in pleasant converse with his young and unsparing antagonist, and at once the servile herd of Tory journalists began to recognise Mr. Healy's talents. The saying of the time is well known, that but three men in the House of Commons knew the Land Bill—Mr. Gladstone, Mr. Law, and Mr. Healy.

A few words as to Mr. Healy's general characteristics. Perhaps the most remarkable of all his qualities is his restless industry. From the moment he crosses the tessellated floor of the lobby, at about four in the evening, till the House rises, he is literally never a moment at rest—excepting the half hour or so he spends at dinner in the restaurant within the House. He has almost as many correspondents as a Minister, and he tries to answer nearly every letter on the day of its receipt. Then he takes an interest in, and knows all about, everything that is going on, great or small, English, or Irish, or Scotch. With eyes ablaze, he comes to tell you of some atrocious job that is perpetrated under sub-section B in the schedule to a Scotch Bill on Hypothec, or a Welsh measure on threshing-machines; and he points out the advantage to an Irish Bill for reforming the grand jury by a 'block' he has put against a Bill for increasing the number of Commissioners in Bankruptcy. The extent of his knowledge of Parliamentary measures is astonishing; many bitter opponents in public policy seek his aid in this regard; and—tell it not in Gath!—there have been occasions when he has been seen explaining in the Library the mysteries of legislation to Mr. Herbert Gladstone. Indeed, Healy holds himself at the service of everybody. A puzzled colleague comes to ask for enlightenment; Healy has put his ideas into the shape of an amendment before he has had time to give them full expression. Besides all this, Healy has frequently to write a column or two for a newspaper in the course of the evening. And he is never absent from the House when anything of importance is going forward. He is, perhaps, the only man in the House, except Mr. Gladstone, who cannot bear a moment's idleness; and, like the late Premier, he is distinguished from other members by the fact that even in the division-lobbies he is to be seen utilizing the precious moments by writing at one of the tables. The characteristics of his oratory are by this time familiar. Often, when he stands up first, he is tame, disjointed, and ineffective; but he is one of the men who gather strength and fire as they go along, and before he has resumed his seat he has said some things that have set all the House laughing, and some that have put all the House into a rage. Finally, Healy has the defects of his qualities. The ardour of his temperament and the fierceness of his convictions often tempt him to exaggeration of language and of conduct. Those who play the complicated game of politics for such mighty stakes as a nation's fate and the destinies of millions ought to keep cool heads and steady hands. A quick temper and a sharp tongue cause many pangs to his friends, but keener tortures to Healy himself. He is betrayed into a rude expression, and then goes home and remains in sleepless contrition throughout the night.

It was, of course, inevitable that, when the Land League agitation broke out, one of these antecedents and of this temperament should throw himself into the movement; and to those who now know Mr. Healy, it will not be surprising to hear that he worked with fierce energy and often spoke with passionate vehemence. Passing through the South of Ireland, Mr. Healy became acquainted with the case of Michael McGrath. McGrath had held for years a farm, but, the rent having been raised from £48 to £105, had at last to yield in a struggle, and was evicted. His land was 'grabbed' by another farmer named Cornelius—or, as he was called in the district, 'Curley'—Mangan, and a decree of ejectment was given against McGrath for the house which had been built by his own hands or by those of his father. McGrath and his family did not tamely submit to the judgment of the law. They stood a siege for some days, and, whenever the evicting party approached near enough, threw boiling water upon them. The family were watched so closely that they were unable even to go out to get a drink of water, and at last were reduced by famine to capitulation. But the struggle was not over. McGrath went back to his farm, and was sent to gaol. His wife took possession, and was sent to gaol. His sister took possession, and was sent to goal. As each member of the family was released he or she went back again, and again they were each in turn sent to gaol. At last they had to give up the struggle for the house, and they then adopted an expedient which, perhaps, could only be resorted to in Ireland, of all civilized lands. McGrath got a boat and turned it upside down, and under this boat lived himself, his wife, his sister, and his children. The many tourists who crowd in the summer season to the beautiful regions of Glengariff were accustomed to stop on the road between Glengariff and Bantry to see this curious household. Mr. Healy was much struck with the story, and he and Mr. J. W. Walsh, then an organizer of the Land League, paid a visit to Mangan to remonstrate with him on the injustice he had done to the tenant, whose property he had helped the landlord to rob.

For his action in this matter Mr. Healy was arrested, and this was the first prominent arrest by the new Chief Secretary of the Liberal Government. Mr. Parnell and his friends at once resolved to make a return blow. The lamented death of Mr. William Redmond left a vacancy for the borough of Wexford. Mr. Healy was immediately nominated, and returned without even the mention of opposition. But he had not yet escaped from Mr. Forster's vengeance. He was charged under one of the Acts in the terrible code known as the Whiteboy Acts. The Acts date from the last century, and the prisoner convicted under them is liable to a lengthened term of penal servitude, and to be once, twice, or thrice publicly or privately whipped, each year. The case came before Judge Fitzgerald, and he joined the prosecuting counsel in exhausting every effort to procure a conviction. The two prisoners, Mr. Healy and Mr. Walsh, were, in the first place, tried at the winter assizes, and this was in itself an unusual and suspicious occurrence. The winter assizes are intended for the relief of prisoners who, being imprisoned, would otherwise have to wait till the spring assizes without having their cases decided; but Mr. Healy and Mr. Walsh were not imprisoned. They were put on bail, and this was perhaps the first instance in which bailed prisoners were tried at these assizes. The disadvantage to Mr. Healy and Mr. Walsh was that they were not tried by a jury of county farmers, many of whom might be in their favour, as their crime, if any, had been committed in defence of the farmers' cause. Then they were tried as misdemeanants, which reduced their power of challenge to six names; and, throughout the trial, Judge Fitzgerald was a far more effective cross-examiner on behalf of the Crown than the prosecuting counsel. But in spite of all these efforts, Mr. Healy and Mr. Walsh were acquitted.

It is, perhaps, as well here to tell the fate of McGrath. He continued in his boat for some years—still pursued by the many agencies that are on the side of the landlords in Ireland. For instance, he was charged by the county surveyor with trespassing on the road on which this boat-house was placed, and he only escaped through the inexhaustible ingenuity of Mr. Maurice Healy, Mr. Healy's brother. But finally, through exposure to the weather, poor McGrath caught typhus fever, passed through the illness under the boat, died under it, and was there waked. Since then neighbours have built a small house for his widow and children.

The scene now changed from the agitation in Ireland and from the State Trials: and interest was transferred from Dublin to Westminster. The result of the trial of Mr. Parnell was regarded as foregone, and excited but a languid interest. The real centre of attraction was the House of Commons. The Government had pledged themselves to propose coercion; the Irish members at their annual meeting, held in the City Hall, Dublin, had, on their side, pledged themselves to exhaust every effort in opposing coercion. Everyone was anxious to see the opening of the portentous struggle.

CHAPTER XI.

THE COERCION STRUGGLE.

PARLIAMENT met on Thursday, January 6. Nobody felt certain as to what would be the fate of the coercion proposals of the Government. The terms of the Queen's Speech were eagerly scanned; the statements with regard to coercion were strong, the allusions to the coming Land Bill were weak. 'Attempts upon life,' said the Queen's Speech, 'have not grown in the same proportions as other offences.' The burden of the charge was that what was called 'an extended system of terror had been established' which had 'paralyzed almost alike the exercise of private rights and the performance of civil duties.'[1] In other words, the main offence was that the organization of the tenantry throughout the country had been made so complete that the landlords found it impossible any longer to get the tenants to play their game by internecine struggle for the privilege of paying a rack-rent for the land. If such a conspiracy existed, it was a national conspiracy; for membership of the Land League at this period was practically coterminous with the citizenhood of four-fifths of the country. The statement was frequently put forward, of course, that the terrorism which existed was the creation of a few agitators who were at the head of the Land League; but this theory was gradually dropped, and war was declared against the Land League as a body—that was, against the Irish people as a nation.

The allusions in the Prime Minister's speech to the coming Land Act were even more vague and unsatisfactory than those of the Queen's Speech. He still stuck to the Act of 1870 as fairly successful.[2] He passed a general eulogium upon the landlords as a class, and he even denied that there had been any general increase of the rents.[3] Probably, for strategical reasons, he also did his best to minimize the reforms which he was about to propose. His legislation was to be nothing better than a development of the principles of the Act of 1870. There were some faint promises of a tribunal for settling fair rent and of free sale, but he studiously avoided all mention of fixity of tenure—the third of the 'three F's.'[4] This speech increased the general alarm; and when the Irish members complained of the insufficiency of the proposals which the Government had shadowed forth, they were received with cheers from the Radical benches.[5]

The Irish members, as has been seen, had pledged themselves to oppose coercion by all the forms of the House, and the plan they adopted was to propose several amendments in succession. Mr. Parnell started by proposing 'That the peace and tranquillity of Ireland cannot be promoted by suspending any of the constitutional rights of the Irish people.' Mr. McCarthy followed with an amendment, 'Humbly to pray her Majesty to refrain from using the naval, military, and constabulary forces of the Crown in enforcing ejectments for non-payment of rent in Ireland, until the measures proposed to be submitted to her Majesty with regard to the ownership of land in Ireland have been decided upon by Parliament.' And finally Mr. Dawson proposed 'That in the opinion of this House it is expedient to submit a measure for the purpose of assimilating the Borough Franchise in Ireland to that in England, as promised in her Majesty's most gracious speech last session.'

This brought the debate on the Queen's Speech up to Thursday, January 20. By this time the aspect of affairs had undergone a considerable change. The exasperation caused by this prolonged resistance created a similar exasperation outside the House of Commons. There was gradually

---

[1] Hansard, vol. cclvii., p. 6.
[2] 'We are not at all prepared to admit that the Land Act has been a failure.'—Hansard, vol. cclvii., p. 119.
[3] 'I do not wish at all to convey that it is my impression that rents in Ireland would in general be described with any fairness as being unfair or exorbitant.'—Ibid., p. 120.
[4] Ibid., pp. 120, 121.　　　　[5] Ibid., p. 222.

rising one of those tempests of popular passion in England which sweep down party ties. The Radicals grew fewer and fainter in their opposition, the two English parties practically coalesced, and the House was united against the little Irish phalanx. The latter, on their part, exhausted, but still angry and determined, resolved to fight on; and they, too, were backed by the rising temper of their own country. The Land League grew daily in power and in resources; the subscriptions from America rose to an amount that a short time before would have been considered fabulous; and on January 13 the treasurer was able to announce that during the week then past there had been received from various sources no less a sum than £4,050. Eviction became daily more impossible, and, though all the forces of the Crown were placed at the disposal of the landlords, the decree frequently had to remain unfulfilled in the presence of crowds of peasants armed with pitchforks, scythes, and pike-heads, and ready to perish in defence of their homesteads. These various circumstances were also aggravated by the daily contests at question-time between Mr. Forster and the Irish representatives. Every act of repression to which he resorted lent fuel to the flame, and from this period forward he took up an ultra-Tory attitude. He admitted no case of exceptional hardship, defended the police through thick and thin, and in fact adopted the policy of repression pure and simple.

At last, on the night of Thursday, January 20, the third Irish amendment was disposed of. On January 12 it was announced that Mr. Shaw had retired from the Home Rule Party. He was followed by all the other Home Rulers who with him had remained seated on the Liberal side of the House; and thus the Irish Party found themselves deserted by their own friends in face of the enemy, and in the very agony of pitched battle.

On Monday, January 24, Mr. Forster introduced the first Coercion Bill. The speech which he delivered was one of the ablest that he ever addressed to the House. The matter was well arranged, the delivery was good, the fierce passion which he felt lent effect to his denunciations, and the speech was full of those asides and suggestions which were natural to one of the greatest masters of adroit suggestiveness the House of Commons ever saw. Its effect upon the House was very great, and the newspapers of the next morning proclaimed with unbroken unanimity that he had clearly and triumphantly proved the case for coercion.

Let me examine rapidly the grounds on which Mr. Forster demanded coercion.

Mr. Forster's first position was that the total of crime was enormous and unprecedented; and this he proceeded to prove by stating that the total number of outrages in the year 1880 was 2,590, and that this was the greatest total of crime ever recorded from the date when agrarian crimes were first distinctly tabulated—which was another way of stating that the crime of 1880 was the largest of any year on record. This statement of the case, if true, gave a strong—almost an unanswerable—argument in favour of coercion. But the statement was entirely untrue. In the first place Mr. Forster had to reduce his big total of 2,590 down to 1,253, for the balance of 1,337 were threatening letters. If the House had been in a reasonable temper this announcement would have been so startling as to make it suspicious of the whole case of Mr. Forster; for, of course, when Mr. Forster spoke to his colleagues of the appalling total of 2,590 crimes, what they would infer was that he was talking of crimes actually perpetrated, not of crimes intended or threatened.

Mr. Forster diverted attention from this astonishing revelation of the weakness of his case by appearing to frankly admit it; and by still contending that even if this distinction were made between actual offences committed and mere threatening letters, still the year 1880 stood out in bold and bad relief from all the other years of Irish crime in the extent of its criminality.

'In 1880 (he said), exclusive of threatening letters, the number of agrarian outrages was 1,253; in 1845, they were 950—that is to say, that they were 32 per cent. higher last year than they were in the largest year of which we have any special record. Hon. members are well aware that there is now a great difference in the population. The population of Ireland is now some 5,000,000, compared with 8,000,000 in 1845. Therefore, taking into account the difference of population, the actual agrarian outrages of last year, exclusive of threatening letters, were more than double what they were in the worst year we have any record of, namely, the year 1845.'[1]

Here again we have a statement which is entirely untrue, to the extent that it gives a grossly—it may be said, a gigantically—false representation of the state of affairs. It is entirely untrue to declare that the year 1880 was more criminal than any year from 1844. It would be far more correct to say that the year 1880 was a year startlingly free from crime in comparison with several of the years from 1844. The criminal character of a year should assuredly be tested, not so much by the number of its crimes as by their character. A year that had a hundred cases of petty larceny and no murder would certainly be less criminal than a year that had fifty-two crimes, of which fifty were petty larceny and two were wilful murder, though there was a difference of forty-eight between the criminal totals of the one year and the other. A test of the criminality of these different years would be a comparison of such serious crimes as homicides, whether murder or manslaughter. Let us apply this test to 1880 and other years, and this is what we find:

HOMICIDES, DESCRIBED AS AGRARIAN.

Year	Count	Year	Count
1844	18	1850	18
1845	18	1851	12
1846	16	1869	10
1847	16	1879	10
1849	15	1880	8

It will be seen from this table that, in serious agrarian crime, the year 1880 bore a most favourable contrast, not merely with many years since 1844, but also with the very year which preceded it.

Let us try another form of comparison between the criminality of 1880 and that of preceding years. The distinction made between agrarian and other outrages would seem to have been very lax in the early years of the statistical records. For instance, in the year 1847 the total outrages in Ireland are set down as 2,986, and of these but 620 are placed to the credit of agrarian outrages. This must, of course, be inaccurate; for 1847, as has been seen, was a year of agrarian upheaval, and, instead of the proportion of crime between agrarian and non-agrarian being fairly represented by 620 on the one side, and the balance of the total of 2,986 on the other, it would seem far more likely that the greater number of the 2,986 crimes

[1] Hansard. vol. cclvii., p. 1209.

were agrarian crimes—the crimes of starving and desperate peasants fighting for their patch of land and their meals of potatoes. In any case, let us now compare the total crime of 1880 with that of other years:

Year.	Total of Outrages.	Year.	Total of Outrages.
1844	6,327	1849	14,908
1845	8,088	1850	10,639
1846	12,374	1851	9,144
1847	20,986	1880	5,609
1848	14,080		

This table will show a startling difference between the crime of 1880 and that of several of the years by which it was preceded.

Finally, let us compare the total of murders of all kinds in 1880 with those of preceding years:

Year.	Homicides.	Year.	Homicides.
1844	146	1851	157
1845	139	1852	140
1846	170	1853	119
1847	212	1870	77
1848	171	1871	71
1849	203	1880	69
1850	139		

But the strongest evidence of the comparative freedom from serious crime of 1880 in comparison with other years in found in the speech of Mr. Forster himself.

'Some honourable members,' he said, 'have said that after all there have been but few cases of murder, or attempt at murder'—and when this statement was received, as was natural, with cheers from the Irish members, the Chief Secretary made the reply—'but they were not necessary;'[1] and this answer was considered so satisfactory by the House generally, that the Ministerialists and Conservatives cheered in accord.

Later on the Marquis of Hartington made exactly the same admission. 'I find,' he said, 'that during the year 1879, when Ireland was ruled by a beneficent Conservative Government, there were ten agrarian homicides or murders, and in the year which has just elapsed there were seven.'

I have now, from the words of the Queen's Speech, from the words of Mr. Forster, from the words of Lord Hartington, and from the figures, proved that in serious crime 1880, instead of being exceptionally criminal, was, compared with years of disturbances, exceptionally innocent; and that disposes of Mr. Forster's first plea for coercion.

The second plea for coercion was the enormous increase of crime in the latter half of the year 1880, and especially in the last three months of that year.

'I am also (said Mr. Forster) obliged to tell the House that there has been a great increase in the last three months of last year. Exclusive of threatening letters, 719 outrages out of the total of 1,253 for the entire year occurred in the three months of October, November, and December; and, including threatening letters, 1,696 out of 2,590. That is to say, two-thirds of the total agrarian outrages occurred within the last quarter of the year, and 58 per cent. of these, exclusive of threatening letters. It

---

[1] Hansard, vol. cclvii., p. 1213.

is also right to say that the number which occurred in the month of December was much more than it is for October and November put together.'¹

This was an argument which carried great weight with the House of Commons, and unquestionably it was the argument that finally induced Mr. Forster's colleagues to accept coercion. And the figures certainly were sufficiently startling. The total for September, 1880, was 167; in October the total had risen to 268, in November to 561, and in December it had reached 867.

With this part of Mr. Forster's case I will not deal just for the moment. The outrages for the year 1880 were published in Blue Books, giving the crimes for each month of the year separately. The first Blue Book was not produced at the opening of the Session, nor for several days after; it was produced at a time when the case of Ireland had already been decided. The story of the Blue Books I will tell a few paragraphs later on; and then it will be seen that the case for the increase of crime in the latter half of 1880, and in the months of October, November, and December, was just as much without real foundation, and was as much a tissue of misrepresentation and false pretences as the representation that 1880 was remarkable for the depth of its criminality above all years from 1844. With the year 1880 considerably under the total of the previous year's murders, and immensely under the total of that of many other years, by what means did Mr. Forster succeed in fooling a body of intelligent men into the belief that Ireland was, in that year, a perfect pandemonium of hideous and revolting crime?

Mr. Forster's chief device was to select some special and isolated case of horrible ill-usage, and represent this as of constant occurrence, and typical of the general condition of the country. For instance, in one of his effective asides he described 'carding':

'I do not know (he said) whether honourable members know what carding means, and perhaps I had better explain it. An iron comb used for agricultural purposes is applied to a man's naked body, and the torture must be very great.'²

The sentence in which he introduces this description will sufficiently prove that he meant to indicate that 'carding' was an extremely common occurrence.

'A disguised party of men (he said), consisting of ten, twenty, or even more, come to a lone farmhouse at night, drag the farmer out of bed, beat him, and card him.'

And he then went on after his dexterous aside:

'Then the man is threatened and warned against disobeying the orders of the organization any longer. Shots are fired over his head, and sometimes at him. Let hon. members think of the terrors thus produced. Imagine a small farmer in a desolate situation—his house on the side of some hill, or near some bog. There is no help near; no police-station is at hand; and the man himself is powerless to resist. Naturally, he submits to this cruel tyranny and intimidation. And no wonder, when such things as these are taking place, that the hon. member for Tipperary (Mr. Dillon) is right, and that the Land League reigns supreme.'³

¹ Hansard, vol. cclvii., pp. 1209, 1210.
² Ibid., p. 1212.   ³ Ibid.

What will be thought of the candour of the Chief Secretary in making such a representation when it is said that in the Blue Book containing the crimes from February, 1880, to October, 1880, there is, in the whole total of 1,048 crimes, just *one* single instance of 'carding'?

But in the absence of murders, and with but one case of 'carding,' Mr. Forster had plenty of stories with regard to the mutilation of cattle. The Chief Secretary relied on the fact that the story of such offences would naturally have great effect upon an audience of Englishmen, with their strong and just hatred of cruelty to animals.

When Mr. Forster had exhausted his harrowing description of these outrages upon animals, what was the dread total he had to bring of such cases before Parliament? 'In 1880,' he said, 'the number of cases of maiming cattle amounted to 101.'[1] With similar reasonableness Sir Charles Dilke, in a speech made during the recess, had suggested the necessity of coercion from the fact that in ten months of 1880 there had been 47 cases of maiming or killing animals. Forty-seven outrages on animals in ten months, 101 in twelve—a small total to destroy a nation's liberties! In 1876 there were in England 2,468 convictions for cruelty to animals; in 1877, 2,726; in 1878, 3,533. In the very month of November of 1880, the Society for the Prevention of Cruelty to Animals was able to advertise 323 convictions, or more than three times the number of cases in all Ireland for the entire year. If the liberties of England were at the mercy of an ignorant and hostile opinion in Ireland, one can well imagine how, by a judicious manipulation of these statistics, the habits of the English people might be falsely illustrated to the Irish people as those of a nation of savages and monsters.

There was one device finally. It was the foundation of the whole case of the Chief Secretary that his legislation was directed, not against the Land League as an organization, nor against the masses of the Irish people. His whole cue was that the Act was directed against the few criminals who with their own hands perpetrated these outrages: the Bills, in fact, were in defence of the nation generally against a few criminals among its population. Answering the argument that they ought to have introduced Land Reform before coercion, the Chief Secretary said: 'My answer is that the Irish people cannot wait for protection, and they ought not to wait for protection.'[2] The criminals, on the other hand, were 'village tyrants,' the '*mauvais sujets*' of their neighbourhood; the 'contemptible, dissolute ruffian and blackguard,' who was 'shunned by every respectable man.'[3]

This miserable minority, too, of persons who committed outrages were well known to the police.

'It is not (said Mr. Forster) that the police do not know who these village tyrants are. The police know perfectly well who plan and perpetrate these outrages, and the perpetrators are perfectly aware of the fact that they are known.'[4]

The moment the Habeas Corpus Act was suspended, these men would either fly the country or be arrested.

'The men who plan and execute these outrages desist from fear of being arrested. They are aware that the police know who they are. My belief

---

[1] Hansard, vol. cclvii., p. 1211.
[2] *Ibid.*, p. 1235.
[3] *Ibid.*, pp. 1226, 1227.
[4] *Ibid.*, p. 1226.

is that if you pass this Act you will cause an immense diminution of crime.'[1]

It will be seen later on in what shameful difference was the application of the Coercion Act and the limitation by the Chief Secretary of the persons to whom it should apply, and in what grotesque and horrible contrast were his expectations of what the fruits of coercion would be and what the fruits of coercion really were.

The Returns on which Mr. Forster had founded his claim for coercion were distributed among members for the first time on the morning of the day on which he asked leave to introduce his Coercion Bill. On Thursday evening, January 27, the analysis of the Returns was in the hands of an able and skilful assailant in the person of Mr. Henry Labouchere. He went through the Returns and exposed astonishing cases of multiplication and exaggeration. Mr. Labouchere picked out some of the most amusing; and his speech was a great success.

In truth, the Returns were so full of incredible absurdities, that several speakers freely resorted to them, certain that quotations from them would be sure to enliven the dulness of the House. This is the very first outrage that stood in the Book:

'A portion of the front wall of an old unoccupied thatched cabin was maliciously thrown down, in consequence of which the roof fell in.'

The 8th outrage reported for the West Riding of Co. Cork was thus described:

'A wooden gate broken up with stones, and half an iron gate taken away, the property of W. S. Bateman.'

Here is the 4th outrage reported for the North Riding of Co. Tipperary:

'A small wooden gate, the property of Lord Dunally, was taken off its hinges, brought into a field, and broken with large stones.'

The 41st outrage reported in the County Cavan is as follows:

'Several panes of glass were maliciously broken in the windows of an unoccupied house.'

Here is the 6th outrage reported for the County Derry:

'Three perches of a wall maliciously thrown down.'

Here is the 100th outrage in the West Riding of County Galway:

'A barrel of coal tar maliciously spilled.'

These discoveries of the true character of the outrages by which Mr. Forster had been able to draw his lurid picture of the state of Ireland were sufficiently startling; but a more bewildering and a more disturbing discovery was the manner in which one offence was manufactured into several. Sometimes the one outrage was made to do duty for two or more. Thus in page 120 of the Return an outrage in the County Mayo is described as follows:

'A party of men came to Tighe's house at night, and warned him that they would kill him unless he gave up a meadow which he bought.

'Same party before leaving broke Tighe's window.'

[1] Hansard, vol. cclvii., p. 1231.

This occurrence figures as two outrages. As 'intimidation' it is outrage No. 104; as injury to property, it is outrage No. 105.

In the same page of the Return there are these two separate records:

'Mr. Walsh was fired at when returning from his lodge from Achill Sound, by one of four men whom he passed on the road; he was not injured.'

And:

'Mr. Walsh, when fired at, at once dismounted from his horse, and, while doing so, was struck with a stick and knocked down.'

This occurrence also figures as two outrages. As 'firing at the person' it is outrage No. 110; as 'aggravated assault' it is outrage No. 111.

Sometimes the same occurrence is manufactured into five crimes, thus:

No. of Outrage.	Names of injured persons.	Offence: Description.	Short details.
87	Thomas R. Talbot and caretakers.	Taking and holding forcible possession.	Mr. Talbot took a farm from which James Murphy (accused) was evicted, and placed caretakers in charge of it. About 2 a.m. an armed party forcibly reinstated Murphy and family, swore him not to leave it, assaulted caretakers, set fire to about £60 worth of property, and robbed the caretakers of their arms—three loaded guns.[1]
88	Ditto.	Administering unlawful oaths.	
89	Ditto.	Assault on caretakers.	
90	Ditto.	Incendiary fire.	
91	Ditto.	Robbery of arms.	

And finally, that grotesque absurdity might reach its climax, an assault by a man is represented as one outrage, and then the assault on him by those whom he attacked figures as another. Here is the entry:

No. of Outrage.	Date.	Names of injured persons.	Nature of offence.	Short details.
36	April 3.	Margaret Lydon. Patt Whalen. Bridget Whalen.	Aggravated assault.	A dispute arose about the possession of a small plot of ground. John Lydon assaulted the injured persons.
37	April 3.	John Lydon.	Ditto.	Lydon was assaulted at the time of the above dispute about the land.[2]

When the Returns for November and December were published, a considerable time afterwards, there were the same extraordinary phenomena.

In page 15 of the Return for November, the 9th crime is:

'At an early hour four locks were maliciously broken off gates at James Fenton's farm.'

In page 39, the 7th crime and outrage in the County of Tipperary is thus described:

'On the night of the 20th November the windows of the injured man's house were broken, and the tops knocked off two corn ricks.'

[1] Return, Agrarian Crime (Ireland), part i., p. 54. [2] Ibid.

The 9th outrage on the same page is thus described:

'Four panes of glass were broken in the injured man's house on the night of the 20th November.'

In the Return for December, in page 9, the second crime and outrage in the King's County is in these words:

'The head of a large cock of hay, the property of Mr. Gaynor, was knocked off, causing considerable damage to the hay; also an iron gate was carried away and his cattle driven into the road.'

In page 43 the 83rd agrarian outrage was described:

'Three beehives and some shrubs were maliciously injured.'

It would be rash to say that, if these false Returns had been presented to Parliament at an early period of the session, they would have largely increased the number of opponents to coercion; but if, at the time of the struggle within the bosom of the Cabinet itself for and against the adoption of repressive measures, Mr. Forster had not confined himself to laying before his colleagues the simple total of increased crimes, it seems hardly open to doubt that the opponents of coercion would have been able to continue their resistance. That he submitted only the totals to his colleagues was clearly manifest. During the delivery of Mr. Labouchere's speech the face of the Prime Minister grew clouded and disturbed. He asked for the Returns just published, and was observed to scan them eagerly and anxiously.

Mr. Gladstone spoke on the third night of the debate. It is worth while quoting a couple of passages to show the honest intentions with which Mr. Gladstone supported coercion, and how Mr. Forster had succeeded in completely misrepresenting the case of Ireland to him. 'We aim by this Bill,' said Mr. Gladstone, 'and aim solely at the perpetrators and abettors of outrage.'[1]

'I stand (continued Mr. Gladstone) upon the words of the legislation we propose, and I say that they do not in the slightest degree justify the suspicion that we are interfering with the liberty of discussion. I will go further. We are not attempting to interfere with the license of discussion. There is no interference here with the liberty to propose the most subversive and revolutionary changes. There is no interference here with the right of associating in the furtherance of those changes, provided the furtherance is by peaceful means. There is no interference here with whatever right hon. gentlemen may think they possess to recommend, and to bring about, not only changes of the law, *but in certain cases breaches of positive contract*. I am not stating these things as a matter of boast, I am stating them as matter of fact. I must say it appears to me that it is a very liberal state of law which permits hon. gentlemen to meet *together to break a contract into which they have entered*.'[2]

These words clearly prove that Mr. Gladstone was as averse then as he is now to the prosecution of combination in political opposition. If the Coercion Act afterwards falsified these predictions of Mr. Gladstone, as it did, that does not prove the non-existence or the insincerity of Mr. Gladstone's intentions. Mr. Forster was the man responsible for the working of the Coercion Act, and, besides, pledges as to how coercion will be carried out, made in the bland serenity of Parliamentary debate, can never be fulfilled amid the fierce passion of the social war

[1] Hansard, vol. cclvii., p. 1086.   [2] *Ibid*., pp. 1086, 1087.

which coercion begets. The contrast between the purposes to which Mr. Gladstone thought coercion should be devoted and its actual operation is one of the strongest arguments against coercion, and not, as is stupidly or dishonestly argued, an argument in favour of its renewal.

The debate was resumed on Monday, January 31. Mr. Gladstone announced that the first stage of the Bill—that of the introduction—should be finished at that sitting. The Prime Minister made this announcement, as it were, carelessly; but there was a portentous underswell in his voice which showed the supreme importance he attached to it. The Ministerialists, of course, understood the *mot d'ordre* of the speech, and loudly cheered; the Conservatives, equally exasperated against the Irish, and equally delighted at the success of their efforts in hounding on the Government, shouted their applause, and the small Parnellite band, quite as quick as anybody else to see the dire significance of the Premier's announcement, set up a cry not as loud, but quite as defiant, as any that had come from either of the other parties.

The debate resumed its course with apparent placidity. The House was almost empty during the whole evening, and it was not until one o'clock that the contest began. At that hour the usual motion for adjournment was made. The reply of the Prime Minister was laconic and emphatic. 'I beg to say,' he answered, 'on the part of the Government, that we propose to resist that motion.'[1] The strange calm that had reigned over the House during the evening was now broken. Passion was let loose, and active steps were taken on both sides for hot and sharp encounter. The Ministerialists, on their side, had begun their preparations for the coming contest at an early hour. About half-past ten there began to be a gradual melting away of the House, and there were left no more than half a score of the dullest and drowsiest, the most reticent and most docile members of the Ministerial Party. Of the men thus told off to remain through the sitting, the majority left the House and were lost to observation in the various departments of the building. The Irish members settled down steadily to their work, and followed each other in the empty House in monotonous succession. During the first night the proceedings were not ill-humoured on either side. Mr. Biggar was grotesquely humorous after his fashion, and the few English members in the House sympathized with his mood. When he declared that the Irish members were accused of wasting time, there came from English members a deprecatory 'No, no,' whereupon the member for Cavan beamed on the House, and the House beamed back upon the member for Cavan.

The struggle continued all through Tuesday, Dr. Lyon Playfair taking the place of the Speaker when the latter became exhausted. About eleven o'clock on Tuesday night an appeal was made by Sir Richard Cross, on the part of the Conservatives, to the Speaker to put in use the rule against wilful obstruction. The Speaker did not think the time had come for putting this rule into operation, but at the same time hinted very plainly that in his view there was very strong evidence of 'combination for the purpose of wilful and persistent obstruction.' After giving this ruling, Mr. Brand retired from the chair, and Dr. Lyon Playfair again took his place. For a while the point as to 'obstruction' was dropped; but soon Sir Stafford Northcote came forward, and again urged the Chair to deal summarily with the Irish members. But Dr. Playfair still refused to take action; and when, finally, an appeal was made to him by Sir Stafford

[1] Hansard, vo' cclv.i., p. 1809.

Northcote to name Mr. Parnell, and he still refused to act, Sir Stafford and the Conservative Party left the House in a body.

The Irish members now changed their course, and, abandoning any further motions for adjournment, proceeded to debate the main question, which was an amendment on the part of Dr. Lyons in opposition to Mr. Forster's demand for leave to introduce the Coercion Bill. Each member spoke at the greatest length that either his physical or his mental resources would permit. Under this change the House became transformed: the heat and excitement of a crowded Chamber gave place to the languor, silence, and calm consistent with a House of but eight or nine members, most of them either fast asleep or in broken slumber. The visitors, whose attendance throughout the scene had been marvellously regular, broke down under disappointment of the hope of further excitement; the Ladies' Gallery became absolutely deserted; there were vacancies even in the Strangers' Gallery, which had up to this remained crowded; and but one or two persons remained in the gallery for distinguished strangers. The mournful silence of the Chamber was broken only by the voice of the Irish member and the snore of a sleepy member. It was something of a relief to the dread quiet when Sir William Harcourt now and then carried on a low but audible conversation with some of his colleagues. It was on this morning that Mr. Sexton delivered the second of the remarkable speeches by which he was at last forcing himself into the position of one of the most adroit and most eloquent orators of the House. He spoke from a quarter to five until twenty minutes to eight. This speech, delivered to an audience of seven or eight people, nearly every one of them in a state of complete or partial slumber, was complete in every one of its sentences, had every idea well worked out, every word happily chosen. Mr. Shaw-Lefevre, one of the few representatives of the Ministry who remained on the Treasury bench throughout the night, afterwards declared that he had listened to every word that Mr. Sexton had uttered, and that there was not throughout it all a superfluous syllable.

Meantime other Irish members were preparing to follow, and to continue the struggle as long as their physical strength would hold out. Some of them had taken broken snatches of sleep while one of their comrades was speaking, and at this time were washing off in the lavatories around the House the fatigues of the night. Inside and outside the House a state of electrical excitement prevailed that can only be appreciated by those who passed through these scenes. There were affrighting whispers of what might be done by savage mobs of Englishmen on the one side, by Irish desperadoes on the other. Some of the Irish members had been subjected to a certain amount of inconvenience as they walked home in the early hours of the morning. No one, in fact, knew what was going to happen, but everybody had a vague feeling that something was about to occur, and something of a startling character. Inside the House there was a vague suspicion of an impending catastrophe. An English member informed Mr. Sexton, when the member for Sligo, after his speech, dragged himself down to the smoking-room, that 'something' would take place at nine o'clock.

Mr. Leamy followed Mr. Sexton, and about a quarter to nine Mr. Biggar stood up. Meantime there were many signs that the dreaded 'something' was about to take place. As if by some mysterious and occult influence, the House filled with extraordinary rapidity. As the clock approached the hour of nine, Dr. (now Sir Lyon) Playfair began to look very anxious and expectant. Mr. Gladstone and Sir Stafford Northcote had come in, and at nine o'clock the Speaker made his appearance. He was received with a burst of enthusiastic cheers, and it was evident from the benches on both sides, which were now almost crowded, that both the English parties had been told of what was about to come. Mr. Biggar had resumed his seat when the Speaker came in, and now rose to continue his speech, but the Speaker, who had entered with an air of strange determination, and with an ominous roll of paper in his hand, remained standing and refused to see the member for Cavan. He then read the historic declaration that he would now close the discussion. Each sentence of his speech was received with boisterous applause from both Liberals and Conservatives. It is still painful to recall the looks of furious hate with which the Tory members looked towards the Irish benches. Meantime, the latter were without the assistance of their leader, for Mr. Parnell had gone to snatch a few hours' sleep at the Westminster Palace Hotel close by. Their hasty consultation was not concluded when the Speaker had put the question whether Mr. Forster's motion or Dr. Lyons' amendment should be accepted. In the midst of this uncertainty the precious seconds passed away. At last the doors of the House were closed, and nothing remained but to take part in the division. In sullenness and silence on both sides the division was taken. It was noticeable that, as the members passed each other to go into the different lobbies, there was not even a single exchange of the passing word between men of the opposite camps which usually relieves in an agreeable manner the conflict of parties. The Speaker then announced the numbers : For the original question, 164 ; against, 19 ; majority for the Government, 145.

The Speaker immediately afterwards proposed to put the original question, that leave be given to bring in the Bill. Mr. Justin McCarthy, as deputy-chairman of the party, rose to protest. The Speaker took no notice, and the member for Longford and he were standing and speaking at the same time, but not a word of either could be heard. The Irish representative was met with a storm of interruption which was almost deafening. Mr. McCarthy, with a tranquil and resolute smile, still held his ground. By a happy inspiration the Irish members determined not to go through the farce of a second division. First two, then two or three more, and finally all of them jumped to their feet, raised their hands—in most cases clenched in passion—and shouted, 'Privilege ! privilege !' for several seconds, many shaking their clenched fists with desperate anger, and moving their lips as if they were accompanying these menacing gestures with words of violence. Mr. Gladstone was notably pale and disturbed. The Speaker still remained standing, saying nothing, and the House became somewhat less vehement. At last the Irish members brought the painful incident to a conclusion by walking out of the House in single file, Mr. McCarthy leading the way, and bowing to the Speaker as they left. Some of the younger members of the House slightly cheered, but the Assembly generally remained silent. Then the original question was put, and it was carried without dissent. Immediately afterwards enthusiasm and excitement once more broke forth, and the cheering became still louder when Mr. Forster, in the usual manner, walked up the floor of the House from the bar with his Bill in his hand. Then there was a renewal of cheers when the measure passed its first reading without any dissent, and the sitting, after its forty-one hours' duration, came to an end.

The Irish members retired from the House to the conference-room, to consider their course of action. They had scarcely arrived there when Mr. Parnell, to whom Mr. Healy had conveyed the news of these stirring events, entered. He wore his usual placid smile; but his followers, hot from their wild encounter, under the influence of one of those crises which draw tight the ties between leader and followers, burst into spontaneous cheers. The Irish Party was young in those days, and this fact will account for their gravely discussing one of the most foolish propositions ever submitted to a body of politicians. Mr. O'Connor Power proposed the following resolution:

'That the irregular and unprecedented course adopted by Mr. Speaker in summarily closing the debate on the Coercion Bill, by which the Irish members have been deprived of the opportunity of protesting against the suspension of constitutional liberty in Ireland, requires to be taken notice of; and that a protest, signed by Irish members, be forwarded to Mr. Speaker and circulated in the public press; and that we, the Irish members, retire from the House pending the result of a consultation with our constituents.'[1]

The debate was most interesting and most able. All the speakers who took part in it put their cases with vigour, and, indeed, in most cases with vehemence. The long vigils of so many days and nights had begun to tell on the nerves of most of them, and there was a certain shrillness in the voices, a certain feverishness in the language and gestures of the debaters, that told of systems which had been subjected to too severe and too prolonged a strain. But these were the very things which lent passion and force to the debate, and therefore it is, probably, that it remains so distinctly in the memories of all who were present. After a lengthy discussion, it was decided that it was the duty of the Irish members to remain in their places in Parliament and to go on with the struggle.

The Wednesday immediately following the close of the forty-one hours' sitting was again wasted in motions for adjournment. Just before the sitting on Thursday there came the stunning report that Mr. Davitt had been arrested. Mr. Davitt had now been more than three years out of prison. He had already, as the reader knows, passed through the hideous tortures of seven years' confinement. The Coercion Bill was passed soon after this, and, though the expectation was general that he might be placed under restraint under the new legislation, nobody suspected that the Government would have proceeded to lengths so great as to send back to penal servitude one of the leaders of the agitation. The news deeply affected Mr. Parnell and the other Irish members. When the House met, however, there was no indication of the coming storm. Mr. Parnell rose from his seat in his usual tranquil fashion, and asked, in a tone of apparently no great concern, whether it was true that Mr. Davitt had been arrested. 'Yes, sir!'[2] was the laconic reply. It speaks eloquently of the hideous passions which coercion begets that this intelligence was received with a tempest of cheers that would have formed a fitting welcome to a mighty victor in the field or the accomplishment of a momentous popular reform.

When, a few minutes after, Mr. Gladstone rose to propose the Rules of Urgency, Mr. Dillon rose at the same time. The Speaker called upon Mr. Dillon to sit down, and that gentleman shouted above the tumult of 'Order, order!' and 'Name, name!' the words, 'I rise to a point of order.'[3] The Speaker resolutely refused to allow Mr. Dillon to proceed. Mr.

[1] *Freeman's Journal*, February 3, 1881.   [2] Hansard, vol. cclviii., p. 66.   [3] *Ibid.*, p. 69.

Dillon thereupon folded his arms, and he and the Speaker remained standing for some minutes at the same time. At last the Speaker was understood to name Mr. Dillon, though the decree could not be heard above the wild din. His suspension having been carried, Mr. Dillon was called upon to withdraw; he refused, and a noisy scene took place. Then the Sergeant-at-Arms invited Mr. Dillon to withdraw, and when the latter still refused, the Sergeant again advanced with the principal doorkeeper and a number of messengers, placed his hand on Mr. Dillon's shoulder, and requested him to obey the order of the Speaker. 'If you employ force I must yield,'[1] said Mr. Dillon, and then withdrew.

The Prime Minister had scarcely again risen when Mr. Parnell stood up at the same time, and made the motion that the right honourable gentleman be no longer heard. The Speaker, however, refused to accept the motion, and threatened Mr. Parnell with suspension in case he continued. Again Mr. Gladstone got up, and resumed the sentence which had so frequently been interrupted. Mr. Parnell again rose. The Speaker declared that the conduct of the member for Cork was wilful and deliberate obstruction, and named him. When the division took place in the case of Mr. Dillon, the Irish members had not yet made up their minds as to what was the proper course to adopt; but by the time that Mr. Parnell was named their tactics had been resolved upon. When the division upon Mr. Parnell's suspension was called, they refused to quit their seats. The division went on without them, and the House presented a curious spectacle with the Speaker left alone with the Irish Party. The deserted and tranquil appearance of the House might have encouraged the illusion that the storm of passion had subsided, and given place to perfect quiet. The Speaker warned the Irish members of the consequences that might result upon what they were doing; Mr. Sullivan declared that they contested the legality of the proceeding. This exchange of language between the Speaker and the Parnellites was mild and courteous. The division over, Mr. Parnell was ordered to withdraw; but he refused to go unless compelled by force, and again the Sergeant-at-Arms and the messengers came forward and touched his shoulder. The Irish leader slowly descended the gangway, bowed to the Speaker, and walked out of the House with head erect and amid the ringing cheers of his supporters. Once more Mr. Gladstone resumed the unfortunate sentence, that, as he himself said, had been bisected and trisected already; but again he was not allowed to proceed, for Mr. Finigan rose and proposed the same motion that Mr. Parnell had proposed, that the Prime Minister be no longer heard. Once more a division was taken, and once more the Irish members refused to leave their places. The tellers and clerks took down the names of the contumacious members, and after the withdrawal of Mr. Finigan the Speaker read out their names and suspended them all. The names were: Messrs. Barry, Biggar, Byrne, Corbet, Daly, Dawson, Gill, Gray, Healy, Lalor, Leamy, Leahy, Justin McCarthy, McCoan, Marum, Metge, Nelson, Arthur O'Connor, T. P. O'Connor, The O'Donoghue, The O'Gorman Mahon, W. H. O'Sullivan, O'Connor Power, Redmond, Sexton, Smithwick, A. M. Sullivan, and T. D. Sullivan.

By this time the passion of the House was to some extent exhausted, and there was even some return of good-humour; but Mr. Gladstone remained grave, and proposed the suspension of the twenty-eight members with an air of painful preoccupation. Then the division was taken, and

---

[1] Hansard, vol. cclviii., p. 70.

once more the Irish members refused to leave their places. The Speaker then called upon the different members in their turns to withdraw, and each in turn, and in practically identical language, refused to do so unless compelled by force, and protested against the legality of the whole proceedings. The protests of the expelled members varied slightly, and there was also a difference in the manner of their exit. Some hurried away; while others, following the example of Mr. Parnell, bowed with gravity and solemnity to the Chair. The demeanour of the House varied from moment to moment: sometimes it laughed, sometimes it cheered; finally, it settled down into allowing the incident to pass off in grave silence.

The debates dragged on, and the third reading of the Coercion Bill at last took place on February 25, 1881. At this stage Mr. Forster indulged in triumphant phrases that sound somewhat strangely at this time. As through the whole debate, he made the claim that he was acting for the interests and speaking the voice of the majority of the Irish people. 'We have,' he said, 'been delivering Ireland, or trying our best to deliver Ireland, from a great grievance, and we have been saving her, or believing we are saving her, from a still greater peril.'[1] And then he said, looking at the Irish members, and in final victory over their efforts to arrest Coercion: 'They have tried to prevent it, and they have failed.' Even some of the English papers thought this boastful harangue over the destruction of the liberties of Ireland a little too strong. 'We do not see much ground,' says the *Pall Mall Gazette*, 'for Mr. Forster's rather uncouth exultation. It is true that the Irish members have failed to stop the Bill, but we do not know that it is a good reason why a Liberal Minister should feel particularly triumphant because he has passed a measure over the heads of all the Liberal representatives of the country concerned.'

Almost immediately afterwards a second Coercion Bill, in the shape of the Arms Bill—Peace Preservation (Ireland) Bill—was proposed. This also was steadily resisted, and it was March 11 when the third reading was carried. Again Mr. Forster took up the theme that he was acting in accordance with the wishes of the majority of the Irish people. 'He should not object,' he said, . . . 'to appeal from hon. gentlemen opposite to the people of Ireland. . . . He was sure that he could venture to appeal with confidence from hon. members below the gangway opposite to their constituents.'[2]

These sentences are quoted to illustrate the length to which Mr. Forster was prepared to go. While he was thus claiming to represent the majority of the Irish people, he must have known that he was laying up for himself stores of hatred in their hearts that no length of time will ever exhaust. While he claimed to represent the constituencies of his Irish opponents better than they did themselves, he must have seen that every member of the Irish Party became more popular in exact proportion to the amount of resistance he offered to Mr. Forster's proposals. The quotations have an additional interest to-day as guides to the statesmanship of Mr. Forster.

By this time exhaustion had completely set in on both sides, and the House was more concerned at the time with the decision of one of his many law cases against Mr. Bradlaugh and the report that the Government were going to ask urgency for Supply. There were three divisions—thin, heartless, and shadowy things in a poorly attended House; and the announcement that the Arms Bill had passed, and that thus the long, chequered, and passionate battle between coercion and obstruction was at

---

[1] Hansard vol., cclviii., p. 1820.   [2] *Ibid.*, vol. cclix., p. 863.

an end, was received in an unbroken silence that was evidently international, and that marked a praiseworthy desire on all sides to escape from the bad and bitter passions of the struggle.

Thus, after nine weeks, the great fight came to an end. The merits of the struggle can now be surveyed with the calmness of an historical retrospect. Many critics, then and since, have blamed the Irish Party for the violence and the vehemence of their action, and for their prolongation of the struggle. But if all these objections and a great many more were true, subsequent events have justified the wisdom of the tactics that were adopted. The nine weeks' coercion struggle *made* the Irish Party, and thereby gave unity, cohesion, and resistless strength to the great movement for the restoration of national rights. The first necessity at that period was to kindle into flames of enthusiasm the faith of the Irish people in themselves, in their representatives, and in the results that might be achieved by Parliamentary warfare. The struggle that was going on at the time, too, in Ireland for the possession of the land was one which required all the strength of revolutionary enthusiasm to carry it to anything like a successful issue. With all the mighty forces that were arrayed against the cause of the tenant, the tenant could win by determination and by passion alone. Every scene of violence in the House of Commons roused still higher the temper of the Irish people, and if that temper had not reached fever heat, the Land Bill of 1881 would have gone to the same bourne of rejected proposals as the Compensation for Disturbance Bill and the thousand and one other proposals for the reform of the land tenure in Ireland had gone before. The power, too, which the Coercion Act placed in the hands of Mr. Forster, and the use which Mr. Forster made of this power, must always be considered as among the greatest forces in bringing the Irish cause to its present position.

The Land Bill was introduced on April 7. The first impression produced upon the Irish members was one of pleased surprise. It was seen that the proposals were bold and sweeping. During the Easter recess, which came immediately after Mr. Gladstone's introduction of the measure, the Irish members proceeded to Dublin to consult with the country. A convention of the branches of the Land League was called, and was held in Dublin during two days. The two parties which existed in the Land League, as in every organization, were inclined to take up different attitudes upon the Bill. The majority of the Parliamentary Party were strongly in favour of accepting the Bill and of making it the starting-point of a new movement. Another section—resolute, bold, vehement—held as its fundamental belief that the Land struggle should now be pushed on to the bitter end until it was closed for ever, and that it was in the power of the Irish people, by the maintenance of a determined and united front, to bring matters to that triumphant issue. The weapon which this section had in view, probably from the beginning, was a universal refusal to pay rent. The success which had attended a similar movement against the tithes was the precedent chiefly relied upon. The discussion occupied two days, and for some time the result seemed doubtful. Finally, a resolution was passed which left Irish members freedom either to oppose or support the second reading of the measure.

This was the instruction from the National Convention with which Mr. Parnell and his colleagues returned to Parliament; but meantime events had been happening which had been doing a great deal to force the hands of the Irish leader. When the Coercion Act was passed, the state of

Ireland was one of almost complete tranquillity. The improvement in its condition had been further helped by the character of the Land Bill. But the Chief Secretary was soon to bring disturbance out of tranquillity, for he and the Irish officials throughout the country began to take steps which were calculated to drive even a less excited people into frenzy. He began to put the powers of the Coercion Act into operation; and he displayed a sinister ingenuity in discovering the men who were least fitted to be entrusted with the large and arbitrary powers of such an Act. The most prominent of these officials were men who had already given abundant testimony of their unfitness for delicate duties and large authority. Major Bond had been dismissed from the police force of Birmingham; Major Traill was an officer who had been publicly reprimanded by the Commander-in-Chief; and his removal from his regiment had been requested by his commanding officer.[1] The character of Mr. Clifford Lloyd is now so notorious that it would be a waste of words to argue the gross blunder and even shameful outrage of sending such a man to administer a Coercion Act. Since his career in Ireland he has been tested in Egypt, and in the Mauritius, and, as everybody knows, was found to be a person with whom no other colleague could work in harmony, and had to leave the country and his office. But before he was taken up as a special *protégé* by Mr. Forster, he had already given indications of the kind of man he was. On January 1, 1881, he bore down upon a meeting in Drogheda with a large body of police with fixed bayonets, and dispersed the meeting forcibly; and even after he had thus succeeded in accomplishing his purpose, shouted to the people: 'If you do not be off at once, I will have you shot down.'[2] For his conduct on this occasion he was denounced by Mr. Whitworth, brother of the then member for Drogheda, as a 'firebrand';[3] and the member for Drogheda himself—and no man was a more bitter opponent of the Irish Party and the popular movement—declared in a debate his great surprise that the Government had employed Mr. Lloyd. 'A more dangerous man,' said Mr. Whitworth, 'they could not send to the South of Ireland. His (Mr. Whitworth's) brother, who was a magistrate in Drogheda, told him that if this man were sent to disturbed districts, there would be bloodshed.'[4]

Major Bond, in spite of his antecedents, seems to have conducted himself with more discretion than might have been anticipated; but Major Traill and Mr. Clifford Lloyd raged through the population with a perfect frenzy for insult, lawlessness, and cruelty. One of Major Traill's exploits was to go to a police barrack on a Sunday, where some men were in custody, to hold a court there and then, with himself as sole magistrate, and to impose on the men sentences varying from eight days to one month with hard labour. Of course, when the case was brought before the Superior Courts, the action of Major Traill was overruled. Baron Fitzgerald, the presiding judge—a strong Conservative—declared 'that he (Major Traill) had sentenced three several men to imprisonment illegally;' and the defence made by Major Traill's counsel was that, being only a major in the army, 'he

---

[1] Mr. Forster, Hansard, vol. cclviii., pp. 1067, 1068.
[2] Mr. Healy, *Ibid.*, vol. cclxiii., p. 1255.
[3] *Ibid.*, p. 639. Mr. Clifford Lloyd wrote to the papers afterwards to deny that he ever used this expression; but Mr. Healy and several Catholic clergymen who were present declared that they heard it. In nearly all such cases in which Mr. Clifford Lloyd was arraigned, he gave a version different from that of the persons who made the complaint.
[4] *Ibid.*, vol. cclvi., pp. 998, 999.

could not be expected to know the law accurately, as he was not a lawyer.' But, meantime, the persons who had thus been illegally convicted had served the whole term of their imprisonment, and had taken their sleep upon plank beds. Mr. Forster thought, when the matter was brought before him, that Major Traill 'had been sufficiently penalised for the error he made, by becoming the defendant in three actions.'[1]

But the exploits of Mr. Clifford Lloyd in Kilmallock and the other places to which he was sent leave in the shade everything done by his colleagues. On the first day on which he made his appearance in the town of Kilmallock, he ordered the people who were talking in groups around the town to disperse to their homes, and when they did not immediately obey, struck them furiously with his cane. Shortly afterwards a band, which was playing as it passed through the streets, was attacked by the police under the direction of Mr. Lloyd, and the people were clubbed with the ends of the rifles.[2] Mr. Lloyd next attacked the women of Kilmallock. One evening a number of young ladies were standing in the street. The police ordered them to disperse on the ground that they were obstructing the highway, a charge of strange absurdity in the ghastly loneliness of a small Irish town. They were brought up before Mr. Lloyd and several other magistrates, and the police-constable who acted under Mr. Lloyd's orders accused the ladies of using insulting language, as well as of obstructing the highway. When the constable was examined, his complaint was found to be that he had been called 'Clifford Lloyd's pet.' Both the charge and the police-constable, as well as Mr. Clifford Lloyd, were laughed at, and the young ladies had to be discharged. Mr. Lloyd was more successful in his operations under the Coercion Act. He had inflicted fines upon two men and a married woman, and public sympathy went so strongly with these people that a subscription was raised to pay the fine, rather than allow them to go to prison. Andrew Mortel and Edmund O'Neill were the two men who carried around the subscription list. They were arrested and placed in prison under the Coercion Act on the ground of intimidation. Mr. O'Sullivan, then member for the County of Limerick and a resident in Kilmallock, got a declaration from all the persons who gave subscriptions that they had given the money voluntarily. Mr. Mortel and Mr. O'Neill, however, remained in prison.[3] Finally Mr. Lloyd obtained the arrest of Father Sheehy, and this arrest of a priest, eminent for his abilities and for his character, and with a strong hold upon the affections of the masses by his fearless spirit, added enormously to the exasperation of the country. It will be seen by-and-by that though at this period Mr. Lloyd had not succeeded in his crusade against women, he was more successful when the *régime* of coercion was entirely unchecked, and Mr. Forster set himself without shame or scruple to the dragooning of Ireland.

And these offences were aggravated by the fact that every single act of police tyranny, petty or large, found a staunch advocate in the House of Commons in Mr. Forster. The landlords at the same time, too, proceeded to justify the worst anticipations of the Land Leaguers. It had been over and over again pointed out that the effect of the Coercion Act, coming as it did on the threshold of the Land Bill, would be to inspire the landlords with the idea that the tenants, once more terrorised and broken, could be treated with the cruelty of the old times. Large numbers of the tenants

---

[1] Hansard, vol. ccxli., pp. 11, 12.
[2] *Ibid.*, p. 904. Letter of Father Sheehy to Mr. Parnell.
[3] *Ibid.*, vol. cclxiii., pp. 1000, 1001.

had not recovered from the reeling shock of 1879, had not paid their rent, and could not pay it; and even in the Land Bill that was coming there was no provision for them. The result was that evictions, which had been brought down when the Land League was completely triumphant, now made a sudden bound upwards. In the quarter of 1880 ending March 31, 2,748 persons had been evicted; in the second quarter, ending June 30, 3,508 persons; in the third quarter, ending September 30, 3,447 persons; and in the fourth quarter, ending December 31, when the strong arm of the Land League stood between the landlord and the tenant, the number of persons evicted had fallen to 954.[1] The first quarter of 1881 showed the effect upon landlords of the promise of coercion, and the number of persons evicted rose to 1,732. When the Coercion Act began to be applied, and the various local defenders of the tenants began to be imprisoned by the Clifford Lloyds and the Traills, the evictions gave a sudden rise from 1,732 to 5,262.

So strongly was public opinion, even in Parliament, impressed with these facts, that Mr. Labouchere proposed a clause in the Coercion Act suspending evictions; but, of course, it was rejected. Mr. Forster himself, lapsing into a moment of sympathy with the oppressed, as in the session of 1880, when he declared that he would resign rather than carry out cruel evictions, confessed that many of the persons about to be evicted were unable to pay their rents. At the same time he stated that many who were able to pay their rents were ordered by the Land League leaders to withhold them. Mr. Parnell at once accepted the implied suggestion, and for two hours the question was discussed in Parliament whether the Government would refuse to lend the aid of military and police in throwing out the distressed on the roadside if the Land League leaders would respond by advising the payment of rent in cases where it could be paid. But the proposed compromise came to nothing. Evictions, accordingly, proceeded apace; and the suffering of eviction was aggravated by the gradually increasing severity of the police *régime*. Finally, matters reached a climax when the city of Dublin was proclaimed under the new Act, although up to this time not a single political crime had been committed by any one of its three hundred thousand inhabitants. Mr. Forster had to confess that the sole object of proclaiming the city was to bring the meetings of the Land League held there within the provisions of the Coercion Act. A short time afterwards Mr. John Dillon was arrested, and so the work of driving the country into madness went on.

The first effect was upon the Parliamentary Party. The arrest of Mr. Dillon was announced immediately before the second reading of the Land Bill. The Irish Party were called together to decide upon their plan of action. Again in the conference-room thirty of them met under the presidency of Mr. Parnell. A discussion, the full gravity of which was felt by all, occupied the party during three hours. Mr. Parnell himself proposed from the chair a resolution in favour of abstention, and this resolution was carried by 17 votes against 12. This decision produced a feeling of dismay in many sections in Ireland, was bitterly criticised, and was openly disobeyed by some members of the party. In fact, it may now be admitted that this was one of the very darkest hours through which the Irish Party had passed; yet there will be few to deny now that the decision to abstain

---

[1] A considerable number of those persons were afterwards admitted as caretakers; but, as everybody knows, this deprived them of their status as tenants, and left them at the mercy of the landlords.

was the only expedient and consistent course which the Irish Party could
have adopted. That course left the party complete freedom of action in
the future; it expressed in the most emphatic manner the conviction that
the Land Bill was not the final settlement of the Land Question; and,
above all, it helped the chances of the measure with the House of Lords by
raising in the background the spectre of a 'No-Rent' manifesto.

This will appear more clearly by-and-by. For the present it will suffice
to say here that the Land Bill was objected to on the following grounds:
First, that it would establish an impracticable and inconvenient state of
relations between landlord and tenant by endeavouring to fix a partnership
in the soil between two persons of opposing interests, and that the only
solution which would be just, complete, and final would be the solution
proposed by the Land League—the transformation of rent-paying tenants
into peasant proprietors; secondly, that the Land Courts would not make
such reductions in the rents as were required by the circumstances of the
case; thirdly, that, as a large number of tenants were, owing to bad
seasons and by the legacy of the 'hanging gale' and other arrears from the
period of the Great Famine, entirely unable to pay their rent, the new legislation could do them no good, and that they would be just as much at the
mercy of the landlords as if no legislation at all were passed; fourthly,
that the leaseholders were excluded; fifthly, that due provision was not
made for saving the improvements effected by the tenant from confiscation
in the shape of rent; sixthly, the clause in favour of emigration; and,
seventhly, the absence of provision for the labourers.

These objections were met in the same spirit as the objections made by
the Irish Parliamentary Party to the Land Bill of 1870; and subsequent
events have, in the case of the Bill of 1881 as in that of 1870, proved the
unwisdom of English statesmen and the wisdom of the Irish representatives. There is not one of these objections which has not been proved
sound, and most of them will reappear shortly when they pass from the
mouths of Irish representatives into measures passed by both Houses of
Parliament. The Irish members endeavoured in vain, in the course of the
proceedings in Parliament, to introduce amendments which would have
the effect of making the Bill a better settlement; but these amendments
were almost invariably rejected. One amendment, however, was carried
which was destined to play a most important part in the entire future of
the Land Question. Mr. Healy stuck to his place throughout the discussion
of the Bill, and the debates were often wholly carried on by him, Mr. Law,
and Mr. Gibson. The present writer was sitting next to Mr. Healy on the
night when the famous Healy Clause, declaring that in future no rent should
be chargeable on the tenants' improvements, was carried. Mr. Healy
made his proposal in mild and almost careless terms, and Mr. Law got up
and accepted the principle with scarcely the appearance even of demur.
But there was a little confusion about the exact wording, and, in order to
give time for collecting thought, Dr. Playfair remembered that he wanted
his tea, and adjourned the House for a quarter of an hour. The clause
was drafted meantime, and was added to the Bill. Apparently nothing
very particular had occurred, the whole business had passed off in unbroken
tranquillity and overflowing amicability; but the prime mover in the business knew well what he had done. With a face of sphinx-like severity
Mr. Healy whispered to the friend by his side: 'These words will put
millions in the pockets of the tenants.'

The Land Bill received the royal assent on August 22. The Irish

leaders were now face to face with the gravest problem they had yet to
encounter. This was in regard to the attitude they should assume towards
the new Act. There were many things in the state of Ireland at that
period to tempt to extreme resolves. The Land League had gone on daily
increasing in power; coercion, instead of diminishing, seemed to add to
its influence and its prestige. Though Parliament was engaged in the
passage of a measure in many respects as stupendous as the Land Act of
1881, the centre of political gravity and political interest was in the operations of the Land League in Ireland rather than in the debates and proceedings at St. Stephen's. The Irish farmer could not be blamed if he
observed with exultation the absolutely revolutionary change which had
come over his prospects. In this hour he recalled with bitter satisfaction
that long list of modest proposals for his relief which the Imperial Parliament had ever rejected, and the gloom, unbroken by one word of sympathy
or one statesmanlike proposal, from the passage of the Union till the Land
Bill of 1870. The reader has had set forth in previous pages the history of
all these futile appeals to the Legislature for relief, and also a picture of
the awful evils for which relief was sought. He will not have forgotten
the dread *régime* of famine and fever, the wholesale clearances, the merciless rack-renting, the tyranny omnipotent, mean, and ubiquitous, the wholesale emigration, which formed the one side of the picture, and the ignorance,
the insolence, the light-hearted neglect, or the mocking insult of English Ministers and Parliaments, which formed the other; and is the
hope vain that, whatever be his nationality, he will feel some sympathy
with the reversal of the two parts at this moment—the Legislature eager
with gifts, the farmer turning away in the scorn of self-dependence? In
any case, the Irish farmers understood the change. They saw that the
success of a Bill proposing changes against which all the statesmen, the
whole press, and the entire landlord party of England and Ireland would
have risen in revolt a few years before, was longed for with far greater
eagerness by their hereditary and hitherto omnipotent oppressors than it
was by themselves. In short, the slave had become the master; the
suppliant was transformed into the victor dictating terms. On the other
hand, Mr. Parnell had placed before himself, as a central point of policy,
by no word or act of his to abate one jot of the victory which the people
might be able to wring from their enemies. At this moment the situation,
as it presented itself to his mind, was this: the Land Courts had practically
the entire settlement of the rental of Ireland in their hands; the changes
required in that rental, according to the views of Mr. Parnell, were not
small, nor narrow, nor sporadic, but revolutionary, wholesale, and thorough.
But what were the chances of a revolutionary reduction of rents? The
whole character of the Land Court forbade any such expectation. Judge
O'Hagan, the chief of the court, was well known to be a man of pliant and
timid character. Of his two colleagues, Mr. Litton was a lawyer who had
never got beyond the peddling proposals of Ulster Tenant Leagues, and a
man utterly devoid of any boldness or initiative; while Mr. Vernon, the
third member of the commission, was agent for several large landed proprietors, was himself a landed proprietor, and had besides the reputation of
being much stronger willed than either of his colleagues. Apart from their
own weakness of character, the two legal members of the chief commission
were men who had grown old in all the ideas and traditions of the ancient
laws with regard to the tenure of land in Ireland. To the generation to
which the youth of Mr. Justice O'Hagan and Mr. Litton belonged, the

proprietorship of the tenant in the soil was the code only of the Ribbon Lodge, and had its only statutable sanction in the blunderbuss.

Again, when Mr. Parnell and the other leaders of the Land League sought for the probable effects of the rent-fixing clauses of the Land Act, they naturally turned to the prophecies of the men by whom the Land Act had been framed and had been carried through both Houses of Parliament.

'If (said Lord Selborne) you compare the state of things under the Bill with that which would exist if nothing of the kind were done, the Bill may be expected to restore, and, moreover, not diminish, the value of the landlords' property.'[1] 'I deny (he said again) that it will diminish, in any degree whatever, the rights of the landlord or the value of the interest he possesses.'[2]

Lord Carlingford was still more explicit:

'My lords (he said), I maintain that the provisions of this Bill will cause the landlords no money loss whatever.'[3]

These prophecies Mr. Parnell and his colleagues were certainly bound to take as sincere. Furthermore, every care had been taken that the decisions of the Land Courts should be subject to Parliamentary criticism. The courts were bound to present to Parliament almost every detail of every single one of the cases brought before them. A considerable number of the sub-commissioners held but temporary appointments, and, as a matter of fact, some were removed under a continual hailstorm of Parliamentary criticism; and the Parliamentary criticism that they had to dread was not that of the small minority who defended the interests of the tenant in Parliament, but that of the overwhelming majority of the two parties in both Houses of the Legislature—the majority which represented the interests of the landlords. If the Land Court were subject to the pressure of the landlords of the House of Commons and of the House of Lords, and bound by the declaration of the Ministers on the one side, it was necessary to procure counterbalancing pressure on the side of the tenants; in other words, to make the court fair to the tenants by making the tenants to some extent independent of the court. These were the steps of reasoning by which the Irish leaders arrived at the conviction that by organization and unity alone could the farmer maintain the ground he had gained; that without this organization and unity the Land Courts would become but a new machinery for perpetuating the yoke of impossible rents, and the Land Act turn out, like so many other previous statutes, but Dead Sea fruit that turned to ashes at the touch.

At the same time there were the Land Courts with their doors open. The extreme section of the Land Leaguers were so convinced of the omnipotence of the League, and of the futility and treachery of the Land Act, that they strongly urged the policy of keeping the tenants out of the courts altogether. But it was perceived by Mr. Parnell that such a policy was impracticable; and, therefore, his policy was, not to prevent, but to regulate, the appeal to these courts. To him the best plan of doing this appeared to be to place in the courts a certain number of typical cases. The cases were not to be those which exhibited the most flagrant instances of rack-renting. This proviso in the selection of cases was fiercely denounced, but the justice of the proviso requires very little defence. Obviously an extravagantly rack-

---

[1] Hansard, vol. cclxiv., p. 534. [2] Ibid., p. 532. [3] Ibid., p. 252.

rented property would not supply to the court a fair and average case. A large reduction might be made in such a case, and at the same time the general scale of rent in Ireland might remain too high. There was the danger of the tenants being deceived, by the reduction in such a case, into a false estimate of what the general attitude of the Land Courts would be. A reduction of fifty per cent. on a hopelessly rack-rented estate might well dazzle the farmers into the belief that a reduction of fifty per cent. would be made all round. They would, of course, have discovered their mistake in time, but they would not have discovered it until, by their appeal to the Land Court, they had disintegrated the organization which ought still to remain their main safeguard and buttress. In this way what was known as the 'Test-Case' policy came to be adopted.

A second great convention was held in the Rotunda on September 15 and the two following days. Upwards of a thousand branches were represented, the tone of the speeches was triumphant, and the whole assembly breathed a spirit of exultation. The members of the extreme section formed no inconsiderable portion of the delegates. To this section enormous strength had been added by the use to which Mr. Forster had put his Coercion Acts. By this time a large number of the men who had been most active in building up the mighty organization were in gaol. From their cells these men appealed to their colleagues not to give up the fruits of the victory for which they had consented to struggle and to suffer, and the advocates of extreme courses found the most telling argument in favour of their policy in the sufferings of Mr. Davitt and Father Sheehy. The proposal of this section was, that the tenantry should have nothing whatever to do with the Act; that they should continue the organization and the agitation, and go on to the bitter end, until landlordism was completely crushed, and the Government could have no choice but to accept the programme of the Land League and purchase peace by the expropriation of the landlords and the creation of a peasant proprietary. The weapon which this section held to be the means of bringing about this final consummation was a 'No-Rent' manifesto; but to this course Mr. Parnell and the greater number of his colleagues were at this moment opposed. They were in favour of the middle course which I have described. They thought it possible at the same time to maintain the organization and to test the Land Court. Their policy was well summed up by Mr. Parnell himself, as that of 'testing and not using the Land Act.' The influence of Mr. Parnell and his colleagues prevailed, and the 'Test-Case' policy was sanctioned by the convention. It was often suggested, immediately afterwards, that this policy was never really believed in by Mr. Parnell. I can bear personal testimony to the fact that he proceeded at once to take the means necessary for carrying the policy into practical effect. I sat by his side for nights in succession, as he extracted from the books of the Land League cases which appeared to him to be such as would fairly test the disposition of the court, and Mr. Healy went down to the South of Ireland to visit the homes and to investigate the farms of some whose cases had thus been selected. On the day on which the forms for application to the new Land Court were issued, Mr. Parnell was so eager to be among the first applicants that he visited the house of the Land Commission no less than three times. In fact, he had resolved to give the fair 'Test-Case' policy a *bonâ-fide* trial.

But this was not to be.

Mr. Gladstone spoke at Leeds on October 7. He made an attack on the

Irish leader, which was certainly strong; but was, at the same time, not too strong if the central position of Mr. Gladstone were correct. It was Mr. Gladstone's case that Mr. Parnell represented not the majority, but a minority, of the Irish people; and that the majority were being terrorised by the minority. In short, Mr. Gladstone thought at this period that the Irish people and Mr. Parnell, instead of being at one, were at variance. This opinion he has since found out to be mistaken; but that it was honestly his opinion at this time the following extract from the speech will prove:

'The people of Ireland, we believe (said Mr. Gladstone), desire, in conformity with the advice of the old patriots, and their bishops and their best friends . . . to make a full trial of the Land Act; and if they do make a full trial of that Act, you may rely upon it, it is as certain as human contingencies can be to give peace to the country. We shall rely on the good sense of the people, because we are determined that no force, or fear of ruin through force, shall as far as we are concerned, and as it is in our power to decide the question, prevent the Irish people having the full and free benefit of the Land Act.'[1]

A good deal of hopeless nonsense has been spoken about this and further passages in the same speech. The real and candid explanation of the difference in the attitude of Mr. Gladstone then and now is not merely the difference—and that is great—in the tactics of Mr. Parnell and the condition of Ireland, but in the difference in the Parliamentary position of the Irish Party. Mr. Parnell then had 35 followers out of 103 members; and Mr. Gladstone might well deny that Mr. Parnell was representative of the majority of the Irish people. Such a denial became impossible as soon as Mr. Parnell's followers numbered 85 out of 103 of a total representation. Finally, Mr. Gladstone wound up with this ominous passage:

'When we have that short further experience to which I have referred, if it should then appear that there is still to be fought a final conflict in Ireland between law on the one side and sheer lawlessness on the other—if the law, still purged from defects, is still to be rejected and refused, the first condition of political society remains unfulfilled, and then, I say without hesitation, the resources of civilization against its enemies are not yet exhausted.'[2]

To that speech on Sunday, October 9, Mr. Parnell replied at Wexford. The reception given to Mr. Parnell at this Wexford meeting is described by those who saw it as perhaps the most enthusiastic of the many receptions of almost frenzied enthusiasm which he received during this momentous year. Triumphal arches spanned the streets, evergreens and flowers covered the windows and doorways and lamp-posts. Bands came from several parts of the country, and special trains brought thousands from the surrounding districts. The speech of Mr. Parnell was in the same passionate tones as that to which it was a reply. Mr. Gladstone, in the course of his speech, had complained of the want of all support to the efforts of Government by the landlords and other classes threatened, and then had dropped into the astonishing confession that the 'Government are expected to keep the peace with no moral force behind them.'

'The Government (said Mr. Parnell, taking up this point) have no moral force behind them in Ireland. The whole Irish people are against them.

[1] *Freeman's Journal*, October 10, 1881.   [2] *Ibid.*

They have to depend for their support upon the interest of a very small minority of the people of this country, and, therefore, they have no moral force behind them, and Mr. Gladstone, in these few short words, admits that English government has failed in Ireland. . . . I say it is not in his power to trample on the aspirations and the rights of the Irish nation with no moral force behind him.'

On the Monday following his speech Mr. Parnell was entertained at a banquet, and in his speech he used some words which showed he had some presentiment of what was coming.

'I am frequently disposed to think,' he said, 'that Ireland has not yet got through the troubled waters of affliction to be crossed before we reach the promised land of prosperity to Ireland. . . . There may be—probably there will be—more stringent coercion before us than we have yet experienced.'

The next day he went to his home in Avondale, and he reached Dublin by the last train on Wednesday night, having promised to attend the Kildare County Convention, which was to be held at Naas on the following day. He was to have left Kingsbridge Station by the 10.15 a.m. train. On that same Wednesday a Cabinet Council had been held in England, and in the evening Mr. Forster had crossed over, authorized to arrest his chief opponent. Here is Mr. Parnell's own account of what actually occurred:

'Intending to proceed to Naas this morning, I ordered, before retiring to bed on Wednesday night, that I should be called at half-past eight o'clock. When the man came to my bedroom to awaken me, he told me that two gentlemen were waiting below who wanted to see me. I told him to ask their names and business. Having gone out, he came back in a few moments, and said that one was the superintendent of police and the other was a policeman. I told him to say that I would be dressed in half an hour, and would see them then. He went away, but came back again to tell me that he had been downstairs to see the gentlemen, and had told them I was not stopping at that hotel. He then said that I should get out through the back part of the house, and not allow them to catch me. I told him that I would not do that, even if it were possible, because the police authorities would be sure to have every way most closely watched. He again went down, and this time showed the detectives up to my bedroom.'

The *Freeman's Journal*,[1] from which this is quoted, continues:

'In Foster Place there was a force of one hundred policemen held in readiness in case of any emergency. Mr. Mallon, when he entered the bedroom, found Mr. C. S. Parnell in the act of dressing, and immediately presented him with two warrants. He did not state their purport, but Mr. Parnell understood the situation without any intimation. It is not true to state that he exhibited surprise, or that he looked puzzled. The documents were presented to him with gentlemanly courtesy by Mr. Mallon, and the hon. gentleman who was about to be arrested received them with perfect calmness and deliberation. He had had private advices from England regarding the Cabinet Council, and was well aware that the Government meditated some *coup d'état*.

'Two copies of the warrants had also been sent to the Kingsbridge Terminus, to be served on Mr. Parnell in case he should go to Sallins

[1] October 14, 1881.

by an early train. Superintendent Mallon expressed some anxiety lest a crowd should collect and interfere with the arrest, and he requested Mr. Parnell to come away as quickly as possible. Mr. Parnell responded to his anxiety. A cab was called, and the two detectives with the honourable prisoner drove away. When the party reached the Bank of Ireland, at which but a fortnight previously Mr. Parnell had directed the attention of many thousands to its former memories and future prospects, five or six metropolitan police, evidently by preconcerted arrangement, jumped upon two outside cars and drove in front of the party. On reaching the quays at the foot of Parliament Street, a number of horse police joined the procession at the rear. In this order the four vehicles drove to Kilmainham. This strange procession passed along the thoroughfares without creating any remarkable notice. A few people did stop to look at it on part of the route, and then pursued the vehicles. But their curiosity was probably aroused by the presence of 'the force' rather than by any knowledge that, after a short lull, the Coercion Act was again being applied to the *élite* of the League. They stopped their chase after going a few perches, and at half-past nine o'clock Mr. Parnell appeared in front of the dark portals of Kilmainham.'

A few hours afterwards he was interviewed by a reporter of the *Freeman's Journal*. The interview closed with one of those *mots* by which Mr. Parnell has marked important epochs in his career. 'As I rose to leave,' says the reporter, 'Mr. Parnell stated, "I shall take it as an evidence that the people did not do their duty if I am speedily released."

In Ireland the arrest of Mr. Parnell was mourned throughout the country as a national calamity. Indignation meetings were held, unless they were dispersed by the police or the soldiery, in every town and village in the country, and in most cases the shutters were put on the windows as in times of death and funerals. The country was swept by a passion of anger and grief, the more bitter because it had to be suppressed. Troops were poured into the country, and, by way of striking wholesome terror, Dublin was given over for two days to the police; and then occurred scenes of brutality the records of which it is not possible to read even at this distance without bitter anger. Under the pretext that there was danger of a riot in O'Connell—then Sackville—Street, it was taken possession of by large bodies of police, and when a crowd of boys, attracted by this curious spectacle, began to jeer and groan, the police made charges, struck the people with their *bâtons* and clenched fists, and kicked those whom they felled.

'Their conduct,' writes the *Weekly Irish Times*,[1] a Conservative organ in Dublin, 'was such as to appear almost incredible to all who had not been to witness it. . . . After every charge they made, men, amongst them respectable citizens, were left lying in the streets, blood pouring from the wounds they received on the head from the *bâtons* of the police, while others were covered with severe bruises from the kicks and blows of clenched fists, delivered with all the strength that powerful men could exert.'

This was before ten o'clock. Later on, another and perhaps even worse scene was enacted:

'The police drew their *bâtons*, and the scene which followed beggars description. Charging headlong into the people, the constables struck

[1] October 22, 1881.

right and left, and men and women fell under their blows. No quarter was given. The roadway was strewn with the bodies of the people. From the Ballast Office to the Bridge, and from the Bridge to Sackville Street, the charge was continued with fury. Women fled shrieking, and their cries rendered even more painful the scene of barbarity which was being enacted. All was confusion, and nought could be seen but the police mercilessly batoning the people. Some few of the people threw stones, of which fact the broken gas-lamps bear testimony; but, with this exception, no resistance was offered. Gentlemen and respectable working men, returning homewards from theatres or the houses of friends, fell victims to the attack; and as an incident of the conduct of the police it may be mentioned that, besides numerous others, more than a dozen students of Trinity College and a militia officer—unoffending passers-by—were knocked down and kicked, and two postal telegraph messengers, engaged in carrying telegrams, were barbarously assailed. When the people were felled, they were kicked on the ground; and when they again rose, they were again knocked down by any constable who met them.[1]

Nor is it on newspaper accounts only that we have to rely for a record of the brutality of the police on this occasion. 'I have seen,' said Mr. Dwyer Gray, M.P., at a meeting of the Dublin Corporation, at which the question was discussed—'I have seen the conduct of the police. . . . I saw them beating children, and acting in the most wanton and shameful way: attacking respectable men, beating them, striking them on the face, when going on their way quietly and peaceably as they had a perfect right to do.'[2] 'I can speak from personal observation,' declared Alderman Harris, '. . . as to the gravity of the result produced by whoever had the command of the police making that immense display of force last Saturday. . . . The police were running after and beating respectable men.'[3] When these facts were brought before the Chief Secretary by a deputation from the Corporation of Dublin, his calm reply was, 'It cannot be altogether a milk-and-water business, clearing streets.'[4] Is it possible that Joe Brady or some other of the 'Invincibles' was in the crowd, and thus saw the Metropolis of Ireland given over to this savagery?

It was assuredly a strange proof of the idea that the Irish longed to be liberated from the tyranny of Mr. Parnell that the population had to be dragooned by overwhelming military and police forces into the tame acceptance of Mr. Parnell's imprisonment. The two nations, in fact, stood opposite each other—both unanimous. Not a voice in England was raised in defence of Mr. Parnell; not a voice in Ireland was raised in favour of Mr. Forster. Ireland and England confronted one another in universal and undisguised hatred. This was the strange pass to which Mr. Forster's statesmanship had brought the two countries.

The arrest of Mr. Parnell was followed by that of Mr. Dillon and Mr. O'Kelly. Mr. Sexton was lying ill in bed when the warrant came for his arrest also, and he rose immediately and accompanied the police to Kilmainham. Warrants were also issued for the arrest of Mr. Healy, Mr. Arthur O'Connor, and Mr. Biggar. Mr. Healy was on his way to Ireland to give himself up, when he was met at Holyhead by an official of

---

[1] *Weekly Irish Times*, October 22, 1881.
[2] *Freeman's Journal*, October 18, 1881.   [3] *Ibid.*   [4] *Ibid.*

the League and ordered to remain in England. Mr. Arthur O'Connor was also ordered by Mr. Parnell to escape arrest if he could, and so was Mr. Biggar. The realistic leader of the Irish movement was anxious that as many of his followers as possible should remain outside the gaols, so as to carry on the war against the enemy ; and his followers, though reluctantly, accepted his mandate. In Dublin and throughout the country every person in any way connected with the League was arrested. It was evidently the resolve of the Government to destroy the organization by the removal of its most active members. Finally, the Land League was suppressed.

At last the extremists, whom Mr. Parnell had successfully opposed, were victorious. When Mr. Forster became their ally they were for the first time irresistible. The Land League leaders, now inside gaol, were brought face to face with a situation in which moderation was no longer possible. Resort was had to the final weapon, and, after various consultations, the 'No-Rent' manifesto was issued.

CHAPTER XII.

THE FRUITS OF COERCION.

To appreciate properly the effect of the coercion *régime* which now followed, it is necessary to recall to the reader the state of Ireland as it was when Parliament met in January, 1881, with Ireland as it became during the six months that followed the arrest of Mr. Parnell. It will be remembered that Mr. Forster himself had to acknowledge that the country at that period was comparatively quiet ; that the Returns, when dissected, proved that the real amount of crime was much less than the gross total led one to believe ; and that it was repeated so often, and by so many different speakers, as to become a platitude of debate, that the number of murders, instead of having increased, had actually been less during the days of the Land League supremacy than at any previous period of great political excitement and impending social changes. The time had come when the Government resolved to apply coercion in earnest, when every restraint of decency or prudence was cast aside, and Ireland was ruled with a rod of iron indeed. It is hard even now to write of the acts perpetrated at this period under the direction of Mr. Forster without some display of temper or some heat of language. The pretences on which the Coercion Acts had been originally obtained from Parliament were completely forgotten. The Acts, as I have shown by extract after extract from the Ministerial speeches, were obtained for the purpose of putting down crime or the incitement to crime, and for that alone. They were employed—openly and avowedly employed—for the purpose of compelling the payment of rent. The warrants of arrest contained the confession of this entire change of purpose and breach of faith. Thus in one of the warrants against Mr. Parnell, the charge was that he had intimidated divers persons to compel them to abstain from doing what they had a legal right to do—namely, to pay rents lawfully due by them. The non-payment of rent may be a moral offence, but assuredly it was not the kind of crime and outrage for the perpetration or abetting of which Mr. Gladstone declared the Coercion Act was required. Mr. Forster had declared that the Acts were required not against any large section of the population, but against the *mauvais sujets*, the village tyrants, and a few scattered miscreants throughout the country; and writs were issued against men in almost every class of society!

The proceedings taken against women did perhaps more than anything else to expose the savage character of the *régime* now established, and to create the fiercest popular passion. A number of ladies had taken up the work of the organization as it fell from the hands of the men whom Mr. Forster had sent to gaol. What that work was will presently appear. Against several of these ladies the Chief Secretary ordered legal proceedings. The method of these proceedings was characteristic of a nature at once coarse, clumsy, and savage. In the reign of Edward III. a statute was passed against prostitutes and tramps. It was under a statute like this that young ladies, brought up tenderly and delicately, were tried, and such of them as were convicted were condemned in sentences which cannot be described as lenient. Mr. Clifford Lloyd was now able to enjoy himself to the top of his bent. He pranced around the country with as large an escort as could have been required by the Czar passing through a Polish city; he arrested wholesale; he trampled on the laws of the country, and carried out laws of his own suiting; he employed boldly and shamelessly every weapon of coercion for the purpose of extracting the rent. Thus the Coercion Act became simply one of the additional agencies of the rent office; and the non-payment of rent was raised to the dignity of a criminal offence. One well-authenticated case of this kind will sufficiently exemplify the state of things that existed in Ireland at this horrible period. A Mrs. Moroney was engaged in a fierce struggle with her tenantry in Miltown-Malbay, County Clare. One of her tenants was summoned by Mr. Clifford Lloyd, and was told that unless he paid his rent he would be put in gaol. He refused to pay his rent; Mr. Lloyd kept his word: the man was arrested at daybreak on the following day under one of Mr. Forster's warrants; he was sent to a prison in Ulster, as far removed as possible from his business and his family; and while he was away his wife died, and it was to a desolate home he returned after his release.

Huts were erected by the Ladies' Land League for the purpose of sheltering the evicted, who, as will be presently seen, were reaching at this point numbers that startled and shocked and terrified the whole country. Mr. Lloyd insisted that the huts were for the purpose of intimidation and not for shelter, and arrested and sent every person to gaol who was engaged in their erection. Against women he was at last allowed to have plenary powers. He sent Miss McCormack to gaol for six months; he sent Miss Reynolds to gaol for six months; he sent Miss Kirk to gaol for three months. Of course he always denied that he imprisoned these women at all. All he did was to ask them to promise to keep the peace; and he sent them to gaol in consequence of the refusal. But he knew, and everybody knew, that no man or woman could, with a particle of self-respect, or with any hope of retaining the respect of any of his or her people, submit to any compromise with the brutal tyranny that was then desolating their country. Other magistrates, fired with noble envy of Mr. Lloyd's exploits, also made war upon women. Mrs. Moore was sent to gaol for six months; and Mr. Becket sentenced Miss Mary O'Connor to six months' imprisonment.

Two extracts from the reports of Hansard will complete this part of the picture. When Mr. Forster's attention was called to any of the brutalities of Mr. Clifford Lloyd, this was how he answered:

'When an action is taken up by a magistrate, it is done on his own responsibility; and it would be a most serious matter to suppose that I, as representing the Executive, have power to interfere with the action of the magistrates.'[1]

It is scarcely necessary to remind the historical student that this answer of Mr. Forster is the repetition of a trick venerable in the history of despotisms. The magistrate, who is the tool and the creature of the Government, who carries out its wishes and behests, is represented as a perfectly independent judicial functionary, with whom the Executive would not, and even dare not, interfere. Mr. Clifford Lloyd and the other magistrates who were carrying out this work throughout Ireland, were as much the servants and creatures of Mr. Forster as the smallest messenger in his office or the chambermaid in his house. They were appointed by the Lord-Lieutenant; they could be dismissed by the Lord-Lieutenant. Most of them held appointments that were distinctly temporary, and renewable at short periods—from quarter to quarter—and with large emoluments dependent on the continuance of the agitation, of which they were among the most unholy brood. And these were the gentlemen from interference with whom Mr. Forster shrank with the delicate respect for constitutional forms which he was displaying in so many ways at that moment.

A second extract from Hansard will describe the treatment to which the ladies were subjected who were sentenced to be imprisoned by Mr. Clifford Lloyd and the other magistrates:

'Mr. Labouchere asked the Chief Secretary to the Lord-Lieutenant of Ireland whether it is true that Mrs. Moore, Miss Kirk, and Miss O'Connor, who have been sentenced to various terms of imprisonment under an ancient Act for alleged intimidation, by different stipendiary magistrates, are kept in solitude for about twenty-three hours out of twenty-four; and whether the time has arrived when, in the interests of the peace and tranquillity of Ireland, these ladies should be restored to their friends?

'Mr. Trevelyan: Sir, the ladies named in this question have been committed to prison in default of finding bail, and are treated in exact conformity with the prison rules; and, according to the rules for "bailed prisoners," they are allowed two hours for exercise daily, and are therefore in their cells for twenty-two out of twenty-four hours. They can at once return to their friends on tendering the requisite sureties.'[2]

Thus it will be seen that these women were suffering far more severely than the men arrested under the Coercion Act. The prisoners under the Coercion Act were allowed to have communication with each other for six hours out of every day. The young ladies sentenced by Mr. Clifford Lloyd were in solitude throughout the entire day. In the prisons in which they were placed there were none but the degraded of their own sex; and sometimes the young ladies attended their devotions in close proximity to the prostitutes and thieves of their district.

Up and down the country, meantime, the police authorities were pursuing the other methods which are associated with unchecked authority and the efforts to override a people. The same war was made on lads and boys as on women. A lad named Lee was brought before the magistrates

---

[1] Hansard, vol. cclxviii., p. 1071.   [2] Ibid., vol. cclxix., p. 1404.

for whistling.[1] Thomas Wall, another lad, was accused by another constable for the same offence, and in addition was charged with abusive language. The abusive language was whistling 'Harvey Duff,' a song which spoke in satirical terms of the police. 'Do you consider,' the accusing constable was asked, 'that whistling "Harvey Duff" is using abusive language?' 'Yes,' answered the friend of Mr. Forster, 'I do; and I swear it is.'[2] On April 16, 1882, a policeman in Waterford rushed into a shop where a woman was engaged in reading *United Ireland*, threw her down, and, kneeling on her stomach, searched her in an indecent manner.[3] In Cappamore, County Limerick, a sub-constable attacked a girl named Burke, twelve years of age, because she was singing 'Harvey Duff.' He drew his bayonet, and inflicted a wound.[4]

Was it true, asked Mr. Healy with his characteristically grim humour, that Daniel O'Sullivan, aged nine or ten years, 'who appeared before the magistrates crying,' had been prosecuted by the magistrates, under the Whiteboy Act, for having, at two o'clock in the day, by carrying a lighted torch in the public streets at Millstreet, promoted a certain unlawful meeting contrary to the statute made and provided, and against the peace of our Sovereign Lady the Queen, her crown and dignity? Was it not true that the child's offence really consisted in heading a procession of young fellows who were after tilling the farm of a woman whose husband had died?

Mr. Forster found fault with the levity of the question, and then proceeded to state the serious facts of the case. The youth Daniel O'Sullivan was the leader of a party of boys from twelve to seventeen years of age; O'Sullivan himself was about twelve. When their procession was stopped the boys dispersed, but they reassembled at the instigation of grown-up persons.[5]

The police made domiciliary visits by day and by night into the rooms alike of women and of men. They broke into meetings; they stood outside doors and took the names of all persons entering into even the house of a priest to take steps for relieving the tenantry.[6] They tore down a placard in Tipperary calling upon the people to vote for the popular candidates for poor-law guardians;[7] and at a meeting of the Drogheda Corporation the sub-inspector of police interposed in the proceedings with the declaration that he would not allow the word 'coercion' to be used.[8]

Meantime Dublin Castle exhausted the resources of civil power in helping on the now unchecked savagery of the alien oligarchy against the nation. Troops were supplied in abundance; horse, foot, and artillery took part in the work of eviction; and sometimes the blue-jacket and the war-vessel were employed in the unholy task of turning out the starving to die. To make the grotesqueness and horror of the situation complete, it sometimes happened that the vessel which had come to help in evicting had but twelve months before visited the same shore and the same people to distribute among them the food which English charity had bestowed to save them from starvation. It is perhaps only in a system so absurd and unnatural as the Legislative Union between England and Ireland that a contradiction so glaring as generosity in one year and starvation in the next is possible.

[1] Hansard, vol. cclviii., p. 888.
[2] *Ibid.*, vol. cclxv., p. 184.
[3] *Ibid.*, vol. cclxviii., pp. 993, 1266.
[4] *Ibid.*, vol. cclxvii., p. 25.
[5] *Ibid.*, vol. cclx., p. 1543.
[6] *Ibid.*, vol. cclxvii., p. 1277.
[7] *Ibid.*, vol. cclxviii., p. 12.
[8] *Ibid.*, vol. cclxvii., p. 1285.

With the Government making their cause their own; with all the resources of the British Exchequer and the British naval and military forces at their back; with Mr. Forster to imprison every popular journalist and every popular orator; with Mr. Clifford Lloyd to make non-payment of rent a crime, and the erection of huts for the outcast and the dying an act of intimidation—the landlords acted as they have always done at every period when Fate and the British Government have together delivered the Irish tenantry helpless into their hands. They were, too, in the mood to take full advantage of all these things. For the first time in all their annals of power they had been confronted, defied, and beaten. Under the *régime* of the Land League they had been compelled to surrender rights of immemorial date—to lower their rack-rents, to stay eviction, to treat their tenants as fellow-beings, and not as so many ciphers or serfs. The mighty organization which had made this revolutionary change was beaten and dead: they had not only rights to re-conquer, but passion to slake; not only rents to exact, but vengeance to feed.

They went to work with a will that recalled the spirit of the glorious days which followed the Great Famine.

The evictions for the first quarter of 1881 were 1,732 persons; for the second quarter, ending June 30, they had increased to 5,562 persons; for the quarter ending September 30 the evictions were 6,496; and for the quarter ending December 31 they were 3,851. During the entire year of 1881, 17,341 persons had thus been deprived of their rights as tenants, and the greater proportion of them had been absolutely thrown on the roadside. It will be seen that eviction was proceeding for at least six months of the year in geometrical progression, and that the year 1881, under the influence of Mr. Forster's *régime*, was reaching a total of evictions for any approach to which we must go back to the dread years of the Famine.

Nor, of course, did those evictions take place without scenes of heart-rending cruelty or desperate encounter. In County Clare a man was killed by a body of police who were protecting a process-server; in April a policeman and two farmers were killed; in June a police-charge killed a man; in October a man was killed at a Land League meeting by a bayonet-thrust from a policeman; and later on in that month an event occurred which produced widespread and bitter indignation. A body of police were sent to collect poor-rates due by a number of miserable tenants on the estate of a Mr. Blake. Disputes have arisen as to how the struggle between the police and the people began, but the police fired into the people, several were wounded, and two women, Ellen McDonough, a young girl, and Mrs. Deare—a feeble old woman of sixty-five years of age—were wounded, and subsequently died. A verdict of 'Wilful Murder' was given in both cases against the police.

The reader has now the causes which produced the fit of absolute frenzy which passed over Ireland during the winter of 1881 and the spring of 1882. The country stood at bay, and driven from constitutional and open movement, with speech and writing and organization suppressed, with every day adding a new wrong and a new insult, with wholesale eviction, exile, and starvation once more confronting the nation as in the dread past, the population resorted to the secret organization and the revolting crimes which have been the inevitable and hideous brood of despotic *régimes*. A wild and horrible wave of crime passed over the country; the days of 1880 might well have been looked back to as extraordinarily peaceful in comparison with the period which had now set in, and neither the Queen's

Speech nor the Marquis of Hartington could any longer declare that there were but comparatively few murders.

In the year 1880, the number of murders was eight, there was no homicide, and there were twenty-five cases of firing at the person. In 1881, there were seventeen cases of murder, there were five homicides, and sixty-six cases of firing at the person; and in the first six months of 1882 there were fifteen murders, and forty cases of firing at the person. All these crimes, of course, are crimes of an agrarian character. The increase of crime was brought over and over again before Parliament. 'The present measures of coercion,' said Mr. Gorst, on March 28, 1882, 'have entirely failed to restore order in Ireland. The assizes just concluded show that the amount of crime now was more than double what it was in all the various districts last year; in almost every case the juries failed to convict, and therefore there must be some new departure on the part of the Government.'[1]

And on another occasion Mr. Gorst gave from the charges of the judges a proof of his statement, and the proof was startlingly damning.

At the Longford Assizes there were 98 cases of agrarian outrages, against 75 for the preceding year; in the County Clare there were 356 cases, as against 254 in the preceding year; in County Sligo 138 cases, against 97 in the preceding year; in Queen's County 62 cases, against 21 in the preceding year; in County Donegal 4,105 cases, against 645; in County Tipperary 159 crimes, against 75 in the preceding year, and so on.[2]

Curiously enough, crime was more abundant in some of the districts in which coercion had raged in its most active and its most outrageous form. Judge Barry stated at the assizes in the County of Clare that the outrages which had occurred for the two months previous to the assizes were twice as numerous as in the corresponding month of the previous year,[3] and the period of increased crime was the period of Mr. Clifford Lloyd's appearance in County Clare.

Meantime the author of this cycle of eviction, imprisonment, and brutal murder persevered in his system with fatuous obstinacy, every day prophesying that coercion would be triumphant, and that murder or organizations to murder were all but extinct.

At that moment there was, as everybody now knows, right under his feet, within a few yards of his own office, a conspiracy more murderous and more powerful than any that had existed in Ireland for probably half a century. And while the Chief Secretary was grimly congratulating himself, as he passed to the station for England, on the news of complete victory over crime he was bringing to his colleagues, his steps were being dogged by a gang of assassins armed against his life.

But the colleagues of Mr. Forster and the public opinion of England read the signs of the times more intelligently. The daily list of arrests and crime proved at last too sickening, and so strong was the revulsion of feeling, even in England, against the horrible state of things in Ireland, that the Conservatives showed some inclination to put a restraint upon the career of Mr. Forster.

Then these various outrages upon the people were brought constantly before the House of Commons by the Irish members, and naturally began in time to tell. An uneasy feeling grew up that after all such a crusade against every form of free speech, and free meeting, and free action, against

---

[1] Hansard, vol. cclxviii., p. 210.   *Ibid.*, vol. cclxviii., pp. 680, 687.
[3] *Ibid.*, p. 1003.

women and children, was not entirely creditable to the institutions or the reputation of England. The daily increase, at the same time, in the numbers, character, and atrocity of crimes in Ireland, helped to shake Mr. Forster's system; the prevarication of which he was frequently guilty spread uneasy doubts in his official pictures of Ireland. The theory that he was warring, not with the Irish people, but with a certain small and criminal section among the population, received its final overthrow in the local elections throughout Ireland, in every one of which the men whom he had sent into gaol as either abettors or perpetrators of crime were raised to the highest positions in the gift of their fellow-citizens. It was when his position was thus already damaged that Mr. Sexton was able to bring before the House of Commons a startling document. This was a circular issued to the constabulary of the County of Clare by the County Inspector. Beginning with a statement that attempts would probably be made on the life of Mr. Clifford Lloyd, it went on :

'Men proceeding on his (Mr. Clifford Lloyd's) escort should be men of great determination as well as steadiness; and even on suspicion of an attempt, should at once use their firearms, to prevent the bare possibility of an attempt on that gentleman's life. If men should accidentally commit an error in shooting any person on suspicion of that person being about to commit murder, I shall exonerate them by coming forward and producing this document.'[1]

Mr. Forster saw the spectre of coming ruin in the discovery of a document like this; prevaricated, and professed to require time to see whether the document was genuine. The interval he probably hoped to employ in explaining away to his colleagues the damning testimony of the document itself. But Mr. Sexton saw through this expedient, and insisted on raising a discussion at once, and when that discussion was over, Mr. Forster was a ruined man.

At the same moment he was assailed from another quarter. The Conservatives had seen plainly the rise of a tide of popular disgust with Mr. Forster and his system among the British people—who, to do them justice, are but poor hands at a continuance of the brutal methods of despotic countries—and thought the moment had come when a different method might be proposed for dealing with Ireland. The whole legislation of the Ministry had evidently broken down; the Coercion Act had not put down crime; the Land Act had not closed the Land Question; and against both the one measure and the other, Conservative members proposed hostile motions. Sir John Hay gave notice of the following motion :

'That the detention of large numbers of her Majesty's subjects in solitary confinement, without cause assigned, and without trial, is repugnant to the spirit of the Constitution; and that, to enable them to be brought to trial, jury trials should for a limited time (in Ireland), and in regard to crimes of a well-defined character, be replaced by some form of trial less liable to abuse.'[2]

And Mr. W. H. Smith gave notice of his intention 'to ask the First Lord of the Treasury if the Government will take into their consideration the urgent necessity for the introduction of a measure to extend the purchase clauses of the Land Act, and to make effectual provision for facilitating the

---

[1] Hansard, vol. cclxviii., pp. 991, 1000. [2] *Ibid.*, vol. cclxviii., p. 1945.

transfer of the ownership of the land to tenants who are occupiers on terms which would be just and reasonable to the existing landlords.'[1] If the leaders of the Land League required any justification of their policy, here it was. They had declared all along that coercion would fail, and that peasant proprietary was the only final and practical settlement of the Irish Land Question; and while they were in prison, and after their country had passed through the agony of a fierce and bloody strife, two English Conservatives came forward to filch and to adopt their scheme. These are not the only cases, as will be seen by-and-by, in which there existed more than a platonic friendship between the Tories and the Irish Party.

These were the events which prepared the Government on their side for a reconciliation with the Irish leader. On his side the motives for desiring a peace are apparent, and, in spite of all the absurd mystification with which the transaction was surrounded, can be understood by any reasonable person. Mr. Parnell was alarmed at the vast increase in the evictions; the greater number of the evicted he knew were absolutely unable to pay their rents, the arrears which had come as a *damnosa hæreditas* from the Famine years being a burden they were incapable of shaking off; and he was much too clear-headed a man to suppose that in the long-run the purse of the Land League could hold out against the Exchequer of England. The Kilmainham treaty, as it was called, was a great victory for Mr. Parnell. All the forces of the empire had been pitted against him, and he had beaten the empire. The terms of the Government are sufficient proof of this. These terms, summed up briefly, were: First, the failure of coercion was acknowledged frankly and unreservedly. The completeness of the confession involved the sacrifice of the men chiefly responsible for coercion; and accordingly Mr. Forster and Lord Cowper resigned from the Ministry. Then there was to be no renewal of coercion. This is a statement which was much contested during the debates that came soon after; but no man in his senses believes that coercion would have been pressed forward by the Government which had shed Mr. Forster and released Mr. Parnell. It is quite possible that the Crimes Bill would have been introduced, but it would have been hung up after a stage or two, and Ireland would have returned to the ordinary law.[2]

The first indication of the coming resolves of the Government was the reception given by Mr. Gladstone to the new Land Bill brought in by Mr. J. E. Redmond on behalf of the Irish Party. This Bill proposed an amendment of the Healy and the Purchase clauses of the Land Act, the inclusion of leaseholders, but, above all, the remission of those arrears which shut out so many of the tenants from all possible benefit under the Land Act and from all prospect or hope. Mr. Gladstone received the proposals of the Bill with great favour, practically held out that the larger and more remote questions of Land Reform would be favourably considered: and, with regard to the question of the Arrears, made statements amounting to a promise that the Government shared the convictions of the

[1] *Times*, March 11, 1882.

[2] The plan of the Government was to give the Rules of Procedure priority over the renewed coercion, and it was one of Mr. Forster's most bitter charges against the Government, both during that Session and the Session following, when the question was again raised, that Mr. Gladstone did give this priority to the Procedure Rules over coercion. Nobody at all experienced in Parliamentary affairs need be told that if the Procedure Rules had got the priority there would be no more mention of the Crimes Act during the Session. It certainly would have taken from May, the date of Mr. Forster's fall, to the end of the Session to pass the Procedure Rules alone

Irish members, and would be prepared to deal with the question immediately.

Such, then, were the terms of the so-called Kilmainham treaty: abandonment of coercion, the retirement of the coercion Minister, and the acceptance, on the other hand, of the chief demands of Mr. Parnell for amendment of the Land Act in less than a year after it had become law, and the immediate settlement of the burning question of Arrears. The House of Commons certainly fully appreciated the greatness and completeness of Mr. Parnell's victory. The first few days after his release from prison were days of veritable triumph. He received every recognition, public and private, of being master of the situation. Doubtful friends or bitter enemies rushed up to shake his hand and worship the rising sun. He was recognised to be—as beyond all question at that moment he was—the most potent political force in the British Empire. From no man did Mr. Parnell receive a recognition so eloquent, though probably so grudging, of the supremacy of his power and the completeness of his triumph at this moment as from his baffled and beaten opponent. By a singularly dramatic appropriateness, it was during the speech in which Mr. Forster was explaining his resignation that Mr. Parnell entered. 'There are two warrants,' Mr. Forster was saying, 'which I signed in regard to the hon. member for the city of Cork also for intimidation. I have often asserted that these arrests for intimidation were——'

'At this point,' goes on Hansard, 'the entrance of Mr. Parnell into the House, and the cheers with which he was greeted by the Home Rule members, drowned the voice of the right hon. gentleman and prevented the conclusion of the sentence from being heard.'[1]

And then Mr. Forster went on to use the following words, which clearly prove the omnipotence of Mr. Parnell at this moment:

'A surrender (said the Chief Secretary a few moments later) is bad, but a compromise or arrangement is worse. I think we may remember what a Tudor king said to a great Irishman in former times: "If all Ireland cannot govern the Earl of Kildare, then let the Earl of Kildare govern Ireland." The king thought it was better that the Earl of Kildare should govern Ireland than that there should be an arrangement between the Earl of Kildare and his representative. In like manner if all England cannot govern the hon. member for Cork, then let us acknowledge that he is the greatest power in Ireland to-day.'[2]

The prospect of the Irish people was equally bright. With the close of the Land struggle, with the abandonment of coercion and the destruction of the hated coercion Minister, tranquillity promised to immediately return. On this point two authorities as antagonistic as Mr. Forster and Mr. William O'Brien were completely agreed. Finally, in the pages of the *Times*, which so often have been defaced with articles brutally unfair to Ireland, there was this startling confession:

'The recurrence of St. Patrick's Day, with its traditional celebration, its old toasts and its old memories, reminds us that the Irishman of history and of tale is nowhere to be found. . . . The Irishman is becoming like the Englishman, that is, the Englishman of the dull, morose, self-satisfied sort—the man who sees everything and everybody from his own point of view, and pursues his object with a dogged indifference to all reasons, interests, feelings, and beliefs. The Irishman, like the Englishman, is now

---

[1] Hansard, vol. cclxix., p. 108. [2] *Ibid.*, p. 111.

righteous in his own eyes, and his righteousness is to hold money and land, and have the use of it as long as he can. . . . He has actually become a citizen of the world, and a very 'cute fellow. He has played his cards well, and is making a golden harvest. He has beaten a legion of landlords, dowagers, and encumbrances of all sorts, out of the field, and driven them into workhouses. He has baffled the greatest of legislatures, and outflanked the largest British armies in getting what he thinks his due. Had all this wonderful advance been made at the cost of some other country, England would have been the first to offer chaplets, testimonials, and ovations, to the band of patriots who had achieved it. As the sufferers in the material sense are chiefly of English extraction, we cannot help a little soreness. Yet reason compels us to admit that the Irish have dared and done as they never did before. They are welcome to that praise. But they have lost, and it is a loss we all feel. Paddy has got his wish—he is changed into a landowner.'[1]

Everybody knows how in an hour Mr. Parnell was reduced from this eminence of omnipotence to a position of absolute and apparently irretrievable disaster. On May 6 Lord Frederick Cavendish and Mr. Burke were assassinated in Phœnix Park. This tragedy produced a tempest of passion that swept away for the moment the power of Mr. Gladstone and of Mr. Parnell for good to Ireland. Those who remember the fatal Sunday when the news reached London, and saw the Irish leader and his colleagues that day, can find consolation in the reflection that their fortunes can never see a darker or gloomier hour. One of the victims of the knives of the Invincibles was known to and popular with the Irish members, as he was with all sections of the House of Commons, and the kindly feeling was recognised, which impelled him to offer himself as the bearer of a new message of peace to Ireland. Wherever the Irish race lived, the depth and the pitifulness of the tragedy, and the magnitude of the disaster, were felt and appreciated; and in cities as distant as St. Louis, or San Francisco, or Melbourne, or Wellington, the fatal day filled Irish households with mourning.

The Government found themselves unable to resist the tide of passion that passed over the country; there was a hoarse cry for Coercion; and the Ministers felt that, unless Coercion were dealt out with a liberal hand, they could not hold office for twenty-four hours. It must, at the same time, be acknowledged that the English nation, as a body, behaved on this terrible occasion with self-restraint and dignity. The newspapers, it is true, did their best in one or two instances to fan popular excitement into fury. The *Times*—true to its immemorial traditions—suggested that the Irish population of England, unarmed and innocent, should be massacred for a crime which they abhorred, and that the Irish political leaders should be made responsible for a catastrophe which had dashed all their hopes. But these shameful incitements to violence remained innocuous before the good sense of the English people. The most peculiar result of the Phœnix Park assassinations was the change it made in the position of Mr. Forster. The dread tragedy which was the outcome of the frenzy that his policy had generated was taken to be the vindication of that policy, and the undoubted growth of a large and potent murderous conspiracy was held to be the proof of the utility of coercive measures against the preparation and the perpetration of crime. If the Phœnix Park assassination preached

[1] *Times*, March 17, 1882.

with its bloody tongue one doctrine more loudly than another, it was the futility and the wickedness and disaster of the policy for which Mr. Forster was responsible.

In the debates which ensued nothing could be more unanimous than the condemnation of the policy of Mr. Forster himself. It was one of his own colleagues who pronounced the most damning condemnation of himself and his Coercion Act.

'It was assumed (said Sir William Harcourt) . . . that the Protection of Person and Property Bill was an appropriate remedy, and that if we only had the summary power of arrest, it would be sufficient to put down crime. My right honourable friend, who had charge of that measure, said: "We can discover the persons who commit these crimes—these village ruffians; we know them; we can put them in prison; we can put down crime." That turned out not to be so. The men were shut up; more men were shut up time after time; yet crime went on increasing. It was never suggested—nor did it occur to anybody—that that measure would have failed so completely as it did in suppressing crime. The consequence was, that the shutting up of these people did not sensibly diminish crime. On the contrary, the more people were shut up the more crime increased.'[1]

But, in the heat and fury of party conflict, logic is silent. The Conservatives believed, or professed to believe, that Mr. Forster and his policy had been vindicated by the murder of Lord Frederick Cavendish and Mr. Burke. Mr. Forster was doubly interested in turning the outburst of popular anger and sorrow over the Phœnix Park assassinations to his own justification, and proceeded to make as much capital as he could out of the tragedy. He attacked his former colleagues, he made questionable use of Cabinet communications, he did everything he could, while professing friendship for Mr. Gladstone and the other members of the Ministry, to deal them as many and as deadly stabs as it was in his power to do.

The Crimes Bill, which followed the Phœnix Park murders, was fought by the Irish members doggedly, and was marked by the same scenes as were enacted in the Session of 1881. The progress of the Bill was terribly slow; amendments followed amendments. There came the system of relays, and then an all-night sitting. Once more tempestuous passion was aroused on both sides, and finally on the morning of Saturday, July 1, the following Irish members were declared guilty of obstruction, and suspended *en masse*: Mr. Biggar, Mr. Callan, Dr. Commins, Mr. Dillon, Mr. Healy, Mr. Leamy, Mr. Marum, Mr. Metge, Mr. McCarthy, Mr. T. P. O'Connor, Mr. O'Donnell, Mr. Parnell, Mr. R. Power, Mr. Redmond, Mr. Sullivan, and Mr. Sexton. And later in the day the following members were also suspended: Mr. Byrne, Mr. Corbet, Mr. Gray, Mr. Lalor, Mr. Leahy, Mr. A. O'Connor, Mr. O'Kelly, Mr. W. H. O'Sullivan, and Mr. Sheil.

This had the most extraordinary consequences. Thus Mr. John Dillon had been entirely absent during the night, and when he arrived in the morning to enter the House, he was refused admission, and, for the first time, learnt of his suspension. Similarly, Dr. Commins, Mr. T. D. Sullivan, and Mr. Biggar had been absent during the night. Mr. Richard Power had actually not spoken even once during the debates in Committee

---

[1] Hansard, vol. cclxxvi., pp. 429, 430.

on the Bill, and Mr. Marum had taken so little part that Sir John Hay, a Conservative member, got up and protested against his suspension.

A word is required for another Bill of the Session of 1882. In the latter portion of this session Mr. Gladstone introduced, and, after a short struggle with the Marquis of Salisbury, succeeded in passing, the Arrears Act. If Englishmen were teachable on their Irish mistakes, assuredly the introduction and carriage of this Bill ought to have taught them a great lesson. For it was the Arrears Bill that ought to have brought before the minds of Englishmen the real meaning of the crisis through which Ireland had been passing. The testimony as to the circumstances which necessitated the Arrears Bill comes from many different sources. Mr. Gladstone spoke in favour of the Bill. Mr. Forster spoke in favour of the Bill. It was the great anxiety of Mr. Parnell in Kilmainham, and afterwards of Mr. Trevelyan in Dublin Castle.

'Never mind the "suspects,"' said Mr. Parnell to Captain O'Shea in Kilmainham ; 'we can well afford to see the Coercion Act out. If you have any influence, do not fritter it away upon us ; use it to get the arrears practically adjusted. The great object of my life (added the hon. member) is to settle the Land Question. Now that the Tories have adopted my view as to peasant proprietary, the extension of the Purchase clauses is safe. You have always supported the leaseholders as strongly as myself ; but the great object now is to stay eviction by the introduction of an Arrears Bill.'[1]

'He had felt (Mr. Parnell said in the same debate) with reference to the question of Arrears in Ireland, as relating to the situation of the smaller tenants, the very gravest anxiety and responsibility for many months ; and he was rejoiced that the hon. member had found some way of placing the views of himself and those with him before the Government. They had been aware from what they had seen in the newspapers, and from the information of prisoners who came in from time to time, and who received letters from different parts of the country, that evictions in large and very much greater numbers than had occurred up to the present were imminent unless some such proposal as the Prime Minister had announced were made in regard to arrears. They had anticipated that there would be three times as many evictions in the present quarter of the year as there were in the first quarter, when 7,000 persons were turned out of their homes. They had also every reason to believe that, owing to the fact that the smaller tenantry in Mayo, Galway, Sligo, and parts of Roscommon, Donegal, Leitrim, and Kerry were sunk in arrears to the extent of three or four years—in many cases four or five or six years, and in some cases ten or twelve years—the year's or half-year's rent, by the payment of which the tenants had obtained a temporary respite from eviction, would be but a temporary respite, and that the coming winter would see evictions resumed against the smaller tenants to an extent never witnessed in the country since 1848. They feared also that the outrages which had been so numerous during the last six months would increase as the winter came on ; and that a state of affairs in Ireland would follow, owing to the non-settlement of this question, the end of which they could not possibly foresee.'[2]

Equally emphatic is the testimony of Mr. Trevelyan :

'I think those hon. members have left out of sight what is perhaps the governing consideration of this question, why . . . a very large number of

[1] Hansard, vol. cclxix., p. 783.   [2] Ibid., pp. 792, 793.

members think it necessary to assist the tenants in Ireland. It is because the times have been most exceptional. . . . So far as I can remember, no instance of this sort in which money has been asked to assist the tenants of Ireland can be quoted since the Famine of 1846. The reasons why we have come forward now are the bad years of 1878 and 1879. I only put into other words what was said by the right hon. member for Bradford, when I say that the sudden rise in Irish agrarian crime which took place in 1879-80 was connected with the discontent which was fostered in an atmosphere of misery. There were some parts of the country where the people could not pay their rents. They could not keep body and soul together without charitable assistance, and the helplessness and despair of these people gave the first material thirst for agitation.'[1]

Again:

Every day (went on the Chief Secretary) the Government gets reports of evictions, and whenever these evictions are of tenants who can pay their rents and will not, the Government is very carefully informed by their officers. That is not the case with all evictions, and at this moment in one part of the country men are being turned out of their houses, actually by battalions, who are no more able to pay the arrears of these bad years than they are able to pay the National Debt. I have seen a private account from a very trustworthy source—from a source anyone would allow to be trustworthy—of what is going on in Connemara. In three days 150 families were turned out, numbering 750 persons. At the headquarters of the Union, though only one member of each family attended to ask for assistance, there was absolutely a crowd at the door of the workhouse. It was not the case that these poor people belonged to the class of extravagant tenants. They were not whisky-drinkers; they were not in terror of the Land League. One man who owed £8 borrowed it on the promise of repayment in six months with £4 of addition—a rate of interest which hon. members could easily calculate—that he might sit in his home. The cost of the process of eviction amounted to £3 17s. 6d. I am told that in this district there are thousands in this position—people who have been beggared for years, people who have been utterly unable to hold up their heads since those bad years, and whose only resource from expulsion from their homes is the village money-lender.'[2]

And it was the tenantry whose miserable condition is described so eloquently and sympathetically that the landlords of Ireland were evicting during 1881 and 1882, at the time of the suppression of the Land League. It was tenants of this kind, 17,341 of whom were cast from their homes in the year 1881. It was to evict tenants of this kind Mr. Forster was filling the gaols, was arming the landlords with soldiers and police. It was to evict miserable and despairing wretches like these that the mighty forces of the British Empire were pitted against Ireland and Mr. Parnell. Assuredly it is not too much to ask, when these were the issues on both sides, that the sympathies of all real haters of wrong and suffering should rejoice that the final victory remained with Mr. Parnell and the tenantry, instead of with Mr. Forster, coercion, and the evicting landlords.

On the Arrears Bill Mr. Gladstone staked the existence of his Government, and even risked a collision with the House of Lords; but that Bill was the grant in 1882 of a demand contemptuously rejected in 1881. The

---

[1] Hansard, vol. cclxix., pp. 1327, 1328.   [2] Ibid., pp. 1328, 1329.

Bill itself was an adaptation of one brought in by Mr. Redmond, and again the Bill brought in by Mr. Redmond had been drafted, every clause and every line of it, within the walls of Kilmainham by Mr. Parnell. This is another of the many proofs that it is only through the suffering of Irish leaders that the dull, cold ear of Parliamentary ignorance can be penetrated. Mr. Parnell was quite content, of course, that his scheme should be taken up by the Government and passed into law; but it seemed a little hard that he should have had to go through six months' imprisonment in order to educate the mind of the Ministry.

It were bootless here to enter into the fierce controversies that arose between Lord Spencer and the Irish Party in reference to the administration of the Arrears Act. That particular struggle happily belongs to the past, with acts done and words spoken on both sides that each willingly consigns to oblivion. Suffice it here to introduce one of the men whom this struggle brought into fierce prominence.

William O'Brien comes from a good stock, and was brought up from his earliest years in those principles of which he has become so prominent and so vigorous an advocate. On the day his elder brother was born, in 1848, the sub-inspector of police in Mallow had a warrant to search the house for firearms, but desisted from using it because of Mrs. O'Brien's illness, and on Mr. O'Brien giving his word that there were no arms in the house. O'Brien's father was one of the fiercest and most resolute spirits of the Young Ireland Party, but afterwards, like so many of the men who survived the terrible abortiveness of that time, was by no means friendly to physical force movements. In time he had to remonstrate with some of his own offspring for their adhesion to Fenianism; but his mouth was closed, whenever his remonstrances became too vehement, by an allusion to this episode in the days of his own haughty youth.

William was born on October 2, 1852, in Mallow, with which town his family on the mother's side has been connected from time immemorial. He received his education at Cloyne Diocesan College. This was a mixed school, attended by both Catholic and Protestant children. There was not the slightest sectarian animosity between the children of the different creeds, but there was plenty of political argument and differences. The Catholic Nationalists in the school formed a sort of small Irish Party, and held their own; William O'Brien being successful in carrying off the class-prizes, while his brothers and others carried off the honours in cricket, football, and the like. William from his earliest years had the same principles as he professes to-day. Apart from the example of his father, he had in his brother a strong apostle of the epistle of national rights. To this brother, his senior by some years, he looked up with that mixture of affection and awe which an elder brother often inspires in a younger. This brother was indeed of a type to captivate the imagination of such a nature as that of his younger brother. He was a man of inflexible resolution, great daring, and boundless enthusiasm. Among the revolutionaries of his district he was the chief figure, and there was no raid for arms too desperate, or no expedition too risky, for his spirit. He took part with Captain Mackay, who was one of the boldest of the Fenian leaders, in many of the raids for arms on police barracks and other places in the County of Cork. He was arrested, of course, when the Habeas Corpus Act was suspended, and underwent the misery and tortures which, as has already been described, were inflicted on untried prisoners under the best of possible Constitutions and the freest of possible Governments. With this episode in the life of the elder brother, the brightness of the life of William O'Brien for many a long day ceased. His family history is strangely and terribly sad. In the O'Brien household there were at the one moment three members of the family dying. The father of the family had died before, and now two of his sons and his daughter were lying on their death-beds at the same time. The two brothers died on the one day, and a fortnight afterwards the sister died also. The shock to a nature so fiercely and intensely affectionate as that of William O'Brien can well be imagined. The death of his father and the illness of his brothers had thrown, to a large extent, the support of the entire family on his hands, and to them he was not merely a brother, but to a certain extent a helpful parent. It seemed for a time as if he were to be swept away by the same disease which had proved fatal to so many of his kin. He was only saved from death by a journey to Egypt, but he has never really recovered from the shock to his mind and heart which this family tragedy caused, and he is, and will be for ever, haunted by its memory.

The first thing which William O'Brien ever wrote was a sketch of the trial of Captain Mackay. This attracted the attention of Alderman Nagle, the proprietor of the *Cork Daily Herald*, and he was offered an engagement upon that paper. There he remained until somewhere towards 1876, when he became a member of the reporting staff of the *Freeman's Journal*. He had become, meantime, and remains, an expert shorthand writer. He did the ordinary work of the reporter for several years, with occasional dashes into more congenial occupation in special descriptions of particular picturesque incidents. Whenever his work had any connection with the politics, condition, or prospects of his country, he devoted himself to it with a special fervour. It was his descriptions of the County of Mayo in the great distress of 1879 which first concentrated the attention of the Irish people on the calamity impending over the country. While he was working with an energy as great as that of any other journalist in Dublin at his own profession, his heart was in the cause of his people. When the Coercion Act was passed in 1880, he thought the moment had come for him to offer his services to maintain the fight in face of threats of danger, and he proposed through Mr. Davitt and Mr. Egan that he should take up some of the work of the League. His health, however, was at the time so weak that his friends feared that the imprisonment which was almost certain to follow employment by the League would prove fatal to his constitution, and he was dissuaded from joining the ranks of the movement. In June, 1881, when the conflict between Mr. Forster and the Land League was at its fiercest, the idea occurred of establishing a newspaper as an organ of the League and Parnellite Party. At once the thoughts of several people turned to the able and brilliant writer on the *Freeman's Journal*, and he was invited by Mr. Parnell to found *United Ireland* and to become its editor.

It was then for the first time that the higher powers of O'Brien were discovered. Great as was his reputation as a writer of nervous and picturesque English, he had hitherto been unknown as the author of editorial and purely political articles, and few were prepared for the political grasp and feverish and bewildering force of the editorials he contributed to the new journal. He had now been placed in the position for which his whole character and gifts especially fitted him. O'Brien is the very embodiment of the militant journalist. In some respects, indeed, his character resembles that of the French, rather than of the Irish, *littérateur*. Though he has keen literary instincts and a fine soul, his work is important to him mainly because of its political result. Fragile in frame and weak in health, he is yet above all things a combatant, ready and almost eager to meet danger. If he had been born in Paris, he would probably have been found at the top of a barricade, or, like Armand Carrel, might have perished in a political duel. A long, thin face, deep-set and piercing eyes, flashing out from behind spectacles, sharp features, and quick, feverish walk—the whole appearance of the man speaks of a restless, fierce, and enthusiastic character.

The times were such as to bring out to the full all his qualities of mind and character. As has been said, the foundation of *United Ireland* came in the agony of the struggle against coercion. Its tone was a trumpet-call to further and fiercer advance instead of an appeal to retreat, and naturally, before long, Mr. Forster knew that either *United Ireland* should be crushed or the spirit of revolt would grow daily fiercer and more unbending. Mr. O'Brien was accordingly arrested the day after Mr. Parnell, under an Act which was obtained for imprisoning *mauvais sujets* and village tyrants, the perpetrators and participators in crime! It was a part of the sadness that has followed his whole life that at the very moment of his arrest his mother was seriously ill, a woman whose nobility of character deserved the affection she received from her son. During his imprisonment the authorities were gracious enough to allow him out under escort to pay a visit to her, and he was released the day before her death. After various attempts to have the paper published in different places, sometimes in England and sometimes in France, *United Ireland* was finally suppressed by Mr. Forster. With the overthrow of Mr. Forster, the paper was again revived. Then began a long and lonely duel between Mr. O'Brien and the Administration, which lasted with scarce an interruption for three of the fiercest years in Irish history.

While Mr. O'Brien was being tried for a 'seditious libel,' a vacancy arose in the representation of Mallow, through the promotion of Mr. Johnston, the Attorney-General, to a judgeship. It had been arranged before, that whenever the General Election came Mr. O'Brien, as a Mallow man, should appeal to the town to throw off its servitude to Whiggery and join the rest of the country in the new demand for the restoration of Irish rights. The opportunity for the appeal had come sooner than anybody had anticipated. The prosecution of O'Brien by the Government lent a singular opportuneness to the struggle, and a still further element of significance was added to the contest by the Government sending down Mr. Naish, their new Attorney-General, as his opponent. Mallow, in some respects, has a history similar to that of Athlone, Sligo, and some other small constituencies of Ireland. During the dread interregnum between the betrayal of Keogh and the rise of Butt, it had followed the example of the other small constituencies in sending into Parliament the worthless representatives of Whiggery or Tories. The representatives of Mallow, like the representatives of Galway and Athlone, and of Sligo and Carlow, bought that they might sell. The contest for Mallow, under circumstances like these, attracted an immense amount of attention, and all Ireland looked to the result with feverish eagerness. The reputation of Mallow had been so bad for so many years that there were doubts mixed with hope, and the utmost expectation was that Mr. O'Brien would be returned by a small majority. The full significance of the change that had come over all Ireland was shown when the result was announced, and it was found that O'Brien had been returned by a majority of 72—161 to 89.

The Session of 1883 opened in strange gloom. But meantime there had come to Dublin Castle aid from an unexpected quarter. On January 21 a number of men were arrested on a charge of being concerned in the murder of Lord Frederick Cavendish and Mr. Burke, and some days after the trial opened the whole world was startled by the appearance of James Carey, the chief of the gang, in the witness-box. Speakers did not scruple to suggest that while it was Joe Brady that used the knife, the Irish members were the men who had supplied the funds. Under the influence of speeches like this public passion in England once more became fiercely aroused, and the majority of the English people were firmly convinced, in all probability, that before many days Mr. Parnell would take his place beside the murderers of Lord Frederick Cavendish and Mr. Burke. Irish members are sometimes accused of being venomous, violent, and unscrupulous in their attacks upon their political opponents. Their speeches in this respect were once compared by Mr. Chamberlain to the use of explosive bullets in civilized warfare. This charge is conveniently but characteristically forgetful of the things Irish members have had to bear from the tongues of their English opponents and the pens of English journalists.

There was one man who was again dragged from the depths to the surface by the new revelations as to the state of Ireland. By the same strange logic which had made the hideous outcome of Mr. Forster's policy in the assassinations its defence and not its most eloquent condemnation, the revelations of the trials became again, amid the fury of English passion, to be the vindication of his wisdom. After his fashion he resolved to take full advantage of the tide of passion that was running so high. Mr. Gorst proposed:

'And we venture to express our earnest hope that the policy which has produced these results will be maintained, and that no further attempts will be made to purchase the support of persons disaffected to her Majesty's rule by concessions to lawless agitation; and that the existence of dangerous secret societies in Dublin, and other parts of the country, will continue to be met by unremitting energy and vigilance on the part of the Executive.'[1]

On February 22, 1883, Mr. Forster took part in this debate, and at once resolved to make it the occasion of having it out with his old and triumphant enemy. He had carefully prepared himself for the occasion. His notes were voluminous; every sentence in his long indictment had been carefully weighed; the speech was full of the adroit innuendo and the deeply laid though apparently casual asides of which the member for Bradford was a master. The attack on Mr. Parnell was made the more palatable to the House by its being dexterously sandwiched between attacks on Mr. Forster's former colleagues, against whom at this moment the tide ran almost as high as against Mr. Parnell himself.

The indictment was a great, an immense Parliamentary success. The House, swept by its invective, was lashed into fury, and there were loud cries for Mr. Parnell's immediate rise. This demand was a sufficient proof of the fairness of the temper of the House. Mr. Forster had delivered a speech which he had prepared for weeks; the speech had been extended into the dinner hour; and it was this famished and impatient assembly that Mr. Parnell was expected to address with an impromptu reply to a most elaborately prepared attack. Mr. Parnell, of course, declined to be bullied into premature speech; and, indeed, contemptuous of this as he is

[1] Hansard, vol. cclxxvi. p. 414.

of every attack, he for some time was doubtful whether he should take the trouble of replying at all. The English press, meantime, was in exultant delight. 'Mr. Forster's stern interrogatories,' said the *Times*, 'fell on Mr. Parnell like the lash of a whip on a man's face.'

It is worth pausing for a moment here to say that the whole cause of the tempest against Mr. Parnell and the Land League, which raged for weeks in England and threatened the liberty if not the life of some of the Irish leaders, was the result of a couple of sentences of an informer. The following are the sentences referred to. Carey is being examined by the Crown prosecutor:

'What was the opinion amongst some of them as to where the money came from ?—There were different ideas. Some said it came from America ; I said I did not believe that it came from America.

'Where did you say you believed it came from ?—I said I did not think from America. I think I expressed myself, but I know between the whole of us it was repeatedly said, " Perhaps they are getting it from the Land League." '[1]

From this it will be seen that all Carey ventured to say was that he or some other members of his gang had a suspicion that the money came from the Land League. The subject was never recurred to in his evidence, and, of course, it was never recurred to for the reason that the Crown authorities knew that a connection between the Land League and the 'Invincibles' could not be established. Attention would have been more fitly directed to another portion of the evidence of Carey which spoke in trumpet tones against Mr. Forster. The 'Invincibles' were the same dread brood that despotism always begets, were as much the children of Mr. Forster's *régime* as the Nihilists are of the autocracy of Russia, and Carey himself was the strongest witness in proof of this.

James Carey cross-examined by Mr. Walsh :

'When you became a member of the Order of Invincibles, was it for the object of serving your country that you joined ?—Well, yes.

'And at that time when you joined with the object of serving your country, in what state was Ireland ?—In a very bad state.

' A famine, I think, was just passing over her ?—Yes.

'The Coercion Bill was in force, and the popular leaders were in prison ? —Yes.

'And was it because you despaired of any constitutional means of serving Ireland that you joined the Society of Invincibles ?—I believe so.'[2]

It was, of course, assumed that Mr. Parnell would go down under this flood of hatred and calumny. The only effect in Ireland was to attract to him the more passionate affection of his people. The idea had long been familiar to the minds of his admirers that he should be relieved from some of the pecuniary embarrassments which he inherited, and which he had himself largely increased by his generosity to his tenants both during and before the Land League agitation. The attack of Mr. Forster brought this idea to practical shape, and the Parnell Tribute was started with a letter from Archbishop Croke. One thing only was wanted to its success— that was another attack. This came as a result of the sinister counsels of a renegade Nationalist at the Vatican. The tribute went on apace, and

---

[1] *United Ireland*, February 24, 1883. [2] *Ibid.*

when it was closed it had reached close upon the handsome amount of £40,000.

Another incident of this period must be mentioned, in order to introduce another prominent figure in the struggle of to-day. Mr. Timothy Harrington was one of the prominent Land Leaguers of County Kerry in the days of Mr. Forster, and, after some shorter terms of imprisonment, was confined for twelve months in Galway Gaol under the Coercion Act of 1881. In October, 1882, a new political and agrarian organization was established, and Mr. Harrington was appointed as the secretary. Soon after, he had to deliver a speech in Westmeath, and in the course of his observations used this language : ' Now, I ask the tenant farmers to come forward generously and give the labourers a fair day's wages for a fair day's work. If not, the agitation which has been carried on in their behalf will be turned against them if they do not come forward and assist the labourers here in their hour of need.' A couple of those precious resident magistrates, who have become so prominent of late, held this language to be calculated to intimidate the farmers of County Westmeath, and sentenced him to two months' imprisonment. Mr. Harrington appealed to the County Court Judge, and his appeal came before Mr. J. Chute Neligan. Mr. Neligan is a Kerry landlord ; Mr. Harrington is the proprietor of the *Kerry Sentinel*, which has waged fierce war upon the oppression of the landlords of the County Kerry ; and the conviction was confirmed. Mr. Harrington was subjected to the punishment of the plank-bed for a month, and underwent all the other hardships that are meted out to the worst criminals. This sentence, severe enough, was aggravated by the determination of the prison authorities to render his stay in prison as odious as possible. He was asked to perform a duty the description of which is not permissible ; some of the landlords of the county could see their hated and fallen foe thus menially and disgustingly employed from the window of the governor's house, and Mr. Harrington refused to give his enemies the spectacle of his degradation. In consequence, he was condemned by the governor to the loss of the two hours' recreation he was allowed by the prison rules, and for six days he had to remain within his cell, without even once tasting a breath of fresh air or enjoying a moment's exercise. It was while he was thus in the solitude of his cell that he received news which was his vindication. A vacancy had been made in the representation of County Westmeath by the retirement of Mr. Gill. Mullingar, the town in which Mr. Harrington was imprisoned, is the capital town of County Westmeath, and here the nomination of candidates had to take place. The constituency, up to the passage of the Franchise Act, consisted exclusively, or almost exclusively, of farmers ; probably there was not a single labourer on the whole electoral roll. In other words, the constituency consisted exclusively of the class whom Mr. Harrington was convicted of having intimidated, and excluded every one of the class in whose interest he was accused of having employed intimidation. Yet it came to pass that no less than three nomination-papers were sent in signed by farmers, and Mr. Harrington's popularity was so great that nobody attempted to oppose him. It had been arranged that a signal from the railway embankment, from which the cell of Mr. Harrington was visible, should announce the result of the election. It is thus that Irish leaders learn the difference between the esteem of their own people and the hatred of their oppressors. Since that period Mr. Harrington has worked indefatigably as Secretary of the National League. In this great office he has as much to do with the popular government of Ireland as the Lord-Lieutenant, the Chief Secretary, and all Dublin Castle have with the government of Ireland against her will. Under his guidance, at once active and sagacious, the organization has grown to be one of the most powerful in all Irish history. At this moment it numbers close upon fifteen hundred branches. To stimulate popular courage and restrain popular excesses has been the terribly difficult task of Mr. Harrington; and so well has he performed it that he was able to meet and contradict all the statements of Mr. Balfour recently as to illegal conduct on the part of the League. Mr. Harrington is a born organizer. He has much of the iron spirit of the American 'boss,' dashed with the kindliness of a good-humoured Irishman. His frame, hardy, firm-set, is capable of any amount of physical or mental effort. He grew fat on the plank-bed, and cheerful in solitary confinement. Throughout his whole life he has never once tasted stimulant, and this perhaps accounts to some extent for his splendid health. He is a curious mixture of the intense pietist and the personal Puritan with the keen, tolerant, and good-humoured man of the world. No man fights so fierce a battle, and no man has fewer enduring enmities. At one time we think of him as a latter-day Vincent de Paul; at another, as of the most modern of machine politicians and ward-bosses.

A more important victory than even that in Westmeath soon came. The promotion of Mr. Givan to a Government situation left a vacancy in the County of Monaghan. It was at once resolved that the seat should be contested by Mr. Healy, whose great services in amending the Land Act, and especially in obtaining the clause called after his name, marked him out as the strongest candidate for such a contest. The attempt to gain a seat in one of the Ulster constituencies was regarded as insane impudence. The Whigs demanded that, though representative of a miserable minority of the popular party, they should be allowed their traditional place as the officers of the army of which the rank and file were almost entirely composed of Nationalists.[1] These impudent pretensions were for once rejected, and the Nationalists determined to win or lose with their own man. The Tories, on their side, felt the full importance of the contest, and put forward one of their ablest representatives in Mr. John Monroe, an eminent Queen's Counsel. The three parties were thus represented—the Nationalists by Mr. Healy, the Liberals by Mr. Pringle, and the Conservatives by Mr. Monroe. The contest was fought with considerable spirit on all sides, and in the end the National candidate won. The Liberal candidate exposed the emptiness of the pretensions on which his party had held the monopoly of political power for so long. Mr. Pringle had but 274 votes; Mr. Monroe received 2,011 votes; Mr. Healy, with 2,376 votes, had a clear majority over the candidates of the two parties combined. A few weeks afterwards Whiggery received an even more crushing blow. For the vacancy made by Mr. Healy there came forward The O'Conor Don and Mr. W. H. K. Redmond. Mr. Redmond was a young man, scarcely of legal age at the time of the contest, and he was absent in Australia. The O'Conor Don, on the other hand, was a trained and mature politician; and, though he had joined the ranks of his country's enemies, came from

---

[1] Ulster (said the *Northern Whig*) is not National and cannot be made National... The loyal Ulster electors, Protestant and Catholic, Liberal and Conservative, have only to come to an understanding to divide the representation. Under such an arrangement not one Nationalist candidate could be returned for Ulster.—(Quoted in *Pall Mall Gazette*, June 27, 1883.)

an old Irish stock. But in the struggle he was beaten ignominiously. The numbers were: Redmond, 307; O'Conor Don, 126.

In the autumn of this year an attempt was made from another of the anti-National forces to arrest the tide of National victory. The province of Ulster has, with a characteristic ignorance of Irish affairs, been always regarded by the English public as forming a solid mass unanimously in favour of the perpetuation of English domination and against the restoration of Irish liberties. This absurd misrepresentation of the real state of Ulster obtained even among a portion of the Irish public. To the southern Nationalist the north was chiefly known as the home of the most rabid religious and political intolerance perhaps in the whole Christian world; it was designated by the comprehensive title of the 'Black North.' But it was not always so. In the days of 1798 the most stubborn resistance to the success of the English forces was made in Ulster. It was Ulster Presbyterians who, banished from Ireland by laws that worked oppression without regard to religion, gave to the American Revolution its most steadfast counsellors and some of its best generals and bravest soldiers. It was among Ulster Presbyterians that the foundation was laid of the association known as the United Irishmen, who formed, up to the days of Fenianism, the most formidable conspiracy against English rule. In more modern times Ulster Presbyterians formed one of the strongest elements of the Tenant Right Party. It is true that, in the course of time, the Presbyterians forgot the more robust faith of their ancestors, were in some instances carried away by the tide of religious bigotry, and in a large degree lapsed to the ignoble compromise of Whiggery; but at all times in the history of Ulster the Catholics formed nearly a half of the entire population. These Catholics were Nationalists to a man; and, living in the midst of a population which the law permitted to insult, to persecute, and often to murder them with perfect impunity, they held to their faith with a fervour unknown in the almost exclusively Catholic parts of the country. But the landlords belonged to the anti-Nationalist Party; the boards were all manned by members of the anti-Nationalist Party; the occupants of the Bench were gathered from the ranks of an organization sworn to persecution and hatred of the Catholics; and, finally, under a restricted franchise, the Parliamentary representatives were taken exclusively from the two English parties. Under these circumstances the National Party in Ulster still remained inarticulate, and Ulster continued to present to the outside world a solid front of fierce antagonism to everything Irish and National.

After the Monaghan election the Ulster Nationalists decided that they should hold meetings in different parts of the country for the purpose of preparing for the General Election by establishing registration associations. The object was unquestionably legitimate and even praiseworthy. It was in the highest sense legal, and these meetings were organized and upheld by something like 48 per cent. of the population generally in Ulster, and in some of the counties where the meetings were to be held, by 70 per cent. of the population. The meetings, which were protested against by Orangemen as an invasion, were summoned, among other places, for the County of Cavan, and Cavan, both in the election of 1880 and in the last two elections, returned two National representatives; in Monaghan, and Monaghan is now represented by two National members; in Tyrone, and two out of four seats in Tyrone are represented by Nationalists; in Fermanagh, and the two seats in Fermanagh are represented by two Nationalists; in Newry, and the return of a Nationalist in Newry was not even opposed. The statistics of population show with equal clearness the impudence of the Orange claim. In Strabane, where a meeting was called, out of the total population of 4,196, 2,720 are Catholics, and there are only 693 of the Episcopalian Protestants, from whom Orangeism is largely recruited, and 685 Presbyterians. Out of the entire population of 5,231 in Pomeroy, 3,537 are Catholics, 734 Episcopalian Protestants, and 892 Presbyterians. Out of the entire population of Castle Derg, 3,748 are Catholics, 940 Episcopalian Protestants, and 505 Presbyterians. And, finally, out of the entire population of 6,069 in Rosslea, where there was a most violent attempt to break up the Nationalist meeting, 4,394 are Catholics, 1,357 Protestant Episcopalians, and 258 Presbyterians.[1]

The landlords resolved to make a last desperate effort for the preservation of their power, and organized a movement perhaps as wicked and as shameful as any known to the modern history of Ireland. They openly proclaimed that they would put down, by force of arms if necessary, these meetings of their fellow-citizens. They organized bodies which had all the appurtenances as well as the spirit of armies. Wherever a Nationalist meeting was arranged they organized a counter-demonstration. Their followers went to these demonstrations as heavily armed as if they were marching to the field of battle, and the orators of the day made speeches openly inciting to wholesale murder.

'With no uncertain sound,' said an Orange placard published in Omagh, 'compel the rebel conspirators to return to their haunts in the south and west, and under a guard of military and police, as in Dungannon on Thursday.'[2] 'It was a great pity,' said Lord Rossmore, 'that the so-called Government of England stopped loyal men from assembling to uphold their institutions here, and had sent down a handful of soldiers whom they could eat up in a second or two if they thought fit.'[3] 'The Orangemen,' said Captain Barton, 'if they liked, could be the Government themselves. . . . He only wished they were allowed, and they could soon drive the rebels, like Parnell and his followers, out of their sight.'[4] Major Saunderson wondered 'why those rebels abused the police and soldiers; only for them, where would they have been in Dungannon? They would have been in the nearest river (cheers), and at Omagh and Aughnacloy they would have been in the same place.'[5] The Rev. Mr. Jagoe 'would conclude by telling them what John Dillon, another rebel, said in a speech in the House of Commons, and which he took from a report in the *Freeman's Journal*, and which he had in his pocket: "That he would advise the people to shoot down every Protestant in Ireland." (Groans, and cries of "We'll shoot them.")'[6] 'Theirs was no aggressive party,' exclaimed Mr. Murray Ker, D.L. . . . 'Let there be no revolver practice.' (Cheers.) 'His advice to them about revolvers was, never use a revolver except they were firing at some one.' (Laughter and cheers.)[7] 'If the Government,' said Lord Claud Hamilton, 'fail to prevent Mr. Parnell and Co. from making inroads into Ulster . . . if they do not prevent those hordes of ruffians from invading us, we will take the law into our own hands, and we ourselves will.'[8] 'Keep the cartridge in the rifle,' said Colonel King-Harman at Rathmines.'[9] 'Keep a firm grip on your sticks,' said Mr. Archdale at Dromore.[10] The

---

[1] 'Loyalty plus Murder,' p. 10. By Mr. T. M. Healy, M.P.
[2] *Ibid.*, p. 7. [3] *Ibid.*, p. 18. [4] *Ibid.*, p. 22.
[5] *Ibid.*, p. 23. [6] *Ibid.* [7] *Ibid.*, p. 41.
[8] *Ibid.*, p. 42. [9] *Ibid.*, title-page. [10] *Ibid.*

Daily Express, the organ of law and order and of the landlords, whose editor is the well-known Dr. Patton, Dublin correspondent of the *Times*, filled its columns with direct incitements to murder which would have landed, and justly landed, a Nationalist editor in penal servitude.

'This new attempt (it wrote of the Nationalist meetings in Ulster) . . . will be repelled, and the hireling disturbers of the peace of Ulster hurled back ignominiously from the frontier by the loyal men of Fermanagh. . . . They have at length aroused a spirit in the north which will no longer submit to insult. The alarm is sounded, and the determination of the Loyalists of the country expressed in another column. It is a warning which they will do well to respect. Let them call it a threat if they choose. There it is to be read and pondered. It is no time to quibble about words. The meaning is clear and plain, and the men to whom it is addressed do not shrink from the avowal of their final determination. They plainly tell the disturbers of the peace . . . that they are determined to take effectual measures to put a stop to every attempt to disseminate pernicious doctrines in their midst.'[1]

Commenting on the death of an unfortunate creature named Giffen, who was killed by the police at Dromore, the same organ wrote:

'As it was, the fact that a couple of men on the Loyalist side were wounded with lances or bayonets is most unlucky. The men may have misbehaved, they may have deserved what they got, but it is very painful to the feelings of all people to find the Queen's troops charging and cutting down even rioters *who are urged on to riot by loyalty.*'[2]

When at last he found that these outrages could no longer be permitted, Lord Spencer took active measures. Police shorthand writers were sent to some of the Orange, as previously they had been sent to all of the Nationalist meetings, and the peers and the deputy lieutenants and the magistrates at once abandoned the tone of murderous incitement. A body of police was ordered to prevent the breaking up of a meeting by Orange rowdies, and the rowdies, of course, flew pell-mell before the first charge of the police. There never was a movement so blustering and so cruel that vanished with such rapidity before the first show of determination on the part of the Government. Under a National Government such a movement would be almost unimaginable.[3]

---

[1] 'Loyalty plus Murder,' pp. 32, 33.   [2] *Ibid.*, p. 53.

[3] It is well to quote Sir George Trevelyan's description of the character and purpose of the Orange counter-demonstrations: 'Unfortunately, however, the counter-demonstrations of the Orangemen were, to a great extent, demonstrations of bodies of armed men. At their last meeting at Dromore *sackfuls of revolvers were left behind close to the place of meeting.* The reason that they were so left was that a shrewd and energetic officer who was present was seen to search the Orangemen as they came along. The Orange meetings, therefore, were bodies of armed men, many of whom came prepared to use their arms; some of them prepared to make a murderous attack upon the Nationalists.' ('No! No!') 'So far as the Government knew, it was not the custom of the Nationalists to go armed to their meetings until the bad example was set by the Orangemen.' (Hansard, vol. cclxxxiv., p. 383.) And here is his description of the state to which the Orange firebrands had brought Ulster: 'In spite of the fact that Ulster was full of armed men, who were excited to an extreme degree by the violent speeches of their leaders; that every hand brandished a cudgel; that tens of thousands of revolvers were being carried about; and that the leaders of the men were telling them to take a firm grip of their sticks, and not to fire their pistols except when they were certain of hitting somebody, the winter had so far passed with no great or striking disaster.' (*Ibid.*, p. 384.)

This was the last effort of ascendency in Ireland. In the next Session of Parliament the Irish masses were offered for the first time in all their history an opportunity of being truly represented in an Imperial Parliament. To the acquisition of their rights by their countrymen the Irish Tory Party offered a frantic resistance, but Sir Stafford Northcote and several other leaders of the party refused to join in the demand for excluding Ireland. Mr. Chaplin proposed an amendment the object of which was to exclude Ireland from the franchise. He was able to quote in favour of his proposition the words of the Marquis of Hartington—not more than twelve months old—which described this very measure—the measure which the Liberal Government, with the Marquis of Hartington as one of its members, were now bringing in—as an act little short of madness. But his arguments fell, as he knew, upon deaf ears; and after the House had listened for nearly half an hour to his speech, he ran away from his own amendment.[1] Mr. Brodrick, who, though sitting for an English constituency, is the son of an Irish landlord, rushed in where English Tories feared to tread, proposed a similar amendment, was backed again by all the forces of the Irish landlord party, and, having foolishly given a pledge at the beginning of his speech that he would go to a division, was compelled to test the opinion of the House. The attempt to deprive Ireland of her rights was rejected by 332 to 137—probably the largest majority ever recorded in favour of an extension of popular liberties.

The next attack upon the rights of Ireland was upon the question as to whether she should retain her 103 seats. Mr. Forster brought forward the reduction in her population—a reduction caused by evil land laws and the Act of Union—as a reason why she should be less potent in the future for protecting her rights against the more powerful nation. He set down the number of representatives to which Ireland was entitled as eighty-one.[2] In this crusade against Ireland Mr. Forster found a willing ally in Mr. Goschen. When the second reading of the Franchise Bill was proposed, Mr. Goschen asked whether the number of Irish seats was to be reduced, and emphatically declared that if no guarantee were given by the Ministry on this point he would be compelled to vote against the measure. But neither the Irish landlords, nor Mr. Forster, nor Mr. Goschen could prevail against the forces which had now been arrayed on the side of Ireland, and amid the practically universal assent of the House of Commons, Mr. Gladstone announced, on introducing the Redistribution Bill, that Ireland was to retain the full measure of her seats. In Ireland itself, meantime, other victories had followed. The nominal Home Rulers, at the time of their secession, were loaded with the praises of English Ministers, and were described by the English press as the real representatives of Irish feeling, and upright, outspoken, and reasonable men. They belonged, as everybody in Ireland knew, and the people of England were taught to ignore, to the class of office-seekers, the analysis of whose mischievous influence forms so large a portion of this volume. In due time they sought for the rewards of their treason; the result in every case was their replacement by men pledged to the National principles, to the leadership of Mr. Parnell, and to entire co-operation with the Irish Party. Mr. O'Shaughnessy, promoted to the Registrarship of Petty Sessions Clerks, was succeeded by Mr. MacMahon. Mr. P. J. Smyth, made Secretary of the Loan Fund, was succeeded by Mr. John O'Connor. Two other constituencies, whose names occur in the shameful and painful record of the days when Rabagas was

---

[1] Hansard, vol. ccliii., p. 1080.   [2] *Times*, March 1, 1884.

supreme, joined as heartily as the other constituencies of the country in returning National representatives. Mr. Kenny, opposed by a Conservative in Ennis, a town which formerly had the shame of having elected Lord Fitzgerald, had been returned by an overwhelming majority. Athlone, which must be irrevocably associated with the name and the treason of Judge Keogh, returned Mr. Justin Huntly McCarthy without a contest. Thus Ireland proved its solid unity.

CHAPTER XIII.

THE TORY-PARNELL COMBINATION.

THROUGHOUT the whole Parliament of 1880 to 1885, the Tories and the Irish Party acted in close combination, except when the Government was proposing coercion. On coercion the Tories and the Parnellites parted company, for when a Liberal Government proposed coercion, it was filching a Tory policy, and naturally found Tory support. But even on coercion there was some joint action. Lord Randolph Churchill, it is known, began making his political career in the Parliament of 1880, as leader of a small band of Tory obstructionists who came to be known as the Fourth Party. The Irish members were, doubtless, in orthodox Conservative eyes, a disreputable lot; but to a young ambitious aspirant, they might be made useful, and for five years it was the central note of Lord Randolph Churchill's whole political action to maintain the most close and the most friendly relations with the Irish members. He gave the first indication of this policy on the Coercion Bill of Mr. Forster. He did not dare to openly oppose it, but he threw cold water upon it, and when it was about to pass its third reading, after the fierce conflict which has already been described, he made a speech which he himself described as giving the Bill 'a parting kick.' This attitude he maintained throughout the whole Parliament, and afterwards, as will be seen.

The Irish Party, on the other hand, were quite ready to accept this alliance. The Liberal Government had proposed coercion, and had carried it out with vigour. Coercion is the negation of the equality of Irish citizenhood; and therefore the Irish Party were bound to resist, and, if possible, destroy any and every Government which carried coercion. It was quite true that between the Liberals and the Irish Party there was absolute agreement on nine questions out of ten outside the Irish Question, and it was with no feeling of satisfaction, but in obedience to the sternest sense of duty, that the Irish members took up an attitude of hostility to the Liberal leaders. In fact, the position of the two parties was in many respects similar. Coercion to the Liberal leaders—or at least to some of them—was 'an odious and a hateful incident,' but they felt bound to propose it. To the Irish Party hostility to the democratic forces of this country was an odious and a hateful, but also a necessary, incident in the work of emancipating their country.

Whether wise or unwise, however, the fact remains that the Irish Party acted in strict combination with the Tory Party throughout the whole Parliament of 1880. In every great division the two parties voted solidly together, and every victory which stirred Tory hearts and menaced the Liberal Ministry was won by the help of the Irish vote, and would have been impossible without that help. Let us run rapidly through the chief divisions of the Parliament. According to a Liberal organ,[1] the strength of the different parties at the beginning of the Parliament of 1880 was: Liberals, 350; Conservatives, 238; Home Rulers, 64. There must be one slight correction made in this; the number of Home Rulers was but 63. The mistake of the *Daily News* probably arose from the fact that it classed Mr. Whitworth as a Home Ruler, because Mr. Whitworth had made promises so studiously ambiguous as to leave him free to be regarded either as an orthodox English Liberal or a sound Irish Nationalist. Under the circumstances let Mr. Whitworth pass into the Liberal camp. The figures then should stand: Liberals, 351; Conservatives, 238; Home Rulers, 63. Thus the Liberals had a majority over the Conservatives of 113, counting 226 on a division, and the Liberals had over the Conservatives and Home Rulers combined a majority of 50, counting 100 on a division. But, as everybody knows, the Home Rulers did not remain a united party. From almost the start of the Parliament of 1880 they divided into two bodies—those who sat with the Liberal Ministers and generally supported them, and those who, following the example of Mr. Parnell, sat on the Opposition benches and generally acted as a portion of the regular Opposition to the Ministry. Dividing the Irish representation according to these different sections, it stood thus: Irish Liberals, 14; Irish Conservatives, 25; Home Rulers, 37; Nominal Home Rulers, 26.[2] This makes a total of 102; the remaining member, the Rev. Isaac Nelson, could not be counted as a supporter of any section; after a few appearances in the House he disappeared to Belfast, and neither entreaty, nor threat, nor duty could ever attract him therefrom again during the entire Parliament. Of the 26 Nominal Home Rulers, the Liberal Party could count in every political division on the support of at least 23 (exclusive of Mr. Bellingham and Sir J. Ennis, who usually voted with the Conservatives, and Captain O'Shea, who in Irish divisions usually voted with the Irish Party). These 23, therefore, must be taken from the Home Rule total of 63, and added to the Liberal total of 351; and the struggle then was between a Liberal Party with a nominal strength of 374, and an Opposition consisting of 238 Conservatives and 37 Home Rulers—374 against 275, or a majority of 101 over the combined Opposition.

Bearing these figures always in mind, let us see how they worked out on a few great political divisions. In 1882 there was a division on the Clôture. The Ministry, with a majority of 101 over all Oppositions combined, escaped by a majority of 39. On May 12, 1884, a vote of want of confidence was proposed in the Egyptian policy of the Ministry. The division took place on May 13: the Irish members voted in a body against the Government, and the result was that the Ministerial majority sank to 28.

In 1885 a Conservative had been replaced by a Home Ruler in Athlone and a Liberal by a Home Ruler in Monaghan. But altogether there had been no very great change in the strength of the different sections. The number added to the Irish Party was altogether seven, raising their strength to forty-four; and the number lost by the Liberals altogether was but three, and these must be further reduced to two, because they had succeeded in returning Mr. Sinclair in the place of Mr. Chaine for County Antrim. On February 27, 1885, a division took place on a vote of censure

[1] Supplement to the *Daily News*, December 24, 1885.
[2] The epithet 'nominal' was first applied to these gentlemen by Mr. Gladstone in his Leeds speech of October, 1881. The phrase was immediately taken up in Ireland, and became at once not only an appellation but an epitaph.

proposed on the conduct of the Government in reference to General Gordon. The Irish members voted in a body against the Government, and the Ministerial majority was reduced to 14. On May 13, 1885, the Prime Minister rose and made the announcement that the Government intended to propose the re-enactment of 'certain valuable and equitable' provisions of the Crimes Act of 1882. Nothing further was done until the night of Friday, June 5, when Mr. Gladstone announced that on the following Thursday the new Coercion Bill would be introduced. But on Monday, June 8, came the division on the second reading of the Budget Bill. The general public probably did not know that on that night the apparently invincible Government were in any danger; but shrewd onlookers had smelt the danger from afar, and knew that the night would probably seal the fate of the Ministry.

The Irish members had little doubt as to the course they should take; but if they had any doubt, the Tories had taken care to remove it. Lord Randolph Churchill was again prominent in forecasting the necessity of an alliance between his party and the party of Mr. Parnell. Before Mr. Gladstone finally agreed to propose the renewal of some of the clauses of the Crimes Act, there was, as everybody knows, a struggle inside the Cabinet, Mr. Chamberlain, Sir Charles Dilke and Mr. Shaw-Lefevre leading the hostility to coercion. In the very midst of this struggle Lord Randolph Churchill made a speech in the St. Stephen's Club, strongly denouncing the idea of renewing coercion. He began by the statement that he was 'shocked' that the announcement of a renewal of coercion had been 'received very much as a matter of course.' 'I lay this down,' he went on, 'without any hesitation, as an absolute and unimpeachable constitutional doctrine, that while any British Government may reasonably, and with perfect confidence, apply to Parliament in times of great popular disorder for exceptional and unconstitutional powers, at the same time, when that popular disorder has passed away, the Government is bound by the highest considerations of public policy and of constitutional doctrine to return to and to rely on the ordinary law.' Then he proceeded to explain the state of circumstances which ought to exist to justify the announcement of the Government. 'It means,' he said, 'that her Majesty's Government have terrible facts, terrible evidence to adduce to Parliament in support of their demand as to the real condition of Ireland. It means that the Government will tell you that the hearts of the Irish people are full of treason, that everywhere in Ireland there are bands of assassins and midnight marauders, and of desperate men who may be controlled by no ordinary law, lying in wait ready to burst forth into malignant life and malevolent activity. It means that these desperadoes will enjoy to a great extent the sympathy of the Irish people.' But no such state of things existed in the opinion of Lord Randolph Churchill. 'The published returns presented to Parliament,' he declared, 'showed no abnormal amount of crime.' And thus he wound up his assault on the policy of the Government. 'This demand for peculiar penal laws for Ireland at the present moment would be an act in the highest degree impolitic unless supported by overwhelming and overpowering evidence which no one could resist. Because what has been the attitude of Parliament in the last year? Parliament has just enfranchised considerably over half a million of the Irish people, and has declared them capable citizens fit to take part in the Government of this empire. In a few months these new voters will exercise their rights for the first time. Now, I ask you, would it not have been well, would it not have been hopeful, would it not have been cheering, if you could have tried to put some kind thoughts towards England into their minds by using the last days of this unlucky Parliament to abrogate all that harsh legislation which is so odious to Englishmen, and which undoubtedly abridges the freedom and insults the dignity of a sensitive and an imaginative race? How do you suppose all these 700,000 new electors will go to the poll? What thoughts will they have in their minds? Will they not go to the poll with the knowledge that the Parliament of England in its last dying days, in a moment when they were unrepresented who had been declared to be capable citizens, had given them what they will think a parting kick.'[1]

Such a speech pretty plainly indicated that Lord Randolph Churchill would oppose the coercive proposals of the existing Government, and that if he had any voice in the policy of the next Tory Government—and everybody knew that he was bound to have a potent voice—there would be no coercion from the Tory Government either. But with even so strong an assumption, the cautious and realistic leader of the Irish Party was not satisfied; and the Irish members did not go into the lobby to vote against a Liberal Ministry about to propose coercion until there was an assurance, definite, distinct, unmistakable, that there would be no coercion from their successors. It was under these circumstances that the momentous division of June 8, 1885, was taken. 'It was only,' I wrote in a description of the historic scene immediately after its occurrence, 'as the division was approaching its end that some suspicion of the truth began to dawn upon the Tories. At once a state of unusual and fierce excitement supervened. Lord Randolph Churchill was particularly vehement. It was seen that the stream from the Government lobby was getting thinner, while that from the Opposition was still flowing in full tide; and each successive Tory, as he got into the House, was almost torn to pieces as he was asked what was his number. There were hoarse whispers, and eager demands, and a slight and tremulous cheer. But it was too soon as yet to give way to a joy that might be premature. At last certainty began to come in thickening signs. Lord Kensington walked to the table from the Government lobby and stated the numbers to the clerk. This was almost decisive, as it showed the exhaustion of the numbers of the Government; and here were the Conservatives still coming in. The number of the Government was now known to be 252, and the great question was whether the Conservatives had beaten this. It was soon known that 252 had been beaten, and then the floodgates were opened. Lord Randolph Churchill was the leader of the uproar; and Gavroche celebrating a victory at the barricades, or an old Eton boy triumphing over success at football, could not have been more juvenile in the extravagance of his joy. He took up his hat and began to move it madly, and soon he had actually got up and was standing on his seat, and from this point of vantage kept waving his hat. Some younger Tories sitting beside him imitated this mad example and waved their hats.'[2] Here we have the Tories rejoicing over a victory which was obtained for them by the Irish vote; and in a very few days afterwards they were enjoying the spoils of office which the same Irish vote had bestowed upon them.

Lord Salisbury succeeded to Mr. Gladstone. Lord Randolph Churchill was Secretary for India, and Sir William Dyke was sent as Chief Secretary to Ireland. The new Tory Cabinet honourably and promptly fulfilled their

[1] *Times*, May 21, 1885.   [2] 'Gladstone's House of Commons.' pp. 553, 554.

engagements to the allies who had brought them into office. Coercion was at once dropped. A still more difficult demand was soon after made. There was a strong feeling in Ireland that Myles Joyce—one of the men hanged for participation in the hideous Maamtrasna massacre—was innocent, and also some others who were still in penal servitude. Several times during the existence of the Ministry of Mr. Gladstone an attempt had been made to have the question reopened; but the Government had always steadily refused. The attempt was renewed when there came the change of Administration. The position of the new Government was very difficult. The acceptance of the Irish demand meant the throwing over of Lord Spencer; and Lord Spencer had carried out the policy of coercion in Ireland with an energy and courage that had won him the admiration of all Englishmen. But the Government had no choice; they promised an inquiry. It was not for the Irish Party to condemn the Tory Administration for doing their work; but Englishmen generally joined in the condemnation of this vile abandonment of principle and this shameful desertion of the brave Englishman who had passed for years through hourly risk of his life, a fierceness of attack, a universality of popular hate, more killing than even the assassin's knife. A burst of indignation came from all sides, and even so tepid a Liberal as Mr. Goschen was provoked into excited comment on the 'Maamtrasna alliance.' Soon after, the new Government gave a further proof of their resolve to please the Irish members. The plan of the Irish Party for the settlement of the Irish Land Question has always been peasant proprietary. At the first conference of the Land League—that much-abused body—peasant proprietary, and peasant proprietary by purchase, was set forth as the proper solution. It is worth while reproducing here the programme of a body that has been represented as proposing nothing but confiscation and plunder. This was the programme of the Land League:

'To carry out the permanent reform of land tenure, we propose the creation of a Department or Commission of Land Administration for Ireland. This Department would be invested with ample powers to deal with all questions relating to land in Ireland. (1) Where the landlord and tenant of any holding had agreed for the sale to the tenant of the said holding, the Department would execute the necessary conveyance to the tenant, and advance him the whole or part of the purchase-money; and upon such advance being made by the Department, such holding would be deemed to be charged with an annuity of £5 for every £100 of such advance, and so in proportion for any less sum, such annuity to be limited in favour of the Department, and to be declared to be repayable in the term of thirty-five years.

'(2) When a tenant tendered to the landlord for the purchase of his holding a sum equal to twenty years of the Poor Law valuation thereof, the Department would execute the conveyance of the said holding to the tenant, and would be empowered to advance to the tenant the whole or any part of the purchase-money, the repayment of which would be secured as set forth in the case of voluntary sales.

'(3) The Department would be empowered to acquire the ownership of any estate upon tendering to the owner thereof a sum equal to twenty years of the Poor Law valuation of such estate, and to let said estate to the tenants at a rent equal to $3\frac{1}{2}$ per cent. of the purchase-money thereof.

'(4) The Department of the Court having jurisdiction in this matter would be empowered to determine the rights and priorities of the several persons entitled to, or having charges upon, or otherwise interested in, any holding conveyed as above mentioned, and would distribute the purchase-money in accordance with such rights and priorities; and when any moneys arising from a sale were not immediately distributed, the Department would have a right to invest the said moneys for the benefit of the parties entitled thereto. Provision would be made whereby the Treasury would from time to time advance to the Department such sums of money as would be required for the purchases above mentioned.'

These proposals were made as far back as 1880. It is scarcely necessary to say that they encountered fierce opposition and denunciation from the British press. 'They were,' said the *Times*,[1] 'clearly confiscation, pure and undisguised.' These also were the proposals which were put forward by the Irish Party when the Land Question was taken up by Mr. Gladstone. They were rejected at that time, with the result that they were taken up by all parties at a later period. It has been seen that Mr. W. H. Smith, in 1882, proposed a resolution which demanded exactly the same settlement for the Land Question as had been demanded by the Land League in 1880. In the excitement caused by the assassination in Phœnix Park, coupled with the Crimes Act, the question was then dropped; but on June 12 of the following year it was once more taken up, and on this occasion the sponsor of the Land League settlement of the Irish Land Question was no less a person than Lord George Hamilton, a leader among the Conservatives, and the son of an Irish landlord. One English journal at least appreciated the significance of this appropriation of Land League doctrines by Conservative leaders and by Parliament generally; for the motion of Lord George practically commanded universal assent.

In 1884 Mr. Trevelyan brought forward a Bill the principle of which was the principle of the Land League; but the measure proposed was so impracticable that the Bill was still-born. In 1885 the Government showed no signs of touching the question, and Irish members had despaired of seeing any attempt to make even the beginning of its settlement. But the change of Administration produced on the Land Question, as well as on the question of coercion, a surprising transformation of the political prospect. The Conservatives had scarcely got into office when Lord Ashbourne—as Mr. Gibson had become—brought in a Bill of a more practical character, and in a comparatively short time the Bill passed into law, and the programme of the Land League, five years after its publication, and with all the savage and dread incidents crowded into the dreary interval, was embodied in the statute-book of England.

It was in Ireland, however, that the Government gave the most eloquent proofs of its changing spirit. Lord Carnarvon, a Conservative of kindly temper and Liberal views, was sent as Viceroy. Owing to the change in the policy of the Goverment, he was able to dispense with the dragoons and foot-soldiers and police, and to go unattended through the country and among the people. His reception everywhere, if not cordial, was at least not hostile. In the loneliest parts of the country he found himself perfectly safe from blow or from insult; and, to make the transformation which the change of Government had produced in Ireland dramatically complete, on one occasion he was driven through the country by Bryan Kilmartin, a man who, having been sentenced to penal servitude for life, had been released on his innocence being clearly proved. Crime at the same time sank

[1] May 5, 1881.

to almost infinitesimal proportions. The sympathy which it was able to command when innocent and guilty were alike oppressed and harried, was denied now that the country was once more free. The severity of the agrarian crisis was mitigated by the reductions which good landlords made voluntarily and bad landlords made in obedience to pressure from the Government and to organization as firmly knit as the trades' unions which extort fair wages and honourable treatment for English workmen; and the bitterness which had sprung up between the peoples of England and Ireland became in some degree at least softened. In this mood the Irish people approached the great turning-point in their history, and entered upon the general election of 1885.

The incidents of the election were but too well calculated to maintain the confidence which the Irish Party had in the good intentions of the Tory Ministers and the Tory Party. There could not be the smallest mistake as to the demands of the Irish Party; and, indeed, if the consistent pursuit of the same policy for years had not been sufficient to teach the Tories what the Irishmen really wanted, there was a distinct and outspoken utterance at the very beginning of the electoral campaign. At a banquet given in his honour in Dublin, Mr. Parnell declared that the time had come when the Irish Party should put forward one plank, and one only, in its platform; and that that plank was Home Rule. This was a challenge to English statesmen; and so it was interpreted by more than one of them. Mr. Chamberlain met Mr. Parnell's demand with a negative which surprised very much all those who had made themselves acquainted with his antecedents and his previous utterances upon the question of Irish self-government. His attitude, however, whether inconsistent or not with previous utterances, was clear, and, moreover, invited clearness on the part of others. To Lord Randolph Churchill he issued a challenge over and over again to declare whether he agreed with or accepted the views of Mr. Parnell, but Lord Randolph Churchill held his peace. Mr. Parnell's views might mean, as Mr. Chamberlain asserted, separation, dismemberment, the oppression of Ulster: Lord Randolph Churchill refused to utter one word against them. It was evident that the Tory leaders desired to keep themselves entirely free on the question of Home Rule, so as to be able, when the elections were over, to take the course which the fortunes of the ballot-box might dictate.

The Irish leaders were not alone in placing this interpretation upon the attitude of Lord Randolph Churchill and the other Tory leaders. The Tory candidates throughout the country took the hint, and acted accordingly. In a large number of cases either the scruples of conscience or the determination to avoid any form of inconvenient pledge, induced the Tory candidate not to say one word on the Irish Question. Indeed, an examination of the Tory addresses at the election of 1885 will reveal the astonishing fact that in, if not the majority, at least almost the majority of them, there was no mention whatever of the burning question of Home Rule. This was especially the case in constituencies where, there being an Irish vote, the Tory candidate was anxious, while leaving himself unpledged, at the same time not to say anything which would estrange an Irish elector. The Houghton-le-Spring division of Durham contains a large number of Irish voters. The Irish voters had resolved to support the Tory candidate, and Colonel Nicholas Wood accordingly did not say a word about Ireland. In the West Toxteth Division of Liverpool there is a considerable Irish vote, and the Irish voters had resolved to support the Tory candidate, and Mr.

Royden in return left them to draw their own conclusions as to his Irish policy by not even mentioning the name of Ireland. In other districts bolder spirits not only mentioned Ireland, but came forward with a programme which might be developed into an adoption of Home Rule. Candidate after candidate pledged himself to the support of an extension of local self-government, and an extension of local self-government is a vague term which might dwindle down to a mere extension of county government, or might be enlarged to such a scheme of Home Rule as that proposed by Mr. Gladstone. But this same class of candidates were still more outspoken in their denunciation of coercion ; and, indeed, it was largely on the cry of coercion or no coercion that the Tories fought the General Election of 1885. 'I would give,' said Sir Frederick Milner, the Conservative candidate for York, 'to the Irish every privilege which is extended to the other inhabitants of Great Britain. I am in favour of a measure for the extension of local self-government, and am of opinion that we ought to do our utmost to encourage and develop Irish industries, and to promote the welfare and happiness of her people.' 'I cordially approve,' said Major Dixon, the Conservative candidate for Middlesboro', 'of the conduct of the present Government in not renewing the Crimes Act in Ireland, and hope to see other coercive measures also abandoned ; and I shall be prepared to support any well-devised scheme for giving to Ireland a large amount of self-government.' 'At home, what do we find!' exclaimed Mr. Hammond, the Conservative candidate for Newcastle-on-Tyne. 'Our sister kingdom—Ireland—ruled with the iron rod of coercion.' 'To Ireland,' said Mr. Cumming Macdonald, the Conservative candidate for the Chesterfield Division of Derbyshire, 'I would continue to hold out, with the Conservative Party, the olive-branch of peace, conscious that in times past she has suffered many wrongs.'

In Hyde, Manchester, the Irish electors were asked to 'vote for Flattely ; no Coercion ;' similar placards were posted over Leeds in the interest of Mr. Dawson, the Tory candidate. 'I have declared myself,' said Mr. Jennings, the Tory member for Stockport, when tasked in Parliament with his attitude at the November election of 1885, 'in favour of a Liberal measure of local self-government for Ireland. I have expressed myself as being opposed to Coercion Bills, and such Bills I have said I never would vote for; and I never will.' The name of Mr. Jennings has since appeared in the divisions on the Coercion Bill of the present Government; but that does not alter his own statement as to his attitude during the election of 1885. In one of the Metropolitan constituencies Mr. Wilfrid Blunt stood as an avowed and advanced Home Ruler, and at the same time as a member of the Tory Party. The relation between the two parties, the Irish Nationalists and the Tories, were even more intimate in private than in public. The Tory candidates paid all the expense of printing all the documents of the National League in Bolton, and the money appears in the official return of the election expenses of the two Tory members. At the Flint Burghs I heard the Tory candidate speak to a meeting of Irish Nationalists after I had concluded my own speech. In North Kensington, Sir Roper Lethbridge followed his return as Tory member by paying a visit to a branch of the National League in his constituency and thanking them for his return ; in Kennington, Mr. Gent Davis, the Tory member, declared to one of his Irish electors that if he were ever to vote for coercion the Irishmen would be at liberty to break his windows.

There had, however, been more important evidences of the prevalent opinion of the Tory Party at this crisis. Before finally making up his mind as to what direction the Irish vote ought to go in England, Mr. Parnell had held an interview with Lord Carnarvon. At this interview Mr. Parnell was given by Lord Carnarvon to understand 'that the Conservative Party, if they should be successful at the polls, would offer Ireland a statutory Legislature, with a right to protect her own industries, and that this would be coupled with the settlement of the Irish Land Question on the basis of purchase on a larger scale than that now proposed by the Prime Minister.'[1]

Under all these circumstances it was the conviction of the Irish leaders, and it is their conviction still, that if the Tories had been returned with a small majority, in such numbers as to enable them with the support of the Irish Party to seriously defeat the Liberals, they would have introduced a good measure of Home Rule. And the introduction of such a measure by a Tory Government would have had many advantages over its introduction by a Liberal Ministry, even with so potent a leader as Mr. Gladstone. It is the universal moral of English history that the Tories can pass large and almost revolutionary measures of reform with less difficulty than can Liberals the most modest measures of reform. The reasons are simple and open to every eye. The Tory Government proposing reform is free from obstacles in both Houses of Parliament. In the House of Commons, instead of finding hostility and obstruction to reform from the Liberal Opposition, it receives encouragement and support; and the House of Lords, which would not pass the smallest measure of reform proposed by a Liberal Minister, unless he be backed by revolutionary excitement, swallows any reform, however large, which is backed by a Tory Premier. It is therefore certain, if the Tories had proposed Home Rule after the General Election of 1885, that Ireland would be at the present moment self-governed, and England be spared all the tumult, unrest, delay of urgently needed reform, and all the thousand and one other inconveniences that accompany the present disastrous struggle.

Under the influence of these views the Irish leaders recommended the Irish electors to vote for the Tory candidates, and with considerable effect. In nearly every one of the constituencies where the Irish formed a strong voting power, the Tory candidates were returned.

In Ireland meantime the Irish Party had carried all before it, even beyond the expectation of its most sanguine friends.

A fund had been collected—mostly, it may be assumed, by Englishmen whose venom was greater than their intelligence—for the purpose of supporting so-called Loyalist candidates for the different Irish constituencies. The story is told that Mr. Forster was one of the gentlemen engaged in bringing this statesmanlike enterprise to fruition. The story ought to be true, for the reason that it would crown all his preceding success in bringing about in Ireland the very exact opposite to that which he desired, and by his expedients strengthening and rendering omnipotent the forces he most detested. For these were some of the results of the starting of Loyalist candidates: In South Cork, the Loyalist candidate polled 195 votes; the Nationalist 4,820. In Mid Cork the Loyalist polled 106, the Nationalist 5,033. In North Kilkenny the Loyalist polled 174, the

---

[1] Speech of Mr. Parnell on the second reading of the Government of Ireland Bill, *Times*, June 8. Lord Carnarvon denied some points in this statement in the House of Lords next day. Anybody who reads the denial carefully will see it is in reality a confirmation.

Nationalist 4,084. In West Mayo the Loyalist polled 131, the Nationalist 4,790. In South Mayo the Loyalist polled 75, the Nationalist 4,900. In East Kerry the Loyalist polled 30 votes, the Nationalist 3,169. In the North of Ireland alone did any contest take place in which the National Party did not win by overwhelming odds. In Derry City Sir C. E. Lewis defeated Mr. Justin McCarthy out of a poll of 3,619, by 29 votes. In West Belfast Mr. Sexton was beaten with a small majority of 35 on a poll of 7,523. In North Tyrone an energetic fight was made by Mr. John Dillon, but he was defeated by a majority of 423. Mr. Healy won South Derry, though the Catholics are in a minority of some thousands in the population and in a minority of some hundreds on the electorate. In South Tyrone, likewise, Protestant farmers enabled Mr. William O'Brien to beat the candidate of the landlords. This gave the Irish Nationalists 17 out of 33 seats in Ulster, thus bringing the 'Black North,' as it used to be called, into line with the rest of the country in demanding self-government. The final result was that the Irish Party fought eighty-nine contests in Ireland and were successful in eighty-five. They had besides won one seat in England, the Scotland Division of Liverpool, and their entire strength then at the end of the election was eighty-six men. Four of these had been elected for two constituencies. Of the eighty-two elected twenty-two were put in gaol by Mr. Forster, warrants were issued against four others, and there were in the number a '48 convict, a '67 convict, and a '67 suspect.

Meantime, everybody in England acknowledged the important aid which the Irish Party had given to the Tory candidates.

'Fair Trade may have deluded a few,' said Mr. Gladstone, commenting on the borough elections while speaking in Flintshire on behalf of Lord Richard Grosvenor, 'as Free Trade has blessed the many, but that has not been the main cause. . . . The main cause is the Irish vote.'[1] 'They' (meaning the Tories),[2] he wrote to the Midlothian electors, 'know that but for the imperative orders, issued on their behalf by Mr. Parnell and his friends, whom they were never tired of denouncing as disloyal men, the Liberal majority of forty-eight would at this moment have been near a hundred.' 'Lancashire,' he said, in the Flintshire speech, 'has returned her voice. She has spoken, but if you listen to her accents you will find that they are tinged strongly with the Irish brogue.'[3] 'We have had,' said Mr. Chamberlain, 'a most unusual and extraordinary combination against us, and I am inclined to describe it as the combination of the five P's, and I shall tell you what the five P's are in the order of their importance, beginning with the least important. They are Priests, Publicans, Parsons, Parnellites, and Protectionists.'[4] 'Whatever else,' wrote the *Birmingham Daily Post*, 'may be the issue of the elections, or however they may benefit by the Parnellite vote, Great Britain has most unquestionably rejected the Tory Party. But for the aid of the Irish allies, their position on the present polls would have been as bad as it was in 1880, if not worse.' 'But for the Nationalist vote in English and Scotch constituencies,' said the *Manchester Examiner*, 'the Liberals would have gone back to Parliament with more than their old numbers.'[5]

But the Irish vote had not succeeded in bringing the Tories to a position in which they would be of any service to Ireland. When the General Election was over, the numbers were: Liberals, 333; Conservatives

---

[1] *Standard*, December 1, 1885. [2] *Ibid.*, December 4. [3] *Ibid.*, December 1.
[4] *Ibid.*, December 4, 1885. [5] Quoted in *Pall Mall Gazette*, December 7, 1885.

(including 2 Independents), 251 ; Nationalists, 86. The Liberals were thus in a majority over the Conservatives of 82. If the Tories got the Irish vote and were able to poll the full strength of their own party, they would have had a majority of but four over the Liberals; and four is not a working majority. Besides, it was more than doubtful if they would have carried the whole of their own party with them on a policy of Home Rule. All or nearly all their supporters from Ireland belonged to that terrible Orange faction which has obstinately opposed every concession to the majority of the Irish nation. A certain number of the same unholy gang had been returned for English constituencies. There can be little doubt under these circumstances that the proposal of Home Rule by the Tory Ministers would have led to a Tory cave which would have placed the Government in a hopeless minority, and have given them the discredit of having proposed Home Rule without the merit of having carried it. The Tory and the Irish leaders had little difficulty in recognising that the stroke of 1885 had not succeeded. A Tory statesman who had acted throughout in a frank and manly spirit gave the word to a prominent Irish member that there was nothing more to be expected from the Tory leaders, and that the Irish Nationalists had better fix their hopes elsewhere. The situation was more frankly put to the same member by Lord Randolph Churchill 'I have done my best for you,' he said, 'and failed ; and now, of course I'll do my best against you.' So ended the Tory-Parnell combination.

CHAPTER XIV.

THE HOME RULE STRUGGLE.

THE Tory-Parnell combination was at an end ; but the Parnellites did not yet recognise that the Tories could be guilty of the deliberate policy of immediately abandoning all the principles which had been preached during the General Election. Above all, they were not prepared for the action of Lord Randolph Churchill. It might be true, they thought, that the Government could not propose Home Rule, because they had no chance of carrying it ; it might be true that they would oppose any scheme of Home Rule brought forward by Mr. Gladstone. These things were part of the game of political life. That did not mean that by-and-by they would not take up Home Rule again, and propose a scheme of their own superior to that of Mr. Gladstone.

Theories founded on the maintenance of the ordinary decencies and the common honesty of political life may now appear very childish ; but the Irish Party had not yet learned all they have since been taught of the vile want of principle and the viler want of shame which characterize the present leaders of the Tory Party. The Tory Government, which had been raised to power on condition of not renewing coercion, and which had pledged itself, through its candidates, against coercion at the election, began its career by announcing its intention of proposing the suppression of the National League. Irish Nationalists heard with a smile of incredulity the report that Lord Randolph Churchill intended to make an attempt to rouse the Orangemen to fury in order to embarrass the movement for Home Rule ; but in a few weeks their doubts were set at nought. Lord Randolph Churchill went to Belfast, accompanied by those very Orangemen whom his lieutenants and himself had so heartily despised in the days of the Tory-Parnell combination, preached a religious war, and so far succeeded as to bring about, a few months afterwards, one of the most brutal, savage, and cruel riots that have ever disgraced even Belfast. When the Tories proposed coercion, the Liberal leaders resolved at once to throw them out of office. An amendment to the Queen's Speech of 1886, proposed by Mr. Jesse Collings, was carried in spite of the violent hostility of the Marquis of Hartington and Mr. Goschen; and the Marquis o Salisbury gave way to Mr. Gladstone.

Prime Minister for the third time, Mr. Gladstone now found himself face to face with the greatest task of his great life; and the obstacles were greater, and not smaller, than those he had ever before encountered. The Marquis of Hartington refused from the start to have anything to do with a Ministry which proposed Home Rule in any shape. Mr. Chamberlain and Sir George Trevelyan had pledged themselves beforehand against certain forms of Home Rule; but they entered the Cabinet, and it was yet to be seen whether Mr. Gladstone could produce a plan which they could accept. For weeks there were contradictory rumours every hour as to how the struggle in the Cabinet was going on; but all doubts were set at rest by Mr. Chamberlain and Sir George Trevelyan taking their seats one evening below the gangway, and so announcing to the world that they had been unable to agree with the plan of Mr. Gladstone. But Mr. Gladstone was not to be turned back from his great purpose by the desertion of any colleagues, however eminent, and went on with the preparation of his Bills. The Tories meantime kept pestering him with questions every day, apparently expecting that such a mighty problem as the constitution of a country could be fixed in a few hours. It was known that Mr. Gladstone intended to deal simultaneously with the National and the Land Question, and the first intention was to bring in the Land Bill first, and then the Home Rule Bill. This plan was changed; and at last, on April 8, the Home Rule Bill was introduced.

The scene was as thrilling as any ever beheld in the House of Commons, and never have there been more abundant signs of absorbing public interest. In order to secure seats, the Irish members began to arrive from six o'clock in the morning, and by eight or nine o'clock every seat in the House was seized. The result was that members spent all the day within the walls of Westminster Palace—breakfasting, lunching, and dining there. When the sitting commenced, a number of members who had remained without seats brought in chairs, and placed them on the floor of the House—a sight unprecedented, I believe, in the history of the Assembly. Mr. Gladstone's entrance was marked by a striking incident. As he sat, pale, panting, and still under the excitement of the great reception he had received from the crowds outside, the whole Liberal Party (with four exceptions) and all the Irish members, sprang to their feet and cheered him enthusiastically. The four exceptions to this general mark of reverence and esteem were the four Dissentient leaders. Lord Hartington, Sir Henry James, Sir George Trevelyan, and Mr. Chamberlain remained sitting, and in a group by themselves they presented a curious look of isolation amid these surroundings. It took Mr. Gladstone upwards of three hours to set forth all the details of his great measure. His voice lasted well to the end, and the attention of the House never relaxed for a moment. The speech was calm in language, and the Tories were decent enough to abstain from any outbursts of impatience. Indeed, the general desire to catch every word of a speech in which every sentence was fateful, produced a reticence from both friend and foe. The main provisions of the Bill are well described in an excellent summary of the measure published by Mr. Sydney Buxton:

'The Bill provides for the constitution of an Irish Parliament sitting in Dublin, with the Queen as its head.

'The Parliament—which is to be quinquennial—is to consist of 309 members, divided into two "orders," 103 members in the "first order," and 206 in the "second order."

'The "first order" is to consist of such or all of the 28 Irish representative peers as choose to serve; the remaining members to be "elective." At the end of 30 years the rights of peerage members will lapse, and the whole of the "first order" will be elective.

'The elective members will sit for 10 years; every five years one-half their number will retire, but are eligible for re-election. They do not vacate their seats on a dissolution.

'They will be elected by constituencies subsequently to be formed. The elective member himself must possess a property qualification equivalent to an income of £200 a year. The franchise is a restricted one, the elector having to possess or occupy land of a net annual value of £25.

'The "second order" is to be elected on the existing franchise, and by the existing constituencies, the representation of each being doubled. For the first Parliament, the Irish members now sitting in the House of Commons will, except such as may resign, constitute one-half the members of the "second order" of the new House.

The two orders shall sit and deliberate together, and, under ordinary circumstances, shall vote together, the majority deciding.

'If, however, on any question (other than a Bill) relating to legislation, or to the regulations and rules of the House, the majority of either order demand a separate vote, a separate vote of each order shall be taken. If the decision of the two orders be different, the matter shall be decided in the negative.

'The Lord-Lieutenant has power given him to arrange for the procedure at the first sitting, the election of Speaker, and other minor matters for carrying the Act into effect.

'If a Bill, or any part of a Bill, is lost by the disagreement of the two orders voting separately, the matter in dispute shall be considered as vetoed, or lost, for a period of three years, or until the next dissolution of the Legislative Body, if longer than three years. After that time, if the question be again raised, and the Bill or provision be adopted by the second order and negatived by the first, it shall be submitted to the Legislative Body as a whole, both orders shall vote together, and the question shall be decided by the simple majority. The Bill then, if within the statutory power of the Parliament, and unless vetoed by the Crown, passes into law.

'The Lord-Lieutenant—who, as Lord-Lieutenant, will not be the representative of any party, and will not quit office with the outgoing English Government, and who in future need not necessarily be a Protestant—is appointed by the Crown, and will represent the Crown in Ireland. Neither his office nor his functions can be altered by the Irish Parliament.

'The responsible Executive in Ireland will be constituted in the same manner as that in England. The leader of the majority will be called upon by the Lord-Lieutenant, as representing the Queen, to form a Government responsible to the Irish Parliament. It will stand and fall by votes of that Parliament.

'The Queen, just as in the case of the Imperial Parliament, retains the right—to be exercised through the Lord-Lieutenant—of giving or withholding her assent to Bills, and can dissolve or summon Parliament when she pleases ; she will probably, as in England, exercise the latter function, and as a rule the former, on the advice of the responsible Irish Executive.

'All constitutional questions which may arise, as to whether the Irish Parliament has exceeded its powers, will be referred to, and decided by, the Judicial Committee of the Privy Council ; their decision will be final, and the Lord-Lieutenant will veto any Bill judged by them to contain provisions in excess of the powers of the Irish Legislature, and such a Bill will be void.

'The prerogatives of the Crown are untouched. The following matters remain intact in the hands of the Imperial Parliament : The dignity of, and succession to, the Crown ; the making of peace or war ; all foreign and colonial relations ; the questions of international law, or violation of treaties ; naturalization ; matters relating to trade, navigation, and quarantine, beacons, lighthouses, etc. ; foreign postal and telegraph service ; coinage, weights and measures ; copyright and patents ; questions of treason, alienage ; the creation of titles of honour. The Imperial Parliament is, moreover, to keep in its own hands the army, navy, militia, volunteers, or other military or naval forces ; is responsible for the defence of the realm ; and may erect all needful buildings or defences for military and naval purposes.

'In addition, the Irish Parliament is not permitted to make laws establishing or endowing any religion, or prohibiting in any way religious freedom, by imposing a disability or conferring any privilege on account of religious belief. Nor may they prejudicially affect the right of any child to avail itself of the "conscience clause" at any school it may attend ; nor of the private right of establishing and maintaining any particular form of denominational education.

'It cannot, without the leave of the Privy Council of England, or the assent of the Corporation itself, in any way impair the rights, property, or privileges of any body created and existing under Royal Charter or Act of Parliament.

'For a time, at all events, the Customs and Excise duties are to be levied by officers appointed, as now, by the British Treasury.

'With these exceptions, all other matters, legislative and administrative, are left absolutely in the power, and to the discretion, of the Irish Parliament and its executive government.

'It will be responsible for law and order, though the Imperial Parliament, by retaining the military forces, holds the ultimate power. It can raise and pay a police force—as in England, under local control.

'The responsible Government will have the appointment of the Judges (to be life appointments, as in England), and of all the other officials throughout the kingdom. The Parliament can make or vary courts of law, legal powers, or authorities, etc.

'On the recommendation of the responsible Government, the Parliament can levy such internal taxes as they please (with the exception of Customs and Excise), and can apply the proceeds to such purposes as they think fit. They can raise loans, and undertake public works of every sort. They can manage their own post-offices, telegraphs, and post-office savings banks.

'They can create such local bodies as they choose. They can regulate education: in a word, they will have the power of legislating on all local Irish matters.

'After the first election, they can alter any matter affecting the constitution or election of the "second order;" the franchise, the constituencies, the mode of election, the system of registration, the laws relating to corrupt and illegal practices, the privileges and immunities of the legislative body and of its members, etc.

'To prevent any breach of continuity, existing laws will remain in force until altered or repealed by the new Parliament.

'All existing rights of civil servants and other officials at present in the employ of the Irish Government are carefully guarded. In order to preserve the continuity of Civil Government, they will continue to hold office at the same salary they now receive, and to perform the same or analogous duties, unless, from incompatibility of temper, or from motives of economy, the Irish Government desire their retirement, when they will receive their pension. In any case if, at the end of two years, they wish to retire, they can do so, and will be then entitled to a pension as though their office had been abolished.

'The judges, and certain permanent officials, can only be retired, or allowed to retire, by "the Crown," and they will then receive their pension as though they had served their full time.

'The existing rights of the constabulary and police to pay, pension, etc., are preserved.

'All these pensions become a charge on the Irish Treasury, but are further guaranteed by the English Treasury.

'It is not intended that the Irish representative Peers should any longer sit in the House of Lords, nor the Irish members in the House of Commons, but that Ireland (with the assent of her present representatives) should be practically unrepresented at Westminster.

'The Act constituting the Irish Parliament cannot be altered in any way, except by an Act passed by the Imperial Parliament, and assented to by the Irish Parliament; or by an Act of the Imperial Parliament, passed after there have been summoned back to it, for that especial purpose, 28 Irish representative Peers, and 103 "second order" members.'

'The Financial arrangements are as follow:

'The imposition and collection of Custom duties and of Excise duties, so far as these are immediately connected with Customs duties, will remain in the hands of the British Treasury. All other taxes will be imposed and collected under the authority of the Irish Parliament. The proceeds of these latter taxes will be paid into the Irish Treasury; the proceeds of the Customs and Excise to a special account of the British Treasury.

'From these receipts, certain deductions are first to be made for the Irish contribution to Imperial Expenditure, etc., and the balance is then to be paid over to the Irish Treasury.

'Ireland is to pay one-fifteenth as her portion of the whole existing Imperial charge for debt (£22,000,000 a year), representing a capital sum of £48,000,000, and in addition a small sinking fund; and one-fifteenth of the normal charge for Army and Navy (£25,000,000), and for Imperial Civil charges (£1,650,000). In addition, until she supersedes the present police force, she is to pay £1,000,000 a year (or less if the cost be less) towards the cost of the Royal Irish Constabulary and the Dublin police.

'Thus the Irish proportion of Imperial expenditure will be as follows:

	£	£
Debt	1,466,000	
Sinking fund	360,000	
		1,826,000
Army and Navy		1,666,000
Civil expenditure		110,000
		£3,602,000
Constabulary and police		1,000,000
		£4,602,000

'This is the maximum amount payable, and it cannot be increased for thirty years, when the question of contribution can be again considered.

'On the other hand, the amount can be reduced. (1) If in any year the charge for the army and navy, or for the Imperial Civil Service, is less than fifteen times the amount of the Irish contribution, then the Irish charge will be reduced proportionately. (2) If the cost of the constabulary or police fall below £1,000,000 a year, then the difference will be saved by the Irish Exchequer.

'The estimated revenue from Irish Customs and Excise Customs, duties, amounts to £6,180,000 annually. From this is to be deducted, by the English Treasury, a sum not exceeding four per cent. for cost of collection, leaving a net amount of £5,933,000.

'The debtor and creditor account, as between England and Ireland, will then stand thus:

Expenditure.	£	Receipts.	£
For Imperial purposes ...	3,602,000	Customs and Excise ...	6,180,000
Constabulary, etc. ...	1,000,000		
Collection of Customs and Excise, maximum 4 per cent.	247,000		
	£4,849,000		£6,180,000

Leaving a balance of £1,331,000 to be handed over by England to the Irish Exchequer.

'The Irish Government will take over all loans due to the British Treasury and advanced for Irish purposes, and shall pay the British Treasury an annual sum equivalent to three per cent. interest on the amount with repayment in thirty years. The total amount outstanding is some six millions, and the receipts and disbursements of the Irish Government under this head will about balance. The balance of the Irish Church surplus fund—about £20,000 a year—is to be handed over to the Irish Government.

'The following will show the further receipts and expenditure of the Irish Government, as estimated by Mr. Gladstone on the basis of existing expenditure and taxation, and may be put in the form of a balance-sheet:

Expenditure.	£	Revenue.	£
Irish Civil charges	2,510,000	Repaid by England	1,331,000
Collection of revenue, etc.	587,000	Stamps	600,000
		Income-tax, at 8d.[1]	550,000
Balance, surplus	404,000	Other sources of revenue —Post Office, etc.	1,020,000
	£3,501,000		£3,501,000

'This gives a surplus of £404,000 to start with. But, in addition, great savings of expenditure can be, and ought to be, made in the Irish Civil charges and collection of revenue. Per head of the population, they are now double what they are in England, and at least £300,000 or £400,000 should be saved. In addition, after a time, the cost of the police ought to fall at least £200,000 or £300,000 below the million allotted to that purpose.

'Thus, with reasonable economy, the surplus at the disposal of the Irish Government ought to amount to some £1,000,000 a year—a sum which will enable it readily to borrow money for public wants and for public improvements.'[1]

On April 16 Mr. Gladstone brought in the second of his great measures: the Bill for the buying out of the Irish landlords. I borrow again from Mr. Buxton an analysis of this measure:

'The object of the Bill is to give to all Irish landlords the option of selling their rented agricultural lands on certain terms. The tenants have no power to force the sale; or to prevent it if the landlord elects to sell, and is willing to accept the price fixed by the Land Court. Only "immediate landlords" have the power of option; encumbrancers cannot, by foreclosing, obtain any right of sale under the Bill.

'The normal price is to be, under ordinary circumstances, "on a fairly well-conditioned estate," 20 years' purchase of the net rental of the estate —equal to about 16 years' purchase of the nominal rental. If, however, the land be especially good, or the estate in an exceptionally good condition, the number of years' purchase can be increased by the Land Commission to 22. On the other hand, where, in the opinion of the Commission, the land is not worth 20 years' purchase, they can fix a lower price; or, if the land be so valueless as to make it inequitable for the State Authority to purchase, they can refuse the offer altogether.

'The *net* rental of the estate is to be fixed by the Land Commission, who, in order to find it, are to deduct from the gross rental—chief rent, tithe rent charge, the average percentage (over the last ten years) of outgoings for bad debts, management, repairs, etc., and for rates and taxes paid by the landlord. In fixing the price, the Commission may take into account any circumstances or surroundings they judge right.

'The *gross* rental of an estate is the gross rent of all the tenanted holdings on the estate, payable in the year ending November, 1885. The gross rent of a holding is the judicial rent, or, if none be fixed, then a fair rent is to be fixed by the Land Commission.

'Arrears of rent becoming due, between November, 1885, and the date of purchase (and which the landlord has endeavoured to obtain) are to be added to the price.

[1] 'Mr. Gladstone's Irish Bills,' pp. 13, 18.

'In the cases of holdings at or under £4 annual value, if the tenant does not desire to become the freeholder, the State Authority shall become the owner, the tenant remaining liable for rent as before.

'It is provided, moreover, that in certain "congested districts"—to be scheduled afterwards—if the State Authority buys the land, it shall retain the ownership and not vest it in the occupiers.

'The whole of the rented estate, including town parks, houses, and villages, if part of the agricultural estate, but excluding the mansion, demesne land, or home farm, must go together. If, however, the landlord desires, and the State Authority agrees, it can buy the mansion, demesne land, and home farm. No estate, which is within the limits of a town, or is not in the main agricultural and pastoral, comes under the Act. Grazing lands of a value of over £50 a year may be excluded by the landlord from the sale, or the purchase can be refused by the State Authority.

'The Land Commissioners are to be appointed by name in the Act. Any vacancy is to be filled up by "her Majesty," and the Commissioners hold office "during her pleasure."

'When the price is fixed, the landlord, and the legal encumbrancers—whose position will not be affected in any way by the Act—will receive the money, and the tenant will at once become the freeholder of his holding, subject to the payment of a terminable annuity for 49 years, equal to 4 per cent. per annum on the capitalized value, at 20 years' purchase, of the old rent.

'This annuity, and the rent in the case of small holdings where the occupier remains as tenant, is to be collected by the department of the Irish Government called the State Authority ; and the surplus (equivalent to 4 per cent. per annum on the difference between the capitalized value of the old rent and that of the redemption money) will be applied, after payment of the interest and repayment on the capital advanced by the British Treasury, to the purposes of the Irish Government.

'The State Authority will be enabled to enforce the payment of its annuities in such manner as is afterwards provided by an Act of the Irish Parliament, and until that provision is made, the present laws relating to the enforcement of the payment of rent, etc., in Ireland will remain in force.

'During the time that the holding is subject to the annuity, the occupier may neither subdivide nor let without the consent of the State Authority. If he does, or in case of bankruptcy, the holding can be sold.

'The State Authority is to pay the British Treasury an annual amount equal to 4 per cent. on the capital sum advanced by the latter and received by the landlord.[1]

'The total liability under the Bill is limited to £50,000,000. as follows :

£10,000,000 in the year ending March, 1887-8
£20,000,000 ,, ,, ,, 1888-9
£20,000,000 ,, ,, ,, 1889-90

'The applications from the landlords will be considered in priority of time.

'No application can be made after March, 1890.

'The money advanced by the British Treasury is to be raised by the

[1] Thus, if the whole £50,000,000 be advanced, the State Authority will receive £2,500,000 a year, subject to cost of collection, etc., and have to pay the British Treasury only £2,000,000. It will thus, if thought necessary or expedient, be able to grant further remission to the occupier.

issue to the landlords of 3 per cent. stock at par. This stock is to be redeemed by the repayment of a terminable annuity for 49 years by the State Authority.

'In order to obtain security for the loan, the British Government appoint a Receiver-General, through whose hands the whole of the Irish revenues are to pass, together with the proceeds of Irish Customs and Excise; but he will have absolutely nothing to do with the levying of the revenue. After deducting from these receipts the amount due from the State Authority for interest and repayment of capital advanced, and after deducting also the Irish contributions to the Imperial charges, the balance of the receipts will be handed over to the Irish Exchequer.

'Assuming that the whole loan is called up, the Irish balance-sheet will then stand as follows:

Expenditure.	£	Revenue.	£
For Imperial purposes	3,602,000	Customs and Excise	6,180,000
Constabulary, etc.	1,000,000	Stamps	600,000
Collection of Customs and Excise	247,000	Income Tax	550,000
Annuity on loan advanced for purchase	2,000,000	Other sources revenue	1,020,000
Irish Civil charges	2,510,000	Rent-charge	2,500,000
Collection of revenue, etc.	587,000		
Collection of rent-charge and expenses, say	100,000		
Surplus	804,000		
	£10,850,000		£10,850,000

'In addition, the Surplus will be increased by the economies made in the Civil Service, Constabulary, etc.'

It would be wearisome to go at any length through the story of the intrigues, negotiations, rise and fall of fortune that characterized the interval between the introduction and the second reading of the Home Rule Bill. It became evident from the start that Mr. Gladstone had enormously increased his difficulties in passing the Home Rule Bill by the introduction of the Land Bill. It was quite true that he had guaranteed the British Exchequer absolutely against loss; but his enemies were either stupid or unscrupulous enough to misrepresent his scheme, and to travesty it into a plan which would lose to the British Exchequer every penny advanced, and ultimately add several millions to the burdens of the British taxpayer. Mr. Gladstone was implored, both then and at a later stage in the struggle, to drop his Land Bill. These appeals might have been addressed with some hope of success to an unscrupulous or a reckless politician; but they were hopeless to a statesman who felt the obligations of honour and the necessities of public interest. Some of Mr. Gladstone's chief opponents were quite ready to denounce Land Purchase at one stage of the controversy—as will presently be seen—and to advocate and propose it at another; but recklessness and indecency of this kind belong to a different order of mind from that of Mr. Gladstone.

Another difficulty of Mr. Gladstone was that his opponents brought entirely opposite objections to his plan. The retention of the Irish members was demanded by Mr. Chamberlain; their exclusion was, according to the Marquis of Hartington, the logical necessity of the plan. Mr. Chamberlain objected to the scheme of Land Purchase; the Marquis of Hartington took very good care to say nothing which might injure the prospects of large monetary relief to the class of which he is a member. The speech of Mr. Gladstone at the Foreign Office to a meeting of his supporters was held to make the second reading of the Bill secure; the same speech on the following day in the House of Commons—Mr. Chamberlain acknowledged that the two speeches were exactly the same—lost the votes of those who the day before, at the Foreign Office, had practically pledged themselves to support the second reading.

Among many of the absurd charges brought against Mr. Gladstone for his conduct of the measure is that he sprang the question upon the country. The charge is entirely untrue. He exhausted every means to keep the question within the control of a united Liberal Party, and to prevent its reference to the tumultuous and passionate tribunal of the ballot-boxes. In those clauses which provoked criticism he promised amendment, and the whole Bill he undertook to postpone till an autumn sitting, after the House had affirmed the principle of Home Rule by passing the second reading. It was those who defeated the second reading of the Bill, and so provoked the General Election, that must bear the responsibility of all that has since happened. If the second reading had been carried, the interval would have been spent in the calm consideration of the various points of difference among those who honestly accepted the principle of an Irish Legislative Assembly, and in all probability a compromise would have been arrived at. There had not arisen at this period any of that fierce bitterness which at present rages between the two sections of the Liberal Party, and so the points of difference could have been debated in calmness and settled by mutual concession.

But it was not to be. The enemies of Mr. Gladstone forced on the contest when they felt sure of victory. A meeting of the Dissentient Liberals was held a few days before the second reading division. A letter was read from Mr. John Bright. The letter has never been produced, though Mr. Chamberlain distinctly undertook to produce it when this fact was commented upon by Mr. John Morley in a speech in the House of Commons; and the world is still ignorant of its character. It was certainly used as an argument in favour of voting against the Bill, and it served more than anything else to bring about that fateful decision; but whether that was the advice of Mr. Bright, or whether he advised abstention, is one of the political mysteries that possibly this generation will never penetrate. The decision of the Dissentient Liberals to vote against the Bill sealed its fate. The division took place on June 7. Mr. Gladstone wound up the debate with one of the most effective, most powerful, most touching speeches he has ever delivered. But his eloquence for once was impotent: the Bill was defeated by a majority of 30.

A few days afterwards Mr. Gladstone announced that the Ministry had resolved to appeal from Parliament to the country; and thus a General Election came. Never perhaps was a General Election fought under such curious circumstances. The leaders of the different sections of the Liberal Party took up hostile positions. Liberal was opposed by Liberal; and in many cases the Tory candidate had the full support of the Dissentient Liberal leaders. There had been a bargain—secret and unavowed at first, but afterwards admitted—between the Tory leaders and the Dissentient

Liberals, that no Liberal who voted against the second reading of Mr. Gladstone's Bill should be opposed; and the bargain was honourably kept by the Tories, except in two cases. Mr. Gladstone acted during the election as he has throughout the struggle. He maintained a strong belief that the Dissentient Liberals, professing to differ from him only on details, would return in time to the party they had deserted. For this reason he did not encourage attacks upon the seats of Dissentient leaders; and thus several were allowed to get in without any contest at all, or after a contest begun too late or too tamely conducted.

The sight of the most eminent men of the Liberal Party differing among themselves naturally bewildered a considerable portion of the country. This fact was bound to have more effect in such a struggle as was then going on than in any other kind of contest. It was a struggle over the Irish Question; and there is no subject so little known in England— perhaps it might be said there are few subjects so little known even in Ireland—as Irish history. The long centuries of wrong, of foul misgovernment, of terrible suffering, which have created the Ireland of to-day, were a sealed book to the English people. The demands of the Irish leaders of to-day they had never before heard spoken of, except with derision or reprobation; and in such circumstances the differences of their leaders might well excuse differences, and doubts, and hesitations of the rank and file. Unhappily the opponents of Mr. Gladstone made full and most unscrupulous use of this ignorance. Never at any General Election was there a more foul and a more full tide of misrepresentation. The election might be described briefly as won by lies addressed to ignorance. The Irish leaders were accused of desiring to destroy the supremacy of the Imperial Parliament, and of working for separation in face of their distinct pledges that they recognised the Legislative Assembly bestowed by Mr. Gladstone's Bill as a subordinate assembly,[1] and in face of the

[1] In his speech on the second reading of the Government of Ireland Bill, Mr. Parnell said: 'Now, sir, the right hon. member for East Edinburgh spoke about the sovereignty of Parliament. I entirely agree upon this point. I entirely accept the definitions given by the Under-Secretary of State for Foreign Affairs the other day. We have always known, since the introduction of this Bill, the difference between a co-ordinate and a subordinate Parliament, and *we have recognised that the Legislature which the Prime Minister proposes to constitute is a subordinate Parliament*, that it is not the same as Grattan's Parliament, which was co-equal with the Imperial Parliament.' In the same speech the Irish leader again said: 'I say that, as far as it is possible for a nation to accept a measure cheerfully, freely, gladly, and without reservation as a final settlement—I say that the Irish people have shown that they have accepted this measure in that sense.' Again he said: 'This settlement I believe will be a final settlement.' (Reported in *Times*, June 8, 1886.) The Chicago Convention, of which so much has been heard, accepted the Bill of Mr. Gladstone with equal emphasis, and by a majority of 971 delegates against one dissentient. In the resolution adopted at the Convention, it spoke of the right of a people 'to frame their own laws,' and it went on to define that right in these significant words: 'A right which lies at the foundation of the prosperity and greatness of this Republic, and *which has been advantageously extended to the colonial possessions of Great Britain*.' Of course, the Home Rule which is given to the colonial possessions of Great Britain is not separation, but such limited Home Rule as would be given by Mr. Gladstone's Bill to Ireland. The Convention still further certified its feelings by expressing hearty approval of the 'course pursued by Charles Stewart Parnell and his associates in the English House of Commons.' As has been seen, the course taken by Mr. Parnell and his colleagues was the acceptance of Mr. Gladstone's Bill. And finally, the sense of the Convention was further expressed by the following resolution: 'That we extend our heartfelt thanks to Mr. Gladstone for his great efforts in behalf of Irish self-government, and we express our gratitude to the English, Scotch, and Welsh democracy, for the support given to the great Liberal leader and his Irish policy during the recent General Elections.' This is the Convention which is represented as consisting of dynamitards.

ample safeguards in Mr. Gladstone's measure for maintaining the control of all the military and naval forces. Lying appeals were made to religious prejudice; and a party led by a Protestant, and manned largely by Protestants, was accused of desiring to persecute the Protestant religion.

But these appeals, powerful as they were, had little effect beside two other factors brought into the election. The first of these was the Land Purchase Bill of Mr. Gladstone. Mr. Gladstone's Bill, in his opinion—and he is generally regarded as some authority on finance—and in the opinion, I think, of every impartial critic, would have taken ample security for every single penny of money advanced to the Irish State for the buying out of the Irish landlords.

But his enemies represented that the money thus lent would be a gift to the Irish landlords out of the pockets of the English tax-payers. Astounding calculations were made as to the additions that would thus be thrown upon the English taxpayers. 'The Land Bill,' said Mr. Alfred Barnes, the Liberal Unionist candidate for Chesterfield Division of Derbyshire, 'which Mr. Gladstone has stated to be inseparable from the Irish Government Bill, would add £150,000,000 to £200,000,000 to the National Debt, and thereby impose a heavy liability and large increase of taxation upon our already overburdened population.' 'I ask you,' said Mr. H. M. Jackson, a Liberal Unionist candidate for the borough of Flintshire, 'to remember that in supporting my opponent you are supporting a measure (declared by the Government to be an inseparable part of their Irish scheme) which if passed will impose upon the National Debt of the country an addition of nearly £200,000,000 (two hundred million pounds), of which each one of you will have to contribute his share.' The credit of having reached perhaps the highest flight in these astonishing calculations belongs to Mr. Baumann, the Tory member for Peckham, 'The Home Rule Bill is only half of Mr. Gladstone's Irish policy. The Prime Minister has also laid before Parliament a Land Purchase Bill which he describes as inseparably connected with the Home Rule Bill, to buy out the Irish landlords by the issue of new British Consols. The precise amount of this addition to the National Debt it is impossible to get at, . . . but it is interesting to note that three years ago Mr. Gladstone put the cost of buying out the Irish landlords at *between three and four hundred million pounds.*'

This was dishonest enough in all conscience; but the dishonesty was in implication as well as in open lie. For while the opponents of Mr. Gladstone were thus attacking his Land Bill, they never breathed a hint that they were favourable themselves to Land Purchase in any shape. On the contrary, the whole tendency and the unmistakable suggestion of all their speeches was that to any money in any form for the buying out of the Irish landlords they were irreconcilably opposed. The contest thus changed its character in the course of the struggle. It was no longer mainly a fight against the Home Rule, but against the Land Bill of Mr. Gladstone. It was whether the British tax-payer should guarantee any money whatever for the buying out of the Irish landlord or not. This is a point to which I direct the especial attention of the reader; he will the more keenly appreciate the grim irony of what immediately followed.

Thus the first great factor in producing the defeat of Mr. Gladstone was the false representation of the issue on the Land Question; the second great factor was an equally false representation of the issue on Home Rule. Mr. Gladstone laid down as the real issue before the country the question whether Ireland was to be governed through herself or by coercion. Between these two courses he declared that there was no halting-ground.

His opponents were shrewd enough to perceive that if this issue were allowed to go before the country in its plainness and nakedness, there could be little doubt as to what would be the result. Between enslaving and liberating a sister-country a nation of freemen could only give one answer; and above all other even free nations the people of England have been distinguished by the readiness and the abundance of sympathy they have extended to other peoples struggling for their rights. Under these circumstances it was felt that the issue should be obscured or the cause of wrong was lost; and the main efforts of Mr. Gladstone's opponents were devoted to showing that the issue was not as he put it—was not the clear, blank, naked issue between Home Rule on the one side, and coercion on the other. It was between Home Rule as Mr. Gladstone proposed, and another and different kind of Home Rule. It was not even an issue between the extreme Home Rule of Mr. Gladstone and the more moderate Home Rule of his opponents. Some of his critics maintained that they were ready to give a wider Home Rule than Mr. Gladstone. Indeed, it was one of the charges against Mr. Gladstone's Bill, which some of his opponents were able to make without laughing, that his Bill gave Ireland too little instead of too much.

'You will doubtless remember,' said Mr. Barnes, the Liberal Unionist member for the Chesterfield Division of Derbyshire, in his election address, 'that both in my addresses and speeches at the last two elections I stated that I was in favour of Home Rule being granted in Ireland in the shape of such a measure of local self-government as could be extended to England, Scotland and Wales, at the same time maintaining the supremacy of the Imperial Parliament and the integrity of the United Kingdom. From that principle I have never receded.' 'It is mere sophistry,' said Sir Henry Havelock Allan, another Liberal Unionist, 'to assert that the only two alternatives are an absolute and abject surrender to the tyranny of the National League on the one hand, or else unmitigated coercion on the other. The legislative wisdom of Parliament is amply able to devise, and I am sure after the last election will devise, a scheme by which, while full scope is given to the legitimate aspirations of the Irish people, as to the local management of their own local affairs, this boon shall be conceded in a shape not dangerous to the unity of the empire or the supremacy of the Imperial Parliament.' Having detailed a different scheme of Home Rule from Mr. Gladstone's, including retention of Irish members, and the appointment of judges by the imperial authority with two legislative bodies, Sir Henry said, 'I think it highly probable that the lines I have indicated represent the precise shape in which Mr. Gladstone's plans will be presented to Parliament in October next. Should that prove to be the case, I need not say what sincere and hearty pleasure it would give me to follow my revered and honoured leader once more at the head of a united Liberal Party.' 'To coercion I object,' exclaimed Colonel Nicholas Wood, Tory member for the Houghton-le-Spring Division of Durham; 'and my firm and hearty support will be given to a considerable extension and improvement of local government alike to the people of England, Scotland, Wales and Ireland, delegated by and under the supreme control of an Imperial Parliament, in which they are fully represented.' 'I indignantly repudiate the imputation,' said Sir Roper Lethbridge, the Tory member for North Kensington, 'that the only alternative policy is one of coercion. On the contrary, all parties in the United Kingdom, with the exception of the extremists led by Mr. Gladstone and Mr. Parnell, are now fairly agreed on the general lines of a policy that shall satisfy all the legitimate aspirations of Irishmen for local self-government, that shall secure the return of law and order in Ireland, that shall treat Ulster as fairly as the other provinces, and that shall at the same time maintain unimpaired the unity of the empire and the supremacy of the Imperial Parliament.' 'It is suggested,' said Mr. Boord, Tory member for Greenwich, 'that coercion is the only alternative to Mr. Gladstone's scheme, and that it is the policy of Lord Salisbury. The suggestion is false. Coercion, if it means anything in this connection, implies the forcible curtailment of the rights and liberties of the Irish people. Lord Salisbury, on the contrary, recommends a firm and constitutional government, such as Ireland has been unused to of late, which, by the suppression of crime, would secure the exercise of their rights and the enjoyment of their liberties to all alike.' Mr. Evelyn, Tory member for Deptford said 'that he could not agree with Mr. Gladstone's statement that there was no alternative between Home Rule and coercion. While he was opposed to Home Rule as revealed in the new Bill, he was also averse to special measures of coercive legislation, unless such were imperatively necessary. He feared if by special legislation they endeavoured to put down the Land League, they would embark on a dangerous enterprise, and secret societies might revive.' Again Mr. Evelyn said: 'I have been asked whether I would vote for coercion in Ireland. I have always considered, long before I ever thought of being a candidate for Deptford, that the Crimes Act which was introduced by Mr. Gladstone and a Whig Government in 1882 was a most abominable and unconstitutional measure.'

So the election was fought. The results were much better than might have been expected. In spite of all opposition, and division, and lies, Mr. Gladstone was able to carry with him the parts of the country where political intelligence is most keen. Scotland gave him 42 supporters to 30 opponents; Wales gave him 24 out of 30 seats; in the North of England the preponderance of his supporters was equally great. Northumberland gave him all the county seats, and three out of the four borough seats; Durham elected 8 Gladstonians to 3 opponents; and of the county seats in Yorkshire the Gladstonians won 18, and the joint opponents, in the shape of Liberal Unionists and Tories, were but 10. It was in Lancashire, and in London and in the South of England that the elections went mainly against Mr. Gladstone. In Lancashire there is a certain amount of that Orangeism which hates an Irishman more because of his religion than even his nationality; in London there was at the election complete disorganization; and the absurd system of registration which deprives a man of a vote if, by crossing the street, he gets into a different constituency, had largely reduced the Liberal strength; for the necessities of their lives make the working class more migratory than other classes; and in the South of England the terrorism of the squire and the parson still largely prevail. In spite of all these things, the results even in these districts of disaster were hopeful. The general result of the election is shown in the following figures: The aggregate Liberal vote was 1,238,342, while the aggregate Unionist vote was 1,316,327, or a difference of but 77,985 in a grand total of 2,554,669 votes. To put it roughly, out of two millions and a half of voters the Unionists had a majority of less than eighty thousand. This was, considering the circumstances, an extraordinarily close fight, and an extraordinarily narrow majority. A look at the election returns, too, will show a great falling-off in the number of votes polled, especially by the

Liberal candidates. This means that the election was lost, not by the number of Tory votes or Liberal votes cast against the policy of Mr. Gladstone—it was lost by the number of Liberals who did not vote at all. In other words, it was lost through the number of Liberals who, through want of knowledge or of boldness of mind, or through the distraction caused by the sight of division among their leaders, the frantic appeals to save their pockets from wholesale plunder, their nation from dismemberment, their co-religionists from annihilation, found themselves unable to make up their minds. In this respect the election and all its disaster told a hopeful lesson. Never before did a great and almost revolutionary reform come for decision before the great tribunal of the people after discussion so brief, and never before in the history of England did a great reform receive so much support in the first shock of battle.[1]

Mr. Gladstone resigned when the elections told that he had not carried the country to his side, and a Tory Administration came into power. With scarcely a day's delay the country had an opportunity of comparing the cries of the General Election and the acts of those whom these cries had made victorious. The country had refused to support Mr. Gladstone because he proposed to buy out the Irish landlords, and because his scheme, they were told, would involve loss to the British taxpayer. The very first night of the new Parliament, the new Ministers declared themselves in favour of a great scheme of Land Purchase. 'I do not believe,' said the Marquis of Salisbury, 'that any tinkering of the land system will have the slightest effect until we can get rid of the duality of ownership which the Land Act of 1881 introduced.' And in the House of Commons Lord Randolph Churchill used language of a similar import. 'The system of single ownership of land in Ireland,' he said, 'we believe, may be the ultimate solution of the difficulties of the Land Question.' This was bad enough: Mr. Gladstone had been defeated in order to prevent Land Purchase, and here were his conquerors proposing Land Purchase the moment they appeared before Parliament. But this was not all. The main argument, as has been seen, against Mr. Gladstone's proposal was that it would impose taxation on the British taxpayer. Mr. Gladstone entirely denied this, and agreed with his opponents in thinking that any burden on the British taxpayer for the payment of the Irish landlord would be monstrously inequitable. But here were his conquerors, and the chief of them laid down that not only would the British taxpayer have to pay for the Irish landlord, but that he ought. Lord Salisbury was dealing with the judicial rents fixed by the Land Courts, and with the demand that these rents should once again be revised. Such a general demand he described the Government as resolved to reject. 'But,' he went on, 'if it should come out that the Courts have made blunders, and that there is that impossibility

---

[1] The reader will not fail to observe that there is an enormous difference between the disparity of the supporters and opponents of Mr. Gladstone's policy, as shown in the vote of the people and in the number of members returned. The discrepancy in numbers is small; the discrepancy in members returned is enormous. In a '*Pall Mall Gazette* extra' on the General Election of 1886, this curious fact is brought out in a very clear manner. The plan of the *Pall Mall Gazette* is to put side by side in all contested elections in England and Scotland an 'ideal' distribution of votes, that is to say, where the number of members is strictly proportioned to the number of votes, and the actual distribution of votes. The result arrived at is that proportional justice would have given, by the contested elections, 209 to the Unionists and 198 to the Liberals; whereas 256 have gone to the Unionists—that is to say, 47 more than their due—and only 151 (47 less than their due) to the Liberals. A verdict which, being analyzed, shows these results is what Tories and Unionists calmly describe as final and irreversible.

in any case of paying rent, I think *it is not the landlords who should bear the loss*. I think this would be one of the cases for the application of the principle of purchase by the State, and *that the State, and not the landlords, must suffer for the errors that have been made.*'

Let me pause for just a moment to examine this astonishing proposition. The assumption is that the rent of the landlord has been fixed too high 'through blunders.' What would be the natural and equitable solution? That as the landlord has been receiving too much, he should be compelled to charge less for the future, if not to restore to the tenant the balance between a fair rent and his rack-rent in the past. The plan of the Marquis of Salisbury is different. Because the landlord is deprived of the excess over a fair rent which he has been taking from his unhappy tenant, he is to be rewarded by the assistance of the British taxpayer. In other words, somebody must be robbed for the landlord; if not his tenant, why, then, the English taxpayer. This was the pretty pass to which Liberal Unionists had brought things by rejecting the Land proposals of Mr. Gladstone.

As time went on, more and more of the idols were shattered which had been held up to the electorate at the General Election. Mr. Chamberlain had gone farther than almost any Irish member in his declarations as to the urgency and the extremeness of the agrarian crisis which had been created in Ireland by the depreciation of agricultural prices. While denouncing the Home Rule Bill of Mr. Gladstone, in 1886, he had proposed to meet the agrarian crisis by suspending all evictions for successive terms of six months, and had gone the length of asking that the British Exchequer should pay to the landlords the rent the suspension of which was thus brought about. Things had not improved since this speech had been made. In the previous Tory Administration, and under the good influence of Lord Carnarvon, the landlords had recognised the change in the situation of the farmers, and had given large reductions, not merely on the ordinary rents, but even on the judicial rents, that is, on the rents already reduced by the Land Courts. In the Autumn Session of 1886 Mr. Parnell, aware of the state of things in Ireland, proposed a Bill the effect of which would have been to allow the tenants to make a claim for a reduction of their rents, even in the cases where the rents had been fixed by the Land Courts. This Bill, of course, has been misrepresented, like all proposals made by the Irish Party. It has been described as confiscation, robbery, and all the rest, and most of its critics have declared that it calmly proposed that the landlords should be robbed of fifty per cent. of their entire rents. The foundation for the latter statement is that the Bill contained a provision that the tenant should deposit fifty per cent. of his rent, but the Bill did not propose that he should only pay fifty per cent. The deposit of the half of his rent was the necessary preliminary to his even getting a chance of being heard by the Court. It was the test and the bond of the tenants' *bona fides*. The Court had perfect liberty afterwards, in case the tenant did not make good his claim for a reduction, to call upon him to give to his landlord every penny of the balance of the fifty per cent. still outstanding. The Tories denied, or explained away, the existence of the depreciation in prices, scouted the claim on behalf of the tenants, and by the assistance of the Liberal Unionists, some of whom voted and some of whom stayed away, were able to reject the measure of the Irish leader.

The inevitable result followed. Sir Michael Hicks-Beach himself found that it was impossible for the tenants to pay the full rents, and accordingly had to resort to threats on the landlords to restrain them from taking advantage of their full legal rights. This he called afterwards 'pressure within the law.' There is no such thing as 'pressure within the law.' The phrase is self-contradictory, and Sir Michael Hicks-Beach was simply doing by his own methods, and at his own caprice, that which Mr. Parnell had asked him to do by the statute of both Houses of the Legislature. The leaders of the tenants followed this excellent example. On many estates the landlords refused to yield to the pressure of the Chief Secretary, and prepared to evict their tenants wholesale for the non-payment of rents, the exorbitance of which has now passed out of the region of controversy, is admitted by landlords and confessed by the report of the Royal Commission, and is the justification for the Legislation proposed by the Government in the House of Lords. The position was exactly the same as in 1880. The grievances of the tenants were admitted; the Legislature had been asked, and had refused, to stand between them and their oppressors, and the people accordingly were thrown upon their own resources. This was the origin of what came to be known as the 'Plan of Campaign.' This 'plan of campaign,' again, has been very much misunderstood in this country. Like Mr. Parnell's Bill, it has been denounced as a measure of pure confiscation, and has been represented as a scheme for the robbing of the landlord of all his rent. As a matter of fact, what took place under the 'Plan of Campaign' was that the landlord was asked to give a reduction as small, and in many cases smaller, than would be given by the Land Court. The tenants were gathered together, and asked, by begging or by borrowing, or by any other means, to collect all their rent, minus the abatement which had been demanded; if the landlord accepted the offer, the money was given to him immediately, and without any abatement whatever. In cases where the landlords refused, the money was employed for the protection of the tenants. This would have been an extreme expedient if the country were in an ordinary condition. But in Ireland, with all the resources of the Government at the back of the landlords, whether right or wrong, whether evicting for just or exorbitant rents, the tenants were perfectly justified in adopting such an extreme method of self-defence. In any case, the 'Plan of Campaign' has done good, and has been justified by the action of the Courts, which in more than one case made reductions larger than those which had been demanded under the 'Plan of Campaign.'

And now we come to the final contrast between the pledges of the Tories and Liberal Unionists in the General Election of 1886 and their subsequent action. I have shown how indignantly the Liberal Unionists and Tories repudiated the idea that the choice of the country was between concession on the one hand and coercion on the other, and how man after man pledged himself against coercion. In face of these facts the Government began the Session of 1887 by the announcement of a Coercion Bill. In this way they were guilty of as flagrant a breach of faith with the constituencies as the annals of this country can show; and, in fact, this Parliament, in proposing coercion, has exceeded, perhaps not its legal powers, but certainly its moral authority. I need only sketch rapidly a measure over which a controversy is still going on. The opinion is universal among all true Liberals that never was a Coercion Bill brought forward with less cause and with less excuse. In all previous instances Ministers have been able to give as an apology for their proposals whole arrays of statistics as proof of the existence of an epidemic of crime. In the case of the present Bill, the Chief Secretary began by producing no statistics at all, and even made it a merit that he had no statistics. 'I stated before,' he said on the motion for leave to introduce the Bill, 'and I state again, that we do not rest our case upon statistics of agrarian crime in Ireland.' The reader has an opportunity of comparing the action of Mr. Balfour in this respect with that of the late Mr. Forster when he brought forward the Coercion Bill of 1881. By-and-by this style of treating the proposals was found too absurd. 'Then the Home Secretary,' said Mr. Morley (speech on going into committee on the Bill) 'and the Attorney-General say, "Oh, by the way, there are statistics of crime which are of great importance." But these statistics, though they were furnished at first with much triumph, did not advance the cause of the Government. What were these statistics? The Government abandoned at the very beginning of the argument any comparison between the amount of crime which justified the Coercion Bill of 1887, and the amount of crime that was held to justify the Coercion Bills of 1881 and 1882. And well they might, for this is how the figures stood:

Year.								Total of agrarian crimes.
1880	...	...	...	...	...	...	...	2,585
1881	...	...	...	...	...	...	...	4,439
1882	...	...	...	...	...	...	...	3,433
1886	...	...	...	...	...	...	...	1,056

The enormous disparity will be at once perceived between the crimes of the years upon which Mr. Forster founded his claim for coercion and the crimes of the year which were held by Mr. Balfour to justify his demand for coercion.

The expedient adopted under these circumstances was to confine the comparison to the three years preceding the proposal of coercion. The result of this comparison was that the crimes of 1884 were found to be 762; of 1885, 916; and of 1886, 1,025. This certainly showed an increase, but it would be the grossest exaggeration to say that it showed that vast increase of crime which alone justifies coercion. The reader has again to be warned against taking these totals as meaning totals of serious, aggravated, heinous crime. In these statistics the pettiest and smallest offence is classed as a 'crime'—a petty larceny, an injury to property to the extent of a few shillings, an assault that in a London police-court would entail no higher penalty than a fine of five shillings or forty-eight hours' imprisonment. This abuse of the word 'crime' has already been adverted to in dealing with Mr. Forster's case for coercion; it is a fact which has to be again and again dwelt upon in dealing with pictures of the state of Ireland; it is this abuse of the word 'crime' that has given to one of the most religious, upright, and peaceful people in the world the blackest criminal character perhaps among any of the other nations of the earth. But taking coercion in its Ministerial and official, and not in its popular sense, the increase of crime in the years 1885 and 1886 over that of 1884 did not justify the demand for coercion. It was his appreciation of the fact that induced the Home Secretary to put forward a discovery which, if well-founded, materially assisted the Government. 'Since October, 1886,' he said, 'outrages in Ireland have risen 83 per cent' (speech on second reading of the Coercion Bill). This statement produced a great effect, and very naturally so; but it involved a suppression of fact that again involved a most flagrant suggestion of what was false. It was quite true that the crimes for the first quarter of 1887 were largely in excess of the crimes of the last quarter of 1886 ; but in the first place, that was no argument in the mouth of the Government. The first quarter of 1887 ends on March 31 ; the Coercion Bill was announced on March 21, and, of course, was contemplated at a much earlier date. In fact, it was resolved and considered upon when the Ministry met Parliament ; and therefore it cannot have been on the crimes of the first quarter of 1887 that the Coercion Bill was founded. The Chief Secretary had not these statistics in his hands when he made his speech introducing the Bill, and as has been seen, expressly stated that he did not found his case on statistics of crime. The second answer to the statistics of the Home Secretary is that his basis of comparison is false. He compared the crimes of the first quarter of 1887 with the crimes of the last quarter of 1886 ; the proper method of comparison is to compare the quarter of one year with the corresponding quarter of the preceding year, where there is something like a similarity of circumstances. The following table shows the crime—or so-called 'crime'—for the four quarters of 1886 and the first quarter of 1887 :

For the quarter ending March 31, 1886	256
For the quarter ending June 30, 1886	297
For the quarter ending September 30, 1886	306
For the quarter ending December 31, 1886	166
For the quarter ending March 31, 1887	241

This is a remarkable table. It shows that the first quarter of 1887, on which the Home Secretary relied as upon a sudden and opportune revelation in favour of the policy of the Government, had less crime than any quarter of the preceding year, except the last quarter. And this last quarter for 1886 deserves special consideration for its own sake, as well as a test of the honesty of the Home Secretary's style of comparison. It had, as has been seen, but 166 crimes ; that is—fewer crimes than the first, fewer than the second, fewer than the third quarter of 1886. All this although the December quarter is nearly always the quarter which, in Irish experience, is most deeply stained with crime. But in 1886 the crime of the December quarter is lower than that of any of the other quarters of the year. It stands out in bold relief as the crimeless winter quarter of its year, which makes two facts the more remarkable. First, that this especially crimeless winter quarter was the quarter when the Plan of Campaign was in fullest operation ; and secondly, was the quarter when the Government resolved that Ireland stood in need of coercion.

In the absence of statistics Mr. Balfour proposed coercion on three other grounds. The first were a series of stories—'narratives,' or 'anecdotes,' Mr. Balfour himself called them—which were not authenticated nor confirmed ; in fact, were the merest gossip. 'On what authority,' interrupted Mr. Parnell, when the Chief-Secretary was telling one of his 'narratives' or 'anecdotes,' 'on what authority does the right hon. gentleman rely for these statements?' 'I am giving the House,' was the reply of Mr. Balfour, 'the facts which I have obtained on my responsibility from what I consider an authentic source!' In other words, the gossip which Mr. Balfour heard, and Mr. Balfour believed, the House of Commons was likewise bound to accept as gospel truth ! Were ever the liberties of a single and a common pickpocket taken away on evidence so flimsy as that which justified the Chief-Secretary in taking away the liberties of a whole nation? But though the Chief-Secretary was vague in his 'anecdotes,' and though the Bill was being hurried through as fast as the Government could manage there was plenty of time to test and to destroy most of the cases brought forward by the Chief-Secretary. One was the case of a farmer named Clarke, indicted for obtaining money by means of a forged document. 'The case,' said Mr. Balfour, 'was proved in the clearest manner. . . . The judge charged strongly for conviction, but the jury, which consisted principally of farmers in the same rank of life as the prisoner, disagreed.' Mr. Parnell was able to prove that Clarke was not a Catholic farmer but a Protestant maltster, was not a National Leaguer, and was acquitted owing to the complicated nature of the accounts in dispute. A second case was that of a man called John Hogan. 'He was charged,' said the Chief Secretary, 'with a most horrible outrage upon a girl. He was acquitted by the jury in face of the clearest evidence. And why? Because he was a well-known leader in that neighbourhood.' The association between an outrage upon a woman and political or agrarian combination, is rather remote, especially in a country where such offences are rare, and are bitterly resented ; but in any case, the whole story was an invention. Hogan was charged with rape ; it came out in evidence that he had been five hours in the company of the woman on the evening when the offence was stated to have been committed ; it was alleged that the consent of the woman was given ; the prisoner himself was examined, and the jury believed his evidence ; and according to a barrister who was present, and who wrote to an Irish member, were completely justified in believing him. A third 'anecdote'—this was given by the Attorney-General—perhaps even more closely shows the kind of case on which the Government made their proposals. 'At the County Kerry Assizes,' said the Attorney-General, 'on March 11, 1887, Patrick Hickey was indicted for a moonlight offence at the house of Mr. Casey, a farmer. During the *mêlée* the disguise of one of the attacking parties fell off, and Casey recognised Hickey, his own cousin. No evidence was called for the defence, and a verdict was given "Not guilty." Here certainly was a very bad case, if true ; but what happened?' 'I rise to order,' said Mr. T. Harrington. 'I defended the prisoner, and I pledge my word to the House, and I am willing to abide by the decision of Mr. Justice O'Brien, if he did not directly charge for the acquittal of the prisoner on the ground that the charge was a fabrication, and if it was not at the judge's instance that I declined to examine any witnesses for the defence.' And the only reply the Attorney-General had to this crushing refutation of this charge was a joke, and the statement that he had founded his assertion on a report of the case in the *Freeman's Journal*.

The second plea of Mr. Balfour was illegal or violent action on the part of branches of the National League. 'Everyone knows,' said Mr. Balfour, 'that boycotting prevails over certain districts of Ireland and makes life perfectly intolerable. Everyone knows that every branch of the National League uses boycotting as the means of carrying out its decrees. . . . I have a good many cases of such occurrences here, which prove that it is done audaciously all over Ireland. One instance is from Mayo, and it is reported in *United Ireland*. In this case a branch of the League passed a resolution 'that no tradesman shall work for any person who cannot produce his card of membership of the League. The hon. member for Cork stated that any branch of the League that put such pressure on would be immediately dissolved.'

Mr. Parnell : 'So it was ; that branch was immediately dissolved.'

Not shamed by this exposure, Mr. Balfour went on to another case, and, it will be seen, with the like result.

Mr. A. J. Balfour: 'Then there was another case in Sligo.'

Mr. T. Harrington: 'Yes, and I called for the resignation of the committee.'

Finally there were the charges of the judges. One case will be sufficient to show the value of this evidence. Of course the hero is Mr. Justice Lawson, one of the sinister brood, the story of whose malign influence runs through so many of my pages. Here was the description of County Mayo in a charge of Judge Lawson which Mr. Balfour quoted in his first speech in favour of his Coercion Bill. 'He regretted to say that on this, the first occasion on which he had the honour of presiding in this court of the County Mayo, he could not say anything to them in favour of the state of things which existed in that county. . . . The present state of things was morally unsatisfactory, and according to the reports made to him, approached as near to rebellion against the authority of the country as anything short of civil war could be.'

This charge was delivered on March 10, and it, therefore, referred to the state of the county in the first quarter of 1887. There was accordingly no opportunity of testing its accuracy until the Government produced the returns of crime for this quarter. When these returns were published, an astonishing discovery was made. The county, as has been seen, was described as being 'as near to rebellion against the authority of the country as anything short of civil war could be.' What were the facts? The county has a population of 230,000; in three months the total number offences in this vast population was 12, and of these 7 were threatening letters! When one looked into the offences, the revelation was still more extraordinary. In a county 'as near to rebellion against the authority of the country as anything short of civil war,' there was not one case of murder, nor of manslaughter, nor firing at the person, nor of suspicion to murder; not one assault on a bailiff, or a police-constable, or a process-server!

Such, then, was the case for coercion; the purposes which it was intended to serve were as difficult to understand, for each different advocate of the Bill gave a different ground for its existence. 'This was a Bill,' said Mr. Balfour in the House of Commons, 'to put down crime. . . . It was not conflicts between landlord and tenant they desired to put down, it was not combinations they desired to crush;' but the Marquis of Salisbury in the House of Lords had quite a different tale to tell. 'Our position,' he said, 'is that the Land War must cease. We have offered to the other House of Parliament a measure, not without hesitation, *in order to put a stop to certain combinations.*' Similarly Mr. Balfour and the other Ministers vehemently denied that the Bill was aimed at political opponents, while the Marquis of Hartington blurted out in a speech at Edinburgh that the main object of the Bill was to put down the Irish Party.*

---

¹ 'I believed, as I still believe, that I have taken many opportunities upon previous occasions of saying that there is in Ireland a revolutionary party which relies upon the support of the still more revolutionary party in America, who have acquired over the minds of the people of Ireland an undue and excessive influence, which has to be contended with and to be overthrown before a final settlement and solution can be arrived at. The conflict with that party was a conflict which was in progress during the whole of these years to which I have referred, when Mr. Gladstone's Government was in power, from 1880 to 1885. That conflict was unhappily suspended when the Conservative Government came into office in 1885; and that conflict was still more unhappily absolutely suspended when the late Government came into power on the basis of surrender and concession. That conflict is now being renewed; that conflict will now have to be decided one way or the other, and it will not be until the final decision of that conflict has taken place that the field will in my judgment be left

When we come to the character of the measure we find that it carries out the views of Lord Salisbury and Lord Hartington, and not the bland pledges of Mr. Balfour. It makes no distinction whatever between ordinary crime and political crime. Under the various clauses of the Bill it is in the power of the Lord-Lieutenant to stop every word written or spoken, and every combination, agrarian or political, which do not recommend themselves to his views. In fact, the Coercion Bill places Ireland under a *régime* as despotic as any that exists in any part of the world. This measure, even at the moment at which I write, is being carried through the House by an abundant use of the closure, and before long it will be passed into law. It is to be accompanied by a Land Bill, the merits of which we cannot finally pronounce upon, but which according to the general impression is as much a sham as the Coercion Bill is a reality. We are thus on the eve once more of a conflict between the Irish people on one side and despotic methods on the other. In that conflict there will be much suffering, and sorrow, and bitterness, but nobody who has read the story in the preceding pages of similar conflicts in the past will have much doubt as to the final result. The Irish people have had to struggle with Coercion Acts before, and have conquered them. This they have done when circumstances were much less favourable than they are at the present moment. Between the present and previous struggles there is a vast, a gigantic and revolutionary difference. In the past England stood solid against Ireland. In the present Ireland has no firmer friends or more ardent sympathisers or more active combatants on her side than large sections of the English people. The hopeful thing about all this controversy is the opportunity it has given of testing the conscience of a democracy, and the fact that the democracy has stood the test. Whatever other classes of British society may do against Ireland, the English masses stand steadily at her back. In the alliance which has thus been produced already a large amount of the old bitterness and the old hatred between the two peoples is perishing. This alliance has done more to obliterate the evil memories of the past than any other event. And so out of the evil sown by the Government good, for once, has come.

I have now traced for the readers of this work the history of the greater part of the period that has elapsed since the Act of Union was passed. These pages are intended as an indictment of the Act. I have proved that that Act has cost the Irish people more than a million of lives by hunger, and upwards of three millions by exile; that it has produced three rebellions and eighty-seven Coercion Acts, and that thus, while called an Act of Union, it has been the cause of separation between the two nations. I close the volume with a strong hope that the last stage of the struggle, though fierce, will be short, that the drear and tragic monotony of famine, emigration, revolt, imprisonment and death will at last be brought to an end, and that before long the hideous facts recorded in the preceding pages will read like the recollections of nightmares that fly before the growing day.

---

clear for any Government or any party to propose either a final solution of the agrarian questions which are the real root of the evils of Ireland, or to make a final offer or proposal for a concession to the Irish people of those extended powers and opportunities for self-government which we, as well as any other portion of the people of this country, are perfectly willing to grant to Ireland, to Scotland, or to the people of England.'—*Times*, April 18, 1887.

INDEX.

A

ABERDEEN, Lord, 104, 106
Absenteeism, 16, 17
Adair, John George, 112, 117, 118, 119
Agrarian crime (Ireland), 214, 215, 216, 217
Agricultural labourers (Irish), 120
Alexander, Mr., 103
Allen, William Philip, 136
Allman, Charlotte, 177
American Irish. *See* Irish Americans
      " Land League, 173
Anglesey, Marquis of, 8
Archdale, Mr., 261
Argyll, Duke of, 197
Arms Act, 15, 20, 21, 227
Arrears Act, 251, 252, 253
Arterial Drainage (Ireland) Act, 17, 21
Ashbourne, Lord. *See* Gibson
Athlone, 89, 90, 100, 101, 264

B.

BALFOUR, Mr. A. J., 259, 290, 291, 292, 293, 294, 295
Ballingarry, 48
Ballot, 139
Bantry, Earl of, 208
Barnes, Mr. A., 285, 286
Barran, Sir H., 75
Barry, John, 195, 196, 209, 226
    " Judge, 123, 245
Barton, Capt., 261
Baumann, Mr., 285
Beaconsfield, Lord, 29, 76, 92, 98, 155, 174.
Belfast, 275
Bellingham, Mr., 265
Bentinck, Lord George, 28, 29, 46, 47
Berkeley, Bishop, 22
Bessborough Commission, 202
Biggar, Joseph Gillis, 141, 146, 147, 148, 149, 154, 155, 156, 157, 158, 159, 161, 173, 196, 207, 222, 223, 224, 226, 239, 250
Blake, Mr., M.P., 196
    " Mrs. James, 113
Blakeney, General, 8
Blosse, Sir Robert, 112
Blunt, Mr. W., 271
Bond, Major, 229, 230
Boord, Mr., 287
Borough Franchise, Irish, 213
Bowyer, Sir George, 141

Boycotting, 203
Boyd, Rochford, 113
Bradlaugh, Mr., 227
Brady, Joe, 239
'Brass Band.' *See* 'Pope's Brass Band
Brennan, Joseph, 207
    " Thomas, 173
Brett, Sergeant, 136
Brewster, Mr., 106
Bright, John, 98, 177, 178, 200, 206, 283
Brodrick, Mr., 263
Brooks, Maurice, 196
Brougham, Lord, 14, 77
Browne, Bishop, 101, 106
Brownlow, Mr., 16, 17, 21
Burke, General Thomas, 136
    " Mr., Assassination of, 249, 256
Butt, Isaac, opposes O'Connell in Repeal debate in Dublin Corporation, 9 ; heads Home Rule movement, 138 ; his early career, 140 ; character and genius, 140, 141, 142 ; political difficulties, 140 ; character of his party, 141 ; his early policy, 144 ; its failure, 145 ; contrasted with Biggar, 156 ; reproves Obstructives, 158 ; denounces their tactics, 158 ; retires from leadership, 162 ; decline and death, 163 ; review of his policy, 163 ; effect of his death, 163.
Buxton, Mr. S., 276, 280
Byrne, Mr. Garrett, 195, 196, 226, 250

C.

CALLAN, Mr., 196, 250
'Carding,' 217, 218
Cardwell, Mr., 126, 127
Carey, James, 195, 196, 257
Carlingford, Lord, 234
Carlisle, Lord, 8, 128, 129
Carnarvon, Lord, 262, 272, 289
Castle. *See* Dublin Castle
Catholic Defence Association, 94, 95, 98
Catholic Emancipation, 8, 11
Catholic Telegraph, 95
Cavendish, Lord Frederick, Assassination of, 249, 256
Census Commissioners', 39, 42, 43
Central Tenants' Defence Association, 170
Chaine, Mr., 265
Challemel-Lacour, M., 179
Chamberlain, Joseph, 164, 202, 206, 256, 266, 270, 273, 283, 289

Chaplin, Mr., 155, 262
Cholera, 42, 54
Christian, Judge, 122
Churchill, Lord R., 264, 266, 267, 270, 274, 288
Civil Bill Ejectments, 17, 18, 20
Clanricarde, Lord, 140
Clarendon, Lord, 48
Clerkenwell Prison, explosion at, 136
Clontarf meeting, 12, 13
Cobbett, William, 22
Coercion, 27
Coercion Acts, 15, 18, 19, 20, 21, 27, 28, 29, 70, 71, 75, 76, 214
Coffins, hinged, 43
Collings, Mr. Jesse, 275
Colthurst, Colonel, 196
Commins, Dr., 196, 250
Compensation for disturbance, 200, 201
Conciliation Hall, 49
Condon, Edward O'Meara, 136, 137
Constabulary Circular, extraordinary, 246
Cook, Dr., 85
Corbet, Mr., 195, 196, 226, 250
Cork Daily Herald, 254
Cork Historical Society, 176
Corn Laws, Abolition of, 19
'Corruption Committee,' 103
Corydon, J., 169
Cowper, Earl, 247
Crawford, Sharman, 17, 21, 73, **74**, 75, 76, 126
Crimes Act, 250, 266
Crimes (Irish), 291, 292
Croke, Archbishop, 257
Cross, Sir R., 222
Crowbar Brigade, 114
Cuban rebellion, 190, 191
Cullen, Cardinal, 93, 94, 101

D.

Daily Express, 261, 262
Daily News, 265
Daily Telegraph, 132, 143
Daly, Mr., M.P., 196, 226
Davis, Thomas, 12
Davitt, Michael, 168, 169, 170, 173, 225, 235, 254
Dawson, Mr. C., 196, 213, 226
Deasy's Act, 127
Deasy, Captain, 136
Denman, Judge, 14
Deputy-Speaker. *See* Playfair
Derby, Lord, 104
Derry Standard, 118
Derryveigh, 117
D'Esterre, 11
Devon Commission, 17, 23, 24
Dilke, Sir Charles, 182, 206, 218, 266
Dillon, Mr. John, 173, 193, 194, 204, 207, 225, 226, 231, 239, 250, 273
Dillon, Mr. John B., 12, 48, 49, 193
Disestablished Irish Church. *See* Irish Church
Disraeli, Mr. *See* Beaconsfield
Dissentient Liberals, 283, 284, 294
Disturbance Bill. *See* 'Compensation for Disturbance'

Doherty, Mr., 17
'Dove of Elphin,' 101, 106
Downing, Captain D. J., 187
Downing, Mr. McCarthy, 96, 156
'Droit de Seigneur,' 116
Drummond, Mr., 8
Dublin Corporation, 9, 25, 26
Duffy, Sir Charles Gavan, 9, 12, 47, 48, 49, 86, 92, 94, 95, 103, 106
Duggan, Bishop, 148
'Durham letter,' 87
'Duty-work,' 16
Dyke, Sir W. H., 267

E.

EBRINGTON, Lord, 8
Ecclesiastical Titles Bill, 92, 93, 98
Edward III., statute of, 241
Egan, Mr. Patrick, 173, 207, 254
Eglinton, Lord, 104, 105
Emigration (Irish), 44, 45, 69, 131
Emigration (Irish) (1849-60 and 1861-70), 131
Emly, Lord, 91, 98
Encumbered Estates Act, 23, 68, 69
  ,,   ,,   Court, 121
Ennis, Sir J., 265
Errington, Mr., 196
Estate Rules. *See* Office Rules
Evelyn, Mr., 287
Evictions, 20, 167, 200, 201, 231, 244
Exports, Irish (1841-49), 79, 80

F.

FAIR rents, 85
Famine, Irish, 16, 21, 22
Fay, Mr. P. McC., 162, 196
Fenianism, 134, 135
Finigan, Mr. Lysaght, 185, 196, 226
Fitzgerald, J. D. (Judge, afterwards Lord), 110, 122, 212, 264
  ,,   Baron, 122, 229
'Five-pound Repealers,' 51
Fixity of tenure, 85
Foley, Mr., 196
Forster, Mr. W. E., 32, 201, 202, 204, 206, 214, 215, 216, 218, 219, 221, 223, 224, 227, 228, 229, 230, 231, 235, 236, 239, 240, 241, 242, 245, 246, 247, 248, 249, 250, 251, 255, 256, 257, 263, 272, 291
Forty-shilling freeholders, 17
Freeman's Journal, 94, 95, 96, 195, 254
Free sale, 85
Free trade, 35

G.

GABBETT, Mr., 196
General Election of 1847, 49
  ,,   ,,   of 1852, 98
  ,,   ,,   of 1874, 140
  ,,   ,,   of 1880, 174
  ,,   ,,   of 1885, 270, 271, 272, 273, 274
  ,,   ,,   of 1886, 283, 284, 285, 286, 287, 288
Gent-Davis, Mr., 271

INDEX

Gibson, Mr. (Lord Ashbourne), 232, 269
Giffen, 262
Gill, Mr. H. J., 188, 196, 226, 258
Givan, Mr., 259
Gladstone, Mr. W. E., 68, 92, 165, 198, 200, 201, 221, 222, 224, 225, 226, 235, 236, 247, 251, 252, 263, 266, 267, 273, 275, 282, 284, 285, 286, 287, 288, 289
Gladstone, Mr. Herbert, 210
Gladstone's Home Rule Bill, 275, 276, 277, 278, 279, 280
Gladstone Land Bill of 1885, 281, 281, 282
Glenbeigh, 117
Glin, Knight of, 36
Godkin, James, 85
Godley, Mr., 70
'God save Ireland,' 137
Gordon, General, 266
Gorst, Mr., 245, 256
Goschen, Mr., 263, 268, 275
Gosset, Capt., 226
Graham, Sir James, 8, 27, 92
'Grahamising letters,' 8
Grattan, Henry, 17, 21
Gray, Mr. E. D., 173, 195, 196, 226, 239, 250
Gray, Sir John, 85, 98, 115, 116, 129, 195
Green Street Court House, 135
Grey, Earl, 28, 71, 76
Grosvenor, Lord R., 273

H.

HABEAS CORPUS Suspension Acts, 18, 19, 20, 21, 76, 135
Hamilton, Lord Claud, 261
" Lord George, 269
Hammond, Mr., 271
'Hanging gale,' 86, 232
Harcourt, Sir W. V., 223, 250
Harrington, Mr. T., 258, 259
Harris, Alderman, 239
" Matthew, 170
Hartington, Lord, 155, 164, 197, 202, 210, 216, 262, 275, 283, 293, 294, 295
Havelock-Allan, Sir H., 286
Hay, Sir John, 246, 251
Healy, Mr. Maurice, M.P., 212
" Miss Kate, 186
" Mr. Timothy, M.P., 196, 208, 209, 210, 211, 212, 225, 226, 232, 235, 239, 240, 250, 259, 273
Healy Clause, 232
Hennessy, Sir J. Pope, 176
Herbert, Sidney, 107
Hicks-Beach, Sir M., 140, 156, 158, 289, 290
'History of our own Times,' 175, 178
Hoey, Mr. J. Cashel, 127
'Home Government Association,' 138
Home Rule, 125, 138, 140, 141, 144, 145, 270, 274, 275, 276, 277, 278, 279, 280, 282, 283, 286
Home Rule Confederation, 162
" League, 149
" Party, 144, 145, 161, 173, 175
Horsman, Mr., 75, 126

I.

INCHIQUIN, Lord, 113
'Incorruptible Parnell,' 150

Independent opposition, 49, 50, 125
Insurrection Acts, 18, 19, 20, 21
Intermediate Education Bill, 164
'Invincibles,' 23, 257
Irish Americans, 78, 133, 134, 135, 166, 167, 173
'Irish Blanqui,' The, 194
Irish Board of Works, 34
'Irish Brigade.' See 'Pope's Brass Band'
Irish Church Disestablishment, 9, 123, 137
Irish Missions, 112
'Irish Committee,' 70
Irish in England, 136, 162
Irish manufactures, 16
Irish Members, suspension of, 226, 250
" Parliamentary Party, 15
Irish People (newspaper), 135, 153
Irish Times, 138

J.

JACKSON, Mr. H. M., 285
Jagoe, Rev. Mr., 261
James, Sir Henry, 275
Jennings, Mr., M.P., 271
Johnston, Attorney-General, 255
" Mr. William, 148
'Journals, etc., relating to Ireland,' 129
Joyce, Myles, 268
Judges, Irish, 88, 122, 123, 124
Jury-packing, 8, 13, 14, 48

K.

KEANE, Mr. Marcus, 114
Kelly, Colonel, 136
Kenny, Mr., M.P., 264
Keogh, Mr. W. (afterwards Judge), 87, 88, 89, 90, 91, 92, 93, 94, 95, 96, 97, 100, 101, 102, 103, 104, 105, 106, 108, 109, 110, 135, 138
Kerr, Mr. M., 261
Kerry Sentinel, 258
Kettle, Mr. A. J., 172, 173
Kildare and Leighlin, Bishop of, 103
Killala, Bishop of, 101
Kilmainham, Treaty, 247, 248
Kilmartin, Bryan, 269
Kilrush Union. Famine and evictions in, 54, 55, 56, 57, 58, 59, 60, 61, 62, 63, 64, 65, 66, 67
King-Harman, Colonel, 138, 144, 181, 261
Kirk, Miss, 241, 242

L.

LABOUCHERE, Mr. H., 219, 221, 231, 242
Labour Rate Act, 34, 35, 37, 44
Ladies' Land League, 241
Lahiff, Mr., 120
Lalor, Mr. J. F., 194
" Mr. R., 194, 196, 226, 250
Land Act of 1870, 165, 197
" 1881, 210, 228, 232
Land Acts and Bills, 20, 74, 75, 143, 228, 280, 285
Land Bill (Mr. Redmond's), 247
" Commission (Bessborough), 202
" Court, 234

Land League, 170, 174, 213, 214, 228, 233, 235, 240, 247, 268, 269
Lansdowne, Lord, 76, 115, 116
Larcom, Sir Thomas, 117
Larkin, Michael, 136
Lavelle, Father, 111, 113
Law, Right Hon. Hugh, 207, 232
Lawson, Judge, 123, 294
Leahy, Mr., 196, 226, 250
Leamy, Mr. E., 196, 223, 226, 250
Leinster, Duke of, 25, 129
Leitrim, Lord, 111, 112, 116
Lethbridge, Mr. R., 271, 286
Letters, Opening of, 8
Lever, Mr. J. O., 174
Levinge, Sir R., 98, 104
Lewis, Sir C., 148, 273
Liberal Unionists, 124, 283, 284, 285, 286, 287
Lincoln, Lord, 17, 71
Litton, Mr., 233
Lloyd, Mr. Clifford, 229, 230, 231, 241, 242, 245, 246
Lowe, Mr., 127
Lowther, Mr. J., 167, 168, 173
Luby, Mr. T. C., 135
Lucan, Lord, 111, 112, 113
Lucas, Mr. F., 85, 97, 98, 106
Lyons, Dr., 223, 224

M.

MACFARLANE, Mr., 196
MacHale, Archbishop, 93, 94, 101, 132
Mackay, Capt., 253
MacKnight, Dr., 85
MacManus, Terence Bellew, 134
MacNevin, R. C., 105
McCarthy, Colour-Sergeant, 169
  ,, Mr. J., 31, 43, 78, 123, 175, 176, 177, 178, 179, 180, 196, 197, 198, 208, 213, 224, 226, 250, 273
McCarthy, Mr. J. H., 264
McCoan, Mr., 196, 226
McCormack, Miss, imprisoned, 241
M'Gee, Mr. T. D., 48, 49
McGrath, M., 211, 212
McKenna, Sir J. N., 196
M'Mahon, Evor, 129
McMahon, Mr., M.P., 263
Magan, Capt., 98
Maguire, John Francis, 85, 97, 126
  ,, Thos., 136
Mahdi, The, 192
Maher, Father, 103
Mahon, The O'Gorman, 194, 196, 226
Mallon, Superintendent, 238
Mallow, 255
'Mambi Land,' 191
Manayunk, 169
Manchester, 136
Marlborough, Duchess of, 173
Martin, John, 149
Marum, Mr., 196, 226, 250, 251
Mathew, Rev. Theobald, 31
Mathews, Henry, Home Secretary, 123, 289, 290
Maynooth, Grant, 15
Mazzini, 8
Meagher, Thomas Francis, 134
Meath, Bishop of, 101
Melbourne, Lord, 9, 17

Meldon, Mr. C., 145, 196
Metge, Mr., 226, 250
Mill, John Stuart, 24, 177
Milner, Sir F., 271
Mitchel, John, 12, 13, 14, 25, 36, 47, 48, 79, 134, 176, 193, 194
Moate, Rector of, 104
Moderate Home Rulers. *See* Nominal Home Rulers
Monaghan, County, 259
Monahan, Judge, 117
Monroe, Mr. J. (Q.C.), 259
Moore, George Henry, 97, 126
  ,, Mrs., 241, 242
Morley, Mr. John, 283, 291
Morning Star, 177, 178
Moroney, Mrs., 241
Murphy, Mr. N. D., 174
  ,, Serjeant, 122, 123
'Murty Hynes,' 188

N.

NAAS, Lord (Earl of Mayo), 105, 107
Nagle, Alderman, 254
Naish, Attorney-General, 255
Napier, Sir J., 126
Nation (newspaper), 12, 45, 46, 47, 86, 87, 95, 96, 109, 110, 125, 180, 181, 187, 208
National meetings in Ulster, 260, 261, 262
Neligan, Mr. J. C., 258
Nelson, Rev. Isaac, 226, 265
Newcastle, Duke of, 104, 107
Newdegate, Mr. 92
Newport, Sir John, 16
New York Herald, 190
Nimmo, Mr. Alexander, 23
Nominal Home Rulers, 263, 265
'No Popery,' 87
'No Rent,' 47, 194, 232
'No-Rent' Manifesto, 235, 240
Normanby, Lord, 8
Norris, Mr., 108
Northcote, Sir S., 158, 159, 181, 223, 224, 263
Northern Times, 177
Norton, Mr. Thomas, 102
Nulty, Bishop, 114

O.

O'BEIRNE, William, 90
  ,, Judge, 123
  ,, M. (*alias* Gould), 136
  ,, Sir Patrick, 141, 196
  ,, William, 253, 254, 255, 273
  ,, William Smith, 17, 21, 48, 134
O'Connell, Daniel, his work for the Irish people, 7; disappointed with Emancipation, 7; starts Repeal agitation, 8; opposed by Liberals, 8; prosecuted, 8; reviles Whigs, 8; his Repeal motion defeated, 8; works for redress of minor grievances, 8; is elected Lord Mayor of Dublin, 9; supports Melbourne Ministry, 9; again starts Repeal agitation, 9; carries Repeal motion in Dublin Corporation, 9; effect on agitation, 9; his action after Tara meeting, 10; habits and daily

life at this time, 11; character of speeches, 11; his attitude towards Young Irelanders, 13, 14; his action at Clontarf, 14; effect on Repeal movement, 14; prosecuted and imprisoned, 14; is released, 14; 'a broken man,' 14; popular opinion, 15; decay of his power, 15; calls attention of Government to impending famine, 25; his proposals for relief of distress, 25; split with Young Irelanders, 46, 47; his great speech on Land Question, 47; his death, 47; character of his Parliamentary supporters, 47; his attitude towards the Russell Ministry, 47; his Parliamentary party, 50

O'Connell, John, 46, 47, 51, 74
O'Connor, Mr. Arthur, 182, 183, 184, 185, 186, 196, 226, 239, 240, 250
O'Connor, Miss Mary, 241, 242
,, Mr. John, 263
,, Mr. T. P., 196, 226, 250
O'Conor, Don, The, 259, 260
O'Donnell, Mr. F. H., 179, 250
O'Donoghue, The, 197, 226
O'Donovan (Rossa), Jeremiah, 134, 135
'Office Rules,' 115, 116
O'Flaherty, Anthony, 91, 98
,, Edmund, 91, 94, 100, 105, 107, 108, 109
O'Gorman, Mahon. *See* Mahon, O'Gorman
O'Grady, Hon. Michael, 119
O'Hagan, Mr. Justice, 233
O'Kelly, James, 137, 188, 189, 190, 191, 192, 193, 196, 239, 250
O'Leary, John, 135
,, Dr., 156
'Old Ironsides,' 151
Orangeism, 8, 9, 14, 48, 49, 261, 262
O'Rourke, Father, 40, 84
Osborne, Mr. Bernal, 18
O'Shaughnessy, Mr., 263
O'Shea, Captain, 196, 251, 265
O'Sullivan, W. H., 173, 196, 226, 230, 250
Outrages, agrarian, 214, 215, 216, 217

P.

PALLES, Chief Baron, 148
Pall Mall Gazette, 227, 288
Palmerstone, Lord, 96, 106, 125, 126, 127
'Parliamentary History of the Irish Land Question,' 17
Parnell, Mr. C. S., 137, 147; contests Dublin County, 149; repugnance to speaking, 150; history of his family, 150; his early years, 152; lessons of youth, 152; hatred of cruelty, 153; turning-point of life, 153; country life, 154; how he took up Obstruction, 154; first efforts in the House, 157; nucleus of his party, 157; attacked by Butt, 158; wrath of the House, 159; motion to suspend him, 159; opposes South African Bill, 159; policy approved in Ireland, 161, 171; elected President of Home Rule Confederation of Great Britain, 162; fights flogging clauses of Army Regulation Bill, 164; opinion of London papers about him, 164; how he became a Land Leaguer, 168; at Westport, 171; declares for 'Peasant Proprietary,' 171; advises farmers 'to keep a firm grip of their homesteads,' 171; effect of his joining Land movement, 171; Land League founded, 171; visits America, 173; founds American Land League, 174; prepares for Election of 1880, 174; his difficulties as to funds and candidates, 174; returned for Cork City, 174; elected leader of Parliamentary Party, 196; speaks on Amendment to Queen's Speech, 199; obtains concession from Government, 200; difficulty as to policy, 201; advises farmers not to give evidence before Land Commission, 203; recommends boycotting, 203; his justification, 204; his attitude towards Shaw's party, 204; opinion on 'Three F's' and 'Peasant Proprietary,' 204, 205; on Irish legislative independence, 205; trial for conspiracy, 207; his amendment to Queen's Speech (1881), 213; raises question about Davitt, 225; moves that Gladstone be no longer heard, 226; 'named,' 226; suspended, 226; proposes abstention from second reading Land Bill, 231; attitude towards Land Courts, 234; adopts Test Case policy, 235; attacked by Gladstone at Leeds, 236; replies to him at Wexford, 236; is arrested and lodged in Kilmainham, 238; his victory over Government in the Kilmainham treaty, 247, 248; Mr. Forster's testimony, 248; suspension of Irish members for opposing Crimes Bill, 250; his anxiety as to Arrears Question, 251; speech on the subject, 251; drafts Mr. Redmond's Land Bill, 253; Mr. Forster's great speech against him, 256; its effect on the Irish people, 257; National Tribute started, 257; declares for Legislative independence, 270

Parnell, John, 150
,, John, 154
,, John Henry, 150
,, Miss Fanny, 153, 160
,, Mrs. 153,
,, Sir Henry, 150, 151
,, Sir John, 150
,, Thomas, 150
Patton, Dr., 262
Peel Sir Robert (late), 9, 10, 11, 15, 19, 20, 26, 27, 30, 33, 67, 68, 69, 70, 76, 78
Pennefather, Judge, 14
Perraud, M., 115
Phœnix Park murders, 249, 250
Phœnix Society, 187
Pigott, Chief Baron, 116
Place-hunting, 50
'Plan of Campaign,' 290
Playfair, Sir L., 222, 223, 232
Plunket, Hon. Mr., 8
,, Lord, 112
Pollock, Mr. Allan, 112, 113

INDEX.

Poor Law Commissioners' Report, 40, 52, 60
Poor Law inquiry of 1835, 24
'Pope's Brass Band,' The, 93, 103
Power, Dr. Maurice, 91, 96
,, Mr. John O'Connor, 161, 170, 225, 226
Power, Mr. Richard, 141, 194, 196, 250
Pringle, Mr., 259
Prisons Bill, 158
Prisons, Death in (in 1846), 41

Q.

QUEEN's Speech (Session of 1845), 27
,, Speech (Session of 1880), 198
,, Speech (Session of 1881), 212, 213

R.

RACK-RENTING, 16
Raikes, Mr., 158, 159
'Realities of Irish Life,' 115
Redistribution Bill, 182, 263
Redmond, Mr. J. E., 226, 247, 250, 253
,, Mr. W. H. K., 259, 260
Reform Act of 1832, 8
Relief Act, 43
,, Committees, 43, 47
Relief of Distress Bill, 174, 202
,, works, 33, 34, 43, 44
Repeal, 8, 9, 11, 12, 46, 51, 52
Reynolds, Miss, imprisoned, 241
'Road Fever,' 38
Roche, Mr. (Lord Fermoy), 98
Roebuck, Mr., 127
Ronayne, Mr., 156
Rosslea, 261
Rossmore, Lord, 261
Russell, Lord John, 25, 26, 28, 30, 33, 34, 35, 47, 48, 51, 67, 70, 71, 72, 73, 74, 75, 76, 79, 87, 92, 96, 98

S.

SADLEIR, James, 98, 107, 108
,, John, 87, 91, 92, 93, 94, 95, 96, 98, 100, 101, 103, 105, 106, 107
Sadleir's Bank, 91, 106, 107, 108, 109, 110
Salisbury, Lord, 251, 267, 275, 288, 289, 294, 295
Saturday Review, 132
Saunderson, Colonel, 261
Scrope, Mr. Poulett, 17
Scully, Mr. Frank, 91, 98
,, Mr. Vincent, 91, 96, 98
Selborne, Lord, 234
Senior, Mr. Nassau, 128, 129
Sergeant-at-Arms. See Gossett
Sexton, Mr. Thomas, 180, 181, 182, 196, 207, 223, 226, 246, 250, 273
Shaw-Lefevre, Mr., 223, 266
Shaw, Mr. William, 164, 196, 199, 200, 213
Shee, Serjeant, 126
Sheehy, Father, 230, 235
Sheil, Mr., M.P., 141, 250
,, Richard Lalor, 50, 51
Sheridan, General, 190

Sinclair, Mr., M.P., 265
'Sitting Bull,' 192
Skibbereen, 38, 43
Sligo, 105
,, Marquis of, 112
Smith, Colonel, 103
Smith, Mr. W. H., 246, 269
Smithwick, Mr., 196, 226
Smyth, Mr. P. J., 196, 263
Somerville, Sir W., 73, 75
'Song from the Backwoods,' 187
'Soup Kitchen Act,' 43, 44
South African Bill, 158, 159, 160
Speaker, The (Sir H. Brand), 159, 222, 224, 225, 226, 227
Special magistrates. See Magistrates
Spencer, Lord, 253, 262, 268
Stanley, Lord, 17, 28
Stephens, Mr. James, 134, 135
Stevens, Mr., 108
Stewart, Commodore, 151, 152
,, Miss, 151
Straid, 168
Sub-letting Act, 7
Sullivan, A. M., 30, 31, 32, 33, 36, 98, 119, 125, 138, 141. 149, 186, 226
Sullivan, Sir Edward, 123
,, Mr. T. D., 125, 137, 186, 187, 188, 196, 207, 226, 250
Suspension of Evictions Bill, 200, 201
,, of Irish Members, 226, 250
Swift, Dean, 'Modest Proposal,' 16, 21
,, Mr. Richard, 107
Synan, Mr., 196

T.

Tablet, 98
Tara, 10
Taylor, Colonel, 147
Tenant Right, 26, 73, 74, 85, 86, 87, 92, 94, 95, 97, 98, 99, 126, 127
'Three F's,' The, 85, 137, 138, 204
Times, The, 69, 131, 132, 248, 249, 262, 269, 294
Torrens, Judge, 110
Traill, Major, 229, 230
Treason Felony Act, 76
Trench, Mr. F., 129
,, Mr. S., 115, 129
Trevelyan, Mr. (afterwards Sir C.), 37, 242
Trevelyan, Sir G. O., 124, 180, 251, 252, 262, 269, 275
Tuke, Mr., 32, 33, 40

U.

ULSTER, 260, 261, 262
,, Custom, 75, 84, 126
,, Nationalists, 260
,, Presbyterians, 260
Union, Act of, 9, 18, 22, 78, 125, 295
Unionists, 125
United Ireland, 254, 255
Unlawful Oaths Act, 21

V.

VATICAN, 15, 257
Vernon, Mr. 233

W.

Walsh, J. W., 211, 212
Weekly News, 181
Wellington, Duke of, 17
Westmeath, 98, 257
    ,, Lord, 104
Wexford People, 100
Whately, Archbishop, 8, 70, 128
Whiggery, 125, 126
Whigs, 8, 29
White, Father, 113
Whiteboy Act, 21
Whitworth, Mr., 229
    ,, Mr. B., 174, 229, 265

Wilde, Sir W., 84
Wilkinson, Mr., 107, 108
Wiseman, Cardinal, 87
Wolseley, General, 192
Women, treatment of, under Coercion Acts, 241, 242
Wood, Colonel, 286
World, The (London), 155, 164

Y.

'Young Ireland' (book), 9
Young Ireland (periodical), 181
Young Ireland Party, 12, 13, 15, 46, 47, 48, 49, 50, 51, 74

THE END.

BILLING AND SONS, PRINTERS, GUILDFORD.

A SELECTION FROM
MESSRS. WARD & DOWNEY'S PUBLICATIONS.
JULY, 1887.

ARNOLD, REV. F.—ROBERTSON OF BRIGHTON: with some Notes of his Times and his Contemporaries. Post 8vo. 9s.

BROGLIE, DUC DE.—THE PERSONAL RECOLLECTIONS OF THE DUC DE BROGLIE. Edited by R. L. de Beaufort. Two vols., demy 8vo. With a portrait on steel.

DAUNT, W. J. O'NEILL.—EIGHTY-FIVE YEARS OF IRISH HISTORY (1800-1885). Two vols. Crown 8vo. 21s.

ELLIOTT, FRANCES.—OLD COURT LIFE IN FRANCE. Royal 8vo. With twenty whole-page engravings. 7s. 6d.

FROST, THOMAS.—RECOLLECTIONS OF A COUNTRY JOURNALIST. Demy 8vo. 12s. 6d.

MOLLOY, J. FITZGERALD.—COURT LIFE BELOW STAIRS; or, London under the Four Georges. Two vols. Crown 8vo. 12s.

———— FAMOUS PLAYS, from Congreve's "Love for Love" to Lytton's "Lady of Lyons." Large post 8vo. [10s. 6d.

———— ROYALTY RESTORED; or, London under Charles II. Two vols. Large crown 8vo. With twelve portraits. 25s.

LEGGE, ALFRED O.—THE UNPOPULAR KING: The Life and Times of Richard III. Two vols. Demy 8vo. With sixteen illustrations. 30s.

O'CONNOR, T. P.—GLADSTONE'S HOUSE OF COMMONS. Demy 8vo. 12s. 6d.

O'SHEA, JOHN AUGUSTUS.—AN IRONBOUND CITY: Five Months of Peril and Privation in Besieged Paris. Two vols. Crown 8vo. 21s.

———— LEAVES FROM THE LIFE OF A SPECIAL CORRESPONDENT. Two vols. Crown 8vo. 21s.

———— ROMANTIC SPAIN: A Record of Personal Experiences. Two vols. Crown 8vo. 21s.

ROOSEVELT, BLANCHE.—VERDI AND 'OTHELLO.' Imp. 16mo. With numerous illustrations.

SAND, GEORGE.—THE LIFE AND LETTERS OF GEORGE SAND: with a Biographical Sketch. Three vols. Demy 8vo. 36s.

SMITH, GEORGE BARNETT.—VICTOR HUGO: His Life and Work. Crown 8vo. With an engraved portrait of Hugo. 6s.

STRAUSS, G. L. M.—THE EMPEROR WILLIAM: The Story of a Great King and a Good Man. [In the Press.

WALL, A. H.—FIFTY YEARS OF A GOOD QUEEN'S REIGN. Imp. 16mo. With six portraits. 3s. 6d. Gilt edges, 4s. 6d.

AN APOLOGY FOR THE LIFE OF MR. GLADSTONE. Crown 8vo. 7s. 6d.

FICTION.

AUTHOR OF 'MEHALAH.'—LITTLE TU'PENNY. 1s.

AUTHOR OF 'MOLLY BAWN.'—A MENTAL STRUGGLE. 6s.

———— MAIDEN ALL FORLORN. 2s.

———— LADY VALWORTH'S DIAMONDS. 1s.

———— HER WEEK'S AMUSEMENT. 2s.

———— A MODERN CIRCE. Three vols.

APPLETON, G. W.—A TERRIBLE LEGACY. 6s.

BARRETT, FRANK.—HIS HELPMATE. 6s.

———— HONEST DAVIE. 2s.

———— JOHN FORD. Two vols. 12s.

———— FOUND GUILTY. Three vols. 31s. 6d.

———— FOLLY MORRISON. 2s.

BETHAM-EDWARDS, M.—THE FLOWER OF DOOM. 2s.

CAMERON, MRS. H. LOVETT.—A LIFE'S MISTAKE. 3s. 6d.

COLLINS, MABEL.—THE PRETTIEST WOMAN IN WARSAW. 6s.

———— LORD VANECOURT'S DAUGHTER. Three vols. 31s. 6d.

CROKER, B. M.—PROPER PRIDE. 2s.

———— PRETTY MISS NEVILLE. 2s.

CROKER, B. M.—A BIRD OF PASSAGE. 6s.
DOWLING, RICHARD.—THE SKELETON KEY. 1s.
——— UNDER ST. PAUL'S. 2s.
——— THE DUKE'S SWEETHEART. 2s.
——— TEMPEST DRIVEN. 6s.
——— FATAL BONDS. Three vols. 31s. 6d.
DOWNEY, EDMUND.—A HOUSE OF TEARS. 1s.
——— IN ONE TOWN. 3s. 6d.
——— ANCHOR WATCH YARNS. 3s. 6d.
FARJEON, B. L.—A SECRET INHERITANCE.
    Three vols. 31s. 6d.   [In August.
——— THE TRAGEDY OF FEATHERSTONE. 3 vols. 31s. 6d.
——— THE SACRED NUGGET. 6s.
——— GREAT PORTER SQUARE. 2s.
——— IN A SILVER SEA. 2s.
——— THE HOUSE OF WHITE SHADOWS. 2s.
——— GRIF. 2s.
——— MOLKA. 1s.
FENN, G. MANVILLE.—THIS MAN'S WIFE. Three vols. 31s. 6d.
——— MASTER OF THE CEREMONIES. 6s.
——— IN JEOPARDY. 6s.
——— DOUBLE CUNNING. 6s.
——— THE BAG OF DIAMONDS. 1s.
——— THE DARK HOUSE. 1s.
——— EVE AT THE WHEEL. 1s.
——— THE CHAPLAIN'S CRAZE. 1s.
FENDALL, PERCY.—SEX TO THE LAST. Three vols. 31s. 6d.
——— SPIDERS AND FLIES. Three vols. 31s. 6d.
FORRESTER, MRS.—VIVA. 2s.
FOTHERGILL, CAROLINE.—AN ENTHUSIAST. 3 vols. 31s. 6d.
GIFT, THEO.—LIL LORIMER. 6s.
GRANT, JAMES.—PLAYING WITH FIRE. Three vols. 31s. 6d.
HARRISON, MRS. BURTON.—FOLK AND FAIRY TALES. 7s. 6d.
HARTE, BRET.—SNOWBOUND AT EAGLE'S. 2s.
HILLARY, MAX.—A DEADLY ERRAND. 1s.
HUGO, VICTOR.—THE OUTLAW OF ICELAND. 2s. 6d.
MACQUOID, KATHARINE S.—AT THE RED GLOVE. Three vols. 31s. 6d.
——— SIR JAMES APPLEBY. Three vols. 31s. 6d.
MOLLOY, J. FITZGERALD.—THAT VILLAIN ROMEO. 6s.
MURRAY, D. CHRISTIE.—A NOVELIST'S NOTE-BOOK. 6s.
    [In the Press.
OLIPHANT, MRS.—OLIVER'S BRIDE. 1s.
PANTON, J. E.—A TANGLED CHAIN. Two vols. 21s.
——— LESS THAN KIN. 3s. 6d.
PAYN, JAMES.—A PRINCE OF THE BLOOD. Three vols. 31s. 6d.   [In preparation.
PHILIPS, F. C.—THE DEAN AND HIS DAUGHTER. 2s.
——— JACK AND THREE JILLS. 2s.
——— A LUCKY YOUNG WOMAN. 6s.
——— AS IN A LOOKING-GLASS. 6s.
——— SOCIAL VICISSITUDES. 2s.
RIDDELL, MRS. J. H.—MISS GASCOIGNE. 2s.
'RITA.'—THE LADYE NANCYE. 2s.   [Shortly.
——— GRETCHEN. Three vols. 31s. 6d.   [In the Press.
THOMAS, ANNIE.—A REIGNING FAVOURITE. 3s. 6d.
TYTLER, SARAH.—LOGIE TOWN. Three vols. 31s. 6d.
WARDEN, FLORENCE.—A PRINCE OF DARKNESS. 1s.

Ward & Downey, Publishers, 12, York St., Covent Garden.

www.ingramcontent.com/pod-product-compliance
Lightning Source LLC
Chambersburg PA
CBHW022059230426
43672CB00008B/1226